FOULED ANCHOR CHRONICLES
"A Sea of Stories"

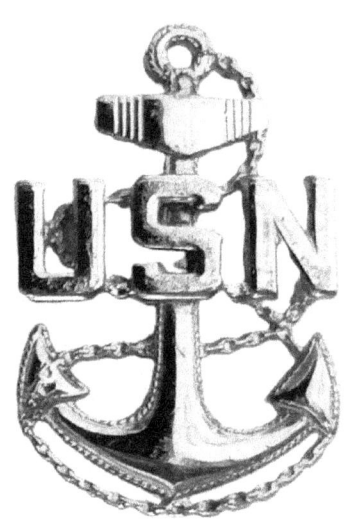

By
George L. Trowbridge

Copyright © 2025 George L. Trowbridge

All rights reserved. In accordance with U.S. Copyright Act of 1976, the scanning, uploading, and electronic sharing of any part of this book without permission of the publisher constitute unlawful piracy and theft of the author's intellectual property. No part of this book may be reproduced in any form by any electronic or mechanical means (including photocopying, recording or information storage and retrieval) without permission in writing from the author or publisher. Thank you for your support of the author's rights. For bulk or wholesale orders, please contact us admin@richterpublishing.com.

Book Cover Design: Jessie Alarcon

Editors: Adriana Hartman, Kaitlyn Sanderson & Steven Tye

Proofreader: Haley Cox

Book Formatting: Kaitlyn Sanderson

Publisher: Richter Publishing LLC www.richterpublishing.com

ISBN-13: 978-1-954094-73-4

DISCLAIMER

This is a fictional autobiography. The stories in this book reflect the author's recollections of actual events, while others may include embellished or entirely fictional incidents created by the author. Names, locations, and identifying details have been altered to protect the privacy of those portrayed. Dialogue has been reconstructed from memory or crafted by the author. Many dates, times, and locations were derived from declassified U.S. Navy records and other documents; however, some may be fictitious. The photographs included are either public domain or owned by the author. Illustrations and maps used were either created by the author or are in the public domain. This information is provided and sold with the knowledge that the publisher and author do not offer any legal or medical advice. In the case of a need for any such expertise, consult with the appropriate professional. This book does not contain all information available on the subject. This book has not been created to be specific to any individual's or organization's situation or needs. Every effort has been made to make this book as accurate as possible. However, there may be typographical and/or content errors. Therefore, this book should serve only as a general guide and not as the ultimate source of subject information. This book contains information that might be dated and is intended only to educate and entertain. The author and publisher shall have no liability or responsibility to any person or entity regarding any loss or damage incurred, or alleged to have incurred, directly or indirectly, by the information contained in this book. You hereby agree to be bound by this disclaimer or you may return this book within the guarantee time period for a full refund. In the interest of full disclosure, this book may contain affiliate links that might pay the author or publisher a commission upon any purchase from the company. While the author and publisher take no responsibility for the business practices of these companies and or the performance of any product or service, the author or publisher has used the product or service and makes a recommendation in good faith based on that experience. All characters appearing in this work are fictitious. Any resemblance to real persons, living or dead, is purely coincidental. The opinions and stories in this book are the views of the author and not that of the publisher.

DEDICATION

To all Navy spouses facing the toughest job in the U.S. Navy: maintaining stability at home while their sailor is deployed around the world. Without the steadfast support and devotion of my wife, Janice, much of what I achieved during my naval career would not have been possible.

Table of Contents

PROLOGUE 1
CHAPTER 1: AN EXCURSION 5
CHAPTER 2: STORMS AHEAD 41
CHAPTER 3: ANOTHER TWIST 79
CHAPTER 4: BACK TO THE FLEET 118
CHAPTER 5: MISJUDGMENTS 157
CHAPTER 6: A TRANSITION 195
CHAPTER 7: THE DITCH AND BEYOND 232
CHAPTER 8: CROSSING THE LINE 273
CHAPTER 9: A CHANGE OF PACE 317
CHAPTER 10: NEXT UP 360
EPILOGUE: GETTING THERE FROM HERE 399
GLOSSARY OF TERMS AND ACRONYMS 405
ABOUT THE AUTHOR 410

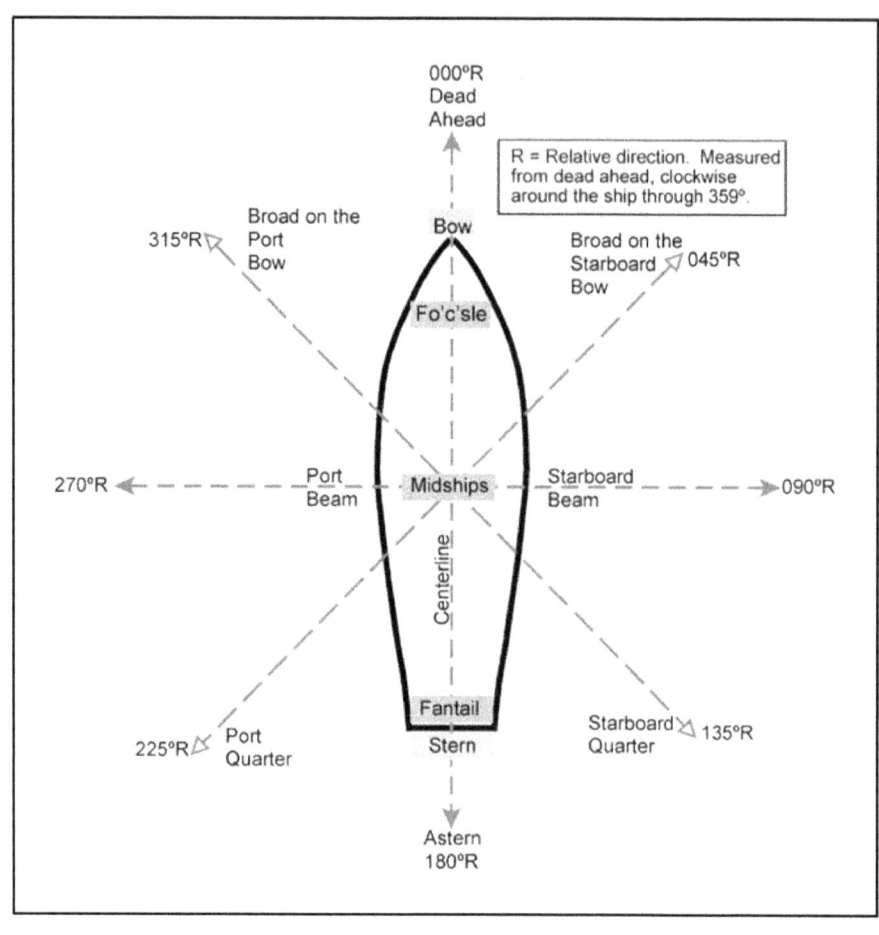

Typical reference directions and commonly used terms on board ships.

PROLOGUE

Our Navy frigate was patrolling the waters outside the entrance to the Gulf of Fonseca along the Eastern Pacific coast of Central America. I would guess that no one in the crew had any idea that we were about to go through a series of unusual and strange events over the next two months. At the Gulf of Fonseca (Spanish: Golfo de Fonseca), the view from seaward was impressive. The landscape is stunning, beautiful, and initially almost breathtaking. The entrance to the Gulf lies between two prominent points of land; to the west is Punta de Amapala, and to the east is Punta Cosiguina. Prominent volcanic peaks rise on both sides of the Gulf's entrance, and several high and conspicuous islands lie within the inner part. Volcan Cosiguina, the tallest peak, rises to 2,860 feet on the southeast side of the entrance, northeast of Punta Cosiguina. On a clear day, Volcan Cosiguina is visible from up to 70 miles offshore.

By May 1983, a decade had passed since my last brushes with war, where I operated in the tumultuous waters off Vietnam. During the war's waning months, my time on USS *Rich* (DD 820), a World War II-era destroyer, left indelible marks on my psyche. The combat experiences I endured aboard that ship were profound events that changed me dramatically and shaped who I would become. During the intervening years since Vietnam, a series of life events had been coincidentally steering me right into a progression of escapades.

So, why were we there in such a beautiful place? It was not because of any single event. The factors leading us there began about four years earlier. In 1979, developments across several Central American countries triggered the United States to pay closer attention to the region. It all started with the leftist revolution in Nicaragua, which resulted in the ousting of the U.S.-backed dictator by the Sandinista National Liberation Front (FSLN). The FSLN quickly established itself as the new Nicaraguan Sandinista government. A few days after taking office, President Reagan accused the Soviet Union and Cuba of sending military supplies to support the Nicaraguan Sandinista government.

In 1981, President Reagan took decisive action by authorizing the Central Intelligence Agency (CIA) to form and support a counterinsurgency army in Nicaragua, known as the Contras. This group conducted operations within Nicaragua and saw factions establishing bases in the neighboring countries of El Salvador, Honduras, and Costa Rica. As the situation evolved, CIA advisors collaborated closely with Contra leaders to establish the Nicaraguan Democratic Force (FDN), which became the principal fighting force of the Contras. By March 1982, the intensity of Contra attacks against the Sandinista government had significantly increased, marking a pivotal escalation in the conflict.

In reality, the United States was waging war against Nicaragua. Initially, the intentions were to keep it secret. When the U.S. media exposed it, the Reagan administration made a concerted effort to win public and congressional support and approval. This conflict was rooted in concerns over the Sandinista government's connection to socialism and its threat to U.S. interests in the region. The administration's clandestine operations were revealed as events unfolded, igniting debates about U.S. foreign policy and interventionism in Central America.

Supporters of the actions argued that they were necessary to curb the spread of communism, while opponents highlighted the ethical implications and consequences for the Nicaraguan people. The situation escalated, leading to significant political and military involvement, not only from the U.S. but also from various regional actors. This backdrop of tension and conflict would come to influence the experiences of those patrolling the waters of the Gulf of Fonseca, shaping the adventures and challenges that lay ahead for the crew of our Navy frigate and for me.

The media began hearing bits of information about the Contra War in early 1982. Rumors churned for a time until a story in *Newsweek* magazine confirmed the existence of the war. The Reagan administration's response was to conduct an information campaign to convince the public and Congress that the Contras deserved our support. What had initially been a covert conflict transformed into an overt one, with U.S. aid to the Contras becoming a matter of congressional policy. Consequently, many operations in Central America involving U.S. military forces became largely transparent, revealing a complex and evolving situation in the region.

One feature of Reagan's strategy was to keep the Sandinista government nervous and force it to allocate limited resources toward military purposes. To advance this strategy, one initiative involved creating the appearance of U.S. preparations to invade Nicaragua.

This context sheds light on our presence here. The stunning landscape and serene waters of the Gulf of Fonseca were juxtaposed with the underlying tension of military posturing. We were not just patrolling picturesque waters; we were part of a broader strategy to destabilize a government that the U.S. perceived as a threat. The tranquility of our surroundings often belied the complex geopolitical realities at play, reminding us that beauty can exist alongside tension and uncertainty.

My journey to reach these Central American waters was far from straightforward. It resembled a winding path, with each twist and turn often feeling aimless, as if my sole objective was to cope and survive in every new location wherever the Navy stationed me. Each experience, though sometimes disorienting, shaped my perspective and resilience in unexpected ways.

Most people would believe that to tell a good story, the storyteller should start at the beginning. However, I've found that sometimes, the best tales include moments that shatter everything you thought you knew. The pieces that fall around you, like dominoes, can often create the most compelling narrative.

In my life, select moments felt like tipping points—when a small decision led to a cascade of events. These moments are what I want to explore. Let me peel back the layers of my experiences, revealing how one choice can pivot a life in an unexpected direction, leaving a trail of memories, lessons, and sometimes regrets in its wake. Each decision, big or small, carries the weight of what could have been, creating a tapestry woven with joy and sorrow.

The stories of my past are not just isolated incidents; they are interconnected threads that shape who I am today. From the paths I chose to the ones I let slip away, every experience adds depth to my understanding of self and the world around me. In embracing the complexity of these choices, I find clarity in my journey, recognizing that each step—whether forward or backward—has contributed to my growth and resilience.

Pivotal events made me question everything and set me on a path I never saw coming, but as it turned out, I was destined to follow. This is the story of how each phase can shift the balance of a life, revealing the intricate design that only hindsight can appreciate.

CHAPTER 1
AN EXCURSION

On May 13, 1983, our Guided Missile Frigate, USS *Estocin* (FFG 15), arrived just off the entrance to the Gulf of Fonseca, relieving USS *Julius A. Furer* (FFG 6). The Gulf of Fonseca area was strategically significant, as it borders El Salvador, Honduras, and Nicaragua. Our mission, referred to in naval terms as "Special Operations (SPECOPS)," was to monitor and report any detected activities of the Sandinistas. Additionally, we were tasked with supporting the CIA and/or special operators in their efforts to assist Contra operations.

By this time, I had become a chief petty officer (pay grade E-7) or Chief Quartermaster (navigation and ship control specialist). Reaching this point in my life has taken me through both good and bad times.

I was raised on a farm in northeast Iowa. Growing up doing farm work, essentially doing man's work from about age 9, convinced me that being a farmer was not for me. In the spring of 1970, after high school, I left the farm behind and soon found work along the Mississippi River in Illinois as a barge deckhand, offloading river barges carrying oats for government storage until the fall harvest. By mid-November, work had slowed with the end of the harvest season, so I quit my job and headed back home to Iowa.

Settling in back home, I felt I deserved some R & R, so I looked up some old high school buddies, and the partying started. After several weeks of fun every night, one of my friends asked me to go to Mason City, Iowa, with him. He had been dating a girl attending Hamilton Business College, who had a friend he thought I would really like. In other words, he needed a wingman.

I figured, why not? So, the next afternoon, in early December 1970, we drove to Mason City, about 50 miles from my hometown, Riceville. We met his girlfriend, and they introduced me to a great girl named Jan (Janice). I was actually meeting my future wife and life partner. Who knew? Jan was also a student at the business college. We double-dated several times with my buddy and his girlfriend. I asked Jan out on a date, just the two of us. I remember we went to see a movie and had a great time together. At the end of the evening, I asked if she would like to go out again, and she said yes. The rest, you could say, was history. Jan and I quickly became a couple. It wasn't long before we were spending time together every day and night. It didn't take long before I realized I was in love. I had been with other girls before, but this was different, and I knew it. We both eventually admitted that we loved each other and were crazy about one another.

It was around the middle of March 1971 when Jan told me she might be pregnant. A visit to the doctor confirmed it. Raised with the idea that we are all responsible for our own actions, along with a strong conviction to do the right thing, I knew what my next step had to be. Without any doubt or hesitation, I asked Jan to marry me, and she accepted. Within a few weeks, we had our wedding date set for late June. At first, the idea of getting married with a baby on the way was a little overwhelming, but the relationship we had quickly built gave me the confidence I needed to move forward.

Janice and I married on June 26, 1971, at the Catholic Church in Stacyville, Iowa, her hometown. That year, summer passed quickly. We settled easily into our new daily routine, while I worked the day shift at a local factory during the week. By late summer, it became clear that Jan was pregnant as our baby grew inside her. On August 5, 1971, the Vietnam draft lottery for those born in 1952 was held. The lottery number for my birthdate was 43. It was reported that numbers up to 50 would be called for physical exams by October 31, 1971. From my perspective, I faced the choice of being drafted into the Army or enlisting in another branch of the Armed Forces. My preference was the U.S. Navy.

We decided to set up an appointment with the nearest Navy Recruiting Office in Mason City. During the last week of August, Jan and I visited the Navy recruiter. By the end of our visit, we agreed that I should go through the full processing to see what I might qualify for.

During the second week of September, I took a bus trip to the Armed Forces Examining and Entrance Station at Fort Des Moines, Iowa. That day, I enlisted in the Navy with a one-month delay before reporting to boot camp. Jan and I decided that she would stay with her parents in Stacyville while I was away. Our baby was due in mid-December, when I would still be in boot camp.

On Wednesday, October 20, I took the bus from Mason City back to Fort Des Moines. From there, I flew to Chicago, Illinois, where Navy personnel met us and transported us to the Recruit Training Center at the Great Lakes Naval Station. Then began the thirteen weeks of boot camp.

After week six of boot camp, we were allowed to make phone calls on Saturday evenings. On the early evening of December 11, my mother-in-law, Ann, answered the phone when I called Jan. Ann told me she had just returned from the local hospital and that I was the father of a healthy baby boy. Our son was born that afternoon, weighing 7 pounds, 10 ounces. Mitchell Thomas Trowbridge, whom we had decided to name after my dad. So now, we were a small family of three.

On Friday, January 14, 1972, I graduated from boot camp. Afterwards, I attended eleven weeks of additional training at Great Lakes. Near the end of training, I received orders to a destroyer homeported in Norfolk, Virginia. Upon completion of training, with my small family, we traveled to Norfolk, and on May 27, I reported on board my first ship, USS *Rich*.

I often joke about that time, saying, "I went on board my first ship, USS *Rich* (DD 820), when I was 19 years old, naïve, wide-eyed, and full of bullshit. I left her at the age of 23, maybe still a little naïve, but the wide-eyed and full of bullshit stuff had long ago been wrung out of me." My time on *Rich* concluded in late 1975; by then, I had advanced to the pay grade of E-5, Petty Officer 2nd Class in the Quartermaster rating (QM2).

I decided to reenlist for six more years in exchange for new orders, and the Navy was offering an attractive monetary bonus. My orders were to a coastal river division at Great Lakes Naval Station, principally operating on Lake Michigan. This assignment was supposed to be a three-year tour, which did not count as shore or sea duty. Jan and I were both excited about these orders, as they would allow me to spend more time at home with her and our young son, Mitch.

I reported to Coastal River Division 21 (CRD 21) during the fall of 1975. The unit operated three Fast Patrol Boats (PTFs), comprised of PTF 17, PTF 18, and PTF 19. The PTFs had all served in the Vietnam War but returned to the United States after the war. In addition, the division also had three Patrol Gunboats (PGs). Moreover, it had its own SEAL Team, a small detachment assigned to the operations department, led by a lieutenant and consisting of five enlisted SEALs, all of whom were Vietnam veterans.

CRD 21 stood out among naval units in a couple of significant ways. All active-duty enlisted personnel were rated petty officers, specifically within pay grades E-4 through E-6, which meant no non-rated personnel (pay grades E-3 and below) in the unit. CRD 21's unique mission also focused on training selected naval reservists.

One downside for active-duty personnel assigned to CRD 21 was that we worked nearly every weekend because our mission was to train reservists. To compensate for working so many weekends, CRD-21 had a very liberal liberty (time off) policy during the week.

On board ships, or in some cases, at shore commands, enlisted personnel generally do not address commissioned naval officers solely by rank. The exceptions are the commanding officer, who is addressed as "captain" or "skipper" regardless of rank, and the executive officer, who is typically referred to as "XO." For the officers, holding the rank of ensign or lieutenant, it is appropriate to address them as "Ensign," "Lieutenant," or "Mister," followed by their surname. Therefore, Lieutenant Williams can be addressed as either "Lieutenant Williams" or "Mr. Williams."

PTF 19 was to become my boat. Lieutenant Bill Knowles was the officer in charge (OIC). After meeting and talking with everyone in the crew, I understood they all enjoyed being there. It was looking to be an excellent assignment.

The PTFs were a little over 80 feet in overall length, with a beam (width) of 24.5 feet and a draft of about 7 feet. They are designated "fast patrol boats" for a reason: their speed capabilities were rated at 44 knots (about 50.6 mph). Twin diesel engines provided the propulsion power, with each main engine capable of generating a maximum of 2,500 horsepower. They featured a twin-propeller system and utilized twin rudders for steering, making them fast and highly maneuverable. The crew size typically consisted of 10 enlisted personnel, plus the OIC.

CRD 21 was located on the Naval Station, specifically in Building 13, which was situated directly on the waterfront at the harbor basin on Lake Michigan. The inner harbor lay in front of the building, while the boat basin stretched along the west side; it accommodated docks for the patrol gunboats (PGs) on the east and PTFs on the west.

There was a traditional event for those new to the command or for individuals being promoted that I learned about in the latter part of my first week. It was an unexpected and memorable experience that highlighted the camaraderie and unique customs of the unit.

Fast Patrol Boat (PTF)

It was Friday afternoon, and everyone was busy on board with cleaning and maintenance tasks in preparation for the weekend. Mr. Knowles came on board, which didn't seem unusual; I assumed he was there to check the boat before letting us off. Larry, the boat's leading petty officer, came around, telling everyone to stow our tools and equipment and then muster on the aft deck. As I walked to the aft deck, I noticed the outboard lifelines were down. Mr. Knowles motioned for us to gather around him.

Once everyone was present, he turned to me. "Trowbridge, we still haven't given you an official welcome." He then looked around at everyone and said, "Do it."

Before I could process what was happening, the whole crew jumped on me and pinned me down on the deck. In unison, they picked me up and threw me over the side. With it being late fall on Lake Michigan, the water was frigid, and I could hear them laughing as I splashed down. I grabbed the life ring buoy they had tossed and watched as a rope ladder was lowered over the boat's side. Mr. Knowles and Larry motioned for me to climb the ladder. As I reached it, I secured my arm through the life ring buoy and started climbing, carrying it with me.

Once I was back on deck, Mr. Knowles said, "Trowbridge, you are now an official crewmember. Congratulations."

He reached out to shake my hand, and I took it as we shared a firm grip. Each crew member came up to shake my hand one by one, making me feel more accepted.

"Liberty call! I'll see all of you on Monday," Mr. Knowles announced.

I was relieved to finally head home, incredibly grateful for the heater in my car. When I arrived, Jan noticed my wet clothes and asked about it. I explained the tradition, and she just shook her head.

"You guys are juveniles," she said.

In early November, we conducted frequent underway periods for training. Underway training for PTF active-duty crews was three or four days in duration. These underway experiences were invaluable, significantly enhancing my understanding of PTF operations. During my first week, Mr. Knowles encouraged me to learn everything I could about the PTF's characteristics, propulsion, auxiliary systems, deck equipment, navigation tools, communication radios, and weapons systems.

Crew members must be familiar with and proficient at doing each other's jobs. Cross-training was imperative. The idea is that in combat, if one crew member is injured or killed, any other crew member should be able to take over the disabled crew member's job.

During the second week of December, while the harbor was still ice-free, the PTFs were lifted out of the water and stored onshore using the synchro-lift facility. With the boat now out of the water for the cold months, we took the chance to focus on hull cleaning, preservation, and general maintenance. The crews settled into their winter routine. Nearby, we had a 12-foot by 60-foot trailer that served as our living space. We ate our lunches in the trailer and spent our duty days living and sleeping there.

The winter daily routine was quite simple. Each day began with morning quarters at 0730 in Building 13, Monday through Friday. After quarters, we typically headed to the boats or the trailer to divide up the daily work tasks. Larry usually determined when we could call it a day, often in the early afternoon. Most Fridays, we would finish up by lunchtime.

I became fast friends with my fellow crew members. Jan and I hosted many gatherings at our apartment, and most of the crew usually came with their wives and girlfriends. We played loud music, consumed many alcoholic beverages, danced, socialized, did stupid shit, and had a lot of fun. We all became good and loyal friends. Life at CRD 21 was great, a piece of cake.

One cold winter morning, during morning quarters, the commanding officer held a short ceremony to promote Chief Boatswain's Mate (BMC) Brown from the maintenance department to Senior Chief Boatswain's Mate. After quarters, Mr. Knowles gathered all of us in an area away from everyone. By now, I had learned that our OIC tended to instigate, and the result of this meeting was no different. The lieutenant started with several questions but was not looking for answers.

"Do you want to continue getting off early? Do you like getting off early on Fridays? Do you enjoy the liberal time off whenever you ask?" He continued, "As you just witnessed, Chief Brown is now Senior Chief Brown. Unless he goes in the water this morning, you can forget about any more extra time off."

Our Engineman 2nd Class, Steve, looked around and returned to Mr. Knowles. "Sir, the basin and harbor are iced over."

The lieutenant surveyed us. "So, you guys can't chop a hole in the ice? Make it happen, or else. Dismissed."

After Mr. Knowles walked away, Larry said, "Shit, we better figure this out. Let's get some shovels, an axe, and find a spot in the boat basin to chop open a hole."

About 15 minutes later, with tools in hand, we all jumped down from the short sea wall onto the ice. We took turns chopping away at the ice, until we had a hole about 4 feet in diameter.

"Let's go get the new senior chief," Larry announced.

Larry and Steve took the lead while the rest of us followed. We entered the back entrance of Building 13 into the maintenance department section. We quickly located Senior Chief Brown seated at his desk in his office. Brown immediately realized what was happening and got up, trying to force his way past us. We all jumped on him, managing to secure his arms and legs, and proceeded to carry him out of the building. There was another struggle getting him off the sea wall, but we eventually got him onto the ice. Once there, it was only a short distance to the hole, and in he went. As he splashed in the cold water, he struggled unsuccessfully to get out, reaching out his hand for someone to pull him up. I think all of us, myself included, thought, No way, he'll try to pull me in. Brown kept struggling; suddenly Max, one of the SEALs, pushed his way through our group.

"Are you guys fucking crazy? You'll kill the guy!" Max shouted.

Max quickly pulled Brown out onto the ice, removing his foul-weather jacket and putting it on the senior chief. "Help me get him inside before he goes into full-on hyperthermia! Jesus Christ, what in the fuck is wrong with you, assholes?" he yelled.

We helped Max with Brown and, within minutes, had him back in his office. One of the maintenance crew brought in a portable electric heater. Max helped the senior chief strip down, and someone produced some towels, coveralls, and blankets.

Once dressed and seated, Brown looked at all of us, while still shivering. "You assholes get out of my sight, don't let me see any of you the rest of the day. Now get the fuck out."

We all looked at each other, turned, and walked out of the building, then headed over to our side of the harbor. Eventually, we all went to work. At lunchtime, I asked Larry if we were in any trouble.

"Haven't heard anything," he answered.

Later that afternoon, Mr. Knowles approached the boat, looked around, and told Larry to let us go home when he was ready, then left. Amazingly, we never heard another word about Brown's dunking. The Navy was much different back then. We saw it as following tradition and the direction of our officer in charge. Oh, and the liberal time-off policies continued.

By mid-March, the ice had broken up along the lakefront, and the harbor was clear. It was time to get the PTFs back in the water. All in one day, each PTF, in turn, with its cradle, was run out on the rail system to the synchro lift, then lowered into the water until the boat's buoyancy took over, freeing it from the cradle. Once our boat was free of the cradle, the shoreline tenders pulled our boat over to the dock, where we made up and secured the mooring lines.

The next day, preparation checks started for all equipment and systems. Once all of the checks were completed, Mr. Knowles ordered the starting of the propulsion diesels. The sound and feel of the big diesel engines, even at idle, were almost sexy. You could feel the entire boat coming to life as engine torque and harmonics reverberated through the boat's structure. It was thrilling to experience the boat come alive. We would kick off the spring underway operations in just a few more days.

On a Friday morning, the word came down for everyone to muster at 1300 in Building 13 for an announcement by the commanding officer. No one, including me, thought there was anything significant regarding the meeting.

Surprise, surprise...the commanding officer had big news; he told us all in a short, direct manner that, effective June 30, the Navy was decommissioning CRD 21, and the unit would be gone. My immediate thought was, shit. And then, more shit. I reenlisted for six years in exchange for this assignment, and within a few months, the Navy was taking it away!

At the end of the meeting, we received a copy of a memorandum. It contained the same information that the commanding officer had previously communicated to us. It also directed each enlisted person to begin working on new orders for post CRD 21 and included a list of phone numbers for our rating detailers. We all took a copy of our memo and returned to the boats. That night, I broke the news to Jan. As always, she accepted the news calmly. We talked a bit about what I thought our options might be. All I knew was to contact the QM Rating detailer immediately.

The following day at quarters, there was more news. The PG and PTF crews would take their boats out of the Great Lakes to the Navy's amphibious base at Little Creek, Virginia. The PGs would depart on June 1, followed by the PTFs on June 16.

Like many situations that appear only to have a downside, there is often a perceived upside as well. That day, I was able to contact the QM Rating detailer, who, to my surprise, informed me that I was eligible for shore duty. He explained that since I was already at Great Lakes, I had two options: (1) a general staff assignment at the Recruit Training Center (RTC) or (2) an assignment to the Navy Recruiting District Chicago as a canvasser/recruiter. He convinced me that the recruiter billet would be the best career move, and like an idiot, I agreed.

I was happy with the idea of staying in the area. We had settled into a very nice housing unit on base and would not have to move again. It also allowed us to see our families more often, as it was only about a six-hour drive to where our families lived in Iowa.

That night, I shared the news with Jan, and her reaction was one of happiness and relief. She had been just as anxious about our situation as I was. Although we had no real clue what recruiting life would entail, we were grateful at that moment. The thought of not returning to sea and having more time at home was a comforting prospect—at least, that's what we had believed.

Despite the turmoil caused by the news of our pending decommissioning, spring boat operations were still a go. However, the underway training regime was adjusted to more closely support the operational tasks foreseen during the upcoming transit through the Great Lakes and ultimately to Little Creek.

During our time underway, Mr. Knowles dedicated a significant amount of effort to training Bobby, the other QM2, and me. His training centered around vessel operations and the standards for watchkeeping. Lt. Knowles wanted to ensure that we were both proficient enough to meet his expectations and standards, emphasizing the importance of rotating wheelhouse watches between us. He made it clear that he couldn't always be in the wheelhouse, so he needed to trust us to navigate and operate the boat safely.

During the last week of May, Mr. Knowles expressed his confidence in both of us and presented each of us with our official letters signed by the commanding officer. These letters certified that we had satisfactorily completed our training and met all the Fast Patrol Boat Coxswain qualification requirements.

The morning of June 16 arrived. After saying our farewells with family, our small flotilla of three PTFs got underway from our dock for the last time and made our way through the harbor breakwaters out onto Lake Michigan. Lieutenant Williams, the OIC of PTF 17, was the senior officer in charge of our three-boat group. The estimate was that the trip would take about four weeks to transit nearly 1,500 nautical miles to Little Creek.

The trip included plans for the boats to stop at several port cities and towns along the route. Most of these port stops assisted Navy recruiting efforts by allowing the public to tour the boats. Additionally, the habitability conditions on the boats were basic and minimal, so some of the stops would enable the crews to stay at local hotels. This would allow everyone to shower, clean up, and do laundry, enhancing the overall experience.

Our basic navigation equipment consisted of a magnetic steering compass, a Mark 27 gyrocompass, a single radar unit, and navigation charts. Our piloting navigation method primarily relied on dead reckoning. The radar unit was an excellent asset for detecting other vessels and obstacles, but it was not infallible. Integration of all tools and methods was essential for ensuring safe and accurate navigation.

The first night out, I took the wheelhouse watch from Bobby at 1800. We were rotating the watch six hours on and six hours off. Our three-boat group made good headway in a loose column, keeping about 2,000 yards apart. All boats were cruising at a steady speed of around 18 knots. PTF 17 was in the lead, followed by PTF 18, while our boat brought up the rear. We were all closely monitoring our very high frequency, frequency modulated (VHF-FM) marine radiotelephones for any vessel traffic on channels 13 and 16. We would initially contact one another on channel 16 for boat-to-boat communications, then switch over to channel 8 for our ongoing discussions. It was a familiar routine, but the night air brought a confident anticipation of what lay ahead.

By early evening, we were in northern Lake Michigan and would soon approach and then transit through the Straits of Mackinac, leaving Lake Michigan behind and entering Lake Huron. We were bound for our first port stop in Port Huron, Michigan, along the St. Clair River.

Mr. Knowles stayed up with me for a while and then told me he was going to get something to eat and try to get some sleep. He asked that we wake him when we were approaching Gull Island light, west of High and Beaver Islands. Once it was fully dark, the soft glow from our navigation lights became apparent. Visibility seemed good, with no moon or other visible vessel traffic, except for the stern light from PTF 18 about a mile ahead of us. It was somewhat windy with maybe 3 to 4-foot waves. All seemed calm; I knew one of the engineman ratings, Donny or Steve, would be up if I needed anything.

I was maintaining a proper lookout, consistently doing a visual scan of the waters around our boat. I monitored to ensure we were on the ordered course and speed. Engine operating temperatures and pressures were all within normal range. Periodically, I would monitor the radar display, looking for possible vessel traffic. Everything appeared normal and as it should be.

Suddenly, out of nowhere, a bright white light—apparently a searchlight—flashed on the port side just forward of the beam, illuminating the wheelhouse. The light's beam quickly moved downward to reveal something in the water about 150 to 200 yards away. Instantly, I recognized the bows of two barges, side-by-side, being pushed ahead by a towboat.

I threw the wheel hard to starboard without hesitation to steer clear of the barges. At a speed of 18 knots, my stern swiftly cleared the barges. Once we were clear, I brought the boat back around to port, passing the barges and towboat on my port side at a safe distance. As the towboat passed, I noticed I couldn't see its red port-side navigation light. As the distance between us widened, the towboat's white stern light finally appeared. I attempted to call the towboat operator on channels 13 and 16, but there was no response.

It was a narrow escape that nearly could have led to a collision. I was a bit shaken up, but I couldn't understand. Why didn't I see the tow on radar? I had checked my radar; nothing. I never saw any navigation lights, despite constantly scanning the area visually. Why were no navigation lights visible except for his stern light? Why didn't the towboat operator call on channels 13 or 16?

Now, I was nervous as hell. It seemed my rapid maneuvers had not alerted anyone. No one called or came to the wheelhouse. It seemed to me the best thing to do was just keep the incident to myself. Right or wrong, that was my decision. However, the incident served as a lifelong lesson regarding vessel operations: never assume all is as it seems.

At about 2100, I called below and asked Donny to wake Mr. Knowles. Mr. Knowles joined me in the wheelhouse a short while later. He looked at the radar for several seconds and asked how things were going.

"Fine," I replied.

He sat on the platform near the ladder well and advised me to continue my watch. Around 2300, we passed under the Mackinac Bridge. The bridge spans the straits between St. Ignace to the north and Mackinaw

City to the south. Once clear of the bridge, I adjusted our course to enter the South Channel, staying south of Bois Blanc Island. Mr. Knowles informed me he was going below, leaving me in command as we transitioned into Lake Huron. Bobby came up just before midnight, so I could hand over the watch to him and relax a bit.

We arrived at Port Huron at noontime; the trip had taken about 26 hours. We tied up at our dock assignment along the south bank of the Black River in downtown Port Huron. We would be here for a couple of days, providing tours to the public starting the next day. Everyone turned to cleaning up the boat to make it presentable.

The following morning at 1000, we opened the boats for tours, and I was taken aback by the long lines of people waiting on the dock. It's important to remember that this was 1976, during the height of the post-Vietnam Era. Many of us believed that most civilians harbored negative feelings towards us. However, in Port Huron, that perception was unfounded. The locals were not only happy to see us, but they were also courteous and respectful of us.

After another day in Port Huron, our PTFs, one at a time, maneuvered away from their mooring back out onto the St. Clair River. On this leg of our trip, we were bound for Lorain, Ohio, on the southern shore of Lake Erie. It was about 132 nautical miles to Lorain. We could typically cover such a distance in open water in less than five hours. However, navigation speeds would be slowed because the first 50 miles or so of the trip involved going southbound down the St. Clair River, then crossing Lake St. Clair to the Detroit River. Once in the Detroit River, it would be another 32 miles to get to Lake Erie. The overall distance from Detroit to Lorain was about 80 nautical miles. Later that afternoon, we entered Lorain Harbor, passing through the breakwater to the mouth of the river. Then we proceeded inbound to our dock assignment at the southwest part of the outer harbor.

Lorain is situated approximately 25 miles west of Cleveland. Our impression of the Lorain harbor area was that it was heavily industrial and dirty. The water is polluted, although one of the locals mentioned that it had improved considerably in recent years. Our reason for being there was to refuel our boats and pick up some repair parts.

The following morning, our boats got underway and proceeded through the channel, navigating past the harbor breakwaters onto Lake Erie. We were bound for Buffalo, New York. All three boats came to a course of 050 degrees and accelerated to 35 knots, roughly 40 mph. The distance to Buffalo was about 170 nautical miles, which meant we could reach our destination in less than five hours. Hauling ass out here in the open water—who doesn't love that? The wind whipped against our faces, the engines roared beneath us, and the thrill of speed filled the air.

By mid-afternoon, we had made the north entrance to Buffalo Harbor, passed the West Breakwater Light, and proceeded to the Buffalo River entrance channel. All three boats docked at a wharf designated as the Buffalo Waterfront along Prime Street downtown.

The prospect of four whole days with the comfort of a hotel felt like a well-deserved treat. I could already imagine the luxury of hot showers, the pleasure of wearing clean clothes, and the comfort of sleeping in nice beds. And let's not forget the allure of the nearby bars! What was there not to like?

The only catch was that one crew member had to remain on board each night. But with our democratic approach, we decided to draw straws for the duty. I held my breath each time, relieved and grateful as I pulled a long straw for every night. With the park service volunteering to provide nighttime security at the wharf, we could relax knowing our boats were safe. Everything had fallen perfectly in place.

Those of us heading to the hotel packed our civilian clothes for later. We arrived still dressed in our boondocker boots, dungarees, foul-weather jackets, and ball caps. The plan was to change after we cleaned up. During check-in, our crew agreed to meet up later for some food and then venture out to find a few good bars. We were all in the mood for some heavy drinking and maybe a little hell-raising. Money wasn't a concern since we'd all received our pay and per diem allowances in cash. We were feeling flush. So far, I hadn't spent a nickel, but that night, I intended to change that.

Larry, Bobby, Frank, and I spent the evening carousing at the bars the city of Buffalo had to offer. All four of us struggled back to the hotel during the early hours to get some sleep before heading to the boats in the morning.

The next day was Tuesday, and it was quite the battle for all of us to get down to the boats; everyone was dealing with varying levels of hangovers. Larry gathered us at 0730, detailing the preparations for the public tours, which were scheduled to start at 1000. Around 0830, some guys from the park service arrived at the wharf area, setting up wooden barricades and direction signs. By 0900, people were lined up along the barricades, stretching out toward Prime Street. It was about this time that Mr. Knowles came on board. I remember telling him it was nice to see him so early in the morning. He looked at me without saying anything, but his facial expression delivered a clear "fuck you" message.

What a marathon day it turned out to be. The advertised tour times were from 1000 to 1600. By 0930, people lined up on the wharf, extending out to the sidewalks along the street as far as we could see. From 1000 on, it was nonstop—one group after another. Most of us had no time for lunch; our only breaks were to use the head. The tour routine we used in Port Huron wasn't working; there were too many people. Each of us took groups of 10 to 15 people around the boat, trying to stay out of each other's way. At one point, it looked as if there may have been more than 100 people on board.

Looking over at PTF 18 docked ahead of us, it was the same; people everywhere. Around 1800, I saw Mr. Knowles and Lieutenants Williams and Henry, the OIC of PTF 18, talking with the park service people on the dock. Mr. Knowles walked across the dock toward our boat; the park service people were moving the barricades around, blocking access to the dock.

Mr. Knowles came on board, pulled Larry aside, and spoke with him briefly. Afterward, Larry came back and told me that when I finished my current tour, I would be done for the day. We finished with our respective groups and saw them off at the gangway. After everyone departed, we tied lines across the gangway handrails, shutting down access. By then, it was close to 1900. We were all tired, hungry, and spent. I went down to the galley to join most of the crew.

Steve looked at me. "Can you believe this? I've never seen that many people wanting a tour, anywhere."

"And will tomorrow be like today?" I replied.

Lt. Knowles shared that he had spoken with representatives from the park service and a Navy recruiting officer, and they were pretty happy with the public turnout and the positive attention it brought to both the Navy and the Naval and Military Park. They estimated that over 1,500 people visited to tour the boats. Lt. Knowles believed it likely set a record for PTF visitors in a single day and mentioned that each day here promised to be just as busy.

The next morning, we returned to the boats, ready to tackle another busy day. After quarters at 0730 with Larry, we began preparing for the tours. It felt like a repeat of the previous day, but the park service had implemented better crowd control measures. They organized groups at the barricades, letting each one proceed to the boats in an orderly manner. While it was still bustling on board, the atmosphere was much less hectic than the day before. However, we ended up providing tours into the early evening hours. Each day, tours opened at 1000, and we wrapped up at about the time of sunset. A vast number of people wanted to tour the boats each day.

A note of historical interest: Buffalo was somewhat enamored with our PTFs, given their history of also operating on the Great Lakes. In 1979, after retirement from active service, the Navy offered PTF 17 to the Buffalo and Erie County Naval & Military Park. To this day, PTF 17 is on display at the waterfront park in Buffalo, now serving as a historical marker of the Vietnam War.

Early Monday morning, around 0600, our boats departed Buffalo, heading for Lake Ontario and our next port visit at Oswego, NY. To travel from Lake Erie to Lake Ontario, we need to transit north through the Welland Canal. The canal entrance is at Port Colborne Harbor in Ontario, about 20 miles west of Buffalo. We arrived at the entrance of Port Colborne harbor shortly after 0700. None of us realized that the best parts of the trip still lay ahead.

The Welland Canal bypasses the Niagara Falls and the rapids of the Niagara River and provides a navigable connection to Lake Ontario from Lake Erie. Lake Erie is approximately 567 feet above sea level, while Lake Ontario is at a much lower elevation, approximately 246 feet above sea level.

The day held two things in store: moving our boats from lock to lock and beautiful scenery everywhere along the 26 miles of canal. We entered the first lock, Lock 8/Guard lock, just north of Port Colborne harbor at about 0730. Moving through the canal waters and around the seven more locks was slow. The PTF design did not allow for slow-speed operation, which meant a commercial tugboat would tow our boats on towing hawsers through the canal and assist in positioning our boats in and out of each lock.

The area surrounding the last three locks is characterized by lowland terrain and is known as the Garden of Canada due to its natural beauty and extensive fruit orchards. We were at Lake Ontario's elevation and proceeded north to Port Weller. The transit through the canal and locks had taken well over 12 hours. It was after 2100 that the tug assisted us in mooring our three boats on the east side of Port Weller Harbor. It had been an exhausting yet fascinating day. Everyone was utterly worn out, hungry, and eager for much-needed rest.

About mid-morning the next day, our PTFs were back under their power. We pulled away from the wharf and made our way around to a heading to proceed north out of Port Weller. Per our standard procedures, PTF 17 took the lead, followed by PTF 18, and then our boat. It was approximately 127 nautical miles from Port Weller to Oswego.

We navigated the channel north through the Port Weller breakwaters. When we were about 1,000 yards (0.5 nautical miles) north of the breakwaters, Mr. Williams called over the radio and ordered all boats to come right to course 049 degrees, maintaining a speed of 25 knots. The lake stretched beyond us, vast and gleaming under the sun, a reminder of the adventures ahead.

Later that afternoon, we arrived at a position about 0.6 miles north of Oswego West Pierhead Light. After navigating south through the breakwaters into the outer harbor, we continued inbound to the inner harbor in the Oswego River. The river empties into Lake Ontario, bringing water from an area south of Oswego called the Lake Ontario Plain. Around 1600, we approached the Port of Oswego Authority East Pier and moored port side to, so that our bows would be headed towards the river channel when we got back underway.

Oswego is not a large city by any means, with a population of around 7,600 at that time. To our surprise, dozens of people were already waiting on the pier for our arrival. They seemed genuinely excited, with barbecue grills sizzling and tables and chairs set up. I spotted a couple of kegs of beer ready to go. After we secured all the mooring lines and shut down the engines, we put our gangway out. All the boat crews disembarked onto the pier, and it felt like we were celebrities. One after another, people approached us, eager to shake our hands. Cheerful groups chanted, "U.S. Navy, welcome to Oswego."

Turning to Bobby, I asked, "Have you ever seen anything like this before?"

He shook his head, indicating no. A fella introduced himself as the "Mayor" and encouraged us to have something to eat and get a beer. A few minutes later, now standing on a chair, the mayor asked for everyone's attention.

Once all quieted down, he announced, "On behalf of the city of Oswego, I want to extend our warmest welcome to the crews of the Navy's fast patrol boats; our fair town is open to you. Have fun and enjoy your stay in Oswego." This time, we joined the locals in cheering the mayor's announcement.

When sailors tell a good story, they often start with the phrase, "Now, this is a no-shitter." This signals that what follows is a genuine account, ensuring listeners know they're about to hear something real.
Bobby was about to get lucky, maybe... A middle-aged man with a big cigar clenched in his teeth walked around and approached different crew members. He would talk to each person for several seconds, and then move on. After a while, he approached Bobby and me.

"Are either of you married, got a girlfriend, or are you single?" he asked.

"I'm married," I answered.

 "I'm single," Bobby replied.

He focused on Bobby and asked, "No girlfriend, right?"

Bobby replied, "No, sir, not at present."

The fella handed Bobby a set of car keys and said, "Here's the keys to my car, see that white Lincoln parked up the street?"

Bobby nodded while taking the keys and said, "Yes."

"Now see that pretty blonde girl over there at the first table wearing the red top?"

Again, Bobby nodded and said, "Yes."

The guy held out a $100 bill, trying to give it to Bobby. "Here's one hundred bucks, that girl is my daughter, her name is Amy. Use my car to take her out tonight and show her a good time. Now go introduce yourself and get acquainted; hopefully, she'll like you."

Bobby turned to face me with a questioning look. Before he could say anything, I told him, "Take the money, take Amy out, have fun. Just don't marry her, okay?"

Bobby accepted the money from her dad, turned, and walked over to where Amy was sitting at the table. I could see him talking to Amy. After about 30 seconds, she motioned to the chair next to her, and Bobby sat down. That was the last I saw of Bobby, except for a few minutes later at the hotel. He had cleaned up, changed into civilian clothes, and looked happy as he headed out for his date with Amy.

The people of Oswego hosted a reception for several more hours. They served us some good food and made sure we drank as much beer as we wanted. Around sunset, they began to pack up and clean the pier area. The reception party was over. I would say we had just received one of the warmest welcomes during our entire trip.

Early the first evening in Oswego, after checking into the hotel, I made my call to Jan, as was my routine everywhere, and, as usual, we talked for some time. Then a group of us were off to check out the local bars in Oswego.

The following day was Wednesday. Opening the boats up for public tours had become routine. Bobby showed up around 0830; we all knew why he was late and had covered for him. His date with Amy either went tremendously well or not so great. Steve asked Bobby how his date had gone.

Bobby grinned. "Man, I don't kiss and tell."

We accepted that Bobby would not spill the beans and returned to work. By 0900, there were lines of people already forming on the pier. Two Navy recruiters had set up their table on the dock at a central location. At 1000, the tours started. Larry was down on the pier at the gangway, organizing people into groups.

We all took our tour stations and greeted the first group as they boarded. Another day of interacting with the public began. Many of the people in the initial groups we recognized from the reception the day before. The day went well. We closed the tours at 1600, then most of us headed to the hotel, about two blocks away, near downtown.

The boats were open to the public for the rest of our time in Oswego. Our stay included plans for the boats to be in town on July 4 for Oswego's Independence Day celebration. We were perfectly fine with the extended stay. Oswego was an enjoyable town; everyone we met was friendly and welcoming. Even the tours we led every day didn't feel like much of a chore due to the people's genuinely pleasant demeanor.

On Monday morning, it was time to go. There were maybe a dozen people on the pier to see us off. Bobby stayed on the dock until the very last minute while saying his long goodbye to, you guessed it, Amy.

We were about to transit southward through the Oswego River/Canal and ultimately enter the Erie Canal (eastern half) at Three Rivers Junction. These waterways are regulated regarding vessel speed restrictions. PTFs, even at engine idle speed, could still produce around 12 knots of speed through the water. Except for certain sections, the New York State Canal System generally has vessel speed limits ranging from 5 to 10 miles per hour (about 4.3 to 8.7 knots). The speed restrictions in the canal systems dictated that a tugboat would be towing our boats for most of the transit.

The tug, *Oklahoma*, appeared and maneuvered along the pier ahead of PTF 17. Our three boat crews worked together using our mooring lines made up into towing bridles and hawsers. The tug passed a towing hawser to PTF 17 (the most forward boat), and they made it off to her bow deck fittings. PTF 17's crew passed a towing bridle and hawser from her stern to PTF 18. Lastly, PTF 18's crew passed another towing bridle and hawser from their stern to our bow, where we made it up to our deck fittings. This towing arrangement simplified the process whenever the tow rig would need to be broken to enter and exit the numerous locks along the canal system.

It wasn't far to the first lock on the Oswego River/Canal, Lock O8, just a short distance upstream, almost immediately after passing under the first bridge. All lock chambers on the Oswego Canal are the same: 328 feet long and 45 feet wide, and they offer fittings on each lock wall for tying off vessels. We were able to fit the tug and all three boats into each lock at the same time and lock through together. Each of the seven locks on the Oswego Canal raised our boats in steps, a total of 118 feet in elevation.

The tug *Oklahoma* had a unique design feature: a retractable wheelhouse. This allowed it to raise the wheelhouse's height using its hydraulic ram system for better visibility and then lower it to ensure clearance under the many low bridges along the canal.

On the Erie Canal from Three Rivers Junction to Troy, NY, there are 23 locks. At Three Rivers Junction, the route into the Erie Canal system is via the Oneida River to the first lock, Lock E23 at Brewerton. After Lock E23, our boats were at Lake Oneida's water level. It is about 25 nautical miles across Lake Oneida to the following two locks at New London, NY. These locks, Lock E22 and E21, would raise the elevation of our boats by about another 50 feet. We were now at the highest elevation above sea level along this section of the Erie Canal.

The journey through the eastbound locks, from Locks E20 to E2, took us progressively lower as we navigated the canal. Traveling through upstate New York along this waterway became a straightforward process of moving from one lock to another. When we finally reached Lock E2 near Waterford, NY, we had descended approximately 380 feet in elevation above sea level after passing through all the locks.

Locking through became quite labor-intensive, as many Lockmasters allowed only two boats to lock through at a time. This decision required us to break apart our towing arrangements, including the bridles and hawsers, to allow each boat to maneuver independently. Consequently, these locking operations were not just labor-intensive but also time-consuming. We anticipated that it would take us two days to transit approximately 135 nautical miles through the Erie Canal, with a contingency plan extending that to three days if weather or other conditions turned unfavorable.

As we progressed along the canal, the countryside in many areas looked much like wilderness. I can say that during the summer months, many places along the canal—the trees, plant life, and flowers—bloomed in their full glory. There were dense trees, green bushes, and lush foliage everywhere one looked. The denseness frequently opened, revealing the vivid colors of wildflowers. The word 'beautiful' doesn't quite capture the radiance of the area. Some spots seemed so remote that it's hard to imagine that Interstate 90 runs almost parallel to the canal in many places.

We passed near Rome and later in the day, Utica. Many locks are located near cities; people would appear on the wall of the lock, watching our boats go through. If we happened to tie up along a wall waiting to go through a lock or after going through, the locals would often approach to get a closer look. It wasn't uncommon to get pelted by their questions; some people thought we were the Army. To clarify, we made a sign from a bed sheet with the words "Go Navy," spray-painted on it, and draped it over the outside front of the wheelhouse.

The vertical clearance under many bridges spanning the canal is barely 20 feet. At least for me, it was somewhat of a novelty watching tug *Oklahoma's* wheelhouse retract to its lowest vertical position to clear under low bridges. Once clear, the hydraulic ram system hoisted the wheelhouse back up. For under-bridge clearance, the low profile of our PTFs allowed us only to lower our mast and radio antennas.

By early evening, *Oklahoma* and our boats were tied up for the night, just past Lock E17 near Little Falls, along the wall. It had been a long day; we had covered just over 100 nautical miles since leaving Oswego that morning. Most of us prepared sandwiches in the galley for dinner, then gathered around to shoot the bull. Mr. Knowles joined us as we discussed what lay ahead to complete the canal transit to Waterford, about 84 miles away. This distance still included passing through another 15 locks, plus the Troy Lock and Dam.

The next morning, it took us only about 10 minutes to arrange the tow to *Oklahoma*. By now, all were well practiced in making up and breaking down the towing arrangement. In early morning fog, our group of boats returned to the canal's channel, bound for E16, the next lock about 8 miles east. We cleared Lock E16 about two hours later. Once back in the channel, the tug *Oklahoma* picked up speed. The low-speed canal restrictions were relaxed for the next 68 miles of the canal until we would reach Lock E6, near Crescent, NY. Instead of speeds around 4 to 5 mph, we were doing closer to 10 mph.

The day shifted seamlessly from one lock to the next as we made our way to the Waterford area. Here, the last four canal locks are closely situated, allowing us to move swiftly from one to the next. By 1700, we had successfully cleared the last lock at Waterford, Lock E2. From this point, we were just 3 nautical miles away from our destination: the Troy Lock and Dam on the Hudson River. We waved farewell to the tug *Oklahoma* and its crew, fully prepared to operate under our power. In less than half an hour, we navigated through the Troy Lock, marking our official entrance onto the Hudson River.

We had done it; we could now say we had been through the Erie Canal or at least the eastern half of it. From the Troy Lock, it is only about 2 miles downstream to the city of Troy on the east bank of the Hudson River. We tied up for the night around 1830 along a wharf near the Riverfront Park, just south of the Troy-Green Island Bridge. We would only stay overnight, then continue downriver to Manhattan in New York City.

From Troy to New York City is about 132 nautical miles down the Hudson River. We estimated that we could achieve an average transit speed of 16 or 17 knots. However, we knew from the Navigation Regulations that there were areas where we had to be mindful of potential wake damage along the shore if our speed was excessive.

We got underway from the wharf at about 0800 and made our way into the river's channel, headed downstream. Unknown to us, the OICs had devised another plan for the day. The U.S. Military Academy at West Point is about 87 nautical miles downriver from Troy. Inter-service rivalry was the driving factor here.

We arrived at Gee's Point shortly after 1300. West Point is easily recognizable with its prominent buildings, the road leading up a hillside from the railroad station, and the wharves along the riverbank.

PTF 17 led as we carefully navigated our boats into the area off the wharfs. Before long, we noticed groups gathering outside several buildings and others approaching the riverbank. Though it wasn't necessary, as we had already attracted attention, all three OICs began sounding repeated, prolonged blasts on our boat horns.

Mr. Knowles told me to take over the helm while he grabbed the loudhailer and shouted toward the campus, "Go Navy, beat Army," over and over.

Then Mr. Williams' voice came over the radio: "Let's go."

Within moments, PTF 17 maneuvered around and headed toward the channel. After PTF 17 cleared, I steered our boat to port and set a course to follow in PTF 17's wake back out to the channel, with PTF 18 coming around and trailing us.

Our fun for the day was over, and it was time to return to the task of heading downriver to Manhattan. There were still 45 nautical miles of river to reach New York City. About 5 miles south of West Point, the river widens significantly near Haverstraw Bay.

From Haverstraw Bay southward, the channels are deeper and the river is wider; all three boats increased their speed to 25 knots. Within two hours, we were tying up at Pier 88, close to the passenger ship terminals in downtown Manhattan. At the head of the pier was 12th Avenue, near the intersection with West 50th Street.

After mooring, we focused on setting up the boat with essential services from the pier, including fresh water and electrical power. Once everything was in place, Mr. Knowles held a crew meeting to share insights about New York. He discussed the location of our hotel, recommended some local restaurants nearby, and outlined the best routes through Hell's Kitchen to reach Times Square and other attractions. Our schedule included a weekend stay in New York, and we anticipated a significant demand for tours.

The hotel was situated on 11th Avenue, just a short distance from the pier. My room was on the seventh floor, allowing me to gaze out the window at our three PTFs below. As I examined a local street map I had grabbed from the lobby, I realized that the hotel was conveniently close to prominent attractions like Times Square, the Theater District, and Broadway.

Bobby, Donny, and I agreed to meet in the hotel lobby at 1800. We planned to get dinner somewhere and then head to Times Square to see the sights. We were all excited about experiencing the city's vibrant atmosphere and bright lights. After discussing a few options, we decided on a local diner known for its classic New York dishes and quick service.

Once we wrapped up dinner and indulged in a few drinks at the restaurant bar, we made our way to Times Square. The hustle and bustle of people, the massive electronic billboards, and the overall energy of the place were captivating. We walked around, snapping photos and soaking it all in.

After a few hours in Times Square, we knew we had to wrap up our night, but the memories of the vibrant city would stay with us. It was a perfect way to wind down after the long journey down the Hudson River.

Early the following day, Larry called my hotel room and told me everyone was to muster back on the boats by 0800. I asked Larry what was up. He said he didn't know, but Mr. Knowles had told him to notify everyone.

We all left the hotel, made our way to the pier, and boarded the boat. Shortly afterward, Mr. Knowles came on board and instructed everyone to meet him in the galley in 20 minutes. Then he left again, returning to the pier, where he walked over to PTF 17 and boarded. About 15 minutes later, Lt. Knowles returned and came down to the galley where we had all gathered.

He gave us a serious look. "Well, it looks like no one at the Navy recruiting command bothered to publicize our visit." Then he smiled. "So, the decision has been made—screw New York, we won't be providing any tours while here. What that means for all of us is that we have time in New York with not much to do." He leaned back, arms crossed. "That also means maximum liberty for everyone. Larry, you guys work out a new duty section schedule; we only need one crew member per duty section."

"Let's make the most of it," Bobby suggested, a mischievous grin on his face. "I'd say we hit the town hard tonight!"

Laughter erupted, and the atmosphere shifted from duty to delight. Plans swirled around—some suggested Broadway shows, others wanted to experience the nightlife, and a few were keen on shopping. For many of us, this was an unexpected gift, a chance to explore and enjoy ourselves. Aside from Steve, who volunteered for the first duty day, the rest of us and Lt. Knowles headed back to the hotel.

When we arrived, Lt. Knowles said, "I don't want you all just hanging out in bars and nightclubs while you're here. This is an excellent opportunity to experience some culture you won't find anywhere else. I've secured tickets from the United Service Organizations (USO) for the afternoon matinee at Radio City Music Hall. That's our plan for today."

What could one do? Mr. Knowles was not someone you could say no to. He was the best officer I'd worked for during my time in the Navy. I believe everyone in the crew felt the same way. The lieutenant was a fun instigator, but he always looked out for our best interests and took great care of his crew.

Larry stepped forward. "What time do we need to leave?"

"All of you meet me here at 1400, wear the best civilian clothes you have with you, okay?" Lt. Knowles replied.

After a light lunch, we all gathered in the lobby, waiting for Lt. Knowles. He arrived right at 1400. We left the hotel and began walking east on West 50th Street as a group. After a few minutes, we crossed Broadway, and in just a few short blocks, we reached the intersection with 6th Avenue. Radio City Music Hall was on the other side of the street. I had heard about the place for most of my life, and now I was seeing it. As we crossed the street, it was hard not to keep looking up at the illuminated Radio City Music Hall signs all over the building's front. Near the entrance, Mr. Knowles distributed tickets to each of us, and we all proceeded to the lobby. An usher handed us matinee programs and escorted us through the sparsely filled hall to our seats up front, close to the orchestra section.

Soon, the stage curtains opened, revealing a large screen. Seconds later, a video began playing that included a brief introduction, detailing that the presentation we were about to see was a roadshow release of "The Sound of Music," combined with a stage show. What an intriguing combination—a film with great audio, interspersed with dancers appearing on stage periodically to perform their routines. It turned out to be quite good. After about an hour and a half, the show's finale brought the Rockettes to the stage. Thirty-six Rockettes entered and danced in unison onto the stage, taking their positions. The Rockettes performed six or seven routines before finishing with the grand finale for which they were famous, the eye-high kicks.

In the matinee program, I learned that the audience was encouraged to count along with their high kicks during the Rockettes' routine. It was suggested that applause should occur between the eighth and twelfth kick, adding an interactive element to the performance. I had to admit that maybe Lt. Knowles was right—the show was fantastic. We all enjoyed it.

Once the show concluded, we all exited Radio City Music Hall and wandered around, soaking in the sights and the vibrant hustle of people on the streets.

The next day, we were on our own. Larry, Bobby, Donny, and I had agreed to meet for breakfast around 0900 to discuss our plans for the day. Larry mentioned that Mr. Knowles had called his room early that morning, letting him know he would be out of touch for a day or two. He said we could leave a message at the hotel desk if needed, as he would check for messages regularly.

Our routine for the remainder of our time in Manhattan was about the same each day. We would meet for breakfast and explore the areas and streets around Times Square. Bobby, Donny, and I made it to the Empire State Building; I always wanted to do that. From the upper-level observation deck, the views are astounding. We also made the trip to Liberty Island and toured the Statue of Liberty. Each evening was spent finding a new bar to haunt until it was time to go back to our hotel. Late Monday afternoon, we all gathered back on board the boats. We would stay on board that night as we would depart early the next day for the final leg of the trip to Little Creek.

The next morning, at about 0630, each boat, in turn, got underway from Pier 88. We maneuvered PTF 19 away from the pier, then turned her around, making our way back out to the Hudson River. PTF 17 took the lead, with PTF 18 next and our boat last. Once southbound on the river, after just a short distance, we passed "The Battery" at the junction of the Hudson and East Rivers.

We were leaving the Hudson River and entering the Upper Bay southbound via the Anchorage Channel. Soon, Governors Island was on our portside, and Liberty Island was on the starboard as we continued down the channel to The Narrows. At The Narrows, we passed under the Verrazzano Narrows Bridge, entering Ambrose Channel. Ambrose Channel took us southeast, passing Sandy Hook, New Jersey, to our starboard, then into the Atlantic Ocean. Once we passed the final whistle buoy marking the exit from Ambrose Channel, all three boats came around to a southeasterly heading, allowing us to follow the New Jersey coastline about 10 miles offshore.

The distance from New York to Chesapeake Bay Entrance was 265 nautical miles. Fortunately, the sea state conditions were favorable, with waves only 2 to 3 feet high. There was very little true wind. Lt. Williams on PTF 17 called over the radio, ordering a speed of 35 knots (about 40 mph). We would reach Chesapeake Bay Entrance at that speed in about eight hours, assuming the weather and sea state remained cooperative. It was a day of good weather and calm seas.

Around 1500, we spotted Chesapeake Light, a massive offshore light structure located about 14 miles east of Cape Henry and the entrance to the bay. By 1600, we were approaching the entrance to Chesapeake Bay. With Cape Henry off our port side, we entered Thimble Shoals Channel, where all boats were required to reduce speed to 15 knots. A few miles later, we passed over the Chesapeake Bay Bridge-Tunnel, a remarkable sight against the vastness of the water.

West of the bridge tunnel, PTF 17 turned to port, leaving Thimble Shoals Channel, and began approaching the southbound channel that would bring us to the entrance of the Navy Amphibious Base at Little Creek. PTF 18 followed in PTF 17's wake, and we trailed behind. All three boats slowed to minimum speed. As we approached the entrance into Little Creek, we could hear Lt. Williams on the radio communicating with Port Control, requesting permission for our three boats to enter. Moments later, we received a reply permitting us to enter the port and providing our berth assignments in the harbor basin at the West Annex, specifically at piers 4 and 5.

Within about 15 minutes, we tossed our mooring lines to the handlers on the dock for the last time. It was over; our long journey had come to an end. Several officers and chiefs from Coastal Squadron Two were there to greet us. Once the engines were shut down and the gangway was in place, one of the chiefs boarded the boat. He saluted Lt. Knowles and requested the crew to gather around. The chief warmly welcomed us and informed us that after we packed our gear and were ready, a bus was standing by to take us to our barracks for the night, while the officers would head to their quarters.

In a short while, we gathered our gear and said our quiet goodbyes to PTF 19 as we walked off her for the last time. We had taken care of her, and she had taken care of us. As a crew, we made our way to the head of the pier and boarded the waiting bus. After a short ride, we checked into the barracks, stowed our gear, and headed to the galley nearby for dinner. This would be our last meal together as the crew of PTF 19. We were instructed to report to the Coastal Squadron Two administrative office at 0800. Most of the night was spent in the barracks lounge watching TV or sitting outside, chatting and relaxing.

The next morning at 0800, all of us gathered at the administrative office to collect our travel orders and flight tickets. Since we only had our work uniforms, we were instructed to wear civilian clothes. Only a few of us were returning to Great Lakes. As for the rest of the crew, each person had their orders and flights to various locations.

That morning, after saying our goodbyes, was the last time we saw each other. Lt. Knowles was there to bid farewell, moving from person to person, shaking hands and thanking each of us for being such great crew members and making his life easier. He repeatedly expressed his gratitude, stating that he was, "grateful for all of us because he could always depend on every one of us." Until the end, Lt. Knowles maintained his class and composure. It was a bittersweet moment, reflecting the reality of Navy life—great friends often separated suddenly, sometimes never to reunite again.

Later, I took a taxi to the Norfolk Airport terminal for the flight home. That afternoon, my plane landed in Chicago. Jan and Mitch were waiting for me at my arrival gate in O'Hare Airport. From the airport, we made the 35-mile drive home to Great Lakes. That day marked the end of what I have always included on my list of great adventures.

I had two weeks of leave ahead of me, and Jan had arranged for a week off from her job. The next morning, we packed our car and drove six hours to Jan's parents' home in Stacyville, Iowa. We planned to spend five days visiting family and friends before returning to Great Lakes. Our time in Stacyville was always a pleasant experience. For the time being, life was good.

Jan and I were unaware that dark, turbulent storms of life were looming just over the horizon. We couldn't see them yet, but they were brewing. Within a few short months, we would find ourselves caught in these storms, feeling as if there were no way out.

CHAPTER 2

STORMS AHEAD

Before I knew it, my leave was over, and I was getting ready to fly to San Diego for the next five weeks for Enlisted Navy Recruiting Orientation (ENRO). It was a bright Friday morning—a day of new beginnings. Jan took the day off from work to drive me to O'Hare Airport, as we shared a quick goodbye in front of the terminal. The last time I visited San Diego was back in 1973, when USS *Rich* made a weekend stop there on our way home from Vietnam. We had to pause after our long journey across the Pacific from Yokosuka, Japan, to refuel and resupply before heading home. I was excited for the next adventure ahead.

It was about a four-hour flight from Chicago to San Diego. At the airport, I could catch a shuttle bus to the 32nd Street Main Gate. I checked in at the gate, showed my orders, and was directed to a bus that took me to the Bachelor Enlisted Quarters (BEQ) designated for ENRO students. I checked in at the BEQ and received my room assignment.

Carrying my bags and gear, I found my room and entered. I was astonished; apparently, West Coast sailors live a whole lot better than East Coast sailors. It was a nice, clean, modern single room with its own head and shower. I was impressed that there was a small refrigerator, a comfortable sitting chair, a desk and chair, and a TV set. This place was more like a hotel. I recall thinking that this recruiting gig might turn out all right!

The next question was what to do over the weekend until school started on Monday. Well, after all, I am a sailor in San Diego. I could easily recall the bars on National Avenue, just up the street from the main gate, but tonight was not the night for that. It had been a long day. Instead of heading into town, I decided to explore the area around the BEQ. It was early evening, and I swung by the galley for dinner.

After finishing my meal, I found a nice common patio area behind the BEQ where two guys were chatting and enjoying some beers. I approached them and asked where I could grab a beer. They informed me about a vending machine inside at the rear of the lobby. Noticing they were drinking Budweiser, I asked if they needed refills, and they both nodded eagerly. I found the vending machine inside and was delighted to see it stocked with Schlitz, my preferred beer. I purchased three beers and headed back outside. I took the beers outside to the patio and sat down. I introduced myself to the guys. Both were friendly. The shorter, stocky guy got up, took his beer, and introduced himself as Barry.

The other guy, a tall, lanky fella, reached over to shake hands. "My name is Henry, but everyone calls me Hank."

After talking for a few minutes, it was no surprise, since we were all at the same BEQ, that they were also there to attend ENRO. Barry was a Storekeeper 2nd Class (SK) from Lawrence, Kansas, while Hank was an Operations Specialist 2nd Class (OS) from Oakland, California. They had both come from the same ship, the aircraft carrier USS *Midway*, which was homeported in Yokosuka, Japan. Given the size of the crew on aircraft carriers, it made sense that they hadn't known each other until that day.

The three of us spent the evening chatting and quickly became friends. We also made several trips to the beer vending machine. Around midnight, we decided to call it a night but not before agreeing to meet up again the next afternoon. I had found my running buddies for the rest of my time in San Diego.

The next afternoon, the three of us met up as planned. Fortunately, Barry had a car, so we didn't have to walk to get into town, which was a great relief. So, where do we head on a Saturday afternoon in San Diego? If you know anything about sailors, you might guess the answer. If you said Tijuana, you would be correct. Once we were off base, it was a quick trip through National City and Chula Vista to San Ysidro, where we crossed the international border.

Tijuana is a vibrant blend of shops, street vendors, stores, food stands, bars, cafés, restaurants, and nightclubs. Brightly colored buses constantly navigate the streets. On one corner, a vendor offered to take our picture with a donkey that was painted white with black zebra stripes. What a fascinating place!

We spent the afternoon exploring the streets and arrived on Avenida Revolución, or "Revolution Avenue," the heart of Tijuana's entertainment district. This thoroughfare was lined with bars, clubs, and restaurants, and from the exteriors, it was clear that each establishment had its own unique atmosphere and style.

As evening approached, Barry expressed his desire to return to San Diego. Hank agreed, noting that the atmosphere could change significantly at night, particularly around the bars. He explained that it was not uncommon for corrupt Tijuana policemen to target sailors, arresting them just to see how much cash they could extort. I didn't object, so we returned to the border crossing.

Upon entering the U.S., we found that the border agents were more thorough, insisting on seeing identification and inspecting our bags, which contained a few souvenirs we had purchased. Once we got back to the car and were en route to San Diego, Barry suggested we check out some good bars he knew of in National City.

"Let's do it," Hank and I agreed.

We spent the night hopping from one bar to another, not looking for much beyond the places that appealed to us the most. After all, we would be there for five weeks, so we needed to find the best watering hole. On Sunday, we all met up and spent the afternoon driving around, exploring different areas of San Diego. We all wanted to be ready to start ENRO training in the morning. None of us had a clear idea of what to expect.

On Monday morning at 0700, my two new friends and I entered the ENRO building. After checking in, we were directed down a hallway to a room with rows of chairs. There were already 30 or more sailors present. Over the next 15 minutes, about 20 more new students arrived. I noticed that the students were a mix of ratings and pay grades, ranging from petty officer second class, like myself, to senior chief petty officers. I was surprised by the number of students present. I remember thinking that the Navy must need a shit-ton of new recruiters.

Within minutes, a senior chief took to the podium at the front of the room. He introduced himself as Senior Chief Goldman, the senior staff instructor. He then turned to introduce the chiefs standing behind him: Chief Belke, Chief Glover, and Chief Williams.

Senior Chief Goldman explained that 60 new students were in our class, but we would be divided into four groups, each with 15 students. Each group would be identified as Alpha, Bravo, Charlie, and Delta.

The senior chief explained that the first 15 names called, in alphabetical order, would be assigned to the Alpha group, with the next 15 called in the Bravo group, and so on. As for me, my last name begins with the letter "T," so I was assigned to the Delta group. It appeared that Chief Williams would be our instructor.

Once we were all divided into our respective groups, Senior Chief Goldman instructed everyone to return to their seats. Just then, a commander entered the room. Senior Chief Goldman called, "Attention on Deck," and we all quickly stood at attention.

As the commander walked to the podium at the front of the room, he said, "At ease, retake your seats."

The commander greeted us with a warm, "Good Morning."

"Good Morning, Sir," the entire room responded.

He started with his welcome message, explaining that he was the officer in charge. He then outlined the purpose and intent of the training experience we were about to embark on.

The commander emphasized several key points during his message. First, he noted that we were selected because our previous commands had identified us as top-performing sailors. In his words, we were the "cream of the crop." Secondly, he explained that participating in ENRO and joining the Navy recruiting force would be a life-changing experience for us, personally and professionally. Lastly, he highlighted that every instructor at ENRO was handpicked from the top tier of the recruiting force, all having a proven record of success as field recruiters and as leaders of recruiting stations or zones. After the commander left the room, the senior chief returned to the podium and instructed each group to follow their instructors.

"Delta group, with me," Chief Williams called out.

It was the first day of ENRO, and our initial steps toward becoming Navy recruiters were about to begin. ENRO consisted of five weeks of training in professional sales, prospecting techniques, marketing, applicant processing, recruiting terminology, leadership, ethical behavior, and activity analysis. The environment here was unlike any that most students had experienced. There were many new terms to master and new skills to acquire. It was a setting where classmates engaged in a mutual learning experience.

We participated in many public speaking classes to develop our communication skills. These skills helped us in recruiting and benefited us throughout the remainder of our naval careers. We were often required to demonstrate what we had learned in the classroom through prepared speeches. Additionally, there was significant role-playing to simulate a sales environment. This role-playing emphasized the importance of helping an applicant (the prospect) make an informed and mutually beneficial decision to join the Navy.

The training stressed the importance of focusing on prospects' needs, facilitating an open exchange of information, and ensuring mutual understanding and agreement throughout the recruiting process. These steps were critical in ensuring prospective applicants fully understood what naval service would entail.

Early in my training, I realized that I had a personal challenge that only I could address: my introverted personality. If I didn't manage it, I often became shy, soft-spoken, withdrawn, and distant. I understood that to succeed in recruiting, I needed to find ways to overcome my introversion and adopt behaviors more aligned with extroversion.

Once I fell into the routine, ENRO seemed easy. Every weekend was off, with very little homework or studying required. Probably for most of us, the biggest challenge was public speaking. The instructor would give you some inanimate item, such as a nail or ball-point pen, then provide 15 or 20 minutes to prepare a presentation precisely three minutes in length, relating whatever item you had to the U.S. Navy. For example, on one occasion, I was given a piece of 2″ x 4″ lumber about six inches long; my presentation focused on becoming a Navy Seabee and learning the construction trades.

I made phone calls home to Jan once or sometimes twice a week. Collect calls could become expensive depending on the day of the week or the time of day, so we were always careful about how long we talked. I considered being able to call Jan that frequently a luxury.

It is essential to consider the context of the times. Just three short years prior, the Cease-Fire Agreement that ended active U.S. combat operations in Vietnam took effect. Almost simultaneously, the Secretary of Defense announced the adoption of the "All-Volunteer Force," which marked the end of the military draft system. This change meant that recruiters for the Navy, Air Force, and Marine Corps could no longer wait for walk-in applicants looking to enlist to avoid being drafted into the Army. They must now proactively seek out prospective applicants.

As each week of ENRO progressed, we all experienced growth. In addition to public speaking, sales prospecting became a significant area of focus. A critical aspect of sales prospecting involves making cold calls by telephone. Recruiters were responsible for generating appointments for interviews with prospective candidates, and cold calling proved to be an effective method for doing this. We learned that each day, recruiters dedicate time to making cold calls to reach out to prospective candidates identified on the Armed Services Vocational-Aptitude Battery (ASVAB), school lists, and other sources.

Week five, the final week of ENRO, had arrived. Graduation day was that Friday, September 3. Each graduate received their U.S. Navy Recruiting Command badge, which is worn on the left side of the uniform shirt, just below our ribbons. It was filled with heartfelt farewells as everyone prepared to be assigned to their respective recruiting districts. We all believed we possessed the necessary tools, skills, and knowledge to become successful recruiters.

I had a flight booked for that afternoon to Chicago, and we arranged for Jan to pick me up at the airport. My orders didn't require me to check in at the Navy Recruiting District (NRD) Chicago headquarters until Wednesday, September 8, the day of my birthday.

Jan and I were delighted to be together now that I was home. After my month-long trip taking the PTFs to Little Creek and spending five weeks in San Diego, the summer months had slipped away.

I was happy because the long Labor Day holiday weekend gave me four days off before I had to report to NRD headquarters at Naval Air Station (NAS) Glenview. I woke up early on Wednesday morning, as my orders instructed me to report by 0800. The drive to NAS Glenview was about 23 miles. I wore my dress white uniform, and arrived by 0730. I quickly found the NRD headquarters building, parked my car, and went inside.

When I walked in, I headed towards the administrative office. The clerk greeted me warmly, took my orders, and then asked me to sit near the door. After about five minutes, a chief entered and introduced himself as Mike Dodge. Mike then gestured toward the passageway and invited me to come with him. He explained that we were going to meet with the chief recruiter (senior enlisted recruiter). Upon entering the chief recruiter's office, a senior chief stood up from his desk and approached me.

He extended his hand. "Welcome, George. We knew you were reporting today. My name is Frank Wilmer." He motioned toward a chair. "Please, have a seat. You've met my assistant, Mike."

This was one aspect I was still getting used to; in recruiting duty, individuals are rarely addressed by their last names or rate; it's generally first names only. Frank sat at his desk while Mike settled into a nearby chair.

Frank glanced at a paper on his desk. "It's a big day for you! Your birthday and first day in recruiting command—can't beat that. It must be a good omen," he remarked.

He informed me that I would be assigned to the Navy Recruiting Station (NRS) in Waukegan, since I was currently living in Great Lakes. I was pleased with this arrangement since Waukegan is only about 10 minutes from my home. Additionally, Frank explained that I would spend most of the day meeting with the enlisted programs officer (EPO), the executive officer (XO), and the commanding officer, which is customary for all new recruiters.

Later that morning, I met with the EPO, Lieutenant Xavier Lincoln. He explained that NRS Waukegan was being expanded to a three-man office and that I would report to Slim Hendrickson, the recruiter in charge. Mr. Lincoln seemed like a decent guy; like most Navy lieutenants, he spent a lot of time telling me things I already knew.

After lunch, I met with the XO, Lieutenant Commander Royce Miller. What I primarily remember about this meeting is my impression of him. The XO struck me as condescending, bitter, and rather unpleasant.

Later, I met with the commanding officer, Commander Daniel J. Bell. What initially caught my attention about the commander wasn't his race (it's worth noting that he is African American) but rather his impressive Afro hairstyle, which was the largest I had ever seen on anyone in the Navy. Beyond this, he appeared reserved and refined. However, I also sensed that he could be condescending and cold.

After meeting with the commanding officer, I returned to the chief recruiter's office. Mike was sitting at his desk when I arrived. I informed him that I had completed my meetings with everyone and asked if there was anything else I needed to do.

Mike stood up. "Yes, one last thing. Tomorrow, you start your first day as an official field recruiter. Be at NRS Waukegan by 0800 in the morning. Slim Hendrickson knows you are coming. Since we're already into September, you won't be assigned enlistment quotas until next month."

I thanked Mike, turned, and left, exiting the building and heading to the parking lot for my car. On my drive home, I began to think that maybe recruiting wouldn't be so bad after all; at least, it's shore duty.

The next morning, I woke up bright and early. As I left, Jan took a picture of me walking out the front door to commemorate my first day as a Navy recruiter. After a short drive, I parked in front of the recruiting station at 209 West Water Street in downtown Waukegan. As I entered, I heard someone talking in the back office. A smiling man with a thick black mustache and piercing blue eyes was seated at a desk just outside the office.

He stood up and extended his hand. "You must be our resident QM."

As we shook hands, he said, "I'm Rob Summers." He then motioned toward the back office. "That's Slim Hendrickson on the phone; he'll be right out. Welcome to NRS Waukegan."

Rob, a Machinist Mate 2nd Class (MM2), was slim and of medium height. His thick black hair complemented his large mustache. It was clear from the beginning that he was a personable individual, and people took an immediate liking to him. I watched as Slim hung up the phone, got up from his desk, and entered the front office.

Slim, a Boiler Technician 1st Class (BT1), was a tall and slender African American with a neat Afro hairstyle, glasses, and a well-groomed goatee.

When Slim introduced himself and we shook hands, I was struck by his demeanor. He came across as well-spoken, friendly, and easygoing.

Slim pointed to a desk and chair near the front office window that faced the street. "We've rearranged things here to create a workspace for you," he explained. "As you may know, I'm the recruiter in charge, and I'll be working with you today to help you get settled and started. Throughout the day, Rob and I will review the routines and outline the daily and weekly activities. Our territory covers all of Lake County, which is quite extensive. Even though having a third recruiter increases our station's monthly quota, we're happy to have the extra help."

Rob piped up, addressing both of us while pointing at me and chuckling, "Hey Slim, look at the size of this guy! I may have found my new steaming (drinking) partner. No one will give me problems as long as he's with me."

Slim looked at me with a smile. "Rob likes to visit the bars occasionally, so I will depend on you to keep him in check. I don't drink much, so it's on you."

I spent the day getting organized and reviewing the suspect and prospect cards. Later, Slim took me into a small room next to his office that had a large, shallow cabinet with double doors mounted on the wall. Slim opened the cabinet doors, revealing a large map of Lake County.

"I know you covered the SMART system at ENRO, and this is ours. I want to show you where we need you to concentrate your efforts in the county," he said.

One of the key tools used at a Navy Recruiting Station is called the "Station Market Analysis and Review Technique" (SMART). The SMART system was designed to identify quality market centers, indicating where recruiting resources should be focused to achieve the best possible results. Most of us referred to it as the SMART board, which was prominently posted in every recruiting station.

Lake County's population was approximately 383,000. Most of this population consisted of active-duty military personnel and their families, particularly near Great Lakes Naval Station. Another part of the county, located south of the naval station along the shores of Lake Michigan, is known as the "Gold Coast." This area is home to many wealthy and affluent families, whose children typically attend Ivy League schools instead of enlisting in the military. Consequently, these two sections of the county influenced the accuracy and reliability of the qualified military applicant numbers for our territory. Slim explained the situation clearly. At that time, the monthly quota for each recruiter was five enlistments.

"Now that you're here, our station's quota has increased from 10 contracts to 15 per month. Typically, Rob and I have been fortunate, with each of us securing three or four contracts each month. I've been here for over a year, and Rob has been here for about 10 months; we've never met our station goal," Slim explained. "Here's how it works: if you can secure at least three contracts monthly, Spence, our zone supervisor, and the district will likely leave you alone. However, if you have three consecutive months without at least three contracts, things could get unpleasant for us all, especially for you. Do we understand each other?"

I responded, "Yes, I understand."

During my conversation with Slim, I realized I was in a no-bullshit situation. The message was clear: I needed to produce results, or there would be consequences. Although none of Slim's comments surprised me, I was still in the naive phase of being a new recruiter. At ENRO, we had been taught that if we used the tools they provided effectively, we would be successful. However, like many recruiters before me, I would soon learn that the idealistic world they depicted at ENRO and the harsh realities of the real world do not coexist in the same realm.

I was about to get my first introduction to the Armed Forces Examining and Entrance Station (AFEES) runs. Around mid-afternoon, Rob mentioned that he had an AFEES run scheduled for the following morning. Since he was only transporting two applicants, he suggested that I accompany him so he could show me how to get to AFEES and explain the process for delivering applicants for processing. He instructed me to meet him at the office by 0430. He emphasized that all applicants needed to check in by 0600; otherwise, they might be turned away. In the Chicago district, AFEES was located in downtown Chicago, on West Van Buren Street in the West Loop, approximately 40 miles from the office.

That night, I set the alarm clock for 3:30 a.m. Jan was surprised by the time. "Are you going to have to get up that early every day?"

I clarified that this was due to the AFEES run and mentioned that our office typically makes these runs once or twice a week, depending on the number of applicants being processed. I also noted that we would rotate the runs among the three of us in the office.

The next morning, I arrived at the office early. Shortly after, Rob walked in and laid out the applicants' paperwork packages on his desk. He quickly explained the details.

"Are you ready?" he asked.

I nodded in agreement. Rob drove as we set off into the darkness of early morning. When we arrived at the first house in Waukegan, Rob asked me to get out and knock on the door. After a moment, a young man emerged. I quickly introduced myself and asked if he was ready. He nodded in response.

Our next pick-up was in Libertyville, roughly 10 miles from Waukegan. Once we had the second applicant in the car, Rob drove out of Libertyville, merging onto I-94 South and heading toward downtown Chicago.

About 30 minutes later, we arrived in front of the AFEES building near the entrance. Rob handed me the paperwork packages and asked me to go inside to ensure the applicants checked in at the Navy desk while he parked the car. The three of us got out and entered the building. Double doors led into a large, empty lobby, and along one wall was a long counter, divided into sections for each service branch.

We approached the Yeoman at the Navy counter and handed him our paperwork. He reviewed everything and then directed our applicants to the stairway on one side. After a few minutes, Rob came in and asked if everything was okay. I told him I thought so and that the applicants had already gone upstairs.

"Would you like some coffee and breakfast?" Rob asked.

I replied, "Definitely coffee."

Rob led the way as we stepped back onto the street, turned, and walked along the front of the building until we reached South Jefferson, where we turned right. About half a block down, there was a restaurant. Although it was still dark outside, the lights from the restaurant and the illuminated sign above the door reading Barney's looked inviting. I was somewhat surprised when we got inside; the place was filled with recruiters from all military branches. It had a greasy spoon vibe that added to its charm. We found an empty table and sat down. This would be the first of many breakfasts I would enjoy at Barney's over the next three years. Barney's served good coffee and hearty breakfasts at affordable prices. After early mornings of rushing to get applicants to AFEES on time, that first sip of fresh, hot coffee was just what I needed to start the rest of the day.

After breakfast, we headed to the car for the trip back to Waukegan. Once back at the station, Slim had brewed coffee, and we chatted a bit before starting our workday. That day, I learned it was a semi-nervous waiting game whenever we had applicants at AFEES. Each time the phone rang, I noticed that both Slim and Rob would momentarily tense up. I would soon understand why, especially when applicants were expected to enlist that day. If someone from AFEES called before early or mid-afternoon, it often meant bad news. The reasons for the calls could vary, ranging from applicants performing poorly on the ASVAB or failing the physical exam to confessing to previous law violations or drug use. While not all calls were negative, most of the time they were. I also would know the disappointment of realizing that all the hard work and time invested in an applicant could lead to nothing.

Before long, my recruiting days evolved into a steady yet diverse routine. Practicing effective time management was of utmost importance. Many days were filled with prospecting activities, handling applicant paperwork, and occasionally attending career days at local high schools or colleges. Towards the end of the day, the final prospecting activity involved making cold calls.

As a new recruiter, I needed to find prospects quickly. In addition to cold calling, I began traveling to different towns. I visited every place I could think of, spoke with people, handed out business cards, and asked those I talked to for potential referrals of anyone they thought might be a candidate for the Navy. I made my rounds, stopping by local high schools, shopping malls, YMCAs, fast-food restaurants, unemployment offices, and job training centers. And, holy crap, it worked—within about two weeks, I was working with around eight potential prospects.

Out of the eight prospects I developed, along with two additional ones I acquired from walk-ins at the office, I sent five of them to AFEES for ASVAB testing and physical examinations by mid-October. By the end of the month, three of them had enlisted, and I was ecstatic! Even though I didn't meet the full quota of five enlistments, Slim and the zone supervisor seemed pleased. No one mentioned it, but I later learned that most new recruiters are fortunate to secure even one enlistment in their first month of production status.

At the same time, I was preparing for the upcoming advancement examination for Quartermaster 1st Class (QM1, pay grade E-6). With the long workdays, the only time I had left for studying was late at night. Balancing my new recruiting responsibilities with exam preparation proved to be a challenge. I dedicated every spare moment I could find to poring over the study materials.

Finally, I sat for the QM1 advancement examination at NAS Glenview in February. I remember walking out after the exam, feeling uncertain and thinking I would be an E-5 for a while longer. Despite all the effort I put into studying, doubts crept in. I tried to reassure myself that I had done my best, but waiting for results always felt excruciating.

The U.S. military strongly encouraged almost every high school in the country to allow the administration of the ASVAB test for its junior and senior students. The ASVAB results shared with all military branches included each participant's personal contact information and highlighted individual test section scores.

Additionally, the military often obtained student lists from high schools that included students' names, home addresses, ages, and telephone numbers. These ASVAB results and school lists were compiled into suspect/prospect lists organized by zip codes.

Generally, cold calling shouldn't begin until late afternoon or early evening, which gives you the best chance of the prospect being home. Making cold calls successfully is part of prospecting, as it combines both art and science. The primary goals of each call are to engage the prospect on the phone and schedule an appointment with them. It's crucial to avoid providing them with an easy way out during the conversation.

As the months passed, our team often worked 10 to 12 hours each day, with AFEES runs regularly extending into 14-hour shifts. Saturdays were usually filled with work as well. However, due to the collaborative efforts of the three of us, we managed to send an average of 10 to 12 applicants to boot camp or into the delayed entry program each month. While this performance wasn't exceptional, it was enough to prevent the recruiting district headquarters from pressuring us. Or so we thought.

Recruiting duty was effective in various ways; unfortunately, one was in straining marriages. The long workdays and weekend commitments tested Jan's patience. Although she knew it was beyond my control, her disappointment in our lack of time together grew. I understood her feelings and felt frustrated as well. Like many married couples, we felt deceived by the Navy. It was supposed to be shore duty, where families had more time together.

"So we're not going to get time together here for three years, then you'll go back to sea duty where we'll have even less time together," Jan said.

Through the General Services Administration (GSA), the command leased a property in Ingleside, located in the western part of Lake County. It was determined that the Ingleside location would serve as a part-time office for NRS Waukegan. This concept would allow prospective applicants to meet with a recruiter closer to home, rather than traveling to the Waukegan location.

In March 1977, headquarters suddenly began paying much more attention to NRS Waukegan and other stations in the northern recruiting zone. Most stations in the Northern Zone had been failing to meet their monthly quotas. The zone supervisor, Spence, was fired and replaced by Senior Chief Chuck Thorton. On his first day, Chuck came to our station and held a closed-door meeting with Slim for several hours. When they emerged from Slim's office, Slim looked tired and dejected. Rob and I exchanged questioning glances. At that moment, the chief recruiter, Frank, Lt. Lincoln, the EPO, and the XO walked through the front door.

They asked Rob and me to stop all work and called us for a meeting. Everyone gathered in the larger front office area. The essence of the meeting, led by Frank and with comments from the EPO and XO, was to express their dissatisfaction with our station's production level. They wanted to determine if there was a systemic problem in our territory or, as the XO said, "Were we just lazy recruiters?" I recognized that mean-spiritedness I had sensed in the XO during our initial meeting. I quickly realized it was best to remain silent and respond to any questions directed at me as briefly as possible. Slim explained that he believed our area's data was flawed and not as substantial as the district thought.

The XO dismissed Slim's argument. "I don't believe what you're saying is true."

Chuck partially defended us, mentioning that he had reviewed the stations and our individual activity records. "It's not that they haven't done the work; the station simply needs guidance," he said.

To my surprise, Frank addressed Rob and me. "George, you're doing a good job, especially considering you've only been here for six months." He paused before adding, "Rob, your production levels are similar to George's. So don't worry; neither of you is being fired." He then turned to Slim and said, "You're not fired either. However, we are going to bring in additional help."

The meeting ended abruptly when the XO stated, "I think we've accomplished what we set out to do."

Without further comments, everyone gathered their belongings and walked out the door. Chuck stayed behind, and once he was sure that everyone else had left, he addressed the three of us. "I'll be back tomorrow. Don't worry; we will fix this, and there will be more news soon. For now, I think all of us—including myself—could use some refreshment."

He turned to Rob. "I know you have the scoop on the best local hangout, so lead the way. It's on me, shipmates."

Just like that, our world was about to change, but not for the better. We went out and had a few drinks with Chuck, putting on what we thought were happy faces. Chuck left after several rounds to head home for the night. Before he departed, he told us to make sure our schedules were clear the next day from 1300 on. Rob, Slim, and I stayed at the bar and ordered another round.

Slim, who had stayed quiet through most of this, turned to Rob and me. "Do either of you feel like we just had a ton of bricks dumped on us?"

Both of us nodded in agreement. After another round, Slim said goodnight and left for home. Rob and I stayed at the bar longer talking; Slim was a good guy, and we both felt bad for him.

In 1973, as part of the movement toward an all-volunteer force, the Navy established a new rating known as the Navy Counselor (NC). The initial goal was for NCs to serve as career counselors for significant shore or afloat commands, with a percentage designated to form the Career Recruiting Force, which emerged during this transition.

The next afternoon, Chuck arrived promptly at 1300 to meet with Slim. Their private discussion lasted about 30 minutes, during which Rob and I waited with increasing curiosity. When they emerged from the back office, Slim approached us with a serious expression. He informed us that a new recruiter in charge would be arriving that same afternoon.

The incoming recruiter in charge was Senior Chief Navy Counselor (NCCS) Blake Gardner. Chuck added that Blake was known as a recruiting legend, particularly celebrated for his remarkable success as a recruiter in the state of Missouri. This was his second tour in recruiting command, and his reputation preceded him. The plan was for Blake to take over at the Waukegan station while Slim and Rob continued in their current roles.

Chuck and Slim both turned to face me. Chuck said, "George, there will be some changes involved here that concern you. First, understand this is somewhat of a promotion and nothing else. You still belong to this NRS, but starting next month, you will be manning the part-time office in Ingleside three to four days each week."

I wasn't sure if this new plan was a good thing or not. I saw it as a disruption to the routine I had settled into over the months. The thought of shifting my focus and spending considerable time in a new location was unsettling. The Ingleside office might bring new opportunities, but it also meant adjusting to a different environment and a new set of prospects. I wondered if I could sustain the momentum I had built in Waukegan.

"Chuck, what does this mean for my current prospects?" I asked, hoping to gain some clarity.

"Your core responsibilities will remain the same," he reassured me. "The Ingleside location will increase our outreach and hopefully improve enlistment numbers in that area."

As he spoke, I could see Slim nodding in agreement; his body language indicated that he supported this decision, yet I sensed he shared my apprehension. The prospect of starting over felt daunting in some ways, but I also knew that adapting was part of the job. With a determined mindset, I resolved to make the best of this situation, regardless of how challenging it might be. It was time to embrace this change and see where it would lead me.

Chuck told us he had to go and that Blake would arrive soon. Blake showed up about an hour later. After making some small talk with all of us, he turned to Rob and me.

"My pickup is in the rear parking lot. In the back, there's a rocking chair and a couple of boxes; would you two bring that stuff in for me?" he asked. Then he turned to me and continued, "I like where your desk is, right up front. When you return, move your stuff out so I can move in."

My only thought was, *Well, hell.* We had already rearranged the office and placed a new desk and phone in a spare back office at the station, assuming a senior chief would want a private office. Instead, Blake pointed to the other back office and told me I could work out of there. I could already feel the tension in the air—his arrival was shifting everything we had arranged.

Blake was a slender man of average height. His face bore small acne scars, and his hairstyle featured a well-groomed comb-over that covered his balding spots. Still, he exuded self-assured confidence and presence, evident in his facial expressions and the way he walked and moved.

The word "eccentric" is a fair description of Blake. After Rob and I brought in his chair and boxes, Blake immediately pushed the desk chair aside and pulled his rocking chair over to the desk. I quickly moved the few items I had stored in the desk to the back office. Blake settled into his seat, pulled a Rolodex from one of his boxes, picked up the phone, and made a call.

We gathered in Slim's office, exchanging quizzical looks but saying nothing. Before long, we overheard Blake on the phone congratulating someone for being promoted to rear admiral. He told the new admiral that he always had full confidence in him and that he would be promoted. Rob leaned over and whispered, "Who is this guy?"

We got back to work, and I noticed Blake was busy making call after call. After finishing his last one, he stood up, informed us he'd see us in the morning, and then walked out. Slim glanced around and repeated Rob's earlier question, "Who is this guy?"

Rob turned to me and said, "I think we need to go have some beers. Are you ready?"

"Yeah, let's get out of here," I answered.

We asked Slim if he wanted to come with us, but he declined and wished us goodnight.

The next morning, we arrived at the office at our usual time. The hours drifted by, but there was no sign of Blake. Finally, around noon, he walked in. After grabbing a cup of coffee and settling into his rocking chair, he signaled for Rob and me to join him at his desk.

As we approached, Blake handed me a matchbook and then produced a napkin for Rob, each with something written on them. The matchbook cover had a name and phone number; the same went for Rob's napkin.

Blake looked at us and said, "Here are some leads I got last night. Call them up, get them in here, and put them in the Navy."

We soon discovered this was Blake's signature modus operandi. He was somewhat of a barstool recruiter. He would often visit bars at night, seek out single, typically divorced women with older children, and persuade them that it might be a good idea for their kids to meet with a recruiter to explore their options. Rob and I called the prospects Blake had given us, and, to my surprise, they both scheduled appointments to come in for an interview.

Later that day, an attractive, middle-aged Filipino woman walked in. Blake immediately got up from his rocking chair and greeted her with a hug and a quick kiss. Slim and I were chatting near Rob's desk when Blake turned to face us, gesturing toward the woman.

"Guys, this is Miss Veronica," he said.

We all exchanged greetings and introduced ourselves in turn. Blake and Veronica chatted briefly before he walked her to the door. After she left, Blake called for everyone's attention.

"Whenever Miss Veronica calls here for me, always tell her I'm not here, and you'll make sure I get the message that she called. Does everyone understand?" he announced.

Rob asked, "Even if you're here?"

"Yes, even if I'm here," Blake replied.

Without further explanation, Blake turned and sat down at his desk. We all exchanged confused looks and returned to work.

Meanwhile, I needed to prepare to open a part-time office in Ingleside. The building in Ingleside had once been a small gas station, but part of it was converted into office space. Directly across the street was a bowling alley, which notably featured a bar and served food. Office furniture needed to be delivered and set up, the phone system had to be installed, and it required equipping with the necessary forms and recruiting aids. The recruiting aids included literature racks, brochures, flyers, posters, signs, and giveaway items.

The downside to Ingleside was that I felt as if I were starting over. I had been informed that there was an expectation for no disruption in my production. So, no break there—essentially, it would mean doing double duty establishing Ingleside while still meeting the monthly quota. What I had learned so far in recruiting duty was that the words "fair" or "fairness" were not in our vocabulary.

Ingleside had its charm, but beneath the surface, a sense of urgency lingered in the air. I couldn't shake off the nagging feeling that time was running out and that I needed to prove myself. Everyone seemed to be in their race, and I was trying to find my footing.

I reminded myself daily that this was part of the process, a stepping stone in my journey. Yet, the duality of feeling both challenged and isolated weighed heavily on me. The uncertainty lingered. I had no choice but to press on. The upside was that I didn't have to spend much time dealing with the daily show hosted by Blake Gardner at Waukegan.

I divided my time between Ingleside and Waukegan for the next five months. Despite the strain on my time and energy, I still managed to find enough prospects to enlist three to five each month. I began to think I could make it work.

To my amazement, the advancement examination results were released in June, and I was selected for advancement to Quartermaster 1st Class. I was set to be frocked to QM1 in July, but I wouldn't begin receiving pay at the E-6 level until October.

When I shared the news with Jan, she was pleased. The pay increase was welcome, especially during the Jimmy Carter era, when high economic inflation strained everyone's budget. Jan also worked full-time, and we could manage financially with both her salary and mine. Additionally, the thought of finally moving up the ranks was exhilarating for me.

One morning during the first week of September, I was at the Ingleside office when I received an unexpected phone call from Chuck, who mentioned he would be stopping by early that afternoon. I initially thought his visit was just another routine check-in, but I was mistaken. When Chuck arrived, he brought along a hefty Boatswain's Mate 1st Class (BM1), whom he introduced: "George, this is Buck Wright."

Chuck wasted no time getting to the point. "George," he said, "it seems you're doing so well out here by yourself that it's time we give you more help. Buck lives right here in Ingleside, so we're moving him here. Ingleside is now a full-time recruiting station, and you're the interim recruiter in charge."

I was left speechless, grappling with the sudden shift in my role. A whirlwind of thoughts raced through my mind. *How can we secure five more monthly contracts to meet Buck's quota?* The weight of expectation settled heavily on my shoulders as I came to understand the implications of what Chuck had just told me.

Chuck wasn't finished. "I don't know if you've heard, but we're opening a new recruiting station in Libertyville. It will be a two-man station, and you are the new recruiter in charge. You have until November 1 to get Buck up to speed here in Ingleside before we move you to Libertyville." Chuck extended his hand to shake as he said, "Congratulations, George! You've earned it."

I remember saying to Chuck, "You're full of surprises today, aren't you? Is there anything else you would like to tell me?"

Chuck chuckled. "That's one thing I like about you: your unique sense of humor."

Recruiting duty was challenging; just when you thought you had everything under control after handling one problem, another would come your way. Sometimes, it felt like they were intentionally trying to make you fail. After Chuck left, I got to know my new recruiter. Ingleside is a small town, and it turned out that his house was only about two blocks from the office. Buck was fresh out of ENRO and had that bright, new look about him—the exact look I probably had just a year before. So, it seemed that Ingleside would be a good fit for Buck.

The main drawback of having Buck with me was that it created a setback in my goal of achieving the coveted award for recruiting excellence, known as the gold wreath. The gold wreath is a physical holder that fits the recruiting badge, making it appear as though the badge is surrounded by a gold wreath when worn. To earn the gold wreath, a recruiter must achieve 15 enlistment contracts over three consecutive months. I had nearly reached this goal twice but fell short by just one contract. No other recruiter in Lake County had a gold wreath—except for Blake. In my view, Blake's achievement didn't truly count since he earned his gold wreaths during his previous recruiting tour in Missouri. Ultimately, one of the main reasons I wanted the gold wreath was that it could provide some protection from being jerked around by the district.

At times, it was challenging, especially when I was at AFEES or having breakfast at Barney's after an AFEES run, to see all the Navy recruiters from the Chicago recruiting stations. They walked around proudly displaying their gold wreaths. It was common knowledge that inner-city stations enjoyed a steady stream of walk-in traffic, which made meeting their goals seem effortless. In contrast, working in suburban stations like mine required relentless effort. We had to "pound the pavement and shake every bush," hoping to find potential recruits.

I started Buck just as Rob had with me: early the following morning, I had him ride along for the AFEES run to Chicago. During Buck's first few weeks, I focused on finding more applicants while also taking the chance to introduce him to my contacts at each high school. We followed my itinerary routes (IT), using the IT log to pinpoint every establishment with literature racks, signage, or posters. Our visits included various businesses, as well as local VFW and American Legion posts, where I established valuable contacts that provided applicant referrals, ultimately leading to enlistments. Additionally, I introduced him to the SMART board system I had set up. We also reviewed the prospecting logs and discussed the progress made with cold calls from the school and ASVAB lists. I felt confident that there wasn't much more I could do to ensure a smooth transition for him.

I assisted Buck during his first month as a recruiter. I had five strong applicants lined up for the month, ready to proceed. I handed over two applicants to Buck to help him get his feet wet. I felt that this was a generous gesture, as no one had helped me in that way when I was a brand-new recruiter. However, I wanted Buck to succeed because I was genuinely excited yet apprehensive about taking over the new station in Libertyville.

When it came to moving to Libertyville, I had mixed feelings. On one hand, it felt like starting over for the third time in just over a year. It was only about 7 miles from home, so the commute wasn't too significant. Adding to my concerns was the fact that it wasn't just the Navy opening a station in Libertyville; the Army and Marine Corps were also setting up offices in the same complex. Additionally, the Air Force had recently established an office in the nearby town of Mundelein, just 3 miles west.

The local population was a factor I could not overlook. To the east lay the Great Lakes Naval Station. The southeastern part of Libertyville's territory was the Gold Coast. Short distances to the south included five other Northern Zone recruiting stations in Palatine, Schaumburg, Glenview, Des Plaines, and Evanston. It felt like a small, somewhat confined area. What concerned me was that it would be a two-man station with a monthly quota of 10 enlistments—five per recruiter.

The Northern Zone was already notorious for chewing through recruiters. Many new recruiters didn't last six months, and recruiter turnover in our zone was higher than anywhere else in the district. After three or four months of poor productivity, many recruiters were labeled as remedial and were squeezed hard. By "squeezed," I mean mandatory working hours became 8 to 8 (0800 to 2000), six, possibly seven days a week, with the zone supervisor calling or visiting daily to track progress and reprimand.

The district's statistician met with remedial recruiters weekly, plying them with data sheets outlining the number of cold calls and ratios the recruiters needed to meet to succeed. I observed instances where the district statistician and zone supervisor required recruiters to make hundreds of cold calls each day, which was an impossible task.

I was glad to be away from my original location at NRS Waukegan. Besides Rob, that place had turned into a revolving door for recruiters. Slim was gone. The infamous Blake, for reasons unknown to me, had transferred to a station in the Central Zone. In less than six months, two more recruiters had arrived and left. For some reason, Waukegan had become even more of a struggling station.

It was striking to see how quickly the district could wear out a recruiter. In many cases, recruiters reached a breaking point, with some openly admitting defeat and asking to return to sea. Generally, when someone was transferred out of recruiting before completing their tour, they were classified as either a "fault" transfer or a "no-fault" transfer. A "fault" transfer typically arose from attitudinal issues or a refusal to meet performance standards, while a "no-fault" transfer resulted from an inability to adjust to the recruiting environment. Surviving a "no-fault" transfer could be feasible for one's career, but a "fault" transfer often spelled the end. The district wielded the threat of a fault transfer like a weapon, routinely using it to undermine and potentially terminate sailors who struggled to adapt.

Therefore, there were two ways out of recruiting duty: (1) finish the three-year tour successfully, or (2) accept the terms of a fault or no-fault transfer. As I mentioned earlier, I realized early at NRS Waukegan that recruiting was a no-bullshit situation. All the reasons I just laid out were collectively on my mind, which gave me pause about the viability of Libertyville's success.

The pressure was palpable, and each day felt like a gamble. I questioned whether I could summon the persistence required, all while battling my doubts and skepticism. The stakes were high, and I understood that the path ahead was challenging. *Would I rise to the occasion, or would I become just another statistic in recruiting history?* The thought weighed heavily on me. But just like many situations I had encountered so far in the Navy, what choice did I have? I was about to enter either a "win-win" or a "lose-lose" situation.

The Ingleside station had been doing well, especially with Buck's confidence growing over the past two months. On November 1, I moved to Libertyville, about 14 miles southeast of Ingleside. The new station was located in a strip mall at 737 North Milwaukee Avenue, the main thoroughfare through downtown Libertyville. Final touches on the offices were still underway, and two recruiting stations—Navy and Army—shared an entrance, front lobby, and restrooms. The Marines had their own office three doors down in the same complex. The grand opening was scheduled for Saturday, November 12.

One thing I noted was that the Army and Marine stations were only one-man offices. The Air Force station at nearby Mundelein was also a one-man office. Nevertheless, the Navy decided Libertyville would be a two-man office. Enter my new recruiting partner, Aviation Warfare Systems Operator 1st Class (AW1) Mack Diedrich. Mack had been transferred from a station in the Central Zone closer to the Chicago metro area, where he had spent the previous six months. Mack was a large, soft-spoken man, standing about 6 feet 3 inches tall, with a big build, blonde hair, and eyeglasses.

Mack and I began transforming our new home into a recruiting station. Unlike in Ingleside, I had Mack's assistance this time, which made dividing the necessary tasks much easier. Public affairs had secured quarter-page ads in local newspapers to promote our grand opening. The district also sent invitations to local high school guidance counselors, principals, and select teachers whom I had suggested. Additionally, Libertyville's mayor, members of the city council, along with the chiefs of the police and fire departments, were invited. I participated in interviews on local radio stations and made several appearances on local TV. Since we were sharing the location with the Army recruiting office, they were also engaging in similar promotional efforts.

Chuck communicated that there were no expectations for production in November. However, we were expected to produce at least three enlistees each in December. By January, the grace period was over; it would be full-on production quota. While getting acquainted with our Army counterpart, a staff sergeant named Bob asked me when the Navy expected us to meet the full quota. When I told him our timeframe, he replied with a surprised facial expression, "You're shitting me! I have until next April."

Always being a sailor, I responded, "Well, that's the difference between sailors and broke-dick ground pounders, I guess." My response had a two-fold purpose: (1) to see if he was bullshitting and (2) to see what kind of sense of humor he had.

Bob laughed. "So, what I've heard about squids is true, you're all full of shit."

I now knew from our conversation that we were going to get along. The big day of our grand opening arrived. The weather was warm, and the skies were clear; one would never guess it was a November day in northern Illinois. The event was an open house, advertised from 10:30 a.m. to 4:00 p.m. Of course, some members from the command attended, including Chuck, the chief recruiter, and our new EPO, Lieutenant Todd Blakely, whom I had yet to meet. I was pleased throughout the day to see several guidance counselors and teachers I knew from the local high schools, the city mayor, and several city council members. A local FM radio station had set up in the parking lot, where I conducted short interviews with them. The turnout wasn't huge, but we estimated that close to 100 members of the public and local businesses attended.

The following Monday, we focused on serious prospecting and established an itinerary route in the area. We kept busy arranging visits to local high schools and building connections with American Legion posts, VFWs, Rotary Clubs, Moose Lodges, and Elks Clubs. As sailors, we also checked out the best spots nearby for after-work beers following our evening cold calls. By early December, Mack and I had started processing several applicants each. Things seemed to be coming together well, but I had some concerns due to the fast-approaching holiday season. It was traditionally tough to find applicants willing to ship out to boot camp in December, as many preferred to wait until January. The solution was to convince them to enlist in the delayed entry program, which would allow them to leave for boot camp later. At least that way, the recruiter would still receive credit for the enlistment.

Chuck walked into our office one afternoon the week before Christmas, but he wasn't alone. He had a chief with him, whom he introduced as Chief Boiler Technician (BTC) Connor Howard. Then Chuck dropped a bombshell: he announced that Chief Howard would be the new Northern Zone supervisor, starting in January.

I asked Chuck, "Where are you going?"

Chuck indicated that he was being moved to the Central Zone in Chicago to replace the zone supervisor who was transferring back to sea duty.

Chief Howard would be my third zone supervisor in just over 15 months. I extended my hand to the chief. "Welcome, chief. My name is George, and as you know, my partner here is Mack."

"If you don't mind, let's keep it military. I'll address you as Petty Officer Trowbridge or as Trowbridge," the chief replied. I shot a questioning glance at Chuck, who shrugged his shoulders.

Then I asked Chief Howard, "I don't believe I've ever heard of you. What station or zone were you at before?" His answer floored me.

"I'm fresh out of ENRO." Then, smugly, he said, "I only took the orders here with the understanding that I would be a zone supervisor."

My response was out of character because I verbalized my thoughts when I said, "Let me get this straight: you've never put a body in the war, but you're going to supervise a zone full of experienced recruiters? Whose dick did you suck?" As the old saying goes, you could have heard a pin drop.

The chief looked at me. "You may require some personal attention."

I responded by laughing at him. As I walked past Chuck, I told him I was stepping outside for a minute. Once outside in the parking lot, I focused on calming myself down. This guy had really pissed me off. I quickly realized I was dealing with a fool, and that's all he was. After a few minutes, I went back inside.

Mack sat at his desk, grinning as he gestured toward the closed door to the back room. Chuck and Howard were in a closed-door session. After about five minutes, they emerged. To my surprise, Chief Howard approached me with a smile and extended his hand.

"George, I think we got off on the wrong foot with each other," he said. I accepted his hand, and we shook. "I'll be back after Christmas, and maybe you can find time to get me up to speed." What could I say to that?

"Sure, we'll see you then," I replied.

With that, Chuck said, "George, Mack, we need to go; I still need to get Connor to the Palatine and Des Plaines stations this afternoon."

They then gathered their things and left. Mack and I had a brief conversation about our new zone supervisor. Mack shared that his assessment of Connor Howard was the same as mine: Connor was a real dick.

"I'm going to make some calls to see what I can find out about him," Mack said.

I shrugged and returned to the tasks I wanted to complete for the day. I had several home appointments scheduled for that afternoon. When I returned to the office, Mack had some news. Mack had contacted a friend of his who worked in the Central Zone. According to Mack's friend, Connor Howard was friends with our outgoing chief recruiter, Frank.

Frank had persuaded the EPO to give Howard a chance at the zone supervisor position.

I remember telling Mack, "Well, that's just great. We're already overwhelmed trying to get this place up and running, and now they saddle us with this prick."

The next time I heard from Connor was around mid-January. He called almost every day around 1700, asking what we had accomplished that day. He wanted reports on various aspects, including the number of prospects we were working with, the number of applicants who had taken the ASVAB or been sent to AFEES for physicals and classification, the number of cold calls we were making each day, and whether we had any school visits scheduled. It seemed to me that he spent all day thinking up pointless questions to ask. Up to this point in recruiting, no one had micromanaged my work. The only recruiters I'd seen manage that way were the ones who were failing.

I recall telling Mack, "My first assessment of Connor was that he was just a fool; let me add he's an idiot."

Several high schools and one junior college in our area experienced changes in their administrative leadership, resulting in unfavorable outcomes. It all began when we were invited to a career day at a local high school. Upon my arrival to set up, the guidance counselor informed me that we were not welcome and had to leave. Mack faced a similar situation at a community college event. Recruiters observed that educators influenced by the post-Vietnam anti-government movement had gained positions of power in many local schools.

The policy required us to report these occurrences to the district, which we did. Many schools receive federal funding, and barring military recruiters from their campuses could jeopardize that funding. The district was supposed to contact the schools on our behalf to address these incidents. However, as has often been the case with the district, we never received any feedback or reports. Overall, support from the district was essentially nonexistent.

During Connor's daily calls, I developed a strategy of asking him a series of questions. For example, I would ask, "What's the status of School X that we reported? When can we expect the ASVAB student lists from Schools Y and Z? Has my request for funding for newspaper advertising been approved? I need supplies from recruiting aids for our itinerary routes; what's the status on that?" I bombarded him with any questions I could think of. It became almost like a game, as I don't recall Connor ever being able to answer any of my inquiries. Ultimately, my strategy succeeded in getting him to reduce the number of his phone calls.

In the longer term, my persistence in changing the situation paid off when Connor informed me that all he needed was a status report every Friday afternoon. It wasn't a victory for me; all I wanted was to be left alone to produce whatever I could.

The upcoming months looked bleak. Walk-in traffic for our station was essentially zero, leaving us with no prospects. Mack and I encountered more frequent hang-ups during cold calls. Parents would sometimes answer the phone and yell at us to leave their kids alone.

One night, a father called and threatened to confront me. I remember telling him our address and that I was 6 feet 3 inches tall, weighed 220 pounds, and looked forward to meeting him in person; he hung up. It seemed that anti-military sentiment had taken a strong hold in the Libertyville area. To gauge the situation, I occasionally discussed it with Bob, our next-door Army recruiter. On several occasions, I think he was genuinely honest when he admitted that he had faced experiences similar to ours.

In the following months, recruiting qualified applicants became increasingly demanding and challenging. Our station operated with three to seven enlistments per month. It seemed that my initial assessment that Libertyville could function as a one-man station rather than a two-man station was proving accurate. Overall, the lack of district support, an incompetent zone supervisor, working in a highly competitive territory, and the pressure to meet impossible quotas were taking a toll on both Mack and me.

To cope with our stress and frustration, our after-work drinking sessions became more frequent. Eventually, we stopped relying on our local bars after work; instead, we began bringing our own spirits to the office, and drinking even started during our cold calls. Thankfully, we had recruiting posters to cover up the occasional hole in the walls created by fists or feet. Instead of going home at 2000, we often stayed later to continue drinking at the office or our local bar. I don't know how Jan managed to tolerate it. Many nights, I would come home drunk around 10 or 11 p.m., say goodnight to her, and then pass out in bed.

Just when I thought the situation couldn't get worse, it did. Connor, or "Howard, the idiot," as most recruiters in our zone had taken to calling him, began making unannounced visits. On several occasions, he made insulting and disparaging comments to either me or Mack. The one that almost pushed me over the edge was when he commented, "Maybe Mack and I weren't the shit hot recruiters everyone told him we were." Most people like me had learned it was best to ignore "Howard the idiot" and just go about our business.

Around the first week of June, the district statistician visited our office. He was Senior Chief Fire Controlman (FCCS) Bill Lane, who had never served as a field recruiter. He reviewed our prospecting and cold call logs, then pulled out his printouts and a spreadsheet to highlight that we weren't generating enough activity.

Bill firmly believed in his formula for success, which he described as a 5-to-1 ratio. According to him, making five cold calls would lead to one appointment. From there, five appointments would result in one interview. He further claimed that five interviews would produce one qualified applicant, and ultimately, five qualified applicants would lead to one enlistment.

He stated that all we needed to do was make enough cold calls each day to schedule twenty-five appointments, averaging five interviews daily. Over a typical month with twenty-four workdays, this strategy would lead to 120 interviews, resulting in approximately twenty-four qualified applicants. Ultimately, this should yield at least 4.8 enlistments each month. He emphasized that failure was not an option if we sustained his outlined activity level.

I pointed out to Bill that making twenty-five appointments daily through cold calling would require not just making 125 phone calls per day but also getting 125 prospects to engage in conversation. Additionally, I noted that I typically averaged around 12 to 15 calls per hour, depending on how many prospects I interacted with. Meeting his call quota would take over eight or nine hours. This left little time for other prospecting methods, conducting interviews, processing applicant paperwork, and managing various other daily tasks.

Bill leaned back in his chair, studying me intently. "George, if I understand you correctly, you're saying you don't want or need my help."

I quickly replied, "No, that's not what I'm saying. I do have a question, though." He nodded, prompting me to continue. "Can you give me the name of one recruiter I can talk to who can confirm that they followed your ratios and it worked for them?"

There was an immediate shift in Bill's demeanor; I realized I had crossed a line. He abruptly stood up, gathering his things and stuffing them into his briefcase.

"I can see I'm wasting both your time and mine," he stated sharply. "I'll discuss this meeting with Connor and Frank; you can expect to hear from the district shortly." With that, he turned and left the station.

Mack, who had been silently observing the whole exchange, finally broke the tension: "I think we're screwed."

The next morning, the phone rang. It was the chief recruiter, Frank. He wanted Mack and me in his office at 1300 that afternoon, and before I could respond, he hung up. After lunch, we closed the office and drove to Glenview, arriving around 1245. We parked and entered the headquarters building, heading straight to Frank's office. Frank, the EPO, Connor Howard, Bill Lane, and the XO were already there, and they wasted no time getting to the point.

Frank said, "George, Mack, we've tolerated your poor performance since opening Libertyville. The time has come for some changes. So, George, you are relieved of your duties and will work downstairs in the recruiting aids department for now. Mack, you're being transferred to the Glenview recruiting office across the street. Return to Libertyville this afternoon, clear out your things, and come back to work at 0800 tomorrow."

I started to respond, but the XO cut me off. "Trowbridge, we're done here. Now go do what the chief recruiter has ordered you to do."

"Yes, sir," I replied.

After a glance at Mack, I turned and left the office, walked out of the building, and waited by the car. Several minutes later, Mack came out and walked over to me. We didn't say much to each other during the drive back. At the office, we packed up our belongings and locked the door. Outside in the parking lot, we said goodbye to each other. We each got in our cars and drove away.

I got home before Jan returned from work. When she walked in, she was surprised to see me. I explained what had happened. As always, she took the news in stride. That night, it almost felt out of character when I had dinner with Jan and Mitch.

The next morning, I drove to Glenview and entered the headquarters building through the side entrance, which had stairs leading down to the basement level where the recruiting aids department was located. An old Chief Storekeeper, Ed Fitzgerald, managed the department. Ed was referred to as a TAR, which stands for Training and Administration of the Reserves. He had been on active and reserve duty since the end of World War II; to me, he seemed ancient.

When I arrived, I found Ed and informed him I was there to work for him, at least for now. Ed gave me a tour of the department and explained what he needed me to do. He mentioned that the working hours were from 8:00 a.m. to 4:00 p.m., Monday through Friday. The primary responsibility he detailed was to answer the door when the bell rang, as that indicated a recruiter coming by to pick up their orders. My job would be to fill their orders and log the items I dispense. That was it; that was the whole job.

Working at Glenview with Ed each day felt almost like a vacation. I was home by 1700 every day and had every weekend off. Some days, there was hardly any activity, so I would sit around and read magazines until it was time to go home. I made it a point to avoid the main floor upstairs; I didn't want to run into any of the shit-heads up there. Being assigned to the recruiting aids department was meant to be some form of punishment, but I was enjoying my time there.

What's that old saying? "All good things must come to an end." I got to work in the morning after the long July 4th weekend. Ed was there and told me that the chief recruiter wanted to see me as soon as I arrived. All I could think was, *Fuck, now what?* I took my time, had coffee, and smoked a cigarette before heading upstairs.

CHAPTER 3

ANOTHER TWIST

I climbed the stairs to the main floor and walked down the hallway to the chief recruiter's office. I knocked on the door and entered. To my surprise, three people were seated in the office. Blake Gardner was at the desk, another chief I didn't recognize was sitting in a chair, and the third chief was Chief Gunner's Mate (GMC) Rhett Klein. I had gotten to know Rhett after meeting him at Barney's restaurant, where we would have coffee or breakfast after an AFEES run. Rhett was the recruiter in charge at the top-producing Clark Street station in Chicago's Loop.

Blake began the conversation. "Good morning, George; how's your wonderful wife Jan doing?"

"Fine, Blake," I replied.

"George, I'm not sure if you know, but Frank is no longer here, and I've taken over as the chief recruiter." Blake gestured to the chief I didn't recognize. "This is Freddy Gowan, an old running mate of mine; he'll be my assistant, and you already know Rhett."

Freddy approached and shook my hand. "I've heard good things about you."

Rhett got up and, in turn, shook my hand. "Good to see you again." Then, chuckling and smiling, he asked, "How's life in recruiting aids?"

"Just great," I replied.

Blake motioned for me to sit and explained why I was there. "You may have heard that there's been a shake-up at West Irving Park Road station, the largest in Chicago. We've relieved everyone there for reasons I won't delve into here. However, the station must be back up and running quickly, and that's where you, Rhett, and several others come in."

In that moment, Rhett took charge. "George, I know you and Mack were treated badly, and when I heard about it, I couldn't believe it. I'm stepping in as the recruiter in charge at West Irving Park Road, and I want you on my team. What do you say?"

I held eye contact with Rhett briefly before answering, "Yes."

I agreed to join Rhett for several reasons: I liked him and recognized him as one of the few honest individuals I had encountered.

Rhett seemed pleased. "Great! We start work tomorrow; I know I can count on you." He said, "Mack has also agreed to come on board, along with two others, Jimmy Hughes and Eddy Cooper, so we'll be a five-man station; together we're going to kick ass."

The West Irving Park Road station is located on Chicago's North Side. I recognized it as a great place for recruiting and was somewhat familiar with the area. However, the daily commute to and from Great Lakes would take about 40 minutes or more. One thing you learn to adapt to in recruiting is that you spend a lot of time driving.

The next morning, at 0730, we gathered at our new station. The building also housed the Marine Corps and Army recruiting offices. The Navy had three areas: an office near the front, another near the back, and a separate testing and workroom. I knew Mack well, and I was familiar with both Jimmy and Eddy. Rhett immediately suggested we all go to breakfast first. He led us outside, down the street to the intersection with North Lincoln Avenue, where there was a small restaurant right across the street. Over coffee and breakfast, he outlined his plan.

Rhett had done his research. He understood that West Irving Park Road is surrounded by diverse ethnic neighborhoods, including Filipino, Asian, Polish, and Irish communities. Additionally, several primary and vocational-technical schools are located near the station. Rhett recognized that the station already enjoys a strong flow of walk-in traffic. Lastly, he noted the presence of street gangs, primarily the Latin Kings, along with the Latin Eagles, Uptown Lords, and some white gangs like the Insane Deuces, who are often in conflict with one another, but we did need to pay attention to them.

I quickly realized that working here would be significantly different from recruiting in the suburbs. The next point Rhett made surprised me.

While exchanging glances with me, Mack, and Eddy, Rhett said, "We can't have anyone here not wearing the gold wreath. I report each recruiter's monthly numbers, so we all share in the success. I'll rotate the gold wreath among you three based on our numbers, but I plan for you to earn your gold wreaths by the end of six months."

Rhett then turned to Jimmy, who already had a gold wreath, and asked, "Jimmy, are you okay with this plan?"

"Hell yeah!" Jimmy replied.

Eddy, who had relocated from Skokie, a suburb of Chicago, faced recruitment challenges similar to those in Lake County. Though, I couldn't speak for Eddy or Mack, I questioned, *Can we pull this off?* Despite my apprehension, being part of a team was refreshing—something I had missed. The military is structured around teamwork, but that idea had since faded away in the recruiting command.

After breakfast, we all headed back to the station. In the lobby, four young men were waiting. Jimmy approached them and asked if he could help and who they wanted to see. All four replied that they were there to inquire about joining the Navy.

Rhett smiled at us. "Time to go to work, guys; you know what to do."

I conducted seven walk-in interviews that first day without leaving the office. By the end of the day, I was processing paperwork for three of them. What a change from Lake County! Being a five-man station meant our monthly quota was 25 enlistments, the highest for any station in the Chicago district. July marked a partial production month for our new team, but we still exceeded our goal by sending 28 young people to boot camp. We performed even better in August, achieving 30 enlistments credited to the station.

Mack and I talked one afternoon, and he said, "It's like we've been traded from the Tampa Bay Buccaneers to the Dallas Cowboys."

September was not as strong, but we still surpassed our goal with 26 enlistments. Despite the considerable amount of work we produced, Rhett enforced a strict rule: the station doors closed at 1700; if you stayed later to work, that was entirely your decision. The options were simple: go home or head to the bar next door for a few beers with him before going home. For the first time, other than those nights I spent having beers with Rhett, I was regularly home by 1800, just in time for dinner. Most importantly, we enjoyed most weekends off. Although we kept the office open for part of the day on Saturdays, we took turns working that day among ourselves. For the first time in two years, life seemed good again.

On Monday morning, October 2, I arrived at the station after a trip to Lakeview High School. The XO, EPO, Blake, and Chuck were in Rhett's office. I planned to pass by and head to the back office when Rhett called, "George, go get Mack and Eddy, and bring them in here."

I found Mack and Eddy in the back office and told them Rhett wanted to see us. With Mack leading the way, we walked in a single file down the hall to Rhett's office. Jimmy was already there, making the room feel crowded. Rhett suggested we move to the front lobby for more space. Once in the lobby, Blake instructed, "George, Mack, Jimmy, and Eddy, form a line and face us."

We complied. I noticed the EPO was holding some small boxes. The XO then approached us. "It is my pleasure to present the gold wreath recruiting excellence award to all four of you," he said.

With that, the EPO handed the XO a new recruiting badge with the gold wreath already mounted. The XO turned to me first, handed me the new badge, and shook my hand. "Congratulations, great job."

He then did the same for Mack, Jimmy, and Eddy. I had missed it, but then I noticed that the Army and Marine recruiters had gathered in the lobby as well. When the XO presented Eddy with his gold wreath, everyone in attendance erupted in applause and cheers. Rhett had kept his promise; we all would earn the gold wreath—not in six months, but in just three.

At the same time, swirling around us were all types of events and occurrences I associate with big cities. The gang activity in our territory that Rhett had described during our first morning was accurate. There were routine shootings and other violent attacks, mostly gang-related. This was also during the time in Chicago when the police patrolled many areas on foot or, as they called it, "walking the beat." Officers from the

Chicago Police Department visited us almost daily because we were friendly and always had fresh, hot coffee for them.

One officer had the nickname "Fuzzy." He visited more often than most other police officers and was always pleasant to talk to; everyone liked him. The rapport we built with these officers was invaluable. They were well-informed about what was happening in our neighborhoods. Their insights kept us updated on the latest events and which gang was active in which area.

We displayed an overlay depicting the territories of each major gang on our SMART board. Some young men would call, telling us it was too dangerous for them to come to our station since they would have to go through gang turf. We would conduct some initial discussions over the phone, and if they appeared to be a potentially viable applicant, we would pick them up, drive them to the office, and then return them home.

Once, eight young men from the Polish neighborhood expressed their desire to enlist in the Navy. They insisted that they would only join if they could go together; otherwise, none of them would enlist. They feared for their lives due to threats from a local gang that was actively pursuing them. Fortunately, all eight passed the ASVAB, successfully completed their physical exams, and enlisted. They left for boot camp on the same day.

There were some tough lessons learned. We had a young Black man who called us, and we picked him up to drive him to our office. After the interview, it seemed he would easily qualify for enlistment. Once we completed his processing and scheduled him for AFEES the next morning, we offered to drive him home. However, he insisted on taking the city bus instead. Tragically, within minutes of leaving our office, he was shot three times at the bus stop on the corner. Fortunately, he survived the shooting. Afterward, Rhett met with us, and we unanimously agreed that in the future, we would insist on driving the applicants home if we believed they were at risk.

We quickly learned to maintain a high level of situational awareness and caution whenever we were on the streets or driving in certain neighborhoods. I experienced some intense moments; bricks, rocks, or cinder blocks were thrown at the vehicle I was driving. The white government vehicles, marked with "Navy" in large blue letters, made us easily recognizable. Once, a brick came crashing through my windshield, hurled from an overpass. On another occasion, during an AFEES run right after picking up three applicants at a predetermined location, I drove away only to have a brick and a sizable rock shatter the rear window.

On another morning, during an AFEES run, while it was still dark, I heard four loud bangs echoing through the car. My rule was simple: whenever I wasn't sure what was happening, I would get the hell out of there as fast as the damn vehicle could go. That morning was no exception; I quickly drove away. Later, after delivering my applicants to AFEES and enjoying the sunrise over coffee at Barney's, I approached my vehicle and noticed three bullet holes in the driver-side rear quarter panel and a fourth in the trunk lid. Looking back, it's incredible to me now how I would nonchalantly shrug off things like that and go about my business.

There weren't just gangs to watch out for. Sometimes, what looked like regular people on the street could be dangerous. On more than one occasion, men would walk up to me, then open their jackets or raise their shirts to show me they were armed. Only one made the threat to shoot me.

I recall what I said to him was something like, "If you pull that thing out, I will make you eat it, now shithead, what do you want to do? Pull it or get the fuck away from me." How I looked at him or something convinced him that I was serious because he turned and walked away. I distinctly remember thinking to myself, *George, you're a dumbass.*

There were other types of interactions; in some ways, they were more unpleasant than someone threatening to kill you. Once, a middle-aged woman approached me on the street, came right up to me, spat in my face, and began screaming over and over, "Baby killer." To me, it was sickening that some people hated us that much.

Our small team recognized the importance of staying vigilant about the various forms of violence that could be directed at us. We also acknowledged the need to stay informed about the latest unrest in the city, as it could impact our safety and recruitment efforts.

On some days, before heading home, we would gather at Whirling Dervishes, a disco club and bar just two doors down. The venue featured a spacious dance floor and disc jockeys spinning the latest disco hits. The bar was nice, and there were always many attractive women to admire. It was a fantastic place to unwind before going home. We visited so often that we got on a first-name basis with the bouncers, bartenders, and other staff members.

Most recruiters did not live in the city, which at times caused a point of contention. There were instances when recruiters would arrive at the station to pick up the government vehicle for an AFEES run, only to find that it had been vandalized and, in many cases, stripped of its tires and vital parts. This situation forced the recruiter to use their vehicle to transport applicants to AFEES, which violated another policy.

One significant issue that we faced was the absence of mileage reimbursement when using personal vehicles for work-related tasks. On several occasions, I arrived early in the morning at the station for an AFEES run, only to discover that our government cars had been stripped or vandalized, rendering them unusable. In some instances, after calling the GSA garage to tow vehicles, the GSA dispatcher would inform us that no replacement vehicles were available, forcing us to use our cars for work-related tasks once more.

Collectively, this may not seem like a big deal. But these were the years described by some economists as the "Great Inflation of the 1970s." In 1978, the annual inflation rate was nearly 9 percent, and inflation in 1979 reached double digits. Annual military pay increases averaged less than 5 percent during the last four years of the decade. Additionally, recruiters faced many other out-of-pocket expenses that were not reimbursable. Overall, it could be costly to do the job.

To address financial pressures, some recruiters turned to entrepreneurial ventures. One individual I know purchased hot beverage vending machines and convinced stores, gas stations, and other commercial locations to allow him to install these machines in exchange for a share of the profits.

Some might remember the video game "Space Invaders." A group of recruiters pooled their resources to purchase several commercial game consoles and placed them in various commercial locations. I once asked one of them how much one machine cost, and I believe he told me it was around $8,000. However, he added that the machines paid for themselves quickly, so after breaking even, everything was profit.

Some people participated in an activity known as "running numbers" for gamblers. This involved collecting bets on specific number combinations and then delivering the total amount and recorded bets to the numbers house. Once the winning combinations were announced, the "runner" returned the winnings to the identified bettors. Runners received a significant cut for their services, but the job was dangerous and risky due to handling large sums of cash.

To supplement my income, I decided to be a numbers runner, but I would only do it once or twice a month, usually on Wednesdays. It was easy; it took about an hour early in the day to collect the bets and another hour or so in the late afternoon to deliver the winnings to the bettors. At times, I was carrying as much as $15,000 in cash. In my view, the more cash I handled, the better. My cut for each job averaged between $250 and $400 for two or three hours of work.

The months of November and December went well, and we met our quotas each month. Everything went great until Sunday night, December 31, New Year's Eve. Jan and I hosted a New Year's Eve party at our house. She had invited some of her work friends, while many of my recruiter friends gathered for the celebration. It was a fun party, and the house was packed. It felt like old times, with dancing, drinking, doing stupid stuff, and having a great time. Around 10 p.m., someone mentioned that it was snowing pretty heavily.

Shortly after we welcomed in the New Year of 1979 at midnight, some guests began to leave and head home. When I went outside to see them off, snow fell heavily, creating a full-blown snowstorm. Our house at Great Lakes was less than a mile from the shore of Lake Michigan, so it was not unusual to experience heavier snowfall during lake storms. I also noticed that the air temperature was dropping at the same time. After the last party guests left around 2:00 a.m., Jan and I went to bed.

I woke up late the next morning on New Year's Day. About 12 inches of snow had accumulated in our front yard, and it was still snowing. After having some coffee and breakfast, I went outside to shovel the driveway and sidewalks, as we were expecting guests for a late afternoon New Year's dinner. Although the snowfall rate had slowed, it continued to snow, and now it was really cold outside. Nobody thought much of it; it was winter in northern Illinois.

I got up early on Tuesday morning, January 2, because I needed to shovel the driveway for Jan before heading to work. The drive into Chicago was long and slow, and I didn't reach West Irving Park Road until around 0830. Finding a parking spot on the street was challenging since the roads still hadn't been plowed. When I arrived at work, the only people there were Rhett and Jimmy. Jimmy had a four-wheel drive vehicle and could get around without any problems. Later, Mack and Eddy also arrived.

The weather did not significantly affect our recruiting efforts. We still had applicants from December that needed processing, and walk-in traffic remained strong. Rhett decided to adjust the office hours, opening one hour later in the morning and closing at 1600 instead of 1700. All of us, except for Jimmy, lived in Lake County, which made our daily commutes longer and more challenging. Almost every night when I got home, it seemed that it had either snowed or was still snowing, and I often had to shovel the driveway before I could pull in and park. We were all originally from different parts of the Midwest, so we took the winter weather in stride.

Then came Friday, January 12; it began to snow heavily that afternoon. None of us knew we were about to experience what came to be known in Chicago as "The Blizzard of '79." By Monday morning, January 14, over 23 inches of snow had fallen over the weekend. The snow from early January was still on the ground, so in many areas, the accumulation was now 3 to 4 feet deep. Most of the snow was compacted and contained a significant amount of ice. In addition to the snow, the weather remained cold, with temperatures staying below average.

After that weekend, conditions in the Chicago metro area became truly miserable. The daily struggle to commute into the city in the morning and back home in the afternoon only added to the discomfort. The streets had not been fully cleared, and there had been little to no snow removal. Finding parking in the mornings felt like a leap of faith; you had to drive your vehicle into a snowdrift far enough to get it out of the roadway, all while hoping there wasn't another car buried in the snow that you were heading toward.

To clarify, we were not saints. We were young men in our mid to late twenties, full of energy and driven by high levels of testosterone, eager to raise hell wherever we could. When you combine these typical traits with the constant stress and pressure to perform at a high level, it creates a volatile situation. In a sense, we were like human nitroglycerin. I believe many others felt like me and sought after-work outlets for pent-up frustrations. My incentive was to relieve my energy in bars and on the streets, rather than at home with my family.

Many government vehicles were Ford models from the late 1960s or early 1970s. These Ford models often featured high-performance police interceptor, 352 cubic inch or 390 cubic inch V-8 engines. Essentially, these Fords were fast cars that seemed to endure substantial abuse.

On numerous occasions, after being properly fueled with alcohol, we would take one of the Fords and play our favorite game in the alleys and streets of Chicago. We called the game "Hump Flying," which, in retrospect, was a suicidal game. Hump flying was even more fun if the alleys and streets were covered in snow. The alleys in our part of town were wide and paved, as they provided rear access to each commercial building.

The game was always played at night, starting at one end of a deserted alley and accelerating the car to its maximum speed. The thrill came from reaching the next intersecting street and launching the car over the street's hump, often becoming airborne and landing in the next alley. We always hoped there wouldn't be any vehicle traffic on the street we were flying over. We would take turns behind the wheel to see who could launch the car the highest.

It may sound crazy, but it was a fantastic stress reliever. We particularly enjoyed the game during the weeks of "The Blizzard of '79," as it was a safer bet that most streets would be deserted after dark. It was often said, "If the GSA vehicles could talk, we would all be in jail."

To my surprise, walk-in traffic at the station increased despite the weather. Many applicants wanted to leave immediately, as long as they could attend boot camp in San Diego or Orlando, but not Great Lakes. Meanwhile, snowfall persisted on most days. Little did we know that we would be dealing with snow and cold weather until the first thaw, which wouldn't begin until mid-March.

We all adapted to the circumstances and did our best. In February, both Mack and I earned our second gold wreaths. Rhett received his seventh, and Jimmy earned his third. In March, Eddy obtained his second. There were several days when AFEES closed due to inclement weather, which created additional challenges in meeting our quotas. We had all achieved superstar status in the district's eyes. Mack and I enjoyed our new non-zero status. Around that time, Rhett called Mack and me into his office and closed the door.

He turned to us. "I thought you'd like to know that Blake fired your old friend Connor Howard as the Northern Zone supervisor." Then Rhett smiled at me and said, "George, Connor now has your old job as the recruiter at Libertyville."

"So there is such a thing as poetic justice," I replied, and Rhett laughed.

Another change was implemented: the West Irving Park Road zone designation was changed to the Northern Zone. The good news is that Chuck, who had previously been our zone supervisor before Connor Howard, was once again appointed. We rarely saw Chuck, so I asked him about his infrequent visits one day.

He simply smiled and said, "Why would I interfere with success?"

Another group active in Chicago was the FALN (Fuerzas Armadas de Liberación Nacional). The FALN was a clandestine paramilitary organization from Puerto Rico that advocated for Puerto Rican independence through direct action. Another contentious issue for Puerto Rico was Vieques Island. For decades, the Navy used the island, located east of Puerto Rico, for missile testing, gunfire support exercises for Navy ships, and as a bombing range. Puerto Rico sought the return of the island from the U.S. government.

One night in late March, I had just gotten home from work and was changing clothes in our upstairs bedroom. Suddenly, Jan yelled for me to get downstairs immediately. Thinking something was wrong, I rushed down to the living room, where Jan pointed at the TV, urging me to hurry. Once there, I focused on the screen: a breaking news report showing my recruiting station on West Irving Park Road. The news was that a bomb had detonated at my office about 30 minutes earlier, blowing out much of the back wall. The report also detailed how the Chicago Police Department stated that the FALN had already claimed responsibility for the bombing. That same night, there were several other bombings at different locations in Chicago.

After the TV report ended, I noticed that Jan was visibly shaken. She asked me what I planned to do next. I told her I would go to work in the morning to find out what needed to be done once I had all the details.

"How can you be so calm? What if you guys had still been there?" she asked.

I reassured her by saying that we weren't there. I was confident that no one else had been present, including the Marine and Army recruiters. Unless someone arrived later, I was certain I was the last one to leave that night.

The next morning, before heading to work, Jan watched the morning news on TV when she suddenly exclaimed, "They bombed the reserve center here last night too!"

The Navy Reserve Center at Great Lakes was less than a mile from our house. This news unsettled me because the FALN had now brought their conflict alarmingly close to my family.

The next morning at work, we all went to the back of the building to assess the damage. The FBI and detectives from the Chicago Police Department were still there investigating. It was believed that Jimmy had interviewed a Puerto Rican couple the day before. The woman had been inquiring about becoming a nurse in the Navy. Jimmy recalled that the man carried a briefcase, and at one point, he asked to use the restroom located at the back of the building. Since it was an older building, it used traditional steam radiators for heating. The FBI determined that a pipe bomb had been placed between the radiator and the back wall.

Based on Jimmy's descriptions of the two individuals, the FBI agent observed that their profiles matched those of operatives known to be linked with the FALN. Later that day, contract workers from GSA came to build a temporary wooden structure. They also set up heavy-duty canvas across the opening in the back wall until permanent repairs could be completed.

In the aftermath of the bombings carried out by the FALN, the district promptly relayed information from the FBI to all recruiting stations regarding known threats against Navy and Marine Corps personnel in Chicago. Recruiters were allowed to wear civilian clothing instead of uniforms if they believed it would enhance their safety. Rhett gathered us to discuss whether we should choose to forgo our uniforms at work.

Jimmy voiced what the rest of us were thinking: "What the hell, why wear civilian clothes then drive around in white vehicles with the word 'Navy' all over them? It makes no sense." We all quickly agreed with Jimmy's perspective.

I had a rule: I would never tell Jan about the negative aspects of my life. I can't speak for others, but I believed there was no reason to worry her. I wanted to avoid adding more stress to our already difficult lives. However, in some cases, such as the FALN bombings, it was impossible to keep everything from her.

I have worked diligently to maintain a separation between my professional and family lives. Whether this was right or wrong, I believed it was for the best. I often had recruiter friends over, and we all understood that it was better not to discuss our challenging experiences in front of our wives, girlfriends, and families.

To be clear and fair, Chicago wasn't all violence. Overall, I enjoyed my time there. In many parts of the city, the communities had a small-town feel. Generally, people were nice and friendly to us. However, just as it is now, it can be a dangerous place.

I've never forgotten the day I walked into an armed robbery in progress. It was a winter afternoon, already dark outside. I was working late at the office and had run out of cigarettes. I decided to take a break and go to the drugstore on the corner to buy a pack. I walked up the street to the store entrance and went inside. Within a few steps, I realized there was a guy about 3 feet ahead of me, pointing a handgun at the female clerk standing behind the counter.

Then the realization hit me: the gunman wasn't even aware I was behind him. This is where being relatively tall and having long arms became an advantage. Without conscious thought, I stepped toward the gunman, reached over his right shoulder, grabbed the gun by the barrel, and pulled hard, bringing his arm straight up. I raised my knee, bracing it against the small of his back, pushing him against the counter and pulling his arm past his head. I heard two sounds in quick succession. First, there was a loud pop as his arm dislocated from his shoulder. The second was the sound of his index finger snapping in the gun's trigger guard as I twisted the gun, breaking his finger. This allowed me to wrestle the gun out of his hand.

To make sure the guy couldn't escape while holding his injured arm behind his head, I kicked him repeatedly behind the knees. This forced him down to the floor into a kneeling position. Finally, since he was screaming and struggling, I palmed the gun and used it to hit him hard on the side of his head. That silenced him because the blow knocked him senseless. I noticed the store clerk putting the phone down, and she told me the police were on their way.

Minutes later, two police officers arrived. I was relieved to see that one of them was Fuzzy. The other officer, whom I didn't recognize, took custody of the robber and handcuffed him.

The gunman, now fully alert, yelled, "Son of a bitch broke my arm! I want to press charges!"

I immediately handed the handgun to Fuzzy, informing him that I had not yet checked whether it was loaded. It looked like a cheap .38 caliber single-action revolver. Fuzzy, pointing the barrel upwards, opened the gun's cylinder and turned it so I could see that it was indeed loaded. Two more police officers arrived and took control of the robber, escorting him out of the store.

Fuzzy turned to me. "George, go back to your office and take a break. We'll come down and get your statement in a short while."

He laughed as I told him I needed cigarettes before leaving. I was vaguely acquainted with the store clerk, but I knew her name was Ann.

I went to the counter and said, "Ann, can I get a pack of Marlboros?"

Ann looked at me for a second, then bent down below the counter, stood up, and set three cartons of Marlboros on the countertop. Before I could say anything, she said, "Here, take them. They're on me. Anytime you need cigarettes, come see me."

At first, I tried to refuse, but Ann insisted that I take the cartons. I finally relented and took the cigarettes.

On the way out, Fuzzy said, "We'll be down shortly."

"Okay," I replied.

As I walked back to the office, I found myself thinking once again, *George, you're a dumbass*. When I arrived, I brewed a fresh pot of coffee and sat down at my desk to wait. For the first time, I noticed that my hands were shaking, and I began to shiver, even though the office was warm. I looked at my right hand and saw that my knuckles were scraped and had been bleeding. About 30 minutes later, Fuzzy came in alone. I informed him that there was fresh coffee and encouraged him to help himself. Fuzzy poured a cup and sat in the chair beside my desk. He brought a clipboard and some paperwork and handed me a form.

"Take your time and write down everything you can remember as it happened," he said.

It took me about 20 minutes to write out my statement. Once I was finished, I handed the form to Fuzzy.

He took a few minutes to read it, smiled at me, and said, "Perfect."

We sat and talked for a short while. I was surprised when Fuzzy told me there were three customers in the store, along with the store clerk. All of them had provided statements about what they had witnessed. I told Fuzzy I hadn't realized there was anyone else there besides the clerk.

"Do I have any legal problems?" I asked him.

Fuzzy replied, "What are you talking about?"

"Well, I did physically hurt the guy, and he was screaming that he wanted to press charges," I explained.

Fuzzy laughed and said, "You have nothing to worry about. My God, George, that guy might have killed someone. You stopped that." With that, Fuzzy stood up. "Man, I can't sit here holding your hand all night. I'll see you next time, my friend. Go home."

I couldn't go home yet; I needed to compose myself a bit more. So, I headed to the bar at Whirling Dervishes. As soon as I sat down, Kurt, the bartender, noticed me and waved. I watched him prepare a rum and Coke. Once the drink was ready, Kurt placed it in front of me. I put a $5 bill on the bar and slid it toward him, but Kurt pushed it back to me.

"You drink free tonight, my friend. Fuzzy came by and told us what you did," he said.

I thanked Kurt and lit a cigarette, savoring the taste of my rum and Coke. After a few more drinks, I headed home. As usual, Jan met me at the door, and we exchanged our greeting kiss. We walked into the dining room, where she turned on the lights.

She surprised me by asking, "What happened to your hand?"

I looked at my right hand, which was bleeding again. I hadn't even realized it until that moment. Although I never wanted to lie to Jan, I found myself doing so then. I made up a story about how my car wouldn't start, claiming I must have hurt my hand while checking the battery under the hood. She seemed to buy it. At the time, my work car was an old Ford Maverick, and it had a reputation for not starting.

The next morning, as I arrived at the office and passed by Rhett's office, he called out, "George, get in here." I walked in and asked what he needed.

"What? Did you think none of us would hear about what happened last night?" he asked.

"I have no clue what you're talking about," I replied.

He looked at me and laughed. "Man, you're such a shit-head."

Keeping the banter going, I replied, "Rhett, I honestly have no idea what you mean."

"Don't play dumb; Fuzzy was already here this morning and filled us in," he responded.

I told Rhett that I preferred to keep what happened private. I didn't want Jan to find out about it. Rhett nodded in agreement, indicating that he understood my position.

Then he laughed again and said, "That's why I like you, George. When you do shit, it's always interesting." After that, I returned to my office to start the day.

Finally, in late March, the city of Chicago began to clear the streets of snow. Heavy equipment was brought in from Buffalo, NY, for snow removal, as the city lacked sufficient resources. In newspapers and on TV news shows, public outrage was directed at Mayor Michael Bilandic. As snow removal progressed, hundreds, if not thousands, of vehicles were found buried in the snow and needed to be towed to whatever suitable location the city could find. One afternoon, while I was driving past Lincoln Park, I was astounded to see vehicles stacked five or six high on top of each other in the park.

The morning that the snow was finally cleared from West Irving Park Road, I stood in our lobby watching a large front-end loader digging through the snow and loading it into massive dump trucks. When the front-end loader began digging into the huge pile of snow in front of our office, I observed that one bucket load of snow also contained a small compact car.

With the arrival of the spring thaw, everyone's circumstances changed significantly. Blake had grown weary of his role as chief recruiter, so he leveraged his connections to secure a staff position at U.S. Second Fleet in Norfolk, VA. Senior Chief Navy Counselor William "Willy" Corwin assumed the role of the new chief recruiter. Meanwhile, Chuck was retiring from the Navy, and Rhett was chosen to succeed him as the Northern Zone supervisor.

Eddy would take over as the recruiter in charge at West Irving Park Road, while Mack and Jimmy would remain in their positions. Additionally, two new recruiters would be assigned to the Irving Park Road station, fresh from ENRO. Rhett, who had recently remarried, wanted to work closer to home in Lake County. As the zone supervisor, he decided to operate out of the Libertyville station and would bring me along. I was set to take over the station from which I had previously been fired, but this time it would be a one-man operation.

The first week of April, I was back in Libertyville. It was bittersweet in some respects. The "prick" Connor Howard, who played a significant role in getting me fired, had skillfully orchestrated his own complete and dismal failure as a field recruiter. As I heard, Connor first started visiting the emergency room at Great Lakes Naval Hospital, complaining of chest pains and expressing concerns that he was going to have a heart attack. When that didn't work, he turned heavily to alcohol. He didn't recruit a single person during his entire time in Libertyville. One night, he was driving drunk and got into a minor car accident, but he ended up getting arrested for driving under the influence. Ultimately, Connor received a "fault" transfer from recruiting duty.

On the morning of my move, I first needed to stop by the district headquarters to pick up a set of keys for the office. When I got to Libertyville and opened the office door, I was taken aback by what I found when I turned on the lights. It seemed that Connor's last day there had been quite chaotic. The front desk and two file cabinets were toppled over, and hundreds of suspect/prospect cards were scattered everywhere. The end tables next to the couch were broken.

As I surveyed the scene, the staff sergeant from the Army office across the hall peeked inside and asked if I was the new Navy guy. I confirmed that I was and inquired about what had happened to Bob. He explained that Bob had been moved to the Chicago Loop office. The sergeant extended his hand and said, "Let me introduce myself, I'm Gene."

All I could say at that point was, "Gene, nice to meet you; as you can see, I have some work to do."

"Yes, you do. Let me know if you need anything," Gene replied. I thanked him and got to work putting the place back together.

Within a few days, I had the station in Libertyville up and running. During my absence, the landlord, funded by GSA, converted the large back room into a separate office space. This would become Rhett's office, where he would work as the zone supervisor. The rest of the station was my domain.

My first order of business was to focus on production. I discovered that Connor had not been entirely idle during my absence. After collecting all the suspect and prospect cards that had been scattered around, I began organizing and reviewing them. Annotations on about two dozen prospect cards indicated that Connor had interviewed some of the individuals, and in a few cases, those individuals had taken the ASVAB. However, for approximately 90 percent of the cards, there was no information showing the prospects' outcomes.

That afternoon and the next day were spent calling the prospects I had identified as good follow-ups. It was not surprising that around 10 or more people were still interested in the Navy. Several expressed their discomfort with the last recruiter, Connor. I was able to persuade all of them to schedule appointments, allowing me to interview them and review their situations. Rhett had granted me the remainder of April as a grace period. However, in May, I was expected to meet the usual quota of five monthly enlistments.

I tried to sandbag a bit. Among the group of prospects, two were very eager to leave for boot camp immediately. I even attempted to persuade them to wait until May, but they preferred to move ahead, so I agreed rather than risk losing them altogether. My reasons for this were that I wanted to meet my quota in May and June, and I had less than five months left in my recruiting tour. I wanted to coast as much as possible until September 1. August 31 would be my last day as a Navy recruiter, and September 1 would be my projected rotation or transfer date.

At the same time, Rhett was finding his footing as the zone supervisor. I'm not sure why, but he always seemed to have my back, which I appreciated. Most of the time, it was me he connected with on the Irving Park Road team! And, I have to say, Rhett lived quite an adventurous love life; during the time I've known him, he got married, divorced, and married again—now on number three! Life around Rhett was never dull, that's for sure!

I never understood how Rhett found the time for his extracurricular activities. He was pretty open with me, mentioning that he was already in the process of kicking wife number three to the curb and working on, in all probability, wife number four. I considered Rhett a friend, so whatever he was involved in regarding that matter, I kept to myself.

During this time frame, I received an envelope from the district in the mail. The envelope contained a district-wide memorandum from the commanding officer addressed to all field recruiters. It began with an introductory paragraph explaining that recruiting commands nationwide faced a shortage of experienced, seasoned, and successful recruiters. The following paragraph indicated that all recruiting districts were directed to encourage field recruiters who wished to extend their tours to do so voluntarily. The final paragraph instructed any interested recruiters to submit their extension requests through the appropriate chain of command.

I remember thinking while crumpling the memorandum into a ball and tossing it in the trash can, *Maybe, if they hadn't shit on so many good sailors, they wouldn't have this problem.* I chuckled about it for a moment before getting back to work, pondering, *What a bunch of out-of-touch pricks. Do they think anyone in their right mind would voluntarily stay in this shit show?*

Meanwhile, I needed to focus on my plans after recruiting duty. I contacted the QM Rating detailer to discuss possible sea duty orders. Ultimately, he offered me orders to a Knox-class frigate based in

Mayport, Florida, and we agreed that I would accept them. My orders to the ship arrived at the district command and were forwarded to me in early June. With new orders in hand, I could finally see the light at the end of the tunnel.

Unbeknownst to anyone other than Jan, my sole intention was to leave the Navy on my EOAS (Expiration of Active Service) date, July 31, 1981. Jan and I had already made plans to move back to her hometown in Iowa. My father-in-law had agreed to rent us a house he owned in the area. We planned for me to return to sea until my EOAS, while Jan and Mitch moved home. Once discharged, I would rejoin them in Iowa.

Aside from my time at West Irving Park Road, my experiences here profoundly shook my faith and confidence in the Navy. I witnessed a troubling level of corruption, deceit, dishonesty, and abuse within the recruiting command, which took a heavy mental toll on me. I had no desire to be part of an organization that tolerated such maltreatment. Looking back on my decision to leave, it seems it was driven more by emotion than by rational thought.

Finally, the first day of August arrived—my last month as a recruiter. As a one-man station, I had easily maintained the monthly quotas, so the summer was going well. Little did I know what was about to happen, which would alter everything.

It was Friday, August 2, and I was working alone in the office. Rhett was out visiting other stations in the zone. Around mid-afternoon, the chief recruiter, Willy Corwin, unexpectedly entered my office. After a few polite exchanges, Willy opened his briefcase, smiled, and handed me a piece of paper.

"I bring good news," he said.

After reading the document, I leaned back in my chair, feeling as though I might pass out. It was a congratulatory letter from the command informing me that I had been nominated and approved for an extension in recruiting due to the "urgent needs of the Navy." The letter indicated that my projected rotation date (PRD) had been extended for one year. The subject line read, "Twelve Month, Involuntary, Meritorious Extension," or words to that effect.

I barely heard Willy as he began to say things like, "Congratulations, we can't afford to lose great field recruiters like you," "Have you considered changing your rate to Navy Counselor (NC)?" and "If you cross-rate to NC, you could probably get another three years on shore duty."

All I could say to him was, "Senior chief, I need to go back to sea. I already have orders, and I've done my time here."

We talked a bit more; I didn't say much else about the extension because I didn't want to irritate him. After a while, Willy packed up his things. As he walked out the office door, he said, "Bravo Zulu, George; think of this as an Atta Boy, because that's what it is."

When Rhett came in later that afternoon, he asked me his usual question: "How goes the war?"

"Willy Corwin was here earlier. Did you know he was coming by?" I replied.

Rhett, surprised, answered, "No, I didn't. What did he want?"

I handed the PRD extension letter to Rhett. "Take a look; I guess they couldn't get enough volunteers."

Rhett actually gasped and let out a big exhale as he read the letter. I knew it could rub him the wrong way, but I had to ask.

"Did you know about this?"

Rhett looked me in the eye as he answered, "George, I swear to you, I had no idea about this. I'm pissed. After all, I'm in your chain of command. They went right around me. I'm sorry, George. I know this is the last thing you want. Let me make some calls and see what I can find out and if anything can be done."

Rhett understood this was a real kick in the ass for me in another way. I had already used my orders to authorize a move of our household belongings to Iowa. Jan and Mitch had moved back home to Iowa the weekend before. Our plan was for me to stay at the housing unit at Great Lakes until I went on permanent change of station (PCS) leave next month, before joining my new ship.

Rhett entered his office and closed the door. After a while, he came out and sat by my desk. "Well, what I have learned is unbeknownst to me or any other zone supervisors: the command sent the Bureau of Naval Personnel a list of recruiters, including you, requesting an extension of everyone's PRD due to the needs of the Navy. They approved all of them and included the stipulation that, if necessary, the extensions could be made involuntarily, but on a meritorious basis," he said. "It was also directed that any recruiter who had already received PCS orders had them canceled effective today."

Rhett looked at me. "George, I'm sorry again. Let's lock this place up and have a drink; we could use it. What do you say?"

"Let's go. It's not like I have anyone at home waiting for me. But give me a little time; I need to call Jan. Go ahead, I'll catch up," I replied. I called Jan to share the news. Her reaction was understandable—one of disbelief.

"Are we ever going to be free from this hell they call recruiting duty?" she asked.

I could only reply, "That it isn't over." I remember saying, "I need a little time to think things over and see if I can find some way out of this."

I tried to cheer her up by reminding her that on weekends, I would be able to come home as often as possible. We ended the call with our usual "I love you."

Later, over drinks at our local bar, Rhett wanted to propose an idea. "I know you like it here in Libertyville. You have a sweet deal as a one-man station, and so far, you've been doing great at making your monthly quota. If this PRD extension sticks, and I think it will, we can make this work, doing the best with what we've got." Then he said, "Before I begin, I need to tell you something. So don't punch me in the face after I tell you, okay?"

"Okay, what's your news?" I answered.

Rhett tipped up his glass, took a long drink of his beer, and then said, "I've requested and received a two-year extension here at NRD Chicago. I only did it because some things in my life have changed, and I don't want to go back to sea. I believe there's a good shot I'll get the chief recruiter job soon."

I had to digest what Rhett just told me for a moment before asking. "Are you fucking high or just crazy?"

He laughed so hard that I thought he would fall off his bar stool. "There's more."

"Please continue," I replied.

"I'm changing my rating from Gunner's Mate to Navy Counselor," he said.

I summarized, "So, I get an involuntary fucking meritorious extension, and you, you fucking moron, requested one. Then on top of that, you're going to become a damn Navy Counselor."

Rhett just kept laughing. I knew Rhett well. I also knew he didn't make any moves unless he was sure it would work. So, after Rhett composed himself, I asked, "Okay, what's your idea?"

Rhett essentially laid out the following: (1) I stay in Libertyville and continue to make my monthly quota. If it looks like I'm going to exceed the five recruits in any given month, Rhett will take those enlistments and assign the credit to another recruiter who may be struggling; (2) the idea of not exceeding quotas is meant to protect me from attaining "superstar status," which could raise the idea at district level about transferring me to a struggling station in another zone; (3) finally, if (1) and (2) are successful, Rhett will ensure that I get as many weekends or long weekends off as possible, allowing me to go to Iowa to spend time with family.

When Rhett finished outlining his plan, he asked me, "What do you think? Does it sound like a workable plan? Do we have a deal?" He added, "It will help me, and it will help you."

"Well, if I have to stay, it seems this would work out for the best," I responded. "Rhett, there's one stipulation."

"What is it?" he asked.

I questioned, "If I figure a way out of here earlier, can you promise me you won't stand in my way?"

Rhett held up his glass of beer and said, "Deal."

I felt better because at least I had an initial action plan. Recruiting had taught me many things. One of those things was always trying to make the bastards feel like they're winning while you find ways to stick it to them.

My next order of business was to find a place to live. While living in government housing, married service members forfeit their monthly Basic Allowance for Quarters (BAQ). Therefore, I needed to give up our housing unit so I could once again receive the monthly BAQ to cover rent back in Iowa. I ended up staying with friends for about a week until I found a decent, affordable, small, furnished efficiency apartment in Libertyville. The best part was that the landlord was willing to rent on a month-to-month basis, rather than requiring a long-term lease agreement.

I watched with some sadness on September 1 as my original rotation date came and went. The arrangement with Rhett proved to be a good one. Throughout the fall months, he upheld his promise about weekends off, enabling me to go home and see Jan and Mitch.

Just before the Thanksgiving holiday, I made a morning AFEES run and was having coffee at Barney's when a recruiter named Dave, whom I knew from the Division Street station, joined me at my table. He surprised me by asking what I was doing about the involuntary extension. I replied that I hadn't figured out how to get around it, so I would probably have to serve the 12 months.

Dave leaned in and, in a quiet voice, said, "Man, write your congressman. I did, and it looks like I'm going to be able to break the extension and get the hell out of here."

It hadn't occurred to me to take the action that Dave suggested. I mulled it over for several days, unsure of what to do. During the long Thanksgiving weekend, I spoke with Jan about it. As usual, she told me to do what I thought was best.

"Try contacting our congressman to see what you can find out; at least we'll know," she advised.

I noted the contact information for our congressional district representative from the phone book. While driving back to Libertyville, I made my decision.

Late Monday afternoon, I drafted a letter to our congressman, clearly and concisely explaining my dilemma. Before mailing the letter, I wanted to talk to Rhett to ensure I wasn't blindsiding him if anything came of it.

The next day, Rhett came into the office. After he settled in, I asked if I could discuss something important. I handed him my letter and requested that he read it and share his thoughts. Rhett took the letter from me and began reading it. When he finished, he returned it.

"George, you're free to do this, and I don't have a problem with it. Just know that if your congressman requests further information or pursues your request, certain people at district command are going to be really pissed off," Rhett said. He explained that he knew of others in my situation who had written to their congressman, and the command wasn't happy. "If anyone asks, I never saw this letter, and I was unaware of it. Are we in agreement?"

"Rhett, you have my word," I replied.

I made several copies of the letter for my records, and then I placed the original letter in an envelope and put it in the lobby's outgoing mailbox. Throughout this process, I couldn't help but think, *I hope this doesn't backfire on me.*

Several weeks later, I was surprised to receive a call from our congressman at the office. He explained that he had read my letter and agreed with my position. He also mentioned that he had forwarded my letter to the Secretary of the Navy, requesting that an investigation be opened. The congressman assured me that I would hear from my command soon, and if I encountered any problems, I should notify his office immediately by telephone. I thanked the congressman for his help and assistance before we ended the call. I knew it was now a waiting game to see what would happen next.

Just over a week later, I received a phone call from the chief recruiter's assistant, informing me that I needed to be at his office at 0800 the following day. When morning came, Rhett wasn't around, so I left him a note saying I had gone to Glenview. I then drove to the district headquarters. Upon arriving at Willy Corwin's office, I found him with a lieutenant I didn't recognize. After reading her name tag, I quickly deduced that she must be the new EPO.

The senior chief got straight to the point. "Why did you involve your congressman?"

I briefly explained my reasoning. He then informed me that they now had to respond to an inquiry from the Secretary of the Navy and that the commanding officer, whom he referred to as the "old man," was not very happy about the situation. The lieutenant stayed silent and let Willy do the talking.

Then an attempt at imitating bullshit came out when Willy said, "You do understand that your extension is a legal order, an order that you don't intend to obey." He continued, "The lieutenant and I are tempted to charge you right now for violating Article 92 of the UCMJ (Uniform Code of Military Justice) and take you to captain's mast (Article 15) this afternoon. What do you say?"

"I'm still here, putting people into the war. I haven't stopped working or producing, so what order am I disobeying?" I said. "Willy, senior chief, you can go ahead and charge me with whatever you want. However, remember that Article 15 also gives me the right to decline captain's mast and instead demand a trial by court-martial." I added, "If you insist on pursuing this, let's proceed to court-martial. I'm confident that the Judge Advocate General will be very interested in hearing about this command's inner workings and operations."

Turning to face the lieutenant, I said, "Ma'am, you are a witness to the fact that I formally decline captain's mast and demand a court-martial." The lieutenant's reaction to my statement was priceless; I thought she might be sick before she could compose herself.

Now red in the face and angry, Willy quickly composed himself. "All right, we all need to cool it. Trowbridge, please wait in the passageway so the lieutenant and I can discuss this."

I replied, "Will do," and walked out.

While I waited, a nagging thought crossed my mind; it seemed like they had circled around Rhett again. My paranoia kicked in—*was it possible Rhett was aware of this and intentionally absent?* After about 45 minutes, an assistant emerged to say that Willy wanted to see me. I made my way back to his office and walked in. Willy sat at his desk, flanked by the lieutenant and the XO in nearby chairs. The XO motioned for me to take an empty chair, and I complied. The scowl on the XO's face left no doubt that he was less than pleased.

He began in a formal tone. "Petty Officer Trowbridge, we have discussed the situation and recommended to the captain that we release you from your extension." He added, "The captain agrees with us, so you can contact your detailer for orders as soon as we receive a reply from the office of the Secretary of the Navy stating that the matter has been closed. You will be notified when that happens."

Finally, the XO asked, "Do you understand, Petty Officer Trowbridge?"

"Yes, sir, I do," I replied.

The XO then said, "You are dismissed." I stood up from my chair, turned, and walked out.

Once out of Willy's office, I left the building, walked to the parking lot, and got into my vehicle. Now out of sight of those sons of bitches, I let myself relax; my hands were shaking, and my stomach hurt. I sat there for a while, chain-smoking cigarettes. My mind swirled with questions such as: Did I dare to trust the bastards? Would they do what they said? What kind of retaliation could I expect? How long will it take to find out, so I can start working on getting new orders? What can I do if it turns out the fuckers are just jerking me around?

I finally started the vehicle and began the drive back to Libertyville. Throughout the drive, a flood of questions kept running through my mind. You would think I would feel a sense of victory, right? Not at all, especially not in recruiting command. My time there taught me one undeniable lesson: other than Rhett, I could never trust anyone in my chain of command. My true victory will come the day I leave recruiting duty behind for good.

When I returned to the station, Rhett was in his office. He came out and handed me some phone messages.

"What's up at Glenview?" he asked.

I looked at him for a second before replying. I was mulling it over in my mind. Could I still trust him? I decided to tell him. I explained everything to Rhett, reviewing what had happened with Willy, the new EPO, and the XO. Rhett listened to everything, remaining silent, but I could see my news upset him.

"Rhett, did you know anything about this?" I asked.

A disappointed look crossed his face as he answered, "George, you know better."

I said, "Rhett, I know, but you also know that sometimes around here, when the shit is flying from all directions, one can get paranoid."

"Yeah, I get it," Rhett replied, adding, "Once again, they jumped around me. They know we're good friends, so I guess that's why they did it, but that doesn't make it right."

Rhett changed the subject. "So you got to meet the new EPO, Lieutenant Elise Kingman, huh?"

"Yes, have you met her yet?" I responded.

"Yeah, I met her a few days ago. I think she may actually be an improvement, but we'll see." Then, being Rhett, he added, "I thought she was kind of hot!"

The holiday season was approaching quickly, and to my surprise, I completed my enlistment quota on the Friday before Christmas week. After discussing it with Rhett, he allowed me to go home to Iowa for Christmas, but I needed to return on the 26th. Consequently, my time off was classified as liberty rather than an authorized leave, which meant it did not exceed the maximum allowable time of 96 hours, or four days. After being back for two days, I was free to leave again, with the understanding that I would return on January 2.

Wednesday, January 2, 1980. A time when I thought recruiting duty would be far behind me. Instead, I was facing at least another nine months of production. I had no choice but to get to work and see what I could do to improve production numbers in January. I didn't have any sandbag applicants from December. If I hadn't made the deal with Rhett, I would have received credit for seven enlistments; instead, I turned the two excess applicants over to Rhett so he could give credit to a recruiter at the Des Plaines station. By the end of the month, I had still not received any information regarding my release from the extension. The one bright spot for the month was my weekend trip home to Iowa.

One cold morning around mid-February, I entered the office at 0800, and no one else was there. When I turned on the office lights, I noticed a bottle of E&J Brandy on my desk with a note taped to it. The note was from Rhett: "Congratulations, wait to drink this later. I'll be in around 1600 this afternoon. Look in the folder under the bottle." I set the brandy bottle aside, picked up the folder, and opened it. There it was: the message from the Bureau of Naval Personnel directing that my projected rotation date had been adjusted to June 1, 1980. My priorities for the day immediately changed, with the top priority being to call home and share the news with Jan. My second priority was to contact the QM Rating detailer and determine what I could obtain for new orders.

Later that morning, I contacted the detailer to discuss my options. After reviewing several possibilities, I accepted orders for another Knox-class fast frigate, USS *Vreeland* (FF 1068), which was homeported in Mayport, Florida. According to policy, the detailer also informed me that I needed to attend a two-week Leadership and Management Education and Training course before reporting to my ship. He mentioned that the course would take place in Mayport and would arrange the dates to be included in my orders. After hanging up with the detailer, I felt ecstatic. I looked at the calendar and realized I had just under three and a half months to get out of there.

When Rhett came in that afternoon, I shared my news with him. I could tell he was genuinely happy for me. He then suggested we go to our bar and celebrate with some drinks instead of drinking my brandy. I barely registered his words when he said, "I have some news too, but I'll tell you later."

We settled into our usual seats on the bar stools when we arrived at the bar. After a few rounds of drinks, Rhett asked, "Do you want to hear my news?"

"Of course!" I replied.

With a smile on his face, he looked at me and said, "You're looking at the next chief recruiter starting on March 1."

I extended my hand to shake his. "Congratulations, Rhett! You deserve it. I know you've wanted this for some time, and I'm sure you'll do great. I also believe you will bring much-needed honesty and integrity to the job." We both had plenty of reasons to celebrate. My next question for Rhett was about Willy Corwin.

Before I could ask, Rhett volunteered, "Willy is moving to Area Recruiting Command in Great Lakes."

Then came my big question, "Who's replacing you?"

Rhett paused and then said, "Temporarily, it will be Bill Lane."

I momentarily glanced at Rhett. "Bill Lane, he's a statistician, not a recruiter. Holy shit, I'm going to be stuck with that shithead as the zone supervisor."

"Well, for you, it's only for three months, but I think you'll see that Bill has been in touch with reality for the last year and will be much more flexible," Rhett replied.

I said, "We'll see. I won't let this ruin our celebration, and I can stand on my head for three months."

The first day of March arrived quickly, and Rhett moved to district headquarters. The station felt empty without him, but for me, it had to be business as usual for the next several months. The following week, I returned to the office from a school visit around late morning. Upon entering the building, I was slightly startled to see a master chief petty officer sitting in the lobby.

I immediately said, "How can I help you, master chief?"

He stood and extended his hand. "I'm Ron Carlson, and I guess I work for you. Didn't anyone tell you I was coming?"

I replied, "No. Let me open up the office, and then we'll talk."

Before starting any discussions with the master chief, I excused myself, went to Rhett's old office, and closed the door. I called Bill Lane, but someone I didn't know told me he was unavailable and took a message for him. After that, I went back to the front office and sat down. I informed Ron that I had contacted Bill's office to try to find out what was happening.

He offered an explanation: "As I understand it, you're moving on in a couple of months. They sent me here for you to train me as a field recruiter, and I'll be taking over the zone from Bill."

This made sense to me since Bill was not a recruiter, and Rhett mentioned that he was only temporary. Later, Bill called me back to confirm that I would be training the master chief. He mentioned he would be visiting the office in a couple of days. With that in mind, I started Ron's training. I had the production schedule for March mostly under control. My initial plan was to handle what I could for production in April and then take it easy in May, leading up to my transfer date on June 1. I figured that if I performed poorly in May, they wouldn't be able to do much—what could they do, fire me? However, I needed to readjust my plans to accommodate training Ron.

As a petty officer first class, I found it somewhat uncomfortable to have a master chief report to me. While it's customary in recruiting duty for less experienced recruiters to report to more experienced ones, regardless of pay grade, I felt the situation was unusual. However, Ron handled it well and demonstrated professionalism throughout the process. He acknowledged his unfamiliarity with certain aspects of recruiting, and we moved forward with that understanding.

In mid-March, I received a copy of my new orders. Upon examining them, one detail stood out: I was to detach from NRD Chicago on May 30 and report to the Fleet Training Center at Naval Station Mayport on June 6. I had expected to take the customary 30-day leave for a permanent change of duty station, but this would leave me with only a few days at home before I had to report to Mayport. I understood the reason for this tight schedule—the two-week training course I was set to attend started on June 9 and was only offered three or four times a year. All I could do was take solace in the fact that I was finally leaving recruiting hell. The other information in the package indicated that USS *Vreeland* had recently begun a Mediterranean deployment, so I would have to catch up with the ship there.

April was a good month. I didn't take credit for my full quota, as I had credited Ron with two of mine to add to his three, allowing him to meet the full quota during his first full month of production. In his role as zone supervisor, Bill remained in character by showcasing his boundless and everyday stupidity and assigned me the task of meeting the full quota in May. I found that pretty funny. I ended the month by ensuring Ron achieved five enlistments; however, I ended up with only two. I really didn't care.

On Friday morning, May 30, I stopped by the station to say goodbye to Ron before driving to Glenview to check out of the command—part of the check-out process involved meeting with the chief recruiter. I entered Rhett's office, and to my surprise, Bill and Lieutenant Kingman were already there. Rhett got up from his chair and immediately came over to me, eager to shake hands.

As we shook hands, Rhett said, "You're finally out of here, you know, old friend. You've been nothing but a pain in my ass. But congratulations anyway."

I remember telling Rhett, "Well, you haven't always been the easiest person to get along with either, so you should be honored that I made an exception in your case by taking you under my wing, just to help you along." Rhett and everyone else burst into laughter.

Rhett took my check-out sheet from me. As he signed it, he said, "George, we have something for you."

Lt. Kingman stepped forward and handed me a gift-wrapped box. "Open it, George."

I took the box and unwrapped it. Inside were three items: a bottle of E&J Brandy, next an award letter, and lastly a smaller box that contained a recruiter badge with a gold wreath and stars indicating a third award.

"I know the third gold wreath probably doesn't mean much to you, but it does to me," Rhett said. I grabbed Rhett's hand, shook it, and thanked him for the brandy. While there, I had the lieutenant sign my check-out sheet and said my goodbyes.

Next, I checked out with the XO, who had me sign my final performance evaluation and other documents. I signed everything without reading a word; I just wanted to be out of there. Later that afternoon, I completed my check-out at district headquarters with my leave papers and official orders in hand. I left the gate at Naval Air Station Glenview and began the six-hour drive to Iowa. Three years and nine months of dealing with constant stress, pressure, chaos, insanity, stupidity, corruption, dishonesty, and nonsense were finally over.

CHAPTER 4

BACK TO THE FLEET

I drove into Stacyville just after midnight. I pulled into our driveway and turned off the engine; I was home. The following night, on Saturday, Jan had organized a party for me, inviting our friends and family. Jan and I were happy and excited that recruiting duty was behind us, but we faced the next year of separation with a sense of remorse.

Early Friday morning, June 6, Jan drove me to the airport in Rochester, Minnesota, where I had a flight to Chicago and then a connecting flight to Jacksonville, Florida. It was a long goodbye at the airport since neither of us knew when we would see each other next. The flights went smoothly that day, and my plane landed at Jacksonville Airport around 1730. I was able to catch a bus to Mayport from the airport. It was after 2100 by the time I checked in at the BEQ.

During those days, Mayport Naval Station was a reasonably small installation compared to other East Coast naval stations. However, for its size, it offered many amenities. Primarily, the climate there is hard to beat. Additionally, the station is located at the intersection of the St. Johns River and the Atlantic Ocean. The river runs along the north side of the base, while the beach is along its east side. I had visited Mayport several times, so I was familiar with the base and knew the locations of the Navy Exchange, the galley, the enlisted club, and the Fleet Training Center. Everything was within easy walking distance from the BEQ. Another aspect I believe most people enjoyed about Mayport was its laid-back, relaxed atmosphere.

The BEQ was located near the beach and offered one-man rooms, each equipped with its own head and shower. Being an older building, the rooms featured traditional crank-operated louvre windows. That night, I opened the windows and enjoyed the cool, pleasant sea breeze; it felt wonderful to breathe in the salt air again. I found a pay phone and called Jan to tell her I had arrived safely.

I reported to the Fleet Training Center on Monday morning at 0700. The Leadership and Management Education and Training (LMET) course would last for two weeks. LMET is a formal, Navy-specific training program designed to prepare supervisors and managers for leadership and management roles at key career points.

For me, the LMET experience was pretty average. After my time on recruiting duty, the training felt somewhat basic. I could tell that the other students were gaining valuable insights, but I felt a bit out of place. Overall, the course was easy, and time passed quickly.

LMET was finished by mid-morning on Friday, June 20, which was fortunate because I needed to be at Jacksonville's Naval Air Station by early afternoon for an overseas flight to Rota, Spain. I took a bus from Mayport to the Naval Air Station and checked in at my flight's Military Airlift Command (MAC) terminal. Our plane took off late that afternoon for the 9-hour flight to Spain. We arrived at the Naval Station Rota air terminal around 0700 local time the next day. I boarded a bus to get to the on-base transient barracks. It was a quick ride since the barracks were about three blocks from the air terminal.

Rota is located on the southwest coast of Spain, about 40 miles north of the Atlantic Ocean entrance to the Strait of Gibraltar. At the barracks, I checked in with the chief at the front desk. He provided an overview of the routine for sailors in transit. His first point was that there wasn't a specific timeframe for my stay; it all depended on the operations department determining where my ship was or would be.

Once the ship was located, a flight to the nearest airport or air terminal would be arranged. He instructed me to check in at the desk every morning by 0800 and showed me a status board indicating whether I was on the flight list and when I needed to report to the air terminal. As a petty officer first class, I wouldn't be assigned to any working parties, so I was free to do as I pleased. Next, he explained that I could get paid each morning at the disbursing office next door if I was short on cash. Finally, he handed me a meal ticket for the galley and gave me my room assignment. A seaman helped me carry my sea bag and other gear to my room on the second deck.

The room was quite nice, and the areas surrounding the barracks building were beautiful. It resembled a resort more than a naval base. I was exhausted from my flight, so I lay down for a nap after showering. When I woke up later and checked my watch, it was nearly 1600.

I decided to go into town; it's a short walk from the main gate. The city of Rota resembled a seaside resort. It was clean, and the streets were lined with bars, cafes, and restaurants. I enjoyed an affordable yet delicious dinner at one of the cafes and then spent the rest of the evening sampling drinks at various bars along the street. Around midnight, I decided to call it a night and head back to the base.

Over the next few days, I quickly settled into a routine. Each morning, I'd go to the front desk by 0800, check the flight status list, and make sure my name wasn't there. After that, the rest of my day was free. Several nights, I went out for dinner and drinks at the local bars. It started to feel more like a vacation than waiting for a flight. This routine continued all week until late Thursday night. As I passed the front desk on my way up to my room, I glanced at the flight status list and was surprised to see my name for a flight the next morning at 0900.

The next morning, I woke up early, took a shower, and put on my dress white summer uniform. After checking out at the barracks desk, I arrived at the air terminal around 0800. A petty officer told me that my ship was in Palma de Mallorca. He checked my bags and directed me to my gate.

A small group of passengers was waiting to board the same plane. At around 0830, we boarded, and by 0900, our plane took off. The flight to Palma lasted about an hour and a half. I could see the harbor below as we circled the island and approached the airport. With clear visibility from my window seat, I spotted two moored Navy frigates. One bore the hull number 1068, and I recognized it as *Vreeland*.

The Balearic Islands are a group of four main islands located in the western Mediterranean Sea. Mallorca is the largest of the Balearic Islands and serves as the capital of the province of Spain. Palma de Mallorca—commonly known as Palma—is the largest city. Puerto de Palma is the main port and harbor on Mallorca.

After landing, I retrieved my bags and gear. I waved down a taxi outside the terminal, and the driver loaded my bags into the trunk. He laughed when I asked him if he knew how to get to the port and where the Navy ships were moored. It was a short ride of about 15 minutes to the pier where *Vreeland* was moored.

After gathering my sea bag and other gear, I paid the taxi driver and made my way to *Vreeland's* gangway. I left my sea bag on the pier at the foot of the gangway and ascended to the ship's quarterdeck. At the top of the gangway, I turned and saluted the U.S. Ensign flying from the staff at the ship's stern. Then, I faced the Officer of the Deck (OOD) on the quarterdeck and saluted, saying, "Request permission to come on board."

The OOD, a petty officer first class, returned my salute and replied, "Permission granted."

With that, I stepped onto the quarterdeck and handed my orders to the OOD, stating, "QM1 Trowbridge, reporting on board."

He accepted my orders, passed them to the Petty Officer of the Watch, and instructed him to log my arrival and to call the duty Master-at-Arms (MAA) to the quarterdeck. I returned to the pier, retrieved my sea bag, and went back on board. I had arrived at my new home away from home.

Within a few minutes, a petty officer first class wearing an MAA badge arrived on the quarterdeck. He introduced himself as Glenn Lund and welcomed me aboard. Glenn helped me with my bags and took me to the ship's office to check in. After we checked in at the ship's office, he led me to the operations department berthing compartment.

In the berthing compartment, he pointed out an empty middle rack and locker. "They cleared this rack out for you. We thought you might be arriving today."

I noticed a name tag on the bottom rack below mine—it belonged to QM2 Vaughn. I was excited to be assigned to a Knox-class frigate. These frigates bore no resemblance to traditional destroyers, featuring a boxy superstructure and a prominent mast-and-stack structure (called the "mack") positioned amidships. The ship's crew comprised 17 officers and 240 enlisted personnel.

Vreeland's propulsion plant was standard for the Knox class. Two boilers, each generating 1,200 pounds per square inch (psi) of pressure, supplied superheated steam to a single Westinghouse turbine, powering a single shaft and propeller that delivered 35,000 shaft horsepower and reached a top speed of 27 knots (31 mph). The ship had a cruising range of 4,500 nautical miles at 20 knots (23 mph). Its overall length was 438 feet, with a beam of 46 feet 9 inches and an average draft of 24 feet 9 inches.

USS Vreeland (FF 1068). A Knox-class fast frigate.

Since it was Friday afternoon and Palma was a liberty port for the crew, I wouldn't be assigned to a duty section until Monday while completing the check-in process. My first order of business was to change into a working uniform and stow my clothes, uniforms, and gear in my locker. Someone had laid out clean linens, a blanket, and a pillow on my mattress, so I made my rack. My next plan was to explore the ship and familiarize myself with the various spaces on board, and I was eager to head up to the bridge to survey the equipment and layout.

After locating our department's head and shower area, I walked around until I found the galley and mess decks. Earlier, while speaking with Glenn, he informed me about a 1st Class Mess on board and its location—

aft on the second deck. I decided to visit the mess later and go to the bridge first.

Once on the bridge, I surveyed the layout. Along the aft bulkhead, I found the door to the chartroom. I opened the door to discover a young petty officer third class sitting on a stool, reading a book. I asked the kid, "Are you a QM?"

He replied, "Yes, my name's Savinsky, but everyone calls me 'Ham' for short, as in Hamilton. Are you the new QM1?"

"Yes, I'm George Trowbridge," I said.

Ham offered his hand, and said as we shook, "Welcome aboard! Do you want me to show you around?"

I replied, "Ham, I would appreciate that."

Ham showed me the electronic navigation systems. First, he showed me the Omega receiver unit in the chartroom, a global-range radio navigation system. Next, he showed me the Loran-C receiver unit mounted above the chart table on the bridge. Loran-C is a hyperbolic radio navigation system that allows a receiver to determine its position by listening to low-frequency radio signals transmitted from fixed, land-based radio beacons. We reviewed the surface search radar repeaters on the bridge, along with the fathometer.

Ham explained that Lieutenant Hayden was the ship's official navigator, but QM2 (Quartermaster 2nd Class) Gregg Vaughn had been serving as the assistant navigator. Now that I was there, the QM team increased to four people. The QMs were in a three-section Quartermaster of the Watch (QMOW) underway watch rotation, which included Ham, QM2 Vaughn, and QMSN (Quartermaster Seaman) Ward. Ham wanted to know if I intended to stand QMOW watches while underway. I told him, "We'll see."

I chatted briefly with Ham, who updated me on the rest of the bridge, navigation equipment, and instruments. Since it was his duty day, he didn't mind hanging around and talking, as he had to be on board anyway. After a while, I told him I'd catch up with him later and left the bridge. I decided to head to the 1st Class Mess to check it out. Once on the second deck, towards the aft section of the ship, I found the door marked as the "1st Class Mess." It was locked when I tried to open it, so I knocked and waited.

Within seconds, the door swung open, revealing Glenn. He welcomed me inside as I stepped in. Two others were with him, and Glenn introduced me to them. They had a pretty nice setup. Several couches and chairs were available for seating. A table with four chairs was ready for eating, working, or playing cards. Glenn proudly showed me the popcorn machine, a small refrigerator, and cabinets stocked with various gedunk (snacks). Additionally, a projector screen was mounted on the bulkhead, along with their movie projector.

One of the guys there was Signalman 1st Class (SM1) Paul Weeks. Paul introduced himself as the current elected President of the Mess. He immediately shared, "The monthly dues to belong to the mess are $15. Every petty officer first class on board is considered a member in good standing as long as they pay their dues."

At that point, the other guy stood up from his seat, walked over to me, extended his hand with a smile. "Welcome! I'm Mike Carmichael, Gunner's Mate. Your last name is Trowbridge, right?"

As I shook Mike's hand, I replied, "Right, call me George. It's good to meet you."

Mike leaned back against the table, a grin spreading across his face as he announced, "I have duty today, but tomorrow is Saturday. A few of us are planning to head into town. Would you like to join?"

I couldn't help but smile as I replied, "Sure, that sounds good."

Paul, seated nearby with a playful glint in his eye, chuckled. "George, be careful! Mike and his friends will corrupt you." His tone was lighthearted, yet there was an undertone of camaraderie. "I'm tagging along—we SMs and QMs need to stick together!"

Glenn chimed in with a mock-seriousness that made us all laugh. "George, I'm an OS (Operations Specialist). It should be QMs and OSs banding together, not those skivvy-waving Signalmen."

Listening to their banter, I felt a warm sense of belonging. They were genuinely good guys, and despite the playful teasing, they clearly shared a strong bond. I made a mental note to address my trust issues, remnants from my past experience as a recruiter, realizing that it might be time to let my guard down and embrace this new friendship.

USS *Vreeland* left Mayport on March 11 and was just past the halfway point of its six-month deployment. I learned that the ship was set to return to Mayport on August 12. More importantly, in early October, I found out that *Vreeland* will undergo a nine-month overhaul at the Bath Iron Works (BIW) shipyard in Bath, Maine. This also means that the ship will still be in Bath when I reach my EOAS on July 31 of next year.

The next afternoon, I changed into civilian clothes for later. I knew there were some international pay phones near the ship's port facility, and I wanted to call Jan. I left the ship and started walking; after a short distance, I spotted a line of phones alongside a building. I waited until about 1330 to call, which was 8:30 a.m. local time back in Iowa. I wanted to call early enough before she left for work. I was relieved when she answered the phone.

Later, back on the ship, I met up with Paul and Mike in the mess, and we left together. Waiting for us on the quarterdeck was another guy. Mike introduced me to Electronic Warfare Technician 2nd Class (EW2) Jerry

Chamberlain. Jerry was a tall, big guy who immediately made it clear that he was from Texas. He struck me like some people do—someone who was always upbeat, happy, fun to be around, and full of energy. Jerry was the proverbial pull-my-finger type, always cheerful and in high spirits.

The four of us left the ship and found a taxi to take us into town. When the driver asked where we wanted to go, Paul replied, "To the Gut, where all the sailor bars are."

The driver nodded to show he understood, and off we went. Perched on the hillside, away from the tourist spots bustling with hotels, beaches, beach clubs, upscale restaurants, and nightclubs, lies an area in Palma commonly referred to as the "Gut." The Gut is located in the oldest part of the city and was once considered suitable only for unsavory characters and criminal elements. It had a reputation for high crime rates and was considered dangerous at night—a perfect setting for sailors looking to enjoy a lively night out.

Almost everyone began their night at a bar called "Texas Jacks," situated in the heart of the Gut. This establishment had been a favored spot for U.S. sailors, Marines, and soldiers for decades. A unique tradition involved patrons carving their names into the wooden bar, walls, and staircase, leading to thousands of names etched throughout the venue. One wall was adorned with hundreds of Navy ship ball caps, while others displayed an array of ship and unit cloth patches as well as wooden plaques.

Jerry insisted we kick off our activities with tequila shots, followed by beer chasers. Luckily, we ordered a platter of tacos and enchiladas upon arrival, which helped mitigate the effects of the alcohol. After about the fifth shot of tequila, the food saved us from total inebriation—at least for a little while.

Around the Gut, many other great bars catered to the Navy fleet ships visiting Palma. You could have a wild time, drink to your heart's content, likely get laid, and do it all for very little money. We spent the night carousing from one bar to another. My best guess is that we returned to the ship around 0200. It was a fun night that ultimately ended without any incidents.

After sleeping in and wrestling with my hangover until lunch the next day, I decided to head to the bridge. I began by reviewing the operating manuals and testing the Omega and Loran-C receivers. Then, I took stock of the navigation equipment. I found the standard operating procedures (SOP) and the captain's standing orders, dedicating significant time to reviewing them.

Around mid-afternoon, QM2 Vaughn arrived on the bridge. He was on board because it was his duty day. After introductions, we spent some time talking. He clarified that he would be leaving the Navy in the fall after the deployment. The ship was scheduled to depart Palma on Tuesday for Tunisia, so I asked Vaughn about the passage plan for the transit.

He seemed to tense before responding, "Mr. Hayden and I will be handling that tomorrow."

One skill I developed as a recruiter was the ability to read people and size them up quickly. I thought Vaughn harbored some veiled animosity toward me, even though he didn't say anything outright. From his perspective, I could see that he had been enjoying running the QM gang and being in charge, and now I was here to take that away from him.

On Monday, after morning quarters with the QMs and Lieutenant Hayden, who was also our division officer, I went to the ship's office to finish processing and start check-in. The check-in includes a brief meeting with each key person in command, including representatives from disbursing, medical, and other departments. During the meeting with the senior watch officer, I was assigned to an in-port duty section. The last three meetings on my list were with the department head, the executive officer, and the captain.

That afternoon, I knocked on the commanding officer's cabin door, opened it, and announced myself before requesting permission to enter. The captain, seated at his desk, rose and extended his hand to shake mine.

"Trowbridge; it's good to meet you. Welcome aboard." He motioned for me to take a seat beside his desk. The captain was Commander Phillip A. Accorsi, a pleasant-looking man with salt-and-pepper hair who seemed very friendly and kind. We conversed for a while, with me primarily responding to his questions about my background.

I noticed he had my service record on his desk. What he said next caught me off guard: "Trowbridge, I see you spent close to three years and nine months in recruiting and earned three gold wreaths. Can you explain why you were given a 'fault' transfer?"

"Captain, I have no idea." Surprised, I replied, "I was initially given a one-year mandatory extension, which I protested by contacting my congressman. I knew that it angered some in the command, but I remained a successful recruiter until I checked out."

He leaned back in his chair and smiled. "My last assignment was at the Bureau of Naval Personnel as an Officer Detailer. Before that, I was the commanding officer of a reserve center in Indiana. I know how the game is played. I suspect this was your XO's way of getting even; it happens." Then he continued, "I'll tell you what: if you deserve it and earn it in 90 days, I'll write you a performance evaluation that will make all of this go away. Does that sound fair?"

My only response was, "Yes, Captain, that sounds good. I appreciate it." We concluded the meeting, and I exited the captain's cabin, shutting the door behind me.

As I stepped into the passageway, a wave of anger washed over me as memories of the people at NRD Chicago flooded my mind. I remembered my last day there, checking out with the XO and signing my final performance evaluation without reading it. I just wanted to leave the whole place behind. I knew that even if I had caught the "fault" transfer at that moment and pointed it out, they wouldn't have changed it, and the situation would likely have become confrontational. I just needed to accept the captain's offer and work to earn his performance evaluation. Even though I didn't plan to stay in the Navy, it was still a matter of pride for me to have a spotless record.

That afternoon, I reviewed the passage plan prepared by Lt. Hayden and QM2 Vaughn. Overall, it was a solid plan, but I identified certain elements that needed adjustment or revision. I discussed my proposed changes with the lieutenant, who agreed with my suggestions. Later, we held a navigation briefing in the wardroom for the key bridge, Combat Information Center (CIC), and deck crew members. Everything went smoothly during the briefing. The only change the captain requested was for me to lead the navigation team during the Sea and Anchor detail for our departure from Palma.

We departed from Palma around 0900 the next morning and began our transit to Tunis, Tunisia. The distance from Palma to Tunis was 435 nautical miles. I assigned Ham and Ward as the port and starboard bearing takers, while Vaughn joined me at the chart plot as the bearing recorder. As the assistant navigator, I maintain the navigation chart plot. I report our ship's position and recommendations to the captain, OOD, and the conning officer at two-minute intervals after each fix position is obtained and evaluated. It appeared that Lt. Hayden's plan was simply to stand by and observe.

Fortunately, navigating the ship out of Palma was easy, with few hazards to navigation. In less than 20 minutes, we were in the open waters of the Mediterranean Sea. We set the ship's course toward Tunisia, secured from the Sea and Anchor detail, and established the normal underway watch sections.

It felt wonderful to be back at sea again. The gentle motion of the ship, as it slowly rose and fell with the waves, made me feel complete once more. I began to realize just how much I had missed this experience.

The transit to Tunisia would take about 27 hours at 16 knots. I spent most of the day finalizing the plan for our arrival in Tunis the next day. We would not be entering the port of Tunis, as the water depths alongside the docks there were too shallow. Instead, we would anchor the ship in deeper water at an anchorage area just north of the port's approach channel. We would use the ship's motor whaleboat and the captain's gig to transfer people to shore and back, and there would also be local water taxis available.

We entered the Gulf of Tunis the next morning and navigated to our designated anchorage area. Just before noon, we let go of the ship's anchor. The ship shuddered from the weight of the anchor chain running up from the chain locker and overboard through the hawse pipe into the water. Once the anchor was on the bottom, we slowly backed the ship while paying out the anchor chain to the desired scope of two and one-half shots (225 feet). The anchor windlass brake was set, securing the anchor chain as we backed down again, slowly, ensuring the anchor was set in the bottom and holding. After fixing the ship's position three or four times in the same spot, I reported to the captain that the anchor appeared to be holding. Following my report, the captain ordered us to secure from the Sea and Anchor detail and set the anchor watch.

As I organized the chart for the navigation anchor watch, the captain walked by on his way off the bridge, tapped me on the shoulder, and said, "Good job."

We would be at anchor for five days. The QMs would stand duty on the bridge, checking the ship's position every 30 minutes to ensure the anchor was holding. I divided us into port and starboard sections, assigning two QMs to each section. Vaughn and Ham would make up one section, while Wade and I would form the other. This way, anyone who wanted to go ashore in Tunis would have the opportunity every other day.

It was July, and Tunisia, located on the northern coast of Africa, is bordered by Algeria to the west and Libya to the east. Geographically, Tunisia is a small country, with much of its southern region covered by the Sahara Desert. As a result, the weather was hot—even on the ship anchored offshore. The landscape visible from the ship primarily consisted of cliffs, rocks, and sand.

Islam is the predominant state religion in Tunisia, with approximately 99 percent of the population being Sunni Muslims. For sailors, this means that Tunisia is a dry country with no alcohol, bars, clubs, or nightlife. One afternoon, I went ashore and discovered some decent shops in the souk area. I understood that there were sightseeing trips available on horseback and tours to several museums. Still, after my brief visit, I felt I had experienced all I wanted to of Tunis.

During my time here, I began reflecting on something else: I was approaching my next birthday. On most Navy ships, the average age of the crew is typically around 21 or 22. At this point, being 27, soon to be 28, I was considered old, and the younger crew members often referred to me and others like me as "lifers"—just as I had when I was a 20-year-old sailor.

I divided my time while anchored in Tunis between developing the passage plan for our next port visit and working on the Personal Qualification Standard (PQS) for Fire Fighting and Damage Control. Every crew member of a U.S. Navy surface combatant ship must be a trained firefighter, capable of extinguishing shipboard fires and performing emergency repairs as part of damage control parties. In addition to completing the necessary PQS, they participate in regular shipboard fire and damage control training and drills. Furthermore, I needed to requalify by completing the PQS for Officer of the Deck (OOD) in port to be assigned to OOD watches in charge of the quarterdeck.

After the stop in Tunis, the next scheduled port was Malaga, Spain, for three days. Malaga is located 58 miles northeast of Great Europa Point, which lies on the northern side of the Strait of Gibraltar, near the famous Rock of Gibraltar.

Many crew members were excited about visiting Malaga. After Malaga, the ship would transit out of the Mediterranean Sea. Then we would head north along the coasts of Spain and France. Our journey would continue northeast through the English Channel and into the southern reaches of the North Sea until we arrive off the coast of Belgium. Our first stop would be at anchor off Oostende, Belgium, where we planned to stay for two days before continuing our transit to Antwerp.

On the morning of July 8, *Vreeland* weighed anchor and set sail from Tunis. The distance to Malaga was approximately 780 nautical miles, but along the way, we conducted several anti-submarine warfare exercises with ships from the Royal and Italian Navies. Once again, the weather in the western Mediterranean Sea was mild, and the sea conditions were quite calm.

On the morning of July 11, *Vreeland* began her approach to the Malaga breakwaters and harbor entrance. Malaga's harbor and port are relatively small, so once the ship was inside the breakwaters, it was only a short distance to our assigned berth at a wharf near Malaga Light, a 125-foot-tall lighthouse known for its white cylindrical masonry structure.

The wharf where we docked was just a short walk from the city's historic areas. A quick stroll to the east of the port led to the beach, lined with hotels, restaurants, shops, and bars. We were scheduled to leave Malaga on July 14 and begin our transit to Belgium. Malaga is a liberty port, so aside from the duty sections, the rest of the crew had maximum liberty time ashore. I planned to split my time between exploring some of the local sights and working on the passage plan for our transit to Belgium.

The next day, my first priority was to find a spot where I could make a phone call home to talk with Jan and enjoy some time in town and at the beach. Malaga is a beautiful, historic Spanish city. The streets are narrow, and the area is filled with historic sites and buildings. I learned that morning where I could make an international call, and early that afternoon, I was able to reach Jan. As always, it was wonderful to talk with her, but most important to me was knowing that everything was well at home for her. After my calls with Jan, I'm always in a better frame of mind.

I returned to the ship to meet Paul, Mike, and Jerry. Together, we left the ship and took a short walk to the beach area of the town. We stumbled upon a café where we had lunch, then found a nice open bar with tables near the beach, where we ordered our first round of beers. The four of us spent the next several hours sipping our beers while enjoying the beach and lovely weather. It was a slow, pleasant afternoon. Later, we left the beach and headed into town. Malaga is known for its lively nightlife, and we had made plans to enjoy it that evening.

Mike and I set out on a walking tour of Malaga the next day. Both Roman and Muslim civilizations had made a significant impact on the city. We explored the Roman theater, Malaga Cathedral, and the Alcazaba, a palace-fortress constructed by the Muslim Moors in the 11th century. Alcazaba is located on the slope of Gibralfaro Mountain, offering a stunning view of Malaga and the port.

I decided to stay on board for the rest of our time in Malaga and get some work done. Specifically, I aimed to complete the necessary research to develop and outline the passage plan for Oostende. It seemed that Lt. Hayden, the navigator, was quite happy to let me take over the passage planning. Early in my Navy career, I adopted a strict philosophy: Either lead, follow, or get the hell out of my way. It appeared that the lieutenant saw his role as allowing me to lead and step aside. This unspoken arrangement suited me just fine.

Though I had only been back at sea briefly, I was beginning to realize what I had gained during my years in recruiting duty. The experience taught me many valuable life and professional lessons and changed me in several ways. For instance, now I seem to have a much higher tolerance when interacting with people, particularly with the occasional difficult individual. Diplomacy and discretion now come naturally when dealing with peers, junior sailors, senior enlisted personnel, and officers.

My work habits and personal performance standards are now higher than ever before. This combination of skills and attributes makes me a more effective manager and leader than I was in the past. At the same time, many of my fellow petty officers first class viewed the workday as ending at 1600, which to me was merely the midpoint of the workday. It quickly became evident that my dedication to succeeding in every endeavor did not go unnoticed.

Although I didn't spend much time in the 1st Class Mess, I occasionally took breaks there. I was sensing negativity directed at me from several members of the mess, who seemed to spend most, if not all, of their time there. I don't care about their opinions, so I shrugged them off.

Several chiefs approached me about taking on some additional duties. One of them was Chief Navy Counselor Spaulding, who was the command's full-time career counselor. Chief Spaulding would be leaving for his first recruiting duty tour in about five months, which prompted him to have many questions for me. During one of our conversations, he suggested that I take over as the operations department's career counselor. It seemed like a natural fit, as there isn't much difference between enlistment programs for recruits and those for service members looking to advance their careers in the Navy. Consequently, I agreed to take on that role.

The other individual was Chief Mess Management Specialist Homer, who also served as the command's Chief Master-at-Arms (MAA). Chief Homer had a friendly demeanor and an engaging personality. The MAA force was made up of volunteer petty officers, either first or second class, with one MAA assigned to each duty section. The chief approached me about volunteering to join the MAA force. I spoke with Jerry, a member of the MAA force, who encouraged me to volunteer. After discussing it with Jerry, I accepted the chief's invitation and became a member of the ship's security team.

I had become a busy person. After years of experience as a recruiter, handling multiple assignments comes almost naturally to me. I had already shaken off much of the rust in my navigation skills and abilities, but what I always enjoyed about navigation was that one never stops learning. I held the responsibilities of being the division's leading petty officer and assistant navigator. I was still working through several PQS qualifications and preparing for the final qualification examination boards. Now, I served as the department career counselor and a member of the ship's MAA force. I enjoyed it; shipboard work felt almost like a vacation after recruiting duty.

In many ways, I was fortunate to receive orders to *Vreeland*. She was under the command of a capable and decent man. The XO was excellent—always fair, friendly, and reasonable. I believed the department heads and all senior lieutenants were competent, proficient, fair, and easy to work with. All the junior officers were respectful and friendly. So far, my interactions with the chief petty officers had been nothing but positive. Being a member of *Vreeland's* crew was vastly different from my experiences on my first ship.

On the afternoon of July 14, we were underway from the port of Malaga and began the transit to Belgium. About three hours from Malaga, the Rock of Gibraltar came into view on the starboard bow as we approached Great Europa Point. Two hours later, we were off Great Europa Point and in the outbound ship traffic lane through the Strait of Gibraltar, leaving behind the warm summer weather of the western Mediterranean Sea and bound for the cooler temperatures found in the North Sea.

The distance from Malaga to Oostende is approximately 1,417 nautical miles. At an average speed of 16 knots, it would take us about 3 days and 17 hours to reach the anchorage area off the port of Oostende.

I was excited about this trip; the ship would travel through the English Channel and ultimately pass through the Dover Strait. The Dover Strait is 18 miles wide at its narrowest point, separating England's southeast coast from France's northern coast. I hoped that visibility would be good enough to see the white cliffs of Dover.

After clearing the Strait of Gibraltar and navigating through the busy marine traffic zone, we adjusted the ship's course to a northwesterly heading. A few hours later, off Cabo de São Vicente at the southwestern tip of Portugal, we changed our direction to sail along the coasts of Portugal and Spain. Late the following afternoon, off Cabo Finisterre, we changed our course to a more northeasterly route to transit through the outer area of the Bay of Biscay and along France's coast.

The next morning, we reached the vicinity of Île d'Ouessant and the Chenal du Four, located on France's northwest coast. There, we entered the marine traffic zone to begin our approach toward the western part of the English Channel. From Île d'Ouessant to Oostende, it's another 365 nautical miles, which would take about 23 hours at our current speed.

I made it a point to be on the bridge before sunrise. I knew we would start seeing the white cliffs of Dover around dawn, and I didn't want to miss it. Shortly after sunrise, there they were, off the port bow. We were about 7 miles from the English coastline. In the soft morning light, the cliff's white chalk gleamed, creating a stunning sight.

Before long, the South Foreland light tower became visible on the headland, and just to the north, we could also see the Dover Patrol

Memorial—a prominent stone monument standing above the cliffs. Witnessing the white cliffs of Dover was one more thing I could check off my bucket list.

Just before noon, we arrived at our designated anchorage position, just north of the entrance to the port of Oostende. After letting go of the anchor and ensuring it was set, the anchor watch was set. Shortly after anchoring, it began to rain. It was a cold rain, and the winds made it feel even colder. I wondered if this was typical July weather for the Netherlands and Belgium.

Several other destroyers and frigates from the Royal Navy, as well as those from France, the Netherlands, and Belgium, were anchored nearby. We were here leading up to Belgium's National Day, with our ship representing the U.S. at the Belgian Naval Review, which celebrated the 105th anniversary of Belgium's independence. While here, the King of Belgium would be aboard one of the frigates to oversee a shipboard passing in review of the assembled vessels. Afterward, the captain would go ashore to attend a celebration and banquet hosted by the Belgian monarchy.

The next day, early in the afternoon, crew members were in their dress blue uniforms. We manned the rails at 1300 to honor the King of Belgium and his royal entourage as their ship passed ours. The weather was cloudy with intermittent rain and chilly winds. The crew took their positions on the starboard side along the rails, starting at the forecastle, on the 02-level of the superstructure behind the bridge, and on the main deck aft of the superstructure. When the command is given over the 1MC (ship's intercom), we would remove our covers and wave them in the air while shouting at the top of our lungs, "Hip, Hip, Hooray!" three times.

The message is relayed over the 1MC: "*Vreeland*, stand by." We can see a Belgian frigate approaching our ship off the starboard bow.

Shortly after, another command came over the 1MC: "*Vreeland*, standby to render honors." Immediately, everyone in line removes their covers and begins waving them.

Then, when prompted by the announcement over the 1MC, "*Vreeland*, execute," the crew erupts into a chorus, shouting, "Hip, Hip, Hooray!" After repeating this three times, three short blasts of a whistle are heard over the 1MC, signaling everyone to stop and resume their positions in ranks.

To my surprise, we see crowds of people waving at us from the deck of the Belgian frigate as it passes by. Once the frigate disappears from view, an announcement is made over the 1MC, dismissing the crew from manning the rails. Little did I know that about an hour later, I would witness an unusual sight.

The word came that a Belgian Navy helicopter was on its way to our ship to pick up the captain and fly him to Oostende for the banquet. Since we had a flight deck large enough to accommodate NATO marine helicopters, we assumed it would land. Soon, we received a radio call that a helicopter was en route to the ship and that our captain should be standing by. I went to the aft section of the superstructure, where I could observe the flight deck.

I see what looks like an Alouette III helicopter approaching. As it gets closer, I notice a crewman hanging about 25 feet below the helicopter on a cable. I glance down at the flight deck, where Captain Accorsi stands in full dress blues, adorned with all his medals and carrying his sword in its scabbard.

Within moments, the helicopter hovered over the deck. The crewman on the cable crab-walked over to the captain, threw a horse collar sling around his torso, wrapped his legs around the captain's legs, and then it was lift-off.

I will never forget the sight of the captain as he was lifted off the deck and into the air. He kept one hand on his cover to prevent it from blowing away, while his other hand gripped the scabbard of his sword. Even though he was in a sling, it almost seemed like the crewman had him in a bear hug. Before long, the helicopter turned and headed toward the shore.

As I turned around to head back to the bridge, I realized Ham had been standing next to me, watching the show. I chuckled after he said, "Man, that was some shit. I bet no one expected that, especially the old man. They better serve him a stiff drink and some good chow."

I missed it when the helicopter delivered the captain back to the ship early in the evening. The next morning, we weighed anchor, got underway, and set a course for Antwerp. We turned the ship to a northern heading to approach Scheur, one of the main buoyed approach channels leading into the Westerschelde. Near the Wandelaar Pilot Station, we slowed just long enough for the pilot to board from his pilot boat alongside. Pilots are experienced, highly skilled mariners with extensive knowledge of the local waterways who assist ships in navigating safely to their destinations. The pilot we took on was a Dutchman who spoke excellent English. One got the sense right away that he was competent, skilled, and knowledgeable about his work.

The morning transit through the Westerschelde was not nearly as navigationally challenging as I had expected. The combination of a competent pilot with the critical parts of the fairways in the main channel are marked by lights and lighted beacons made it easier. Additionally, directional sector lights and lighted ranges indicated where to steer the ship, keeping it in safe waters. As we approach the port of Antwerp, another pilot boat comes alongside, delivering the harbor pilot for docking in Antwerp.

The Westerschelde pilot bid farewell and disembarked, boarding the same pilot boat. The Antwerp harbor pilot turned out to be a skilled ship handler and was familiar with the handling characteristics of Knox-class frigates. He guided two harbor tugs alongside our ship to assist with docking. We docked at the port of Antwerp close to lunchtime, very near the central part of the city.

We would be in Antwerp for five days. Down on the mess decks, many brochures promoting the city's sights were available. The brochures highlighted various attractions, from the stunning Cathedral of Our Lady to the vibrant atmosphere of the old town. Each provided a glimpse into Antwerp's rich history and culture, inviting us to explore the cobblestone streets, sample local delicacies, and visit the famous diamond district.

While on board, I became acquainted and friendly with Electronics Technician 1st Class (ET1) Russ Tomlin. The day after our arrival, Russ, Paul, and I decided to take a walking tour of Antwerp. We discovered a small yet unique-looking castle near the ship called Het Steen. Out front, there was an unusual statue of a character named Lange Wapper, a famous peeping tom. The statue depicted Lange exposing himself to smaller statues representing passersby.

It was just a short walk from the ship to Antwerp's Grote Markt, or town square. A brochure informed us that it dates back to the 16th century and is a stunning example of architecture from that time. The town hall, built in both Renaissance and Gothic styles, serves as the centerpiece of the square. At the center of the square stands a large statue of Brabo, a legendary giant-slayer. I have never seen a city quite like it.

We explored the diamond district and then headed to Antwerp's railway station, known as Antwerpen-Centraal. The only word that truly describes the train station is "beautiful." Directly across from the station is Chocolate Nation, touted as the largest Belgian chocolate museum in the world.

We discovered several frites cafés showcasing the signature Belgian french fries. We chatted with some friendly locals who proudly claimed that the Belgians invented what we call french fries. We all ordered fries, and I must admit that with the various sauce toppings, they were probably the best I've ever tasted.

We also discovered that Belgians take great pride in their beer. It felt rude to visit Antwerp without trying some of their cold brews. We started at the Antwerp Brewery to learn about Belgian beer, where the top local brew is De Koninck, made right on site. Later, we stumbled upon a place called Paters Vaetje near the cathedral. This venue offered dozens of different beers, and we spent the rest of the day there sampling all the varieties.

One thing we all noticed about the Belgians we met was their incredible friendliness. Once they learned we were Americans, they often treated us like we were something special. Several of them pointed out that it was the Americans who liberated them from Nazi Germany during World War II. It was interesting to hear how many spoke about the defeat of the Nazis as if it had happened recently rather than 35 years earlier.

By early evening, all three of us were pretty much wasted from all the beer we had consumed. We found a café, had some dinner, and then decided to head back to the ship to sleep it off. Tomorrow would be another day.

The next day, the weather was cold with intermittent rain since morning. That afternoon, Paul, Jerry, and I went ashore. After wandering for a bit, it started to rain again, prompting us to seek shelter in a café we discovered along one of the side streets.

Following a late lunch, we began sampling the various beers available at the café bar. The café was a charming place, the people were friendly, and we settled in for an enjoyable afternoon of drinks. After a while, I needed to use the head, so I got up from the bar and went to the WC at the back of the café.

I entered the WC and was startled to find a woman sitting on the toilet. My presence didn't seem to bother her, and seeing the urinal trough confirmed I was in the right place. While I stood at the urinal, another man walked in, approached the trough, and stood beside me. Suddenly, he exclaimed in Dutch, "Elkema! Hoe gaat het?"

I looked at him and asked, "What did you say?"

His posture changed as he replied in English, "Oh, you're American, huh?"

I responded, "Yes, but what surprised me is that Elkema is my grandmother's maiden name."

"I have a friend who lives across the river in the Netherlands. His name is Henk Elkema. I thought that's who you were; you could be his twin," he explained.

I glanced at him briefly and asked, "Do you have time for a beer? I'd like to hear more." After leaving the WC and sitting at the bar, I introduced myself.

He extended his hand for a handshake. "My name's Geert Bramm." Paul, Jerry, and I, along with our new friend Geert, took turns buying rounds of beer.

Geert explained that he was raised in the Netherlands and attended school with Henk Elkema. He also emphasized that he wasn't close friends with Henk but did occasionally hang out with him. Throughout our conversation, Geert often remarked on how strange it was that I looked so much like Henk. He even said that my height, build, hair, and facial features could be a double for Henk's. Geert also noted that we must be related since there was a connection between Henk and me through the name Elkema.

Later, at Geert's suggestion, we followed him to some other bars and clubs. Since he was local, we assumed he would know the best places to go. Around midnight, we said our goodbyes to Geert and headed back to the ship. I had duty the next day and didn't want to face it with a severe hangover. Plus, I needed to start working on our departure passage plan from Antwerp and our voyage back into the Mediterranean.

On Friday morning, July 25, we left our berth in Antwerp and began our transit through the Westerschelde waterways. The pilots who assisted us were just as skilled and competent as those who guided us into Antwerp the previous week. After navigating south through the English Channel and reaching the Atlantic waters near the Bay of Biscay, we were scheduled to meet ships from the Royal and French Navies for a two-day anti-submarine warfare exercise before continuing our journey to the Mediterranean.

My relationship with Lt. Hayden seemed to be going well. Each day, he effectively fulfilled his duties as division officer. After officers' call, he would hold morning quarters with the division and briefly meet with me to share information about upcoming transits, port visits, or other ship-related tasks before disappearing.

I offered him several opportunities to lead the navigation team during upcoming navigation or Sea and Anchor details, but he declined each time. During one of our discussions, the lieutenant explained his position, saying, "Trowbridge, why would I interfere? You're doing a better job at navigation than I ever could or would. Besides, the captain is happy with both of us, which means this tour will be successful. So, let's keep everything as it is, okay?"

Our next destination in the Mediterranean was Sardinia. On the morning of July 31, we anchored just outside the port entrance to Cagliari. Later that morning, our boat crew took the captain ashore for an end-of-deployment out-briefing with the NATO naval forces that *Vreeland* had worked with during the deployment. That afternoon, the captain returned to the ship, and within an hour, we weighed anchor and departed Cagliari. We were headed for Rota to refuel, and then we would cross the Atlantic Ocean, with plans to arrive at Mayport on August 12, marking the end of the deployment.

Two days later, in the early morning, we docked in Rota after passing through the Strait of Gibraltar. Right after docking, we began taking on fuel, supplies, and mail bags.

Later that afternoon, we departed Rota and navigated out through the outer breakwaters into the Atlantic Ocean. It would take crossing nearly 3,700 nautical miles of open ocean to reach Mayport from Rota. The passage plan for the Atlantic crossing was straightforward. From Rota, we set a southwesterly course that would lead us to latitude 30° North, where we would then turn to a course of 270 degrees (west) and sail parallel along that latitude toward Mayport. The latitude coordinate for the naval station at Mayport is 30° 23.0' North. This route is favorable during the late summer months, which coincide with hurricane season, as it keeps the ship's position north of the tropical zone and south of the colder, more turbulent waters in the North Atlantic.

The ocean crossing was uneventful, with fair weather and good sea conditions along the route. On the morning of August 12, the ship approached the Florida coast. By observing its radar beacon, I could identify the St. Johns River (STJ) entrance buoy on the radar. I recommended a new course to the OOD to close in on the buoy. Within a short time, we set the Sea and Anchor detail for entering port. The crew, in their dress white uniforms, assumed their stations. It's a reasonably short transit into Mayport. Once the ship passes buoy STJ, the vessel is steered using the navigation range lights and marks for the channel, which is a simple process through the nearly 5 miles of breakwaters on both sides.

As we approached the Mayport basin, it was simply a matter of adjusting course to port to line up with the navigation range lights and marks located at the southwest corner of the basin. We slowed down in the approach channel to take on the docking pilot who boarded from one of the tugboats. We were assigned to dock at Berth B-2 within the basin. The pier where we were to dock was lined with the families of crew members and local media to greet our arrival. Within 15 minutes, the ship was alongside the pier, and all mooring lines were passed and secured. The captain ordered the gangway put out and secured the ship's crew from their Sea and Anchor detail stations. *Vreeland* was home.

It was a bittersweet day for me. I felt happy for the crew members reuniting with their families and friends, but I had no one there to greet me. I took solace in the fact that we were back in the U.S. The good news was that I had something to look forward to: the ship would have a 30-day post-deployment stand-down period. This meant that half of the crew could take 14 days of leave at a time if they chose to. I had volunteered to take my leave during the second half of the stand-down period so that in two weeks, I could go home to Iowa.

My buddy Paul was in a similar situation; he was a geographical bachelor like me. His wife and kids lived in his hometown in Vermont. Fortunately, Paul had a car that he stored at the vehicle compound on base during the deployment. Later that day, I walked with Paul to the compound to retrieve his car. Paul was taking leave at the same time as I was, but he planned to drive home to Vermont and back when the time came.

During the stand-down period for the remainder of the crew, we were assigned to three-section duty. This meant that every third day was a duty day for us. One thing I really enjoyed since returning to the U.S. was the ease of calling home and talking with Jan. We were both looking forward to my coming home.

August 28 finally arrived, marking the start of my leave. I had a morning flight scheduled to Chicago with a connecting flight to Rochester. Paul kindly offered to drive me to Jacksonville Airport on his way to Vermont. That afternoon, my plane landed in Rochester ahead of schedule. I met Jan and Mitch as they walked in. We shared a three-way hug and exchanged kisses; it felt wonderful to be home. Even though it had been just under four months since I left them, it somehow felt much longer. With two weeks at home ahead of us, we needed to make the most of our time together.

Jan took a week off from her job, so we had that time together. While I was home, we celebrated my birthday; I had just turned 28. Before I knew it, my leave was over, and I boarded a plane back to Florida. I returned to the ship and checked in off leave late on Friday night, September 12. I had duty that weekend, which was fine since I wasn't up for much off the ship, anyway.

Vreeland was scheduled to remain in port until October. Its focus was now on preparing for the nine-month overhaul at the Bath Iron Works (BIW) shipyard in Bath, Maine. First, we were set to head to the Naval Weapons Station in Earle, New Jersey, to offload the ship's weapons. The offload in Earle was anticipated to take three days. After Earle, there would be a port visit in New York City.

I wasn't motivated to spend the rest of my enlistment in a shipyard. I did call the QM Rating detailer to explore the possibility of transferring to another ship that was either actively operating or deployed. The detailer was willing to accommodate me but wanted me to agree to a two-year extension to get a new set of orders. Since I planned on getting out, I couldn't agree to an extension. So, I had to settle: Bath, Maine.

During the last part of September, there were some changes in the QM gang. QM2 Vaughn was taking his discharge and getting out, and we received a new QMSN, a young seaman named Mike Austin, fresh out of "A" School. I wasn't all that sorry to see Vaughn go. In certain respects, he had been a pain in my ass. His veiled animosity toward me, coupled with his air of superiority, had tried my patience on a number of occasions. As far as I was concerned, when it came to Vaughn, my thoughts about him and his departure were, *Farewell, happy to see you go.*

By this point, I had been on board for over 90 days. Overall, the transition back to sea duty had gone well for me both personally and professionally. Although I often missed Jan and Mitch terribly, it had significantly improved my quality of life compared to recruiting duty. I enjoyed serving on *Vreeland*, and I appreciated the area around Mayport.

During the first week of October, the captain issued performance evaluation reports for all 20 petty officers first class. Mr. Hayden met with me in his stateroom to discuss my evaluation.

I remember him smiling as he handed me the form. "I believe you're going to be pleased." I took it from him and began reading through the comments and evaluation marks.

The comments in the write-up made it sound like I could walk on water. I received Superior Upper, the highest mark in all evaluation sections. Most importantly, I was ranked number one among members of my grade, meaning I was the highest-performing petty officer first class in the command. The captain also commented in the report: "Petty Officer Trowbridge has my strongest possible recommendation for advancement to Chief Petty Officer. If I had to build a ship or a command around one person, it would be him."

After reading everything, the lieutenant smiled as he handed me a pen. "I'm guessing you have no objections?"

I shook my head to indicate "no." I signed the evaluation form and handed it back to him.

With that, he extended his hand for a shake. "I want to thank you too; since you came on board, you've made my life so much easier. What I have learned from you is invaluable." I accepted his hand, and we shook. After that, I excused myself and thanked him for his kind words.

After exiting the lieutenant's stateroom and stepping into the passageway, I felt satisfied and genuinely happy. After revealing that the recruiting command had given me a "fault" transfer, I recalled what the captain had said: "If you deserve it and earn it in 90 days, I'll write you a performance evaluation that will make all of this go away." I hoped the captain was right in his assessment.

Many married crew members were relocating their families from the Mayport area to Maine. One advantage of the ship's move to Maine was that Naval Air Station (NAS) Brunswick is only about 8 miles from Bath. This allowed flights to and from NAS Jacksonville to be viable options for those whose families remained in Florida. Once shipyard work began, single crew members or geographical bachelors like me would transfer off the ship to stay in barracks at the Topsham Annex of NAS Brunswick.

Vreeland departed from Mayport on Monday, October 6, en route to the Naval Weapons Station in Earle. It would take less than two days to cover the 790 nautical miles from Mayport to Earle. On Wednesday morning, we docked at Earle's long ammunition pier in Sandy Hook Bay. Personnel from the weapons station awaited at the pier and boarded as soon as the gangway was in place. After completing the safety and weapon offload plan briefs, the offload commenced promptly.

Offloading all of our ammunition and weapons continued until late Friday morning. We set the Sea and Anchor detail early that afternoon for our entry into New York. A New York State Pilot boarded while the ship was still at the dock. After a briefing from the pilot, we got underway from Earle and began our northward transit through Chapel Hill South and North Channel to the main entrance of Ambrose Channel in New York's Lower Bay. Once in Ambrose Channel, we proceeded northward to the Verrazzano Narrows Bridge; after passing through The Narrows and under the bridge, we arrived in the Upper Bay.

The Upper Bay is the section of New York Harbor between The Narrows and The Battery. Soon, we found ourselves in the Anchorage Channel, approaching The Battery at the southern tip of Manhattan. Once we reached the Hudson River, we continued north along the Manhattan shoreline to our east. QMSN Austin was stationed as the bearing taker on the starboard bridge wing. As we passed the World Trade Center, he remarked on how King Kong had climbed the towers in the movie.

Later that afternoon, *Vreeland* docked at Pier 88 in downtown Manhattan, the same pier where our fast patrol boats had docked four years earlier. We were going to be in New York for the weekend and would depart for Maine on Monday. Except for those in the duty sections, the crew was granted maximum liberty. I had the duty but could go ashore the next day. I had agreed with Russ to visit Times Square; since I had been there before, I could show him around.

The next day, after lunch, Russ and I left the ship and began our walk to Times Square. We spent most of the afternoon exploring Times Square, where Russ seemed captivated by the area. By early evening, we were both feeling hungry. I spotted the local diner where I had enjoyed some classic New York dishes during my first visit. While we were having dinner, we agreed that once we finished eating, we would head out to explore the local bars.

After dinner, we came across a place about a block west of Times Square and decided to go in. It had a pleasant atmosphere: most patrons were well-dressed, and the environment felt friendly and inviting. We found some open seats at the bar and ordered our first round. The bartender, a tall, slender, well-dressed Black man, introduced himself as Vick. We chatted with Vick for a few minutes, and he mentioned that some talented blues musicians would be playing later in the evening if we were interested. Russ and I settled in, thinking we had found our spot for the night.

One thing about me that sometimes feels like a phenomenon is my innate ability to attract the most bizarre people. I would soon discover that tonight would be one of those occasions. Russ had gone to the back to shoot billiards, so I found myself sitting alone at the bar when an attractive, well-dressed Black woman, who seemed to be in her early thirties, approached me and asked if the bar stool next to me was taken. I told her it was available and invited her to take a seat. I stood up and held the stool for her as she settled in.

I offered to buy her a drink, which she accepted. Then I said to her, "My name is George. What's yours?"

She responded in a surprisingly husky yet warm, feminine voice, "My name is Mary. George, I can already see you're a gentleman. It's so nice to meet you." With that, Mary and I began an evening of lively conversation.

Mary and I enjoyed one round after another. Soon, a small band set up near the bar entrance and began to play. I could tell that Mary really couldn't hold her liquor well and was starting to get a bit tipsy. Then, out of nowhere, she said, "You don't know who I am, do you?"

I replied, smirking, "You're Mary."

"No, I mean who my father is," she said.

"Mary, how would I know that?" I answered.

She leaned over toward me, smiling. "My dad is famous."

Mary went on to tell me about her father. She claimed her father was one of the founding members of a famous vocal group that was extremely popular in the 1950s and 60s, with dozens of hit songs. I won't reveal the group's name here because I don't want to get sued. I was familiar with the group and remembered several of their hits. As a kid, one of my older sisters even owned their record album and played it often at home. At that point, I still wasn't sure if she was being truthful or just making it up.

Mary mentioned that her father's group still went on concert tours, and she traveled with them. She started to explain how she performs with the group, singing backup vocals. To prove her point, she sang several lyrics from songs I immediately recognized. To my surprise, she actually had a really nice voice. I began to think, *Maybe her story was legitimate. It's possible. After all, this is New York.*

We talked some more and had a few more drinks. Around that time, Mary told me she really liked me and that we should leave and go to her place for the night. I declined as politely as I could, explaining that I was married, but I was very flattered that she asked. At first, she seemed to accept my answer.

Mary began to act strangely. She told me several times how much she cared for me and was adamant that we were meant to be together. Then, she laid out her plans for my future. She wanted me to desert the Navy, join her, and tour with her father's group. To help me make money, she offered to find me a job as a roadie, which would enable us to spend all our time together. At that point, I was thinking, *This woman is completely crazy. I need to get away from her now!*

I had noticed earlier that Vick seemed to be spending more time near where I sat with Mary. He would look at Mary and then at me on several occasions before moving away. I didn't think much about what Vick was doing. I put two $20 bills on the bar to pay for the last couple of rounds. I turned to her and said, "Mary, it's been so nice getting to know you, but I need to collect up my friend and get back to the ship. I have really enjoyed the evening; thank you so much."

I started to stand up to move away from the bar when suddenly I felt something hard jab me in the ribs. I looked down. Mary had a small, short-barrel revolver pushed into the side of my chest. I looked at her, and tears streamed down her face as she said, "Sit down, you're not going anywhere. If you try to get up again, I'll shoot you."

All I could think to say was, "Mary, why would you shoot me? I thought you liked me?"

She looked me in the eye. "If you come with me, I won't shoot you; what will you do?"

Just as I was about to speak, I suddenly noticed Vick standing behind us. He reached in, placed his hand over the top of the gun, and said gently yet firmly, "Now, Mary, give it to me. You know I've told you never to bring a gun in here. Now, hand it over." To my surprise, Mary lifted the gun and handed it to Vick. He took it and tucked it into his waistband.

I stood up, facing Vick. "Thank you. I wasn't sure what to do, but I think it's time to go. I need to grab my friend in the back first." Vick nodded in agreement.

I left the bar area and went to the billiards room. Fortunately, Russ had finished playing. I approached him and said, "We need to get out of here; a crazy woman at the bar just threatened to shoot me."

Russ looked at me skeptically. "That's bullshit!"

I insisted, "No, it's not. Let's go." As we headed back to the front to leave, I spotted Mary still sitting at the bar, but now she was smiling and laughing with another guy who had taken my place.

As I walked back to the ship with Russ, I recounted the incident with Mary, explaining how Vick, the bartender, had intervened and taken the gun from her, ultimately saving me. I've never been sure whether Mary would have shot me that night—who knows? It's New York, after all; I'm sure people get shot every night. Fortunately, that evening, it wasn't me.

After my encounter with Mary the night before, I was finished with New York. I stayed on board Sunday and finalized the passage plan to Bath. I worked with Austin to set up the bridge equipment for our departure in the morning. Besides those tasks, I spent the rest of the day relaxing and reading a novel.

The next morning, after the pilot came on board, we got underway and backed the ship out to the channel in the Hudson River. We followed the pilot's ordered course and speed once the ship's bow was clear and heading south. Our route outbound was essentially the reverse of the transit route we had used inbound until we reached Ambrose Channel. Ambrose Channel took us southeast, with Sandy Hook, NJ, on our starboard side before we emerged into the Atlantic Ocean. We slowed down near the final whistle buoy to allow the pilot boat to come alongside and pick up the pilot.

We set an easterly course to navigate the ship into the Ambrose–Nantucket Safety Fairway. We would transit through the fairway to a point southeast of Nantucket Island, then turn north, keeping Cape Cod to our west as we sailed toward Casco Bay and the entrance to the Kennebec River. The distance from New York to the entrance of the Kennebec River is 308 nautical miles, then another 12 nautical miles upriver to the shipyard in Bath.

The lower Kennebec River is a narrow, deep estuary carved into bedrock. It lies along the highly indented central coast of Maine. The eastern banks of the river feature two large islands separated by the Back River. The southernmost is Georgetown Island, while farther north, beyond the Back River, is Arrowsic Island. If I had to choose one word to describe this part of the Maine coast, it would be "astonishing."

Vreeland arrived just south of the entrance to the Kennebec River at 0700 the next morning. We approached while staying east of Seguin Island, positioned between Whaleback Rock and Pond Island, which forms the main channel. The Kennebec River pilot boat waited near a buoy marking a shoal area known as White Ledge. We slowed the ship to 3 knots, while allowing the pilot boat to come alongside and the pilot to board safely.

Within a few minutes, the pilot arrived on the bridge. He requested that the captain, navigator, and OOD gather around the chart table. Mr. Hayden signaled that I should join the briefing instead. The pilot clearly outlined his plan for the transit up the river. He had considered the tide, tidal and river currents, and wind and weather conditions. He explained that much of the transit would require the engine to be at full speed ahead to maximize the rudder's effectiveness for navigating several tight turns in the river.

The pilot turned to me while pointing at the fathometer display and asked, "What is the depth offset on the display?"

"To find the depth beneath the keel, subtract 2.4 feet," I replied.

The pilot then said, "Good. There will be times when I need you to call out the depths. Keep an eye on me, and when I point my finger at you, start calling out the depths."

"No problem," I responded.

The captain then announced, "Attention on the bridge, the pilot has the conn."

The helmsman, lee helmsman, the OOD, the junior officer of the deck, and I all acknowledged with, "Aye, the pilot has the conn."

The pilot replied, "I have the conn. Engine ahead full. Helmsman, rudder amidships." The transit up the Kennebec River to Bath began.

Soon, we entered the mouth of the river, passing Salter and Stage Islands on the starboard side and Pond and Wood Islands on the port side, with Popham Beach visible behind them. This began one of the more scenic river transits I've ever made. The river banks are lined with bedrock shores with dense forest as the backdrop. Like most pilots, this guy knew his river well. He guided the ship strictly using visual cues from navigation aids or geographical points combined with the water depth beneath the ship's keel. He skillfully maneuvered the ship from one channel to the next as we continued upriver.

It was hard not to gaze at the stunning landscape of rocks, trees, and charming small towns that lined the river. The pilot informed us that when we reached the Arrowsic and Lee Islands River segment, the navigable channel narrowed, and depths could be minimal for passage. At Bluff Head, the river constricted even further. Fortunately, the upper part of this section has lighted navigation range marks to guide the ship, helping it to remain in safe waters.

As we approached an area just north of Fiddler Ledge, the channel turned sharply west through Fiddler Reach. The right-angle turn from Fiddler Reach into Long Reach is marked by Doubling Point Light. This appeared to be the most potentially hazardous part of the river. The pilot skillfully navigated the ship through the river's sharp turns. As we rounded Doubling Point, I could see a set of bridges crossing the river ahead. On the port bow, I spotted a tall gantry crane and several other cranes, along with a floating dry dock; it was the shipyard at BIW.

Less than 20 minutes later, with the help of a small tugboat, the ship was moored at North Wharf at BIW. The church steeples and buildings of Bath were visible on the hillside beyond the shipyard. This would be *Vreeland's* home for the next nine months. It was only mid-October, but I quickly felt the distinct chill.

CHAPTER 5

MISJUDGMENTS

When Navy ships undergo major repairs, work at the shipyard typically continues around the clock. It's noisy and chaotic. At times, the sounds of metal grinding, chipping, hammering, and banging can be relentless.

After the initial weeks of the overhaul, the crew members of *Vreeland* could move from the ship to the barracks at the Topsham annex, located near NAS Brunswick. However, there was a delay in relocating our crew from the vessel until another ship's crew, currently residing in Topsham, returned to living on board at the end of its overhaul period. Many married crew members had found apartments or houses to rent in Bath and were in the process of moving their wives and families to Maine.

After several weeks, the crew could finally transition from the ship to the barracks. Each day, the crew was taken to and from the shipyard by Navy buses. Each duty section had several designated "duty drivers," who served as the bus drivers for the crew's transportation.

The Topsham barracks were spacious, clean, and relatively modern. Conveniently located across the street was the galley. Additionally, less than one block away, the Navy Exchange operated a convenience store that sold beer, wine, and various groceries. Each block of eight rooms had heads and showers accessible from the hallway. Senior petty officers had single rooms, while other personnel shared accommodations with two or four individuals, depending on their seniority. Overall, this living arrangement represented a significant improvement over life on the ship, which had become increasingly like an industrial environment.

I'll never forget the morning after my first night at the barracks. As we filed outside to board the buses to the ship, I spotted two cow moose standing in the parking lot near a line of pine trees. One seaman began to approach for a closer look, but thankfully, one of his buddies stopped him and quickly convinced him that getting close to wild moose is not a good idea. Yep, we were definitely in Maine.

During our deployment, as we cruised the waters of the Mediterranean Sea and the Atlantic Ocean, I also recovered my proficiency in celestial navigation. These experiences had prepared me for the upcoming Chief Quartermaster advancement examination in January. Although I had planned to leave the Navy, I still wanted to stay competitive for advancement to chief petty officer.

I kept my intention to leave the Navy entirely to myself during my time on *Vreeland*. Most people assumed that, as a petty officer first class with good prospects for advancement, I would reenlist when the time came. Nevertheless, that was a decision I had made, and Jan agreed with it. I fully intended to stand by that decision.

For sailors like me in seagoing ratings, shipyard periods required significant changes in the type of work we performed. Instead of preparing for the next voyage, our tasks shifted to removing all equipment, gear, and furnishings from our assigned shipboard spaces in preparation for overhaul. Once we completed the space preparations, our focus turned to readying the decks, bulkheads, and overheads for new coverings, paint, or protective coatings.

Many people often misunderstand certain aspects of Navy ships undergoing an overhaul in a shipyard. The crew maintains ownership of the vessel and is responsible for ensuring that the shipyard performs the work as outlined in the contract. They work closely with the shipyard workers to successfully complete each phase of the project. Ultimately, it is the crew that must ensure the overhaul period concludes successfully.

Like the other departments, the operations department organized most of its junior enlisted personnel from each division into "tiger teams." In the Navy, the term "tiger team" refers to a group of individuals assembled to accomplish a specific task or job. As the senior petty officer first class in the department, I was appointed to lead our tiger teams. I divided the teams into three smaller groups, each comprising eight to ten sailors. I assigned Paul and Glenn as team leaders for two groups, while I took charge of the third.

Except for the captain and the XO, most of the ship's officers and some chiefs spent the majority of their workday off the ship in the Ship Superintendent's building. There, the officers and chiefs monitored daily work progress and participated in planning sessions and meetings. Each morning at 0700, I would stop by the Ship Superintendent's building for brief progress meetings. After these morning meetings, I would board the ship and conduct morning quarters with the teams at 0730. Then, our workday would begin.

My daily routine now focused on overseeing the completion of various projects from start to finish. These changes in routine could be just as challenging, if not more so, for junior enlisted sailors. It was common to overhear their remarks expressing frustration, "I didn't sign up for this," or "If I wanted to be a shipyard worker, I would be one." Their frustration was understandable. Much of the work involved getting dirty, enduring extreme temperatures, and tolerating noise that was sometimes deafening, while they often felt like they were constantly cleaning up after the shipyard workers.

For senior petty officers, the question became, How do we keep our people motivated? As supervisors, we couldn't simply focus on task completion. At the same time, we needed to care for our people and serve as advocates looking out for their best interests. My approach was to work alongside them and share the workload while also being their coach and leader.

For many people, including myself, the leaders we become are often influenced by the examples set by our past leaders, both good and bad. I have learned that enduring experiences with poor leaders can ultimately be beneficial. After witnessing ineffective or harmful leadership, I can recall countless times when my thoughts were, *If I ever find myself in their position, I now know what not to do.* Therefore, I believe that we can gain positive leadership skills and knowledge from our experiences with all kinds of leaders.

Since we all worked as quasi shipyard workers, our days on board began at 0700 and lasted until around 1500 or 1600. After finishing our work, we would leave the ship, walk to the main gate, and board the bus for the short commute back to the barracks. Once we arrived at the barracks, it was time to shower and clean up before heading to the galley for dinner before it closed.

The barracks have a large lounge area with a television accessible for everyone to use. At least two evenings each week, I called Jan to catch up on the latest news from home. Most evenings after dinner, unless I had laundry to do, I stayed in my room to read or study until I fell asleep. Each morning, I woke up at 0530 and repeated the same routine as the day before. At times, it felt more like a monk's lifestyle than that of a sailor.

As the days and weeks passed, I began to experience internal struggles. I missed Jan and our son terribly. I didn't fully recognize it at the time, but I was slowly sinking into a state of depression. My time on recruiting duty had taught me how to project a convincing yet false front to others, while inside, I often felt dismal and helpless. Each morning, I got up, went to work, and performed my job, but I started to dread the lonely nights. Almost all my friends on the ship were married and had moved their families to Maine. A few other senior petty officers lived at the barracks, but I preferred not to spend time with them for various reasons. I had a strict rule against socializing with junior enlisted crew members, which meant I spent each night alone and isolated.

I created a calendar for the upcoming months, ending on July 31, 1981—my EOAS. Each night, I would cross off the day on the calendar. On November 1, I still had 243 days left. I contemplated taking leave before July, but I'm hesitant to use leave days.

Jan and I shared a practical approach to life. I planned to sell back my excess leave upon my discharge, providing us with extra funds to support ourselves until I could find a paying job. I convinced myself that I just had to endure the next eight months for my family's sake. I believed I could do it—or so I thought.

It was a Saturday night, and as usual, I was alone in my room when I heard a pounding at the door. I got up and opened it to find Paul standing there. He came in and sat in a chair while I settled onto my bed. At first, we exchanged small talk, but then Paul surprised me by asking, "All right, man, what in the hell is going on with you?"

"What are you talking about?" I questioned.

Paul looked at me for a moment before saying, "George, you've really changed. You never smile anymore, you don't laugh, and you look like you're about to bite someone's head off most of the time. Just yesterday, when I said good morning to you, all you did was grunt and walk away."

He continued, "Even the guys in the department have noticed the change; most of them are scared shitless of you."

Paul had been a good friend, so I decided to be honest with him. I explained that I was struggling with being away from my family and that, aside from work, I had little else to occupy my time.

"Have you considered moving your family here?" Paul asked. "You know where I live; two-bedroom apartments are available, and the rent is reasonable. Most of us from the ship live in the same complex."

I told Paul I would think about it. I added that I just needed to work through my issues and that I would be alright. I tried to lighten the mood by joking, "I don't want people to be scared of me."

Paul and I continued our conversation about various topics. As he was leaving, he said, "I'll stop by tomorrow around 1300. You're coming to my place for dinner, and we'll watch some football. Be ready!" Before I could respond, he walked out, shutting the door behind him.

I spent the next afternoon watching football games on TV with Paul and his family. Later, Paul's wife, Sheila, served a delicious dinner. Shortly after dinner, I made an excuse, saying I was tired and asked Paul if he could take me back to the barracks. After thanking Sheila for the meal and her hospitality, we drove to the barracks. I expressed my gratitude to Paul for the day, and just as I was about to get out of his car, he asked, "Are you feeling any better?"

"I'm fine, thanks again," I replied. I got out of the car and watched as Paul drove away.

Once back at my room, I realized that spending time with Paul's family made me feel sadder rather than happier. Observing how joyful Sheila, Paul, and his kids were only made me miss my own family more. To counter my negative thoughts, I decided to call home. Jan and I talked for a while that evening; I tried to prolong the conversation as long as I could until we had to say our goodbyes. Normally, talking with Jan lifts my spirits, but not that night.

Over the next several days, I made an effort to present a more cheerful and engaging demeanor around others. After work, despite the cold weather, I began taking long walks around the Topsham annex grounds in the early evening. Back at the barracks, I intentionally spent more time in the main lounge, watching TV and engaging in light conversations with crew members. These actions were my attempts to change my routine of self-isolation and see if I could break the mental funk of loneliness.

One morning, just after a progress meeting, Mr. Hayden approached me. "The captain wants to see you this morning in his cabin at 1000."

"Sir, do you know why?" I asked him.

The lieutenant shook his head. "All I know is that the XO told me to inform you of the meeting." I thanked him and then left to conduct morning quarters aboard with the teams. I didn't think much about why the captain wanted to see me; I assumed it was regarding a routine matter.

I liked Captain Accorsi. In my opinion, he was the best commanding officer I served with during my time in the Navy. Senior Quartermasters, who also serve as assistant navigators, develop a good rapport and strong communication with their commanding officers. This is because they work closely together to ensure the safe navigation of the ship. However, I also struggled with trust issues regarding commissioned officers, including commanding officers.

Promptly at 1000, I knocked on the captain's cabin door and opened it. "Good morning, Captain, it's Trowbridge. I understand you want to see me."

The captain was seated at his desk, turning toward me as he rose from his chair. "Good morning, come in." He gestured for me to take a seat beside his desk. Once we were both seated, the captain looked me in the eye and said, "George, there is something we need to talk about."

His statement caught me off guard for two reasons: commanding officers don't address enlisted personnel by their first names, and I had no idea what he wanted to discuss. Before I could respond, he said, "It's been brought to my attention that you are struggling with something, and people have noticed a distinct change in you. I don't mean in your work—that has always been excellent—but in you as a person. I want to know what's going on."

I looked at him briefly before replying, "Captain, I'm not sure what you're referring to."

"I know you're married and have a son. It's fair to assume that you miss being with your family, so I have some questions for you. Have you considered bringing your family to Maine? If not, could you explain why?" He asked. As I contemplated how to answer his questions, I wondered if he was psychic or just exceptionally perceptive.

Before I could respond, he continued, "I understand your story. I'm sure you had very little time for family during your years on recruiting duty. I also know that you had almost no leave before reporting to Mayport and then having to report to the ship during the deployment." He paused, looking directly at me. "Would your wife be willing to join you here in Bath? In my opinion, you need to be reunited with your family. I don't want to see you suffering the way you are now. Have I sized things up accurately?" I knew the jig was up; I needed to be honest with him.

"Yes, you're correct. I am missing my wife, Jan, and our son very much. I'm so miserable without them. As for Jan moving here, I'll need to talk to her about it."

The captain responded, "Before you speak with Jan, let me tell you what I can do to help. I know they're in Iowa; how far do they live from Waterloo?"

"It's about 80 miles to Waterloo," I answered.

He said, "Good. The commanding officer of the reserve center in Waterloo is a friend of mine. Would it help if I sent you TAD (Temporary Additional Duty) to Waterloo to give you time to move your family here?"

"It would, if Jan agrees," I replied.

He said, "With TAD orders, your travel expenses to and from Iowa will be reimbursed. All you'll need to do is check in at the reserve center and check out when you leave. Talk with your wife, then let me know." We concluded the meeting with my agreement to inform him of my decision after speaking with Jan.

Later, I spoke with Paul about the rent costs for his apartment. During lunch, we drove to the complex so I could meet the manager and view one of the furnished units available for month-to-month rental. That evening, I called Jan to present my proposal. As expected, she didn't outright reject it, but she also didn't agree to it. She pointed out that we had already established our long-term plans, and moving to Maine was not part of those plans. We ended the call with her agreeing to think it over for a day or two.

I called Jan the next evening. It was clear she still hadn't made up her mind. We discussed the challenges of having Mitch change schools mid-year, the financial implications, and the costs associated with moving to Maine and then back to Iowa. She needed to talk to her dad about the house we had rented from him and understand his feelings about it being vacant for a while. Additionally, she had questions that needed answers, such as whether she would be able to get her job back upon returning. There were several matters she needed to sort through before making a decision. We ended the call with her asking for another day to find the answers she needed.

I didn't want to pressure her. If her final answer were no, I would have to find a way to handle it. When I returned to the barracks the following evening, I checked the office message board and saw a note indicating that my wife had called and requested me to return her call.

As soon as I could, I called Jan. When she answered, she said, "Alright, let's do it." Her response made me the happiest I had been in a long time. During our conversation, she explained that her dad was okay with us temporarily moving out and that her employer had agreed to take her back. We talked for quite a while, making further plans. After hanging up the phone, I began to figure out what needed to be done to implement our plan.

Several years later, I discovered who had actually encouraged Jan to join me in Maine: her grandmother. Jan had talked to her grandmother for advice, and it seems her grandmother told her, "You two have spent too much time apart. Your man has expressed that he needs you. If you don't go, you may lose him for good."

The next day, around mid-morning, I called the captain to request permission to speak with him. He told me to come by as soon as possible since he had to leave for a meeting shortly. I promptly went to his cabin, knocked on the door, and asked for permission to enter. When I shared my news, he seemed as happy about it as I was.

Apparently, he had already made some preliminary plans for me. The captain informed me that he had briefed the XO, and once I arranged my travel and apartment rental, I should let the XO know so that my TAD orders to Iowa could be issued. When I expressed my gratitude for his kindness and assistance, he simply smiled and laughed before saying, "I'm happy for you; you need this. Now, get out."

I replied, "Yes, sir," as I left his cabin.

At lunch, Paul drove me to the apartment complex, where I paid the deposit and the first month's rent, starting in December. That afternoon, I spoke with the XO about when I could leave. I was surprised when he informed me that my orders would be ready in the morning. He also directed the ship's office personnel to arrange my flight and for me to visit the disbursing office, as he had authorized me to draw advance pay. During that time, there was a popular saying: "The Navy takes care of its own." The way the command was assisting me was a fitting example of how the Navy lived up to that statement.

The next morning, Paul drove me to the airport in Portland, Maine, which is about 35 miles from Bath. I had my airline tickets, TAD orders, and a month's worth of advance pay with me. The XO had instructed me to check in at the reserve center in Waterloo, Iowa, by the next day. I hadn't felt this happy since the day I drove out of the gate at NAS Glenview, leaving recruiting duty behind.

Later that afternoon, my plane arrived in Rochester. After I picked up my bag, I found Jan and Mitch waiting for me. Once again, we shared a three-way hug and exchanged kisses. As always, it felt wonderful to be reunited.

The next day, I drove from Stacyville to Waterloo and checked in at the reserve center. The Yeoman there accepted my orders and provided me with his phone number in case I needed assistance. He also requested that I make a check-in call once a week until I completed my time in Iowa. In less than 30 minutes, I was on my way back to Stacyville.

By the week of Thanksgiving, we were prepared for our move. The apartment I rented in Maine was fully furnished, so all we needed to bring were basic household items, clothing, one of our televisions, and a stereo. We planned to drive our pickup truck while towing a small U-Haul trailer to Bath. Our goal was to start the trip the morning after Thanksgiving and arrive in Bath by Sunday at the latest. We aimed to enroll Mitch in the local elementary school the following Monday, December 1. Since it was a four-day holiday weekend, the Yeoman at the reserve center graciously agreed to come in on Friday morning to check me out.

I contacted the apartment manager in Bath to confirm that we could move in on the weekend, earlier than planned. The manager agreed and said she would arrange to leave the apartment keys with Paul, who would be our neighbor just three units away from us.

Our pickup was a late-model Chevrolet short bed, equipped with an insulated topper we had bought while living in Illinois. I spent time customizing the truck and topper to turn the rig into a small camper. The cab featured a sliding rear window with an airtight seal between the cab and topper, which allowed heat from the cab to flow into the bed area.

On the early morning of November 28, we set out from Stacyville. We made a brief stop at the reserve center in Waterloo, where the Yeoman checked me out as promised. After that, we continued eastward on our trip to Maine. A friend had recommended taking a route through Ontario and Quebec, as it would be faster and slightly shorter.

Overall, most of the drive went well. Mitch spent the majority of his time in the topper playing, reading, or sleeping. As expected in winter, we occasionally drove with light snow falling, but at times, the snow came down heavily. Despite the weather, we made good time and stopped for the night somewhere just east of Toronto. The next day, we completed the trip to Bath, arriving at the apartment complex on Saturday night. We were all dead tired. I went over to Paul's place and returned with the keys to our apartment.

On our first night, we only unloaded what we needed to make the beds and brought in a couple of suitcases. Jan and I worked together the next morning getting the apartment organized, and we were settled into our temporary home until July. I was a happy man now that we were all together under one roof again.

Paul and Sheila invited us over for dinner the next evening. Their son, Chuckie, was the same age as Mitch, and like most kids, they seemed to get along well. Since they would be attending the same school, Mitch would at least have one familiar face when he started.

On Monday, we enrolled Mitch in school. Thankfully, Chuckie was in his class. Jan and I spent the day grocery shopping and purchasing other household items.

On Tuesday, I returned to the ship's temporary administrative office at the Topsham annex. I quickly packed the rest of my gear from my room and loaded it into my truck. I wasn't sad to leave barracks life behind. After that, I drove to Bath, found street parking near the BIW gate, and walked into the shipyard to board the ship.

During the weeks after my return, my workdays became more enjoyable because I no longer spent my nights in a lonely barracks room; I had my family with me. I did have to make some adjustments, having become somewhat out of practice living as part of a family. Most evenings, I would help Mitch with his homework, and then we would watch TV together for a while before going to bed. I also tried to set aside time several nights a week to study for the Chief Quartermaster advancement examination, which was just a few short weeks away.

Many of my friends from *Vreeland* lived in the same apartment complex, allowing Jan to meet several wives. She became friends with Sheila, Glen's wife, and Jerry's wife. It was essentially a small Navy community thriving on a strong military family atmosphere. The wives often went grocery shopping, ran other errands together, or spent time hanging out each day. It seemed like an almost idyllic lifestyle.

I took the Chief Quartermaster advancement examination in the third week of January. After nearly three hours, I walked out of the examination feeling somewhat confident that I had performed well.

The examination was just one of several factors considered when selecting candidates for advancement to chief petty officer. Other factors included performance evaluations, time in service, time in grade, types of previous assignments, sea duty, and more. The chief petty officer selection results would not be released and published until July.

Over the next few months, I came to realize that I genuinely enjoyed living in Maine. The stunning landscapes and the countless opportunities for outdoor activities made it a paradise for sports enthusiasts. There are endless options for fishing, hunting, boating, snow skiing, hiking, and camping.

As winter gave way to milder temperatures in Maine, the promise of spring became clear. Spring also marked a change of command for *Vreeland* and her crew. Commander Accorsi completed his tour as commanding officer and was relieved by Commander Reginald Cameron. The change of command ceremony took place on *Vreeland's* helicopter flight deck. The new commanding officer was a tall, slender man. I had spoken with him several times before he officially assumed command, and he struck me as an honest, honorable, caring individual and a dedicated naval officer.

Before long, it was July, my final month in the Navy. I was set to leave *Vreeland* on July 17, which signified the start of my separation leave. I had accumulated 104 days of leave, but according to regulations, I could only sell back 90 of those days. We planned to rely on Jan's job, our savings, my final separation pay, leave sell-back, and unemployment compensation, which we believed would be enough until I found full-time work.

On the morning of Friday, July 17, I checked out. The last person in the chain of command I spoke with was Captain Cameron. The captain asked me, "Are you sure this is what you want to do?"

I replied, "Yes, sir, I believe so."

He added, "If you change your mind before your EOAS, call me, and we'll figure it out."

As I shook hands with the captain, his final words to me were, "Good luck, Trowbridge. I know you'll do well in whatever you choose to do." Shortly after meeting with the captain, I walked away from *Vreeland* for the last time, with my separation and discharge paperwork in hand.

The night before, we loaded our belongings into a small U-Haul trailer. I arrived at the apartment, changed out of my Navy uniform, and put on civilian clothes. Just before lunchtime, we hit the road for the long drive back to Iowa. I felt a sense of relief and, admittedly, a bit of excitement at the thought of being free. In my mind, the possibilities for the future seemed limitless.

We took our time traveling back to Iowa. Instead of the Canadian route, we opted to go south through New Hampshire into Massachusetts and then take Interstate 90 west through New York. Along the way in New York, we made several stops so I could show Jan parts of the Erie Canal where we had traveled by fast patrol boats five years earlier. Near Buffalo, we took a detour to visit Niagara Falls, spending nearly half the day there. Our journey continued with an overnight stay in Indiana. The following afternoon, we finally pulled up to our house in Stacyville.

The next morning, the telephone rang, and Jan answered. I was sitting at the kitchen table, sipping my coffee. After a moment, Jan covered the receiver and spoke in a low voice, "It's for you; it's Captain Cameron." I got up from the table and rushed over to take the phone from Jan.

I put the phone to my ear and said, "Hello."

The captain replied, "Good morning, Chief Trowbridge. I'm calling to let you know that the chief petty officer selection results are in, and you've been selected for advancement to QMC." Before I could respond, he continued, "I didn't know if being selected would change your mind about leaving the Navy. If it does, I will pay for your flight back to Maine."

I was momentarily speechless but quickly regained my composure. "Captain, when is the ship scheduled to get underway?"

He replied, "Thursday, July 30th."

I paused again, wanting to choose my next words carefully. Finally, I said, "Captain, thank you so much for calling to inform me. However, I just got home yesterday and want to give civilian life a fair shot. I hope you understand."

He clearly hadn't given up entirely, as he responded, "I understand, but do you have my phone number?"

"Yes, sir, I do," I answered.

He continued, "Good. Think it over for a couple of days, and if you change your mind, give me a call. Regardless, I will make sure a copy of the chief selectee message is mailed to you for your records." We ended the call with my expressing gratitude for his call and offer.

Listening to my side of the call, it wasn't clear to Jan what the call was about as she asked, "What was that all about?"

I replied, "He called to let me know I've made chief and whether it changed my mind about getting out."

"My God, you made chief! What do you want to do?" Jan responded.

I paused for a moment. "What would you have me do?"

In true Jan fashion, she replied, "It's your decision. I don't want you to go back, but I'll support you if you do. Whatever you decide, you'll do what's best for us."

One more variable in the mix influenced my decision-making process: my dad. He had been battling lung cancer for several years. Earlier in the spring, my parents traveled to Maine for a week-long visit. I was taken aback by how frail my dad appeared. However, he was also upbeat since tests indicated that his cancer was in remission. He seemed confident, but I wasn't so sure. I viewed this as yet another reason to be closer to home, which wouldn't be feasible if I stayed in the Navy.

I had only a few days to decide whether to return to the Navy. One factor lingered in my mind that had led me down this path: I still harbored strong and bitter resentment toward the Navy from my time on recruiting duty. I couldn't forgive the Navy and the recruiting command for the psychological warfare they inflicted on me as a field recruiter. Enduring their dishonesty and corruption for nearly four years profoundly affected me. However, my time on board *Vreeland* helped me let go of some of that resentment. I found little to complain about during my experience; it was overwhelmingly positive.

Within a few days, I had made my decision. I reasoned that I had come this far and needed to see it through. I pushed the thought of returning to the Navy out of my mind. I applied for unemployment compensation. The current law permitted me to receive up to 13 weeks of unemployment benefits. Meanwhile, I began a serious job search. Remember, this was 1981; the country was still recovering from the economic recession of the 1970s. I quickly discovered that job prospects in northeast Iowa and southern Minnesota were limited. However, many companies were advertising for sales professionals.

Within a week, I received notification that my unemployment compensation had been approved, and a few days later, my first check arrived in the mail. I started inquiring about sales positions at various companies. Unfortunately, most of the companies I contacted were located in Des Moines or near Minneapolis, both around 120 miles away. I interviewed with several companies and received offers, but the commute distances were too far. Then, I sent my Curriculum Vitae to an insurance company based in Edina, Minnesota, because they were advertising positions in southeastern Minnesota. Shortly after, I received a phone call inviting me to an interview. I accepted the invitation and was provided with the details regarding the location, date, and time.

During this time, Pat, the Navy recruiter from Charles City, Iowa, called me. He contacted me as a follow-up to establish communication and inform me that if I were considering reenlisting, he would be my recruiter. Pat was doing precisely what I had often done in my role as a recruiter. Whenever personnel recommended for reenlistment separate from the Navy, the local recruiter is provided with the veteran's home of record and contact information. Calls like Pat's are often worthwhile, as it's not uncommon for recently separated Navy veterans to change their minds about reenlisting. The conversation was pleasant and ended with Pat mentioning that he would send a letter that included his business cards so that I would have his contact information.

I went to Edina on the appointment date and easily found the company's location. I entered the building at the scheduled time and was greeted by a receptionist who led me to a spacious room. To my surprise, nearly 15 other people were already seated. Soon, a well-dressed man came in and introduced himself. His name was Arlo Edwin. It was clear from the start that Arlo was very articulate and possessed a charismatic personality. For quite some time, he didn't discuss the available positions; instead, he emphasized the importance of accumulating financial wealth and prosperity. I could tell from the others' body language that he had captured their full attention.

Finally, Arlo clarified his point: the path to wealth for a select few in the room was to become an insurance agent, selling life, accident, and health insurance policies on behalf of his company. He would provide training for those chosen to help them pass the Minnesota State Insurance License Examination. Once licensed, they would receive additional training alongside one of the company's top agents before being assigned their sales territories. There was no salary; compensation would be strictly commission-based, and they would be self-employed agents.

After the session concluded, about half of the participants left. Those who remained had the opportunity to interview privately with Arlo. For some reason, I chose to stay for the interview. When I met with Arlo, he seemed genuinely impressed with my background and experience, particularly the sales training I received for Navy recruiting. He was also pleased with my time as a recruiter and the awards I earned. After some engaging conversations, Arlo expressed a strong desire for me to join his team. I was surprised when I heard myself agreeing to join his sales force.

The challenging aspect was that I couldn't earn any income until I passed the state insurance licensing examination and received my state-issued license. Additionally, there would be a further training period with another agent, without pay.

We had thought and planned that the combination of income from Jan's job, our savings, and unemployment compensation would allow us to get by for three months or more without me earning any income. However, I received a letter from the State of Iowa unemployment agency informing me about a new law called the 1981 Amendments to the Federal-State Unemployment Insurance Program. The letter stated that, beginning July 1, 1981, "persons who left the military at the end of an enlistment and who were eligible to reenlist were no longer eligible for unemployment benefits under ex-service personnel (UCX)."

After reading and understanding the letter, I was furious. I interpreted its message correctly: if I had acted irresponsibly and had been deemed ineligible for reenlistment, I would qualify for unemployment benefits. What a kick in the teeth. Since I was honorably discharged with the RE-R1 reenlistment code (which indicates that I was highly recommended for retention), I'm not eligible to draw unemployment compensation.

Over the next several weeks, I attended multiple preparatory training sessions with Arlo. Equipped with the study materials he provided, I studied diligently at home each evening. It wasn't long before I felt ready to take the licensing examination. I informed Arlo of my readiness, and although he expressed some concerns, he agreed. The following week, I sat for the licensing examination in Minneapolis. After leaving the examination room that day, I felt confident that I had passed. Several days later, Arlo's office called to inform me that they had my results, that I had scored well, and that my agent's license would arrive at their office the next Monday. Additionally, I was scheduled to be in Edina that Monday to meet the agent I would be training with.

The following week at the office, I was introduced to an agent named Bill. I would work with Bill, learning the ropes of making sales calls to prospective customers. The primary type of insurance policy sold was disability coverage, which provides benefits for income loss due to accidents or illnesses. The main prospective customers were typically self-employed individuals, such as farmers, small business owners, and independent truckers. However, it essentially followed a door-to-door sales approach.

Bill provided numerous pointers and advice on identifying potential customers. I would spend several weeks working with Bill, observing him during sales calls. Generally, people were pleasant and often, out of courtesy, would invite us in. Bill was always smooth, polite, and very professional. It was fascinating to observe how frequently he would fill out the coverage application paperwork at the end of his presentation, obtain signatures, collect the first premium check, and then we would be on our way.

After spending about two weeks with Bill, Arlo assigned me my sales territory. This area included Freeborn, Mower, Dodge, and Steele counties, all of which are located along the Iowa-Minnesota border and are easily accessible from Stacyville. The following Monday, I set out on my own, aiming to make at least 10 daily presentations, which could average three or more sales each day. Achieving 10 presentations in one day typically required visiting at least 20 farmers, homes, or businesses. The sales commission for each policy sold was 55 percent of the first premium amount, potentially resulting in daily earnings of approximately $200.

September marked my first whole month working in my assigned territory, and it was great. I enjoyed being self-employed and found that selling disability insurance was quite simple. It involved meeting my daily presentation goals, which often led to achieving or coming close to my projected sales numbers.

Mondays were typically half-days since I had to visit the Edina office first to submit the previous week's customer documents and premium payments. During my first month, my average daily sales commission earnings were about $170. I was very pleased with my production, especially when my commission checks arrived in the mail every Friday.

I was beginning to see the benefits of my recruiter experience anew. One of the most important skills I developed as a recruiter was overcoming the fear of rejection. Not letting the fear of customer rejection overwhelm you is crucial for success in sales. Prospective customers often express their objections to buying in various ways, with the word "no" being the simplest form of refusal. Learning not to take "no" too literally is essential in sales.

Everything seemed on track, but then I received troubling news about Dad's health. It was feared that his cancer was worsening again. On weekends, we made a concerted effort to visit my parents more often. My relationship with my dad had always been strained; he was hard-headed and outspoken, usually very critical of everything I did, which created constant friction between us. However, I noticed a change in his behavior during my recent visits. He had softened his overly critical attitude and appeared to be making a genuine effort to promote peace between us. During the drive home after a visit, Jan remarked that she noticed a difference in my dad's demeanor.

The following month was good for me in terms of sales and earning a fair income. However, Arlo dropped a bombshell on me during the Monday morning meeting in November. For the top five producers, of which I was now one, our sales commission would be reduced from 55 to 45 percent starting in December—no explanation was provided other than it was necessary for the company's financial needs. Several of us attempted to discuss it with Arlo, but all we received was stonewalling. Arlo's solution was, "Increase your sales by 10 percent, and you won't even notice a difference in your earnings."

My reaction was, "What a bunch of bullshit!"

December was a challenging month for several reasons. First, winter weather fully arrived in northeastern Iowa and southeastern Minnesota, making driving in rural areas difficult. Many roads were nearly impassable due to the recent heavy snowfall and ongoing below-freezing temperatures. Second, Dad's health was rapidly deteriorating; he had been hospitalized in Mason City, Iowa, since before Thanksgiving.

It was the second week of December, mid-morning, and I was trying to make sales calls around Albert Lea, Minnesota. For some reason, I felt compelled to go to Mason City to see Dad. I drove to the hospital in Mason City, parked, and went inside. When I reached the waiting area near Dad's room, it was no surprise that Mom was there, but I was surprised to see two of my sisters as well. Mom asked if I had come because Jan managed to contact me. Apparently, she called Jan earlier in the day to let her know I should come to Mason City. Mom was a bit surprised when I told her I was working, but I felt the need to be there.

Mom told me that the doctors had said Dad's cancer had worsened and spread throughout his body. They guessed he would probably pass away soon. Throughout the day, the rest of the family arrived; by late afternoon, all five of my sisters and my older brother were there. To my surprise, Jan showed up with her sister-in-law late in the afternoon. I never understood why, but I was worried that Jan might be upset with me for being there instead of working.

We all stayed up throughout the night, but most of us struggled to remain awake, especially during the early morning hours. At one point, I must have dozed off while sitting in a chair. It was around 6:30 a.m. when my brother shook me awake and told me that Dad had just passed away. I got up and went into Dad's room alone. The nurses had carefully arranged him in bed, with his head resting on a pillow and the bed sheets neatly made. I looked at him for several minutes and then silently said, "Goodbye, Dad. Now go be at peace." I turned and walked out. I felt sorrow over losing my father, but I've never shed a tear for it—something I'll never understand.

The following Saturday, December 19, funeral services were held in Clear Lake. I was amazed by the number of people from around the area who attended his service. Later that afternoon, we all traveled to Dows, my dad's hometown, where a graveside service took place at Fairview Cemetery. After that, it was over.

My income for the rest of December was low since I wasn't working much. I needed to take time to help Mom with several issues. The winter weather often made it nearly impossible to go out for sales calls. As the holidays approached, prospective customers showed little interest in buying disability insurance.

With the cold winter weather, our old oil-burning furnace quickly drained money as it heated our house. With little income, our finances became tight. I was losing faith in civilian life. 1982 arrived, but the freezing Iowa winter made my work life more complicated day by day.

During the second week of January, it snowed repeatedly. The consistently below-freezing temperatures and persistent northerly winds made the conditions even more miserable. One morning, I shoveled the driveway several times to get my car out. Each time I went back inside to change for work, the wind blew snow back into the driveway, filling it again. Mitch was home since the schools were closed, but Jan had managed to get to work.

During my last attempt to clear the driveway, snow covered the area again before I could finish shoveling. I paused and walked to the south side of the house, where a thermometer was mounted; it showed 5 degrees above zero. As I headed to the car, I opened the trunk and grabbed a hammer from my toolbox. Hammer in hand, I went back to the thermometer and smashed it, breaking the glass. I was done with Iowa and fed up with the terrible weather.

I walked into the house. In a briefcase where I kept Navy records, I found the business card for Pat, the Navy recruiter from Charles City. I went to the phone in the kitchen and dialed Pat's number. As the phone rang, I wondered whether he would be available, given the bad weather conditions. After a few more rings, Pat answered the phone. After our introductions and a reminder of who I was, I told Pat that I wanted to reenlist. He had news, and it wasn't good. He explained that there was currently a five to six-month waiting list for Navy veterans (NAVETS) who had been out for over 90 days, referred to as broken service veterans.

After further discussion, we ended the call. I had information that Pat wasn't aware of: I knew someone who could help with the NAVET waiting list situation. The next person I planned to call was Steve Warden, who was now the National NAVET Coordinator at the Navy Recruiting Command in Washington, D.C.

I knew Steve when he was the NAVET Coordinator at the Navy Recruiting District in Chicago. While recruiting, I referred many Navy veterans to Steve to help them secure the best reenlistment deals. It was mutually beneficial for both of us. Steve managed all the work involved in processing the veterans, assisted with selective reenlistment bonuses when applicable, and advised them on various programs and options. Once Steve completed the necessary tasks, I only needed to provide transportation for the veterans to AFEES for processing and shipping out. When a veteran decided to reenlist, Steve and I received joint credit for the accession.

Steve was named the National NAVET Recruiter of the Year for 1979. As a reward, the Navy Recruiting Command selected him to serve as the NAVET Recruiting Coordinator at the national level. During one of my last visits with Steve before he left Chicago, he expressed his gratitude for all the assistance I had provided. He mentioned that only a few field recruiters had actively supported him, and he counted me among them. Steve also ensured I had his contact information for when he relocated to Washington. His parting words to me were, "George, if there is anything I can ever help you with, don't hesitate to reach out." At the time, I didn't think much of what Steve had said, but now I hoped he could assist me.

One thing about me is that I'm an excellent record keeper. I returned to my records briefcase and quickly found Steve's phone number. I called the number, and within moments, Steve answered. After a brief catch-up conversation, I explained the purpose of my call.

I was relieved when Steve said, "George, don't worry; I can take care of this for you. Call me back if your local recruiter doesn't contact you within the next day." After thanking Steve, we ended the call. I just had to wait for him to handle everything.

The next day, the weather cleared up, but I didn't feel like going to work. Mitch was back in school, Jan was at work, and I was home alone. I hadn't yet told Jan that I was considering reenlisting. I planned to wait until I had something solid before mentioning it to her.

Around mid-morning, the phone rang. When I answered, it was Pat.

"George, I don't know who you know, but my zone supervisor called me this morning and told me to get your ass back in the war ASAP. I want to start your processing. Can you make it to Charles City today?" he asked.

"I can be there in two hours; is that okay?" I replied.

Pat responded, "See you soon. I'm sure you know what to bring with you." As I hung up the phone, I quietly thanked Steve for his help.

I left a note on the kitchen table for Mitch and Jan, saying I would be home in the late afternoon. I gathered all my records and information and headed to the recruiting office in Charles City. I spent most of the afternoon working with Pat to complete all the necessary paperwork. While there, I discovered some great news. Pat contacted the district NAVET coordinator, who informed me that I was eligible for a $10,000 selective reenlistment bonus (SRB). If I had stayed on active duty and reenlisted with continuous service, last year's SRB would have been zero.

While I was on the phone with the NAVET coordinator, I mentioned that I had been selected for chief petty officer just as I was getting out and that I had a copy of the chief selectee message. I wanted to request reinstatement of my advancement to chief petty officer. The coordinator agreed to forward my request. It was arranged for me to process at AFEES in Des Moines the following Tuesday, January 19. If everything went well, I would reenlist that day and leave for the Naval Training Center in Orlando, Florida, for about two weeks of NAVET orientation while waiting for orders to my next permanent station.

During the drive back to Stacyville, I pondered how to tell Jan my news about reenlisting and leaving for Orlando the following week. When I arrived home, Jan was there making dinner. She asked where I had been. I told her about my whereabouts and that I was reenlisting.

She looked at me and said, "I knew it was coming; I just didn't know when you would do it." That was Jan; sometimes I think she understood me better than I did.

Then I shared the rest of the news about my processing next week before heading to Orlando. I saved the most important part for last. I watched her reaction when I mentioned the reenlistment bonus and how much it was, and it felt like watching a heavyweight lift off her shoulders.

She turned to me and said, "Good god, that's fantastic; the bonus will solve all our money problems." Then she laughed. "But, it's not fair you're leaving me here in the snow and cold and going to Florida."

The following Monday morning, I loaded my bags into my car for departure. It was a morning of goodbyes to Jan and Mitch, something I thought I wouldn't have to do again. First, I visited the recruiting office in Charles City to collect the necessary paperwork. Then I proceeded to AFEES at Fort Des Moines, Iowa, for my physical examination and processing on the following day. I arrived late that afternoon at Fort Des Moines and checked in. It felt ironic to spend the night in the same open-bay barracks I had seen just over 10 years before.

I was up at 5:00 a.m., had breakfast, and then entered the AFEES building at 5:30 a.m. The atmosphere was much different than years before. Now, in the era of the all-volunteer force, no military personnel shouted instructions or directed people to waiting areas marked out with colored squares or lines. The place had a more customer-service feel to it. All AFEES staff were pleasant, easygoing, and friendly. Being very familiar with the routine, I anticipated no surprises.

I passed the physical examination without any issues. Later, I met with the classifier for potential reclassification. The classifier wanted to review my ASVAB examination scores. His first statement was, "With your ASVAB scores, do you want to stay in the Quartermaster rating? You can choose any rating you want."

He seemed perplexed when I responded, "I'm not changing anything; I'm a QM." I wanted to know if my request for advancement to chief petty officer had been reinstated. I was disappointed, but not surprised, to learn that my request had been denied.

I finished my meeting with the classifier after we addressed and discussed several other criteria. Our main focus was on the NAVET orientation process in Orlando. I noted that my selective reenlistment bonus of $10,000 would be paid in a lump sum upon completing orientation. Later, I took the enlistment oath and then went to the Navy administrative office to collect my travel orders to Orlando, along with additional paperwork. The final event of the day was receiving my new military identification card. I was once again an active-duty petty officer first class. There was one significant disappointment: it would take three more years in grade to requalify for advancement to chief petty officer.

The allowed travel time was generous since I would be driving to Orlando. I had until midnight on Saturday to report to the naval station in Orlando, which gave me nearly four days of travel time.

Another benefit of reenlisting was that if we did so within one year, the Navy would cover the cost of moving our household effects to our permanent duty station. Once it was decided that I would reenlist, Jan and I made a resolution: other than deployments or when I was at sea, we would never be separated again by choice. We strictly adhered to this decision for the rest of my Navy career.

After calling Jan to let her know everything was fine and that I was officially back in the Navy, I got in my car and left Des Moines. I planned to visit my sister in Albany, Illinois, for a day or two. It was just over 200 miles to Albany, and I arrived by early evening. While in Albany, I visited the local barbershop and got a decent military-style haircut. After a wonderful visit with my sister and her family, I hit the road again early Friday morning. The drive from Albany to Orlando was relatively easy and took two more days.

I stopped that night near Atlanta, Georgia. Early the next morning, I got back on the road, and by late afternoon, I arrived at the main gate of the Naval Training Center in Orlando. I presented my orders to the security guard at the gate, who directed me to the parking area and gave me the building number where I was to report.

I found the building that housed the barracks and training rooms for NAVET orientation and checked in at the front desk. The petty officer there assigned me a room, a parking pass for my car, and a meal ticket for the galley. He then told me that nothing would start until Monday and advised me to hang out for the rest of the weekend. The last thing he said was to muster in my working uniform, if I had one, in the main lobby at 0730 on Monday morning. All that was left was to grab my bags and gear from the car and move into my room. After an early dinner at the galley, my next priority was, as usual, to call Jan to let her know I had arrived safely and that all was well.

I spent the rest of the weekend at the barracks, getting to know other Navy veterans who were there for orientation, just like me. I clicked with a guy named Donny since he was also a Quartermaster 1st Class. Donny had served on only one ship, as most of his prior service had been in special boat units supporting SEAL teams. He hoped to receive orders to another special boat unit. Finally, Monday arrived, and our orientation began.

NAVET orientation began with additional medical and dental examinations and ensuring that everyone was fully equipped with uniform items. The rest of our time was spent attending various classes and seminars focused on benefits, current naval policies, and other rather dull topics.

Donny and I were already buddies, but soon two female petty officers first class, Underwood and Emily, joined our small group. Underwood, who preferred to be called "Woody," was fun and lively. Emily, a Yeoman, was a bit more reserved than Woody, but she was also pleasant and enjoyable to be around. All of us were married, so our relationship was strictly platonic—just friendship, nothing more. Within a few days, the four of us became fast friends.

The first week of orientation went by quickly, and on Saturday morning, we finally had the chance to go on liberty for the weekend. Since I was the only one with a car, we decided to take a trip to Cocoa Beach, which was about an hour away.

Once we arrived in town, we spent most of the day at the beach and explored the area. Later, we checked into a hotel by the beach to have a place to crash in the evening. After settling in, we went out for dinner and enjoyed bar hopping, dancing, and having fun together. We had booked two hotel rooms for the night. I assumed that Donny and I would share one room, while the girls would take the other.

I've neglected to mention this before, but I must say that both Woody and Emily were attractive women and physically fit. That night, as the four of us made our way to our rooms,

Woody grabbed Donny's arm and said, "You're coming with me, boy." Donny willingly followed her to their room.

As I turned to Emily, she took my hand, smiling as we looked into each other's eyes. "It's you and me. You don't mind, do you?"

I could only respond by saying, "No, I don't mind."

The room had double beds; like an idiot, I assumed each of us would take one. Once inside, as we prepared for bed, Emily quickly stripped down to just her panties; she was beautiful, with a body like that of a goddess. Then she got into bed and lifted the covers to invite me to join her. I undressed quickly and climbed in beside her, unsure of what she really expected. Once in bed, she asked, "George, we are friends, right?"

I answered, "Of course we are."

"I really need to be held close by a man. I really like you; can we do just that?" she asked.

I replied, "Yes, I think so."

I was relieved by her request. I love Jan with all my heart. But if Emily had wanted more, it would have been very, and I do mean very, difficult for me to say no. It was a pleasant yet challenging night for me. Emily not only wanted to be held, but she insisted on cuddling close all night. I spent most of the night with my loins telling me they were ready if she wanted more. In the morning, we both woke up around the same time. Before leaving the bed, Emily moved in on me, and we shared a long, passionate kiss.

"I know last night must have been difficult for you. But I appreciate it. You gave me what I needed; only a good man could have done what you did for me," she said.

Later, we all gathered for a late breakfast. Afterward, we relaxed on the beach and browsed the shops along Highway A1A. We stayed in town for dinner that night before heading back to Orlando. I believe everyone had a wonderful weekend.

Woody's remark made us all laugh when she said, "Man, it's nice to be around sailors again, just having fun together without worrying about anyone trying to get in my pants unless I want them to."

It felt like we were almost finished during the latter part of the second week of orientation. We experienced more downtime due to fewer scheduled activities. As sailors, we chose to spend more time at the enlisted club on base. Our small group of four stuck together each day. That weekend, once again, the four of us hung out in the Orlando area, staying at a local hotel instead of returning to the base.

Throughout the week and weekend, Emily's relationship with me became more intimate. Initially, it was merely about companionship for me. However, the intensity between us was growing as we both struggled to keep our relationship nonsexual. From our conversations, I understood that her motivation for reenlisting was similar to mine: to regain financial stability. Although Emily never said it outright, I sensed that her relationship with her husband might be delicate.

Monday marked the start of my third week in Orlando. That same day, Emily received her orders for her duty station and was set to depart the next day, Tuesday. I drove Emily to the Orlando Airport the following afternoon for her flight. Donny and Woody joined us to see her off. After checking her baggage, we all walked together to Emily's departure gate and waited until her flight was called for boarding. Just before she lined up to board, Emily pulled me in for a hug, and we shared a long, passionate kiss.

"I'll never forget you. I love you," she whispered to me.

As she pulled away, I could see tears welling up in her beautiful eyes. With that, she turned, walked to her gate, and in moments, she disappeared through the ramp door.

Donny poked me in the ribs and joked, "Just friends, huh?" I told him to shut up and motioned for us to leave.

Since Emily left, I spent most of my time hanging out with Donny and Woody. I already missed Emily. This happens when you meet someone and form a wonderful connection, only for one of you to leave suddenly. Emily's departure was actually for the best. I'm not sure how things would have turned out if we had more time together.

Do you believe in fate? I do. On Wednesday, as fate would have it, I was informed that Chief Warrant Officer (CWO) Griffin, the officer in charge of NAVET orientation, wanted to see me. I went to his office, knocked on his door, and entered. Upon entering, I said, "Sir, it's Petty Officer Trowbridge; I was told you wanted to see me."

He got up from his desk. "Yes, I do. My name is Griffin, I have orders to USS *Vreeland*, which was your last ship. Can I pick your brain a bit?"

"Sure, what would you like to know?" I replied.

He wanted to learn about the ship's condition and what information I could provide about the captain, officers, chiefs, and crew. After extended discussions, he asked, "So why did you get out?"

I gave him my brief explanation for leaving and how I chose to reenlist. I mentioned being selected for chief petty officer during our discussion, just as I was leaving. With a tone of surprise, he immediately said, "What, and you haven't asked for it back?"

"I did. It was processed through the recruiting command, but it was denied," I replied.

His next question was, "Do you have any documentation showing you were selected?"

"Yes, I have a copy of the chief selectee message that Captain Cameron sent me," I answered.

Mr. Griffin opened one of his desk drawers, retrieved a pad of special request/authorization forms, and slid it across the desktop to me. "Go get your message, fill out the form requesting that your selection to chief petty officer be reinstated, and bring it back to me as soon as you can." He then said., "I will walk your request through the chain of command up to the captain today."

I immediately left his office, went to my room, and retrieved my copy of the chief selectee message. Next, I filled out the request/authorization form and returned to the warrant officer's office. His office door was open, so I walked in and handed him the request form and message. He took the form, checked the approved box in the bottom section, and signed it.

As we left his office, he said, "I've got it from here. I'll be back later, and we'll talk some more." I watched him walk across the lobby area and out the door. I felt skeptical but hopeful that he could really get something done.

I received word that CWO Griffin wanted to see me later that afternoon. I immediately went to his office, knocked on the door, and entered. Standing at his desk, he smiled as he handed me several documents. The first was my copy of the chief selectee message; the second was the request/authorization form approved by the commanding officer of the base; and the third was a message from the Commanding Officer of Naval Training Center Orlando to the Bureau of Naval Personnel, which included an endorsement statement for my advancement to chief petty officer. I thanked him for his help.

"It's not a 100 percent guarantee, but I think the chances are very high that the bureau will agree and approve it," he said.

We sat and discussed USS *Vreeland*, as he had more questions about the ship and crew. Later, I excused myself after thanking him again for his interest in helping me.

As the week passed, Donny and Woody received their orders and departed by Thursday afternoon. Now, it was just me; I no longer had my group of friends. I had requested orders to any ship homeported in Mayport, Florida. I felt a bit anxious about not receiving orders yet. The next day, I was called to the administrative office. Upon arriving there, the Yeoman informed me that my orders were in, and he handed me a copy. I smiled as I read the orders. They assigned me to another Knox-class frigate, USS *W.S. Sims* (FF 1059), homeported in Mayport. I was to report on board no later than midnight the next day, Saturday, February 13.

The last thing the Yeoman did that brought another big smile was hand me a government check for my SRB of $10,000, minus federal income tax withholding. I immediately went to the Navy Federal Credit Union branch office on base and deposited the check into our joint checking account, so Jan could access the funds.

Once I returned to the barracks, I called Jan to share the news about my orders to Mayport and to let her know that I had deposited the SRB money at the credit union. We talked for a while, speculating about when she and Mitch would be able to move to Florida. Jan seemed pleased with how everything was unfolding so far. We ended the call with the promise that I would call again once I was in Mayport.

The following morning, after packing my gear and loading everything into my car, I checked out at the administrative office with my orders in hand. It's about a 150-mile drive from Orlando to Mayport, and I was eager to get going. I was glad that the ship was in port and not underway or deployed. I wanted to reach the ship and check in. I knew that since it was the weekend, I wouldn't be assigned to a duty section until after Monday.

It was late morning when I drove up to the main gate at Mayport Naval Station. After learning from the security guard where USS *W.S. Sims* was docked, I proceeded to her berth. I found a parking spot, grabbed the envelope containing my orders, and headed to the ship's gangway. At the top of the gangway, I turned and faced the U.S. Ensign flying from the staff at the ship's stern. Then, I turned to the OOD while holding up my ID card and said, "Request permission to come on board."

The OOD, a chief petty officer, replied, "Permission granted."

I had arrived at my new home. With that, I stepped onto the quarterdeck and handed my orders to the chief, stating, "QM1 Trowbridge, reporting on board." The chief accepted my orders, passed them to the Petty Officer of the Watch, and instructed him to log my arrival and call the duty Master-at-Arms to report to the quarterdeck. I returned to the pier, retrieved my bags, and boarded again.

Within a few minutes, the duty MAA arrived on the quarterdeck. He introduced himself and welcomed me aboard. The MAA helped me with my bags and guided me to the ship's office to check in. After we checked in at the ship's office, he took me to the operations department berthing compartment. In the berthing compartment, he pointed to an empty middle rack and locker, saying, "Here you go, unless you need anything, I've got to go."

The MAA hurrying away didn't bother me; I knew my way around the ship since *Sims* is the same class of ship as *Vreeland*. Therefore, the layout is almost identical.

I finished stowing my gear and making my rack with clean sheets and a blanket. I planned to find a hotel room on the beach for the night and return late the following afternoon. Once I was ready, I went back to the quarterdeck. The same chief was still on watch, so I chatted with him briefly to become acquainted. After our conversation, I approached the gangway, asked for permission to depart from the ship, and headed out onto the dock to my car.

The drive to the main gate took only a few minutes. After passing through the gate, I headed south on Mayport Road to Atlantic Boulevard, then east toward the Atlantic and Neptune Beach area. I turned south onto Highway A1A, Third Street, toward Jacksonville Beach. At that time, no large condos or hotels lined the beach; instead, many older hotels were situated between Third Street and the beach. These hotels were primarily mom-and-pop operations—affordable and clean.

I checked into a hotel where I had previously stayed and secured a room for the night. My preferred room was available, located at the end closest to the beach. From my room, I could step outside, turn right, and in about 20 steps, be on the beach. After settling in, I called Jan, and as always, we talked for quite a while. Once our conversation ended, I cleaned up, changed my clothes, and headed out. The bars and clubs I preferred were all within walking distance from the hotel, so I didn't have to worry about driving or the risk of getting a DUI.

I had a relaxing and fun night in Jacksonville Beach. The next day, I hung out on the beach until late afternoon. That evening, I returned to the ship. Down in the berthing compartment, several crew members were present, so I introduced myself to everyone. I chatted with a few guys until it was time to hit the rack and get some sleep.

After breakfast on Monday morning, I headed to the bridge, knowing that my division would be gathering there for morning quarters. All the division's personnel assembled on the bridge, which allowed me to introduce myself to everyone before the division officer arrived.

My division's organization differed somewhat from *Vreeland*'s. It was the Navigation/Administrative (NAV/AD) division, comprising a mix of ratings, including Hospital Corpsman, Personnelman, Yeoman, and Quartermasters. This division also included the ship's maintenance coordinator and the command career counselor, both chief petty officers, as well as the ship's Master-at-Arms, who was a petty officer first class (MA1).

Soon, our division officer, Lieutenant Junior Grade (Lt. j.g.) Marsk, arrived. I briefly introduced myself before he began briefing the division personnel. After we concluded quarters, I chatted with him for several minutes to get to know him better. Next, I spent some time getting to know the Quartermasters. The senior person was Quartermaster 2nd Class (QM2) Mike Franklin, along with three Quartermaster Seaman: QMSNs Macron, Hampton, and Davidson. During my conversation with

Franklin, he came across as very sharp and well-organized. After that, I headed to the ship's office to begin the formal check-in process for the rest of the day.

I also learned that the ship would be getting underway the next afternoon for two weeks of local operations and work-up exercises in preparation for an upcoming six-month deployment in May to the Indian Ocean, Arabian Sea, and Persian Gulf (Arabian Gulf).

Later in the day, after meeting and checking in with the operations department head, a lieutenant, I checked in with the XO, Lieutenant Commander Phillip Jones. The XO and I talked at some length. He struck me as a reasonable and amicable person with a hint of formal military bearing. The last person in the chain of command to check in with was the commanding officer, Commander Jamison Macdonald.

I had a long conversation with Captain Macdonald. He had my service record on his desk, showing he had reviewed it earlier. He seemed pleased that I had prior experience on a Knox-class frigate. He concluded with, "Welcome aboard, Trowbridge. You have no idea how happy I am to have you here. With the upcoming deployment, we need an experienced senior Quartermaster." After that, we wrapped up the meeting. I thanked the captain and left his cabin, now officially a full-fledged crew member.

CHAPTER 6

A TRANSITION

One of Jan's favorite sayings was, "Everything happens for a reason." I know Jan firmly believed it. Whenever she mentioned it, it drove me crazy. I disagreed; I thought that the order of events and our choices determined the outcomes of events or fate. I think it's because I interpret the word "reason" as a concept of cause-and-effect in an automatic universe where occurrences seem random. What happened to me next brought me closer to Jan's perspective.

The next day, Tuesday, February 16, just as the division was about to post from morning quarters, Mr. Marsk turned to me and said, "Trowbridge, I have a bone to pick with you."

I looked at him and asked, "What is it, sir?"

Smiling, he replied, "You're out of uniform."

I probably looked confused, which made him laugh. He handed me a sheet of paper and said, "This came in last night. Congratulations, Chief." I looked at the paper, which was a message from the Bureau of Naval Personnel stating that my request for advancement to chief petty officer was approved, with an effective date of February 16, 1982. After reading and fully understanding the message, I realized I had officially been a chief petty officer (CPO) since midnight. I silently thanked CWO Griffin back in Orlando because I wouldn't be holding the message indicating I was now a chief petty officer without him.

Mr. Marsk congratulated me again, then said, "Senior Chief Macrillo wants to see you in the ship's office immediately." Gene Macrillo was the Senior Chief Personnelman (PNCS) and the senior enlisted advisor, also known as the command senior chief. I left the bridge and made my way to the ship's office.

When I arrived, I found the senior chief sitting at his desk. He invited me in and asked me to take a seat. Next, he told the others in the office to take a break. Once it was just the two of us, he first offered his hand to shake. "Congratulations, Chief. You're so new that I haven't even met you yet. I need to discuss something with you as soon as Senior Chief Holloway arrives."

Senior Chief Machinist Mate (MMCS) Mick Holloway entered the office a few minutes later and closed the door behind him. I hadn't met either of the senior chiefs until now. Senior Chief Macrillo said, "We have a bit of a dilemma. Normally, when we have a chief selectee, there is time to put them through the process leading up to their initiation date. In your case, you're technically already advanced to chief as of today. Mick and I have a proposal."

"What is the proposal?" I responded.

Mick took over the conversation at this point. He began by saying, "Gene and I discussed it earlier, and we would like for you to postpone your initiation for two days. This will allow us to take you through the process properly. By doing so, we can honor tradition and ultimately welcome you into the Chiefs Mess the right way."

I had a clear understanding of the long-held process involved in the chief petty officer initiation and the rights of passage into the chief brotherhood. I wanted to honor the process, so my response was simple: "Agreed."

Gene appeared relieved and happy with my response. "Chief Radioman Manny Aaron has agreed to be your sponsor. He will help you set up your charge book and answer any questions you may have. You can find Manny in the Chiefs Mess or Radio Central. We need to get you started immediately, so make sure to see Manny as soon as you leave here, okay?"

"Sure," I replied.

However, my answer seemed to offend Mick. He looked me in the eye and seriously said, "Slug, are you defective in some way? You mean, 'yes, senior chief,' don't you?"

I quickly recovered by standing up, snapping to, and responding, "No, senior chief, I am not defective. Yes, senior chief, I will find my sponsor, Chief Aaron."

Mick continued, "You must be in the Chiefs Mess by 1045. You're mess cooking today and will serve lunch to the chiefs."

"Yes, senior chief, I understand. May I be dismissed, senior chief?" I replied.

Gene, grinning, answered, "Get the fuck out of my office, you low-life scum."

I replied, "Yes, senior chief." Then I turned, walked to the ship's office door, opened it, and stepped out into the passageway.

Inside, I overheard Mick say, "Oh shit, we've got a cocky one." I smiled as I walked down the passageway; my CPO initiation process had begun.

I had several immediate tasks to tackle: First, I needed to prepare for the ship's departure. The ship would be at sea for two weeks. Second, I would need some chief uniform items in two days. Finally, I must call Jan to share the great news with her.

I went to the bridge to meet QM2 Franklin and check on the preparations for our upcoming operations. To my relief, he had everything under control, confirming my initial assessment of his competence. I explained that I needed to visit the uniform shop at the Navy Exchange and that I would return as soon as possible.

Franklin smiled and assured me, "I've got this; it's not much of a passage plan—just heading out to the operating area offshore." I thanked him and then went to the berthing compartment to retrieve my checkbook from my locker. Next, I left the ship and headed to the nearest pay phones on the dock to call Jan.

After dialing our home phone number, Jan answered on the second ring, sounding surprised to hear from me so early in the day. I started with, "I have some excellent news."

She responded, "What's the news?"

"Hon, I got advanced to chief! The message came in last night, and I'm now a chief as of today," I replied.

Then I heard a noise, like a newspaper being crumpled, followed by a bang. After a moment, she returned to the line, exclaiming, "Holy crap, that's not just good news, that's big, big news!"

"What happened just now?" I asked.

She laughed and said, "I was dancing around and dropped the phone!"

I told Jan that I didn't have much time to talk. I explained that the ship would be leaving for two weeks starting later today. I mentioned that the CPO initiation process had already begun and that I would be initiated while the ship was still at sea. This meant I needed to purchase at least some essential uniform items that day.

After finishing my call with Jan, I got into my car and drove to the Navy Exchange. I bought several pairs of khaki uniforms and a few other essential items at the uniform shop. With my purchases in hand, I hurried back to the ship since I still needed to find my sponsor, Chief Aaron, and be ready to serve as a mess cook in the Chiefs Mess by 1045.

If you've never served in the Navy, you might wonder, why is advancing to chief petty officer such a significant achievement? There are several reasons, and each chief may provide a distinct perspective.

Achieving the rate of chief petty officer (pay grade E-7) is a significant milestone in one's naval career. Wearing the fouled anchors that denote a chief petty officer is seen as a pinnacle of success for many sailors. Advancing to and being accepted into the Chiefs Mess in the Navy differs from enlisted promotions in other branches of the armed forces. Becoming a chief is a transformative experience; it profoundly changes your professional life. These changes include your living arrangements on board and the heightened expectations placed upon you by your sailors, fellow chiefs, and both junior and senior officers.

Chiefs mentor junior officers and provide valuable guidance and inspiration to their senior and commanding officers. Most commanding and executive officers encourage junior officers to build productive relationships with chief petty officers. "Ask the Chief" is well-known in the Navy, as chiefs are viewed as the backbone of the organization. Navy chief petty officers hold more authority and responsibilities than noncommissioned officers at pay grade E-7 in other military branches. However, along with this authority and responsibility comes accountability at every level within the command.

Becoming a chief petty officer requires a unique blend of technical expertise, leadership ability, and strong interpersonal skills. For many individuals, achieving this represents the peak of their careers. In contrast, for others, it serves as a stepping stone to further professional opportunities, challenges, and promotions. Now, at 29, I was expected to embody wisdom, knowledge, expertise, and strong leadership abilities.

Once back on board, I sought out my sponsor, Chief Aaron. I went below decks to the Chiefs Mess. I paused at the door, silently thinking, *Let the game begin*. I didn't bother to knock; I just opened the door and walked in. One of the chiefs sitting in the lounge area yelled, "Who in the hell are you?"

"QMC Trowbridge, I'm looking for RMC Aaron," I answered.

The chief who had yelled replied, "We'll see about you being a chief or not."

One of the other chiefs sitting at the mess table got up and approached me, carrying a green government record book in one hand, and said, "I'm your sponsor, Manny Aaron. Where have you been? I've been waiting for an hour." I quickly explained that I had some urgent errands to run and had gotten there as soon as I could.

He shrugged off my answer and said, "We need to talk; we don't have much time." I noticed the record book had about a half-inch diameter hole drilled along the edge and wondered what the hole was for. I found out within several more minutes.

Chief Boatswain's Mate Bill Walker entered the mess and looked at me. "You're our new slug." With that, he tossed a quarter-inch diameter steel chain about 5 feet long, a padlock, and a set of keys onto the deck. Then as he walked away, he said, "When your sponsor is through with you, I want to see that chain padlocked to the book and the chain around your neck at all times."

Manny led me to the couch in the lounge area. "Let's sit down and talk." Once we were seated, Manny began explaining what would happen over the next several days. He showed me the record book, which is actually my "charge book." It's called a charge book because I must present it to any chief who demands it. The chief would then make an entry in the book, accusing me of some transgression. During my initiation trial, the judge would address the charges made by the accusing chief. If I was found guilty of any charge (and I would always be found guilty), the judge would impose a fine or punishment.

On the inside cover and facing page of the charge book, there was a handwritten list of ridiculous rules and tasks I was to perform or complete leading up to my initiation as a CPO.

Manny explained that I needed to find one of the junior officers who was willing to serve as my defense counsel for my initiation trial. He further clarified that during the trial, Senior Chief Macrillo would act as the judge, and Senior Chief Holloway would serve as the sheriff. Although it resembled a typical kangaroo court scenario, I had to take it seriously.

I left with my charge book in hand, secured by the chain padlocked to the book. My priority was to check on the progress of underway preparations. The CPO initiation activities would have to wait until after the ship was underway and in safe waters.

When I arrived at the bridge, Franklin appeared to be in control of everything. Mr. Marsk was also there, so I asked him if he would be interested in serving as my defense counsel for my initiation trial.

To my surprise, he agreed. "It would be an honor to do this for you. I want to witness everything that happens during a CPO initiation," he said.

I warned him that if the judge found me guilty of any charge, he would face the same sentence I would.

He laughed and replied, "Not a problem. I think I can handle it."

That afternoon, the ship set sail from Mayport. I led the navigation team during the Sea and Anchor detail for our departure, with my charge book's chain looped around my neck. Although I was new to the ship, I understood that the captain and other officers would want to observe my performance. I believe this was essential for several reasons: I needed to establish my credibility with the captain while fostering teamwork with the navigation team and the ship's officers responsible for safely handling the vessel.

After the ship cleared the St. Johns River breakwaters while outbound from Mayport, we quickly passed buoy STJ. We were now in the open ocean. The ship began the familiar and comforting motions of being at sea, with the bow pitching upward as it met each wave and then pitching downward as the waves passed under the keel, all while rolling slowly from side to side. It felt good to smell the salt in the air and watch the crests and troughs of the sea waves rolling by. Soon, we spotted a pod of dolphins off the bow, appearing to fly through the water while barely moving their bodies. It felt fantastic to be back; I had forgotten how much I loved the sea.

Once the ship was headed to the operating area, it was time to resume my CPO initiation process and start working on the task list. There was only one task I hadn't figured out how to complete yet: obtaining one of the captain's collar devices. I shrugged it off, believing that I would come up with a solution by the next day.

The rest of that day was mainly enjoyable as I worked through my task list. Eventually, I decided to ask the captain for one of his collar devices. That evening, I knocked on the captain's cabin door, opened it, announced myself, and requested his permission to enter, which he granted.

Once inside, he asked, "What do you need, chief?"

I decided to play along and replied firmly, "Captain, I've been tasked with procuring one of your collar devices as the newest chief on board; I'm asking to borrow one."

Captain Macdonald stared at me for a moment, then smiled. "A real chief would figure out how to get one of my collar devices without asking me. Now, get out."

I could only respond, "Aye, sir." As I turned to leave his cabin, I noticed a khaki uniform shirt with collar devices hanging on the back of the door to the cabin's head. I quickly devised a new plan.

Later that night, I went to the bridge to check on the QMOW and review the operations for the next day. I noticed the captain was on the bridge, relaxing in his chair while observing the bridge team. This was my opportunity. I left the bridge and entered the captain's cabin. The khaki shirt was still hanging on the door. I quickly removed one of the collar devices and put it in my pocket. As I exited the cabin, I carefully closed the door, trying to be as quiet as possible, hoping no one would pass by. Once the door was securely latched, I swiftly walked away, satisfied that I had completed the task.

The next day, February 18, was the day of my CPO initiation. The Chiefs Mess published an internal Plan of the Day outlining my activities, starting at 1500 and concluding at 1845, which marked the beginning of the initiation trial in the Chiefs Mess.

That afternoon was spent completing each task from the CPO Initiation Plan of the Day. I notified Mr. Marsk of when I needed him in the Chiefs Mess to serve as my defense counsel. The disbursing officer, by some miracle, was able to provide me with $200 in one-dollar bills, with sequential serial numbers as directed in my charge book. Finally, at 1845, I arrived wearing a new khaki uniform shirt and trousers. I had my charge book in hand and carried a large, heavy-duty plastic trash bag half full of water to symbolize the rain cloud, as instructed in the task list from the charge book.

When Mr. Marsk and I entered, all the chiefs were present. The mess table and the surrounding deck were covered with clear plastic sheets. Two empty metal trash cans were positioned at one end of the table. Three large pitchers filled with a foul-smelling liquid, along with a stack of paper cups, sat on the table.

Senior Chief Macrillo sat at the far end of the table, where a large sign in front of him read "THE JUDGE." Next to the sign lay a wooden mallet—his gavel. He draped a bedsheet over his shoulder and wore his senior chief hat. Standing next to the judge was Senior Chief Holloway, who had a large star made from yellow cardboard taped to his chest that read "SHERIFF." The sheriff instructed Mr. Marsk and me to stand with a metal trash can placed directly in front of each of us. The judge soon called the kangaroo court into session, and the proceedings began.

The sheriff instructed me to place my stack of one-dollar bills on the table in front of Mr. Marsk and then ordered me to surrender my charge book to him. He handed the charge book to the judge, who then produced a sheet of paper and began reading aloud a list of crimes, infractions, or rules I was being charged with. After he finished reading the list, he opened my charge book and read all the entries as if they were offenses I had supposedly committed.

Then the judge looked at me and asked, "Do you want to plead guilty to all charges now, or do you wish to present a defense?"

My response, "Fuck the judge and the sheriff too, you're all full of shit." I thought Mr. Marsk was going to faint as he whispered, "What are you doing?"

This caused all of the chiefs to start chanting, "Hang the guilty bastard."

The next thing that happened was the judge's challenge regarding Mr. Marsk's qualifications to practice law. To my surprise, Mr. Marsk produced a copy of a diploma from Harvard Law School. However, I noticed that the name on the diploma had been scratched out, with Mr. Marsk's name written over it.

He handed the diploma to the judge. "Judge, I believe a law degree from Harvard qualifies me to practice law in a court such as this."

The judge smiled as he tore up the diploma. "I find this unacceptable, as it is not a valid license to practice law in my court. That will be a $10 fine and a dose of truth serum for you and your client to teach you not to be dishonest in my courtroom."

One of the chiefs filled two paper cups with the contents of one of the pitchers. The sheriff instructed both of us to take a cup and said, "Down the hatch, slugs." I drank mine; it was a terrible concoction.

Mr. Marsk downed his as well, then turned to the judge. "Judge, I challenge your qualifications to preside over this trial competently."

Now it was my turn to wonder what in the world he was doing. The judge replied, "Your challenge is denied; the proceedings will continue."

The judge spoke without hesitation, "Charge number one: impersonating a chief petty officer since February 16, 1982, on board USS *W.S. Sims*. How do you plead?"

Mr. Marsk interjected, "My client pleads not guilty."

The chiefs began chanting repeatedly, "Truth serum, truth serum, make them tell the truth."

The judge said, "To prove he's innocent, both of you bottoms up; if you drink it all, I'll find the slug not guilty."

I downed mine; Mr. Marsk downed his, then he said to the judge, "He's not guilty."

The judge responded to the plea with, "I find him guilty; that'll be a $5 fine."

At this point, I produced the captain's uniform collar device, holding it up for everyone to see. "Judge, the fact that I am in possession of the captain's collar device proves that I am worthy of being a chief petty officer. I demand that you cease this despicable kangaroo court and welcome me into the Chiefs Mess right now."

The judge banged his gavel. "Denied, I charge you and your defense counsel with contempt of court. That's a $5 fine and one dose of truth serum each. Sheriff, carry out the sentence."

"Down the hatch, boys," Mick said as he handed us our cups of truth serum.

The judge would read the next charge, and we would plead not guilty. The judge would find me guilty of the charge, and then came the next round of truth serum, and possibly a fine. Around the sixth or seventh time, as Mr. Marsk set down his cup, he launched a solid stream of vomit into the trash can. The next thing I knew, my gag reflex kicked in, causing me to throw up in my trash can. Without missing a beat, the sheriff handed us both towels and said to the judge, "The court is ready to continue."

The routine of charges read by the judge went on for hours, with my denying guilt, followed by the judge declaring me guilty, then imposing a fine, a dose of truth serum, or both. At one point, I grabbed the water-filled trash bag I had brought as a rain cloud and hurled it forcefully at the judge. I was pleased to see the bag rip open, splashing water everywhere and drenching the judge and the sheriff.

The judge banged his gavel. "I find you guilty of assault on officers of the court, $10 fine."

After some time, I began to grow weary of the entire situation and wondered when it would finally come to an end. It concluded abruptly when the judge asked me, "Do you have some kind of problem?"

My response seemed to signal him, as I said, "No, but if this continues as it has, you're going to be the one with a problem."

Then, he stood up and addressed all the chiefs, asking, "Has this man proven that he is worthy of acceptance into the brotherhood and fraternity of Chief Petty Officers of the United States Navy?"

The mess erupted in celebration, and all the chiefs raised their voices in unison, declaring, "Yes, he is worthy."

The sheriff stepped out of character and, once again becoming Mick Holloway, spoke kindly to Mr. Marsk, "Mister Marsk, would you like to get cleaned up? When Chief Trowbridge has showered and changed, the captain and XO will come down to read the Chief Petty Officer Creed and hold the pinning ceremony."

Mr. Marsk turned to me and asked, "Do you want me here, Chief?"

"Yes, sir, I would be honored to have you here," I replied.

I was taken to the head and shower area, where I disposed of the remnants of my khaki uniform, stained with truth serum, vomit, and who knows what else. Once in the shower, I could smell the strong odor of truth serum lingering. It felt like no amount of scrubbing made me smell much better. When I stepped out of the shower, Manny was waiting for me. He led me to the berthing area, where a khaki shirt and trousers hung on a rack.

Earlier in the day, Manny arranged for the mess cooks to move most of my gear from the operations department berthing to the mess. My shoes and other items were also on the rack. He said, "Get dressed and come out; the captain and XO are already here."

I dressed quickly and headed out to the mess lounge area. It seemed the chiefs had been busy too, as the entire mess area was completely cleaned, except for the lingering smell of truth serum. After several more minutes, Mr. Marsk arrived. Mick showed me where he wanted me to stand, positioned me, and then asked me to stand at attention.

Senior Chief Macrillo, the captain, XO, and Mr. Marsk stood before me. Gene began reading from the United States Navy Chief Petty Officer Creed:

During the course of this day, you have been caused to suffer indignities, to experience humiliations. This you have accomplished with rare good grace and therefore, we now believe it fitting to explain to you why this was done. There was no intent, no desire, to demean. Pointless as it may have seemed to you, there was a valid, time-honored reason behind every single deed, behind each pointed barb.

By experience, by performance and by testing, you have been this day advanced to CHIEF PETTY OFFICER. You have one more hurdle to overcome. In the United States Navy and only in the United States Navy, E-7 carries unique responsibilities. No other armed force throughout the world carries the responsibilities nor grants privileges to its enlisted comparable to the privileges and responsibilities you are now bound to observe and expected to fulfill.

Your entire way of life has now been changed. More will be expected of you, more will be demanded of you. Not because you are an E-7, but because you are now a CHIEF PETTY OFFICER. You have not merely been promoted one pay grade--you have joined an exclusive fraternity, and as in all fraternities, you have a responsibility to your brothers, even as they have a responsibility to you.

Always bear in mind that no other armed force has rate or rank equivalent to that of the United States Navy. Granted that all armed forces have two classes of service: enlisted and commissioned, however, the United States Navy has the distinction of having four i.e., Enlisted, CHIEF PETTY OFFICER, Commissioned Warrant Officer and Commissioned Officer. This is why we in the United States Navy may maintain with pride our feelings of superiority once we have attained the position of E-7.

These privileges, these responsibilities do not appear in print, they have no official standing, they cannot be referred to by name, number nor file. They exist because for over 200 years the CHIEFS before you have freely accepted responsibility beyond call of printed assignment, their actions and their performance, demanded the respect of their seniors as well as their juniors.

It is now required that you be a fountain of wisdom, the ambassador of good will, the authority in personnel relations as well as their technical application. "Ask the Chief" is a household word in and out of the Navy. You are now the "CHIEF".

The exalted-position you have now received, and I use the word "exalted" advisedly, exists because of the attitude, the performance of the Chiefs before you. It shall exist only so long as you and your compatriots maintain these standards.

So this is why you were caused to experience these things. You were subjected to humiliations to prove to you that humility is a good, a great, a necessary change which cannot mar you-which in fact, strengthens you, and in your future as a CHIEF PETTY OFFICER, you will be caused to suffer indignities, to experience humiliations far beyond those imposed upon you today. Bear them with the dignity, and with the same good grace, which you bore these today.

It is our intention that you will never forget this day. It is our intention to test you--to try you--to accept you. Your performance today has assured us that you will wear your hat with aplomb brothers in arms before you.

I take deep, sincere pleasure in clasping your hand, and accepting you into our midst.

With that, Gene extended his hand to shake. "Congratulations, welcome to the mess." Next, the captain and Mick approached me. Each had a CPO collar device.

The captain said, "It's not official until you put on your fouled anchors." The captain pinned on one anchor while Mick pinned on the other. After the anchors were secured on my khaki shirt collar tabs. The captain shook my hand. "Congratulations, chief."

The captain added, while laughing, "Now, where's my goddam collar device?" I happened to have his collar device in my pocket.

I reached into my pocket, held it out to him, and said, "Here it is, Captain. It's been cleaned, so don't worry."

The captain smiled, held up his hand, and said, "No, you keep it for memory's sake."

Next, the XO and then Mr. Marsk offered their handshakes and congratulations. Mick and the other chiefs, one by one, approached me, shaking my hand and offering their congratulatory messages. At that moment, I realized I was now a chief petty officer. It felt great. I also took a moment to silently thank Chief Warrant Officer Griffin for caring enough to advocate for me and help reopen my path to where I am now.

Once it was over, the captain, XO, and Mr. Marsk left; aside from several chiefs, nearly everyone returned to their routines. I sat and chatted with Manny for quite a while, getting to know him and a few others better. Before turning in, I visited the bridge to check on the QMOW and ensure everything was okay. Franklin was on watch; he recognized me as I approached him on the dimly lit bridge and said, "Congratulations, chief! I bet you're glad that part is over, huh?"

I could only chuckle in response, "Yes, I am."

After chatting for a while with Franklin, I went below. As I descended the ladder from the bridge, I realized exhaustion was overtaking me. I had been running on adrenaline, and it was starting to fade. Within a few minutes, I reached the Chiefs Mess, my new home on board. It was late, and the mess area was deserted. I entered the berthing area, found my rack, undressed, and crawled in.

Once I settled into my rack, I quickly realized that the rack and mattress offered a significant upgrade in comfort compared to what I was used to. As I lay there, my thoughts drifted back over the events of the past month: from that cold morning shoveling snow when I decided to reenlist, through NAVET orientation in Orlando, and now here I was, back at sea as a chief petty officer. A comforting feeling washed over me, dispelling any lingering doubts about whether I had made the best choice. I felt sure that I was where I belonged.

For the next several weeks, I faced a minor issue: I didn't have enough uniform items. Fortunately, the XO, along with several officers and chiefs, generously donated shirts, trousers, and other essentials until we returned to port. Once we returned to Mayport, I would have the opportunity to purchase the necessary uniform items.

I was fortunate that the previous assistant navigator had done an excellent job training the Quartermaster team. Over the next several days, I closely monitored each Quartermaster's skills by observing how effectively they performed their watch duties and responsibilities. Even Davidson, the most junior member who had only graduated from "A" school a few months ago, demonstrated proficiency in his role. Most importantly, the OODs and the conning officers from each watch section showed confidence in each QM's abilities. I couldn't have asked for more.

I was gradually getting used to being called "chief" or "QMC" by both enlisted personnel and officers. The chiefs in the mess were a close-knit group marked by strong camaraderie. What pleased me the most was that, except for one or two individuals, these chiefs were proactive leaders who dedicated time to their divisions, focusing on mentoring and training their personnel. In other words, the chiefs were highly visible and accessible to the crew.

I soon realized another person was glad to have me on board: Lt. j.g. Marsk. Mr. Marsk's official title was "Navigation Officer." Our underway period marked his first time at sea in that position. After just over two weeks at sea off the coast, it was time to return to Mayport. The day before our planned arrival back in port, Mr. Marsk approached me and mentioned that the captain wanted him to manage the navigation plot for the Sea and Anchor detail. He also explained that he had never performed that specific task before, having only observed others. I could see that he was visibly nervous about the situation. Before he could ask, I offered that if it was all right with him, I would stay close by and assist him as needed. A look of relief instantly washed over his face as he replied, "Thank you, chief."

The evening before, we held the formal navigation brief for entering port in the wardroom. I led the brief with assistance from Mr. Marsk. All principal bridge and CIC watchstanders, as well as the personnel in charge on deck, attend a navigation brief. The brief covers the details of the navigation plan, the predicted weather forecast, tides, tidal currents, call point locations relayed to port control, pilot boarding areas, and any other details relevant to the ship's safe navigation.

The next day, about 20 nautical miles from the entrance to the St. Johns River and the breakwaters, I set the navigation detail, directing the QMs to their designated stations. After several accurate radar fixes, I had the OOD adjust our course to head directly to buoy STJ and the entrance of the inbound channel, and I requested that he reduce the ship's speed from 20 to 12 knots.

As soon as the captain arrived on the bridge, about 10 nautical miles out, I recommended that the Sea and Anchor detail be set for entering port. The captain instructed the OOD to set the Sea and Anchor detail. This led Mr. Marsk to approach the chart table, where I briefed him on the aids to navigation we were currently using to take gyrocompass bearings and the features on the radar I was using to determine ranges. I asked him if he was ready to take over, and he shook his head, indicating yes.

We shifted positions at the chart table so he could take over. I moved to a nearby spot out of the way. At first, his hands shook, and I could hear the tremor in his voice as he spoke. I encouraged him to start instructing his navigation team to stand by for a round of bearings in the coming minute. Franklin, who was serving as the bearing recorder at the chart table, nodded at me, indicating that he had everything under control. He then began prompting Mr. Marsk on when and what to do. I glanced over at the captain sitting in his chair; although he was turned away from me, I could tell he was paying close attention to everything happening around him.

Entering Mayport is relatively straightforward. Once the ship passes buoy STJ, steering the vessel using the navigation range marks and lights for the channel through the nearly 5 miles of breakwaters on both sides is a simple task. Mr. Marsk struggled to establish accurate fix positions and deliver the verbal reports, along with recommendations to the captain and conning officer. The captain closely monitored the navigation range marks and effectively piloted the ship visually, relying little on any information from Mr. Marsk.

Entering Mayport's ship basin is a matter of adjusting the ship's course to port to align with the navigation range marks and lights situated at the southwest corner of the basin. We slowed down in the approach channel to take on the docking pilot from one of the tugboats. We were assigned to dock at Berth B-1, alongside the pier on the starboard side. Within 15 minutes, the ship was at the dock, and all mooring lines were passed and made secure. The captain ordered the gangway to be put out and secured the crew from their Sea and Anchor detail stations.

As the captain left the bridge, he looked me in the eye and quietly said, "Chief, from now on, you handle the navigation plot, okay?" I nodded, affirming his statement.

A few moments later, Mr. Marsk approached me. "How do you think it went, chief?"

At that moment, I lied, saying, "Sir, I think with more experience, you'll get the hang of it." He seemed satisfied with my answer and turned to leave the bridge.

I spotted Franklin nearby, grinning at me as he said, "Good answer, chief."

Later that day, the mail was delivered to the ship. I received several letters from Jan and one from Emily. I opened and read Jan's letters first. Then, I stared at Emily's envelope for a moment, wondering how she knew where I was. I assumed that since she was in an administrative position, she knew how to track people down. Finally, I opened Emily's letter and began to read—the first couple of paragraphs contained general updates. Then, starting in the third paragraph, she revealed her true reasons for writing. First, she explained that she had decided her marriage was over and mentioned that she and her husband had already separated. Next, she confessed that while we were in Orlando, she had fallen in love with me but was unsure of my feelings for her. She knew about Jan but questioned whether my marriage was solid. In her letter, she was essentially asking if I wanted her; all I had to do was write or call her to share my feelings. She concluded the letter by reminding me of her words from that day at the airport: I'll never forget you. I love you, Emily. At the bottom of the page, she had written her phone number.

I sat for several minutes, staring at the words Emily had written. Suddenly, it felt as if I were holding a live grenade; all I had to do was pull the pin, throw it, and my entire life with Jan would be blown apart. I'll admit, the temptation to call her surged within me for a moment. But then the rational part of my brain took control as I watched myself fold Emily's letter and stuff it back into its envelope. Not entirely sure why, I went to my locker in berthing and placed the letter at the bottom of a drawer before closing the locker door. I knew it was best to leave things there.

I mulled over Emily's words for about a week. I cared about her and her feelings, so the thought of ghosting her seemed low-class. One afternoon, I sat down and wrote her a letter. In the kindest and gentlest terms, I explained why what she proposed wasn't possible for us. I admitted I was tempted, but I could never hurt Jan and my son by tearing their lives apart. I expressed my hope that she would find the love she sought and deserved. I placed the letter in an envelope and mailed it. As expected, I've never heard from Emily again.

We were preparing to deploy to the Arabian Sea, the Persian Gulf, and the Indian Ocean in less than two months. In April, we had three additional weeks of underway time to conduct workup preparations off the Virginia Capes with an aircraft carrier and escort ships, allowing us to become once again accustomed to operating as part of a battle group. The ship was scheduled to depart Mayport for the deployment on May 21.

We weren't going to war, but we were headed to a place where war was happening. In September 1980, Iraqi forces launched a full-scale invasion of neighboring Iran, marking the beginning of the Iran-Iraq War, also referred to as the First Gulf War. Territorial, religious, and political disputes fueled this conflict.

Mindful of Iran's weakened military after its revolution in 1978–79, Saddam Hussein, who became Iraq's president in 1979, opted for a preemptive strike against Iran. On September 22, 1980, Iraq initiated air strikes on Iranian air bases, followed by a ground invasion of the oil-rich border region of Khuzestan.

Shatt Al-'Arab is a river in southeastern Iraq formed by the confluence of the Tigris and Euphrates rivers. It flows southeast, passing the Iraqi port of Basra and the Iranian port of Ābādān before emptying into the Persian Gulf. Along the latter half of its course, the river forms the border between Iraq and Iran. Saddam sought to reassert control over both sides of the Shatt Al-'Arab, Iraq's only access point to the Persian Gulf.

Iran launched a counteroffensive, and by early 1982, it was regaining lost territory. With Iran now on the offensive, Iraqi defenses strengthened, and the conflict settled into a virtual stalemate along a front roughly following the border. Both sides launched air and missile attacks against cities, military sites, oil facilities, and transportation, prompting the United States and other Western powers to send warships to the Persian Gulf to regulate oil output for the global market.

USS *W.S. Sims* was expected to operate mainly in the Persian Gulf, between Iran and Saudi Arabia, as part of the U.S. Middle East Force. It was also anticipated to be in the Gulf from June through September, which are the hottest months of the year.

The ship's two propulsion boilers deliver superheated steam to a gear turbine. Electrical power is produced through steam-driven ship service turbo generators. Generally, steam-propelled ships with steam auxiliary systems generated significant heat that permeated the vessel, particularly in hot tropical climates.

While crew living and many working spaces were equipped with air conditioning systems, these systems were not designed to manage the extreme heat of the areas we were entering. To address the expected heat exposure challenges for the crew, it was announced that uniform modifications would be implemented once the ship reached warmer climates.

The uniform for pay grades E-6 and below includes white T-shirts, dungaree shorts, and white tennis or athletic shoes. Officers and chiefs wear khaki shorts, polo-style shirts, and dockside boat shoes. Wearing socks is optional.

Being in Mayport let me call Jan two or three times a week to stay updated on what's happening back home. Everything had gone my way since reenlisting, except for the fact that I didn't have my family with me. However, we were making plans for them to move to Mayport towards the end of the deployment so that they would be here when I return.

On March 31, the ship departed from Mayport, heading to the Navy's operating area off the Virginia Capes. The Virginia Capes Operating Area is a surface and subsurface operating zone located off the coasts of Virginia and North Carolina. The following afternoon, we met up with the aircraft carrier USS *John F. Kennedy* (CV 67) and her group of destroyers and fast frigate escorts. Additional units, although not visible, included several fast-attack submarines.

After several weeks of participating in the operation, we were released from the battle group with orders to proceed with our assigned duties, meaning we were free to return to Mayport. On the morning of April 20, we arrived in Mayport and would remain in port until our deployment departure date on May 21.

Have I mentioned my weakness? After telling you about Emily, you might have guessed what it is. I've always preferred the company of women over men. As a married man, it's been a complicated struggle for me to stay faithful to Jan, but I've always managed to do so. Another aspect we shared was unconditional trust in each other. Jan knew about my preference for female companionship, yet she always seemed to trust that I would do the right thing.

My view on female companionship is: Why not? Women look better, smell better, and have soft and pleasant skin. They're mostly sweeter in disposition, usually don't like to fight, like to dance, and are smarter and more fun. What's not to like?

However, there's something I never seem to learn about having female friends: it can backfire. What I mean is that everything seems great until the woman drops a bombshell on me. You might be wondering, what could be the bombshell? My answer is three words: "I love you." When that happens, it brings everything to a screeching halt—friendship over, it was nice knowing you, have a nice life.

That very evening, I stumbled into what would become my next dilemma. I was a Fleet Reserve Association (FRA) member and had been since my time in Mayport, while on board USS *Vreeland*. FRA's club is located several miles south of the naval station on Mayport Road.

One day after work, I drove to Atlantic Beach to do some shopping. On the way back to the ship, I decided to stop by the FRA for a couple of beers. When I walked in, I was a bit surprised to see the place was fairly empty; I chalked it up to being a Tuesday night. After taking a seat at the bar, the female bartender caught my full attention. She was new; I had never seen her before. I was duly impressed: she was somewhat short, had long blonde hair that reached her waist, a figure to die for, a beautiful face, a smile just as lovely, and was probably in her early twenties.

Moments later, she approached me and took my order. When she returned with my beer, she smiled and extended her hand over the bar to shake mine.

"Hi, my name is Angie. What's yours?" she asked.

Before I could stop myself, a terrible pick-up line slipped out: "Well, hello, Angie. I'm George. I've been away for a while, but now that I'm meeting you, I'm happy to be back. I hope you know you're a huge improvement around here."

My response seemed to impress her, confirming my thoughts when she replied, "Well, I'm happy to meet you too. You've just made my night and improved it significantly. You've already made me like you right from the start." Since there were very few patrons in the place, Angie pulled up a stool behind the bar, and we sat and chatted on and off for several more hours. One question that never came up: our status—married or single? She didn't ask or offer, and I didn't ask or offer.

I left around 2300 and headed to the ship since I had duty the next day. Angie had told me she would be at the FRA Thursday night, so we agreed to meet up. On Thursday, after dinner, I made my way to the FRA. When I walked in, I was surprised to see Angie sitting at the bar instead of bartending. I asked her if she was working, and she replied, "No, I'm here to meet up with you, not work."

After having drinks at the FRA, we got into my car and visited a few other clubs in the beach area. Later, we returned to the FRA, where Angie had left her car. As I was walking her to her car, she turned to me and said, "Tomorrow night, I have tickets to see Kool & The Gang at the Coliseum. One of my girlfriends was supposed to go, but she can no longer go. Do you want to go with me?"

Jokingly, I replied, "Are you asking me out?"

Angie laughed and said, "Yes, don't be an ass."

I paused for a moment and then said, "Sure, let's do it! What time?" We agreed that I would pick her up at her apartment. Angie then retrieved some paper and a pen from her car, wrote down her address and telephone number, and handed it to me. We said our goodbyes and went our separate ways.

I picked up Angie at her apartment on Friday night and drove to the Coliseum in Jacksonville. Before that night, I had never truly enjoyed Kool & The Gang. However, it was a great concert, and I think we both had a good time. After the concert, we drove back to the beaches, and on the way, Angie asked if I wanted to grab some drinks. I agreed and took her to one of my favorite spots in Jacksonville Beach.

Our club had live music, so we spent the night enjoying drinks and dancing. Later that night, I drove Angie home. When we reached her apartment door, she turned to me and asked, "Do you want to keep seeing me?" Her question caught me by surprise.

"Yes, why?" I replied.

She looked up at me with a serious expression and said, "No, I mean, do you want to keep seeing me, and do you want more?" At that moment, I understood her meaning. I realized it was time to have what I call "The Talk."

"Angie, can we talk for a minute?" I asked.

"Yes," she replied.

"Angie, I'm not looking for a girlfriend, romance, or a committed relationship. I'm not looking just to get laid. What I hope for with you is to have you as a friend. I enjoy being with you." She said nothing but continued to look me in the eyes.

"I love spending time with you. Who wouldn't want to be around a beautiful, kind, and wonderful person like you?" I knew I had to bring things to a close, as she was visibly blushing, and I could see the hint of tears welling up in her eyes.

I asked, "Based on what I just said to you, do you want to keep seeing me? If you don't want to, I'll understand."

She looked up at me, reached up, put her arms around my neck, and said, "Bend down and kiss me, will you?" I complied, and we shared a long, passionate kiss. Thoughts raced through my mind about telling her to disregard everything I just said and let's go for it. Luckily, I managed to rein myself in mentally before I made a huge mistake.

As we parted after the kiss, she said, "George, I really, really like you. If you want to keep seeing me, I want to see you too. For now, I'm willing to be just friends. Agreed?"

"Yes," I replied.

She began to giggle and asked, "So, when will I see you next?"

Instead of simply telling her I would call and walking away, I foolishly suggested, "I have duty tomorrow, so how about Sunday? We can go to lunch and then visit St. Augustine to see some sights. I'll pick you up at 1130. How does that sound?"

Smiling and giggling, she answered, "Yes, that sounds great, it's a date." As I turned to leave, she grabbed me, threw her arms around my neck, and pulled me down for another long kiss. When we parted, she smiled and said, "Goodnight, friend." As I walked to the car, I thought, *Man, I need to tread carefully.*

As promised, I picked up Angie late Sunday morning at her apartment. We found a nice spot for lunch on the beach. After lunch, we drove 40 miles to St. Augustine and spent the afternoon exploring the sights of the town. Throughout the afternoon, we talked and got to know each other better. I learned that she was only 23 and attending college part-time. She worked part-time at the FRA and at a retail shop in Atlantic Beach to support herself. She shared her apartment with two college friends, which explained why she hadn't invited me in when I picked her up or dropped her off.

Spending the afternoon with her was relaxing, laid-back, and enjoyable, but I sensed that something was on her mind. We had an early dinner in St. Augustine and then drove to her place in Atlantic Beach. I planned to keep the evening short since the next day would be busy on the ship. To my surprise, when we arrived at her door, Angie asked if I wanted to come in for a bit before heading to the ship. I agreed to stay a little longer, and we went inside. One of her roommates was home, and after we introduced ourselves, she retreated to her bedroom.

Angie asked me to sit on the couch with her, saying she had something she wanted to discuss. Once seated, she began, "I've thought a lot about what you said to me about just being friends. I had assumed you wanted more from me, but I was wrong. I'm okay with your terms if it means I can keep seeing you. What do you say?"

I paused momentarily before responding, feeling as if pressure was being released. I smiled and said, "Yes, I want to keep seeing you. As I've told you, I enjoy my time with you and like you very much."

She seemed happy with my answer and said, "Good, me too."

The foundation of our relationship felt securely established. We talked a little longer before I decided it was time to leave. At the door, Angie asked, "Will I see you this week? I'm working nights at the FRA from Tuesday to Thursday, but I'm free other than that."

"How about I drop by the FRA on Tuesday night, and we can plan something?" I asked.

She smiled and said, "Great."

As I turned to leave, she suddenly grabbed me. "I forgot to tell you, we're friends who kiss each other." Once again, she wrapped her arms around my neck and pulled me down for a long goodbye kiss. As I walked to my car, I couldn't help but think maybe I should break things off. But I shrugged off the thought, rationalizing that everything would be just fine.

Onboard activities were progressing well to prepare for deployment. Each department works to ensure that sufficient equipment, materials, and supplies are available to address every foreseeable circumstance.

Training often disrupts work, and emergency drills for onboard fire, flooding, and battle damage are conducted during the day with the entire crew and at night with the duty sections.

As a geographical bachelor, I willingly took on duty nights for several chiefs so they could be at home with their families. That is what shipmates do; however, this also reduced the number of nights I could go out.

One evening, Angie expressed her desire for us to spend more time together, as I would soon be away for six months. I felt terrible knowing that once the deployment began, it would mean the end of Angie and me. I naively thought Angie would disappear from my life once the ship was gone.

The day before our departure came quickly. Fortunately, one of the other chiefs, Mike, let me leave my car at his house instead of in the large vehicle compound on the base. I was all set. Later that evening, I went to the phones on the dock and made my last call to Jan for a while.

On Friday morning, May 21, with groups of families and friends on the pier to see us off, we brought in the mooring lines and maneuvered the ship away from the dock. Once clear of the docks, we set our course to take us out of Mayport basin and into the St. Johns River. Once in the river, we changed course to position the ship in the middle of the outbound channel. Soon, we passed buoy STJ on our starboard side. Our deployment had begun.

Once out in the seaway, the familiar rhythm began, with the ship pitching slowly up and down and rolling from side to side. We wouldn't be crossing the Atlantic Ocean right away. First, we were headed for the Virginia Capes Operating Area to conduct several exercises with the aircraft carrier USS *America* (CV 66) and her battle group escorts. We set a course east of north to take us along the coast, heading northward to the operating area.

The next afternoon, we were operating off the Virginia Capes. A deck seaman working on the main deck near the stern of the ship saw someone jump from the starboard main deck into the water.

The seaman began yelling repeatedly, "Man overboard, starboard side," at the top of his lungs while running to the nearest sound-powered phone station to call the bridge.

Upon hearing the alert of a man overboard, several people rushed to the nearest life ring stowage locations on the starboard side and threw them over the side. Luckily, one of the life ring buoys had an automatic smoke float attached, which activated once the buoy hit the water. As the person in the water passed down the ship's side, the deck seaman recognized him. When the bridge answered the phone, he repeated the message, "Man overboard, starboard side." Then he added, "It's Haney."

The OOD immediately announced on the bridge, "Man overboard, starboard side," and began issuing orders to sound the emergency signal on the ship's whistle and pass the word over the 1MC. At the same time, the conning officer ordered the engine to full speed ahead to increase the ship's speed and ordered the helmsman to apply right full rudder.

The most efficient man overboard recovery maneuver for smaller, maneuverable ships like ours is the Single turn or Anderson turn. The conning officer executed the turn after deviation from the original heading reached 240 degrees. He ordered "rudder amidships" and initiated stopping maneuvers on the engine. Personnel on deck had the man in the water in sight, and many were pointing to indicate the direction to him.

By this point, the captain was on the bridge, directing the conning officer's maneuvers to ensure that when the ship stopped, it would be upwind from the man in the water, positioning the ship between the man in the water and the wind. This is done so the ship can drift down onto the man in the water, making recovery by deck personnel much easier and safer.

From the bridge's vantage point, we could clearly see Haney in the water. Initially, he refused to grab the additional life ring buoys with lifelines that were thrown to him. The captain ordered the ship's rescue swimmer to enter the water. Moments later, the swimmer jumped into the water and swam to Haney. He urged Haney to grab the life ring buoy, then put an arm around him while signaling the deck crew to haul in the buoy. Within minutes, Haney and the swimmer were safely back on board.

The ship's hospital corpsman took custody of Haney and, with help from several others, escorted him to the sick bay for examination. It was clear by now that Haney hadn't fallen overboard; he had intentionally jumped from the ship. The burning question was, why? Meanwhile, the captain contacted the senior officer in tactical command on USS *America* about the man overboard and the safe recovery, reporting that our ship was returning to its assigned station in the group.

About an hour later, we received the answer to the question. I was talking with the captain when Chief Hospital Corpsman Tim Stein (Doc) came onto the bridge. He informed us that he had completed his medical evaluation of Haney and that he had suffered no serious physical injuries. Then he added that Haney had deliberately jumped, convinced that if he did so, people would think he was crazy and the captain would want him off the ship.

The captain, who had been patiently listening, said, "Haney's right, we can't have him on board. I'm calling to arrange a medical evacuation to the carrier. The kid needs a psychological evaluation. Doc, get him ready to go."

"Yes, captain, we can have him ready in about 15 minutes," Doc replied.

The captain left the bridge and went to CIC to call for Haney's evacuation. About 30 minutes later, the ship went to "Flight Quarters" to receive the carrier's helicopter. Once the SH-60 "Seahawk" helicopter hovered over our deck, the flight deck crew escorted Haney out onto the flight deck. The helicopter had lowered a hoisting sling on a cable to the deck. Our crew helped Haney into the sling, and moments later, he was hoisted up to the helicopter's doorway, where the crewman pulled him inside. The SH-60 turned and headed outbound back to the carrier.

Junior enlisted in pay grades E-3 and below may find themselves temporarily assigned to the ship's galley and mess decks for 90 days. This assignment is called "Mess Cooking." Mess cooking assignments vary; they can include helping the cooks in the galley, keeping the mess decks clean and sanitary, or scrubbing pots, pans, trays, and utensils in the scullery. If one is lucky, they might be selected to mess cook in the officers' wardroom or the Chiefs Mess.

Working in the scullery is considered the worst assignment. The mess cook spends 12 to 14 hours a day in the hot, humid scullery, scrubbing, cleaning, and sanitizing. Usually, the scullery assignment is rotated among the mess cooks on a weekly basis. Keeping someone on scullery duty for more than five or six days can border on mental cruelty. It's not uncommon for a sailor to be assigned to the scullery as punishment for breaking rules.

This was the situation with Haney, the man overboard. Doc learned from speaking with Haney that he was clearly experiencing mental depression. Doc also discovered that Haney had been a disciplinary problem, consistently arriving late for his shifts and intentionally underperforming. What was the consequence for his infractions? His assignment to the scullery was extended several times.

We learned that evening that the doctors on USS *America* decided to send Haney to the Naval Hospital in Portsmouth, VA, for a psychological evaluation. Haney got what he wanted: to be off the ship.

The next afternoon, the senior officer in tactical command on board USS *America* released our ship to proceed on duties as previously assigned, which meant we were released to carry on with our deployment. I was on the bridge at the time; the OOD adjusted our course and speed to begin the first leg of our journey across the Atlantic Ocean. Our destination was Ireland Island, Bermuda, where we would refuel at the Naval Facility.

The distance from our departure point to Bermuda is only 510 nautical miles. We adjusted our speed to ensure an early morning arrival on May 24. Great springtime weather prevailed, with clear skies, comfortable air temperatures, and mild sea state conditions. The North Atlantic weather god was kind to us as we embarked on the long passage across her waters.

It may be difficult for those who have not experienced being at sea on naval destroyers or frigates to understand how exaggerated the vessel motions are in a seaway as compared to larger ships. When these ships are at sea, they are in constant motion.

When a ship rolls from side to side, it will also sway due to wind, currents, or the ship's own propulsion exerting forces on the hull. A roll of 15 to 20 degrees on a frigate in a seaway is normal. Simultaneously, the ship will pitch, heave, and surge. Pitch refers to the up-and-down rotation of the vessel around its fore and aft axis, heave describes the vertical motion, and surge involves linear movements forward and aft caused by wind-generated sea waves.

New sailors often experience bouts of seasickness due to the motions of the vessel. When the weather and sea state conditions worsen, particularly during high winds or storms, the ship's movements become more intense.

The waters surrounding the Bermuda Islands present navigational hazards for ships due to the reefs, particularly to the north and northeast of the islands. These reefs can extend up to 12 miles from the visible land and are primarily unmarked by navigational aids at their outer edges. To safely enter and exit the harbor, the assistance of Bermuda pilots is required.

On the morning of May 24, we approached Bermuda from the east as the sun rose. The pilot boarding station is located well offshore from the entrance to the channel. Shortly thereafter, the pilot boat came alongside, and the Bermuda pilot boarded. One of our junior officers was present to greet the pilot and escort him to the bridge.

The pilot took control of the ship and began navigating past Five Fathom Hole, the main entrance through the reefs to "The Narrows." The Narrows leads to the North Channel. Although the North Channel is a more roundabout route between The Narrows and Great Sound, it offers deeper water depths. The channel winds through the Bermuda Great Reef Lagoon for about 12 nautical miles. Approximately two-thirds of the way from The Narrows, there is a section called The Crescent, where the channel shifts from a primarily east-to-west direction to a general north-to-south trend.

Our ship soon approached the North Basin of Ireland Island. As we passed the breakwaters and entered the basin, two Navy tugboats stood by to assist with docking at Flagship Berth. In about 20 minutes, the ship was securely moored at her berth in the North Basin of Freeport.

I felt relieved to be moored. The entire approach and transit through the Great Sound made me nervous. The waters here are crystal clear, and during the transit, I could see reefs and sunken shipwrecks encroaching on the channel boundaries. Later, we had to retrace our route and safely navigate the ship back out to sea and into the deep ocean waters.

By early afternoon, refueling was complete, and the ship was ready to depart. The Bermuda pilot boarded shortly after the Sea and Anchor detail was set. Within minutes, the ship was underway, maneuvering away from the dock, and then we were outbound from the basin, heading toward the first channel leading to The Crescent. It didn't take long before we had transited The Crescent and were outbound in the North Channel, which took us north of the Bermuda Great Reef Lagoon. About an hour later, after navigating through The Narrows and passing Five Fathom Hole, we slowed the ship to allow the pilot to disembark to a waiting boat.

Once again, I sighed in relief; the ship was now in deep, safe waters. According to the passage plan, the OOD instructed the conning officer to have the helmsman steer a course of 080 degrees. The next leg of our journey would take us another 1,960 nautical miles northeastward to Ponta Delgada, Azores. It would take over five days to reach Ponta Delgada. Stopping in Ponta Delgada was for refueling the ship again before continuing our passage across the North Atlantic to Brest, France.

We were three days out from Bermuda. So far, the passage to the Azores had been uneventful, except for the steady increase in sustained winds. The wind gradually raised the height of the sea waves—nothing out of the ordinary for mid-spring North Atlantic weather.

The Azores Archipelago is located 770 miles off the coast of Portugal. The port of Ponta Delgada is situated at the southwest tip of São Miguel Island. On the morning of May 29, we commenced our approach to the harbor entrance of the port of Ponta Delgada from the southwest. The port of Ponta Delgada is the only fueling station and port of refuge in the central North Atlantic region.

From a navigational perspective, entering the port's inner harbor is fairly uncomplicated. The Ponta Delgada pilot boarded about 1 mile southeast of the breakwaters. Following the pilot's direction, we entered the port, passing the outer breakwaters along our port side. Once inside the port, with the assistance of tugboats, we maneuvered the ship to turn and moor with our starboard side facing the refueling wharf. This way, when we were ready to depart, it would be easy to maneuver away from the wharf and navigate the ship along the breakwaters back out to sea.

Navigating through the port to the wharf was somewhat distracting. The town of Ponta Delgada is visually stunning, showcasing a striking and distinctive Portuguese architectural style. Many of the buildings are white with black trim, and a prominent clock and bell tower stands out among the old structures lining the waterfront.

By early afternoon, the ship had been refueled, and it was time to leave. Shortly after we set the Sea and Anchor detail, the pilot came on board. Within minutes, all mooring lines had been taken in, and we were underway. We passed the outer breakwater and were back in the Atlantic waters, where the pilot disembarked. We set an easterly course along the southern coast of São Miguel Island for the first 45 nautical miles.

Once the eastern end of São Miguel Island was abaft our port beam, the OOD instructed the conning officer to have the helmsman steer a course of 055 degrees. The next leg of our journey would take us another 1,125 nautical miles northeast to Brest. It would take about three days of steaming at 16 knots (18.4 mph) to reach Brest on May 31.

The following three days of our journey were relatively uneventful. Everyone noticed that air temperatures gradually dropped as we sailed farther northeast into higher latitudes. In the North Atlantic Ocean, north latitudes ranging from 35° to 65° are typically dominated by westerly winds, known as the Westerlies. These winds carry warm tropical waters north and east across the North Atlantic, bringing warmer air to the northern regions. However, based on our observations, the warm air had not yet arrived this year.

Shortly after midnight on May 31, we entered the western reaches of the Bay of Biscay. This bay is bordered to the east by the west coast of France and to the south by the north coast of Spain. The waters here are typically clear and deep throughout.

The next morning, we approached Goulet de Brest, the outer entrance to Rade de Brest. The Port of Brest sits on the north side of the roadstead, just inside the entrance. Approximately 7 miles from the entrance, the lookout spotted the Brest pilot boat as it approached the ship. Once the pilot boat came alongside, the pilot boarded and was escorted to the bridge.

The passage to the Port of Brest took less than 30 minutes. We navigated the ship through the port's breakwaters. Then we approached the piers of the French naval base in the southwestern part of the harbor, where we moored with our port side to a very long pier. Once the gangway was in place, we secured the Sea and Anchor detail and set the in-port watch sections. Many crew members were excited to experience France; however, we soon would discover that the residents of Brest were not particularly enthusiastic about us being there.

CHAPTER 7

THE DITCH AND BEYOND

Our visit to Brest was not intended to be purely a liberty port; the primary purpose was to represent the United States diplomatically by promoting our country's cooperation and willingness to collaborate with European Navies. As part of this mission, those going ashore the first evening must wear their dress uniforms instead of civilian clothing.

That evening, I went into town with some of my fellow chiefs, wearing our summer dress white uniforms. We planned to find a café or restaurant for dinner. After dinner, we intended to explore some of the local bars or clubs to see what the nightlife was like in Brest.

We quickly realized that the people of Brest were unhappy about our presence in their town. At the first restaurant we approached, we were refused entry; we all understood part of the waiter's rant, "Fuck the USA and you." We then tried a café down the street, where the waiter, begrudgingly, allowed us to sit at a table. However, no one came to take our orders or serve us. After about 20 minutes, we got up and left.

We decided to skip dinner and look for a bar. We found one down the street and went inside. The place was pretty empty, with only a few customers. Since there were five of us, we settled at the bar. The bartender initially tried to ignore us and stayed at the far end. By this point, I'd had enough. An empty glass was sitting on the bar, so I grabbed it and started banging it loudly on the bar top, saying, "We would like some service down here."

Another one of my traits, or weaknesses depending on how you look at it, is my low tolerance for bullshit. In response to my noise-making, the bartender slowly made his way to our spot along the bar.

He looked at me and said, "Je ne parle pas anglais."

During our Atlantic crossing, I had found a French-English dictionary in the Chiefs Mess and had been teaching myself some basic French phrases.

Remembering some of them, I replied to him, "Je sais que vous parlez anglais." Meaning, "I know you speak English," and then I added, "Est-ce que vous me comprenez?" Meaning, "Do you understand me?"

The bartender answered, "Oui."

"You can speak French?" my buddy Mike asked.

I smiled at him, shook my head, and replied, "Not much, but you can bet he can speak English."

I turned my attention back to the bartender and said in English, "You will serve us now, right?"

He responded, "Oui, what do you men want to drink?"

I replied, "Merci beaucoup." Then I added, "Now that's better. Give my friends and me a round of your best draft beer." The bartender nodded, indicating he understood, and went to get our beers. I turned to Mike and smiled. "That's how you handle these uppity French ass wipes."

I managed to get the bartender's name: Michel. When he asked for my name, I replied, "Chief George." From that moment on, Michel referred to me as Chief George. After enjoying seven or eight rounds of beer, we decided to explore and see what else Brest had to offer.

Eventually, we found another bar where the staff seemed more welcoming to our presence and served us without issue. However, some patrons gave off a vibe of disdain. As one guy walked by on his way out, he shot us a glare filled with annoyance and disgust.

After a while, Mike said, "I don't think Brest is worth spending any more of our time or money. Let's go back to the ship." The rest of us agreed, finished our drinks, and left the bar, starting the walk back to the ship. Apparently, many of the crew felt the same way; on our way back, we ran into groups of crew members heading back to the ship as well.

The next day, word spread around the ship that liberty in Brest was disappointing and not worth the time or effort to go ashore. Not many went into town that evening, and the crew had already given up on Brest. The place was a bust. For me, the only positive aspect of Brest was that I could call home and speak to Jan.

There is one thing about Brest that was impressive: a massive concrete structure you can't miss when walking from the dock area to town. It measures roughly 1,000 by 650 feet, with a roof about 20 feet thick. This structure served as the German U-boat bunker, or submarine pens, during World War II. Scattered around the exterior of the bunker, some damage from the Allied bombings during the war is still visible.

The next morning, we got underway and left Brest behind. Once we were well offshore in the Bay of Biscay, we rendezvoused with ships from the Navies of France, Britain, the Netherlands, and Portugal. It marked the beginning of the French multinational naval exercise called "Suroit 82."

The stated purpose of these types of exercises is to allow the naval forces of different countries to practice and refine their tactics, strategies, and interoperability in a controlled environment. Participation in naval exercises bolsters a country's ability to respond to potential maritime threats and enhances overall operational capabilities.

We spent most of the next two weeks conducting various exercises with ships from different Navies. Finally, on June 15, we detached from the multinational force and began a two-day transit south to Rota, Spain. The stop in Rota was mainly for refueling. After refueling, we would leave Rota and transit through the Strait of Gibraltar, then across the Mediterranean Sea to Port Said, Egypt, the Mediterranean entrance to the Suez Canal.

In the late afternoon of June 17, we departed from Rota and headed toward the inbound shipping traffic lane leading to the Strait of Gibraltar, located about 45 nautical miles away. By early evening, we had entered the traffic lane for the strait.

I set the navigation detail for the transit through the strait. My previous passages on board USS *Vreeland* taught me that the heavy marine traffic from shipping and ferries can be highly challenging for the OOD and the conning officer during night passages. Manning the navigation detail and maintaining precise knowledge of the ship's actual position alleviates some of the burden on the OOD, allowing him and the conning officer to concentrate on avoiding collisions with other vessels.

The distance from the Strait of Gibraltar to Port Said is 1,945 nautical miles. To achieve the necessary time of arrival at the anchorage waiting areas outside Port Said on June 22, we must maintain an average speed of 17 knots over the ground.

The passage through the Mediterranean Sea went well. As it was June, the warm summer weather was in full swing. The sea waves were only 3 to 5 feet high and fairly calm. Visibility was sometimes reduced due to dust circulating over the sea from the Sahara Desert in North Africa. Off the coasts of Algeria and Tunisia, the haze caused by the desert dust persisted for several days until we passed through the Strait of Sicily and arrived south of Malta.

We approached the anchorage areas north of Port Said in the early afternoon of June 22. After contacting the Suez Canal authorities by radiotelephone, we were given a position to anchor. I quickly developed an anchorage plan on the navigation chart.

It was tense. Rows of deep-draft vessels were anchored in long lines. On arriving at our designated anchorage point, it seemed there was barely enough room for us to anchor between two other large ships. We carefully and slowly maneuvered the ship to the anchorage point and let go of the anchor. Once the anchor was on the bottom, we slowly backed the ship down to set the anchor. Once I was sure the anchor was holding, I notified the captain and recommended that we secure from the Sea and Anchor detail and set the anchor watch.

Within minutes, small boats filled with Egyptians approached the ship, seeking to come alongside and board. Some claimed to be electricians there for safety inspections, while others identified themselves as health inspectors or mooring line handlers. They wanted to board the ship to sell their products to the crew. It was difficult to distinguish between legitimate canal representatives and those who sought to gain unauthorized access to the vessel.

Corruption and bribery among Suez Canal officials are widely acknowledged. They usually prefer bribes such as Marlboro cigarettes,

Zippo lighters, or other valuable items. They will quickly steal radios, calculators, or any other item that can be easily taken.

Eventually, some bona fide canal officials arrived to brief us on the transit through the Suez Canal and to inspect our ship's documentation. To ensure a smooth inspection process, we presented each official with cartons of Marlboro cigarettes, Zippo lighters, our ship's coffee mugs, and ball caps. They seemed pleased with the gifts as they left the ship.

We remained anchored until that evening. Around 2200, the canal authorities contacted us via radiotelephone, instructing us to proceed to the canal pilot boarding area near the fairway lighted buoy that marks the entrance to the approach channel into Port Said. After weighing anchor and getting the ship underway, we carefully navigated through the congested anchorage area to reach the designated pilot pick-up location.

Vessels transiting through the Suez Canal are facilitated using a convoy system. The convoy system consists of one southbound convoy and one northbound convoy. Our ship was assigned to the southbound convoy group 'A.'

The waterway surrounding the fairway lighted buoy was busy with pilot boats navigating the area, delivering canal pilots to their respective ships. We maneuvered into the channel, where several ships were already approaching. More vessels were astern of us also entering the channel. Soon, a pilot boat came alongside to deliver our pilots. One of the junior officers met them on deck and escorted them to the bridge.

The captain greeted the pilots as they entered the bridge and presented them with their gratuities, which included Marlboros, Zippo lighters, and other small gifts. One thing that immediately struck everyone on the bridge was the strong odor of the pilots. In Middle Eastern and Arab countries, men and women commonly wear perfume. The pilots had clearly applied a generous amount of perfume before boarding. For

Westerners in confined spaces, the smell can be overpowering and distracting.

Suez Canal pilots are typically incompetent. Their primary role is to advise on maneuvering the vessel and determining its course. In theory, these pilots offer the captain their experience and practical knowledge of canal navigation. Additionally, pilots must have a cabin or space to rest during waiting periods. If a ship cannot accommodate this requirement, it may result in delays and additional pilotage fees. It's quite a racket.

The Suez Canal is 89 miles long and connects the Mediterranean Sea to the Gulf of Suez, which leads into the Red Sea. Starting from Port Said, the canal runs nearly straight to Lake Timsah. From there, it bends towards Great Bitter Lake and Little Bitter Lake. The canal continues south past Port Suez until it reaches the Gulf of Suez at Port Taufiq. To the west of the canal lies the low-lying Nile River delta, while to the east is the higher, rugged, and arid Sinai Peninsula.

With our convoy of ships assembled, we headed south through Port Said and then entered the lengthy stretch of the canal, often referred to as "The Ditch." The canal has no locks and can accommodate very large vessels. Transit times typically range from 12 to 16 hours; since it was midnight, we were in for a long day ahead.

We had to reach the bypass anchorage areas in Great Bitter Lake early in the morning and anchor outside the channel to allow the northbound convoys from Port Taufiq to pass. As the first light of dawn appeared, the canal's banks became more visible. The west bank of the canal has patches of greenery, including trees and irrigated crop fields. Scattered structures show signs that people live and work in these areas.

In contrast, the east bank mainly features tall sand dunes, with occasional access roads leading to the canal. On some of these dunes, small, run-down structures show signs of damage. Abandoned military vehicles, such as tanks and artillery, can be seen in various spots.

We were seeing remnants from the October 1973 Yom Kippur War. During this conflict, Egyptian forces crossed the Suez Canal and the cease-fire line with Israel, advancing into the Sinai Peninsula to establish positions. Egypt aimed to secure a foothold on the eastern bank of the Suez Canal to negotiate the return of the Sinai Peninsula. After three days, Israel stopped the Egyptian advance and initiated a series of counterattacks along the canal.

It was close to 0830 when we anchored the ship in the bypass anchorage in Great Bitter Lake. We were to wait at the anchorage for roughly three or more hours until the northbound convoy of vessels passed. The captain offered the canal pilots breakfast and the use of his cabin to rest until it was time to get back underway.

From Great Bitter Lake, about 25 miles of canal remain to Port Taufiq. There, we would disembark the canal pilots and begin the transit southward through the Gulf of Suez. The distance through the Gulf of Suez to the Red Sea is 160 nautical miles.

At around 1130, the ship weighed anchor and resumed its journey. We carefully navigated southbound back into the channel heading for Port Taufiq. Along the canal's east bank, we passed more abandoned structures and vehicles, which served as further remnants and testaments to the fighting that occurred during the Yom Kippur War.

It was mid-afternoon when we finally disembarked the canal pilots and began our passage south to the Gulf of Suez, leaving the canal behind. I had carefully planned our route, as it is densely populated with heavy shipping traffic using the Suez Canal. Additionally, we had to consider the numerous oil fields and oil production platforms, as well as the surface and submerged pipelines in and around the waterway. There were approximately 20 different oil fields scattered along the length of the Gulf of Suez.

As late afternoon turned into sunset, darkness enveloped us as we navigated through the Gulf. The flares from oil rigs burning off escaping gases cast an eerie glow in the night. Some rigs and platforms were marked with lights, while others were not. We initially planned to proceed at a speed of 16 knots, but we quickly realized this was too slow to avoid the other ships around us, which were traveling at speeds exceeding 20 knots. The OOD determined that a speed of 22 knots was more efficient for maneuvering and executing collision avoidance with nearby vessels.

As we approached midnight, the southern tip of the Sinai Peninsula passed by our port side, and we entered the northern waters of the Red Sea. The distance to Djibouti, our next refueling destination, is 1,125 nautical miles.

Once in the Red Sea, the density of shipping traffic had decreased significantly, so we reduced our speed to the planned transit speed of 16 knots. It would take us three more days to reach the port in Djibouti, where we would take on fuel and supplies and potentially receive some mail.

We transit through the Red Sea, specifically in an area known as the "Central Passage." This central passage offers approximately 830 nautical miles of safe navigation. However, the direct course is much closer to the Red Sea's east side than the west.

The southern exit from the Red Sea is through the Bab al-Mandeb strait. Ras Bab al-Mandeb is a prominent wedge-shaped headland in Yemen. Shaykh Malu (Oyster Island) lies on the coastal reef just west-southwest of the headland. It connects to the mainland by a rocky ledge. It was from Oyster Island that Yemen had previously fired on naval shipping that was transiting Bab al-Mandeb, the narrow waterway with Yemen to the east and the shore of Djibouti to the west. Bab al-Mandeb translates to "Gate of Tears" in Arabic.

The transit of Bab al-Mandeb would occur during the early morning hours after midnight. The captain wanted to err on the side of caution, so it was decided that the ship would be at Condition II of readiness, wartime steaming, just in case we were fired on from Yemen. Luckily, the transit of Bab al-Mandeb was uneventful, and we continued on to arrive at Port de Djibouti early the next morning.

Port de Djibouti, the principal roadstead of Djibouti, the former French Territory of Afars and Issas, stands on the southeast side of Golfe de Tadjoura at the far western reaches of the Gulf of Aden. Navigation into the port is relatively easy with a well-marked channel to assist in staying away from the underwater reefs. The Djibouti pilot boarded about 1 mile north of the port entrance, and we docked without incident about 30 minutes later.

The first thing that struck us was the enormous stockpiles of food from the U.N. World Food Program rotting on the dock. The reason, as we understood it, was that the Somali rebel groups frequently prevented food shipments from entering their country. This was all part of the rebels' efforts to force the collapse of the Somali government. What a waste.

We would stay in Djibouti overnight and wouldn't set out until late the next morning. The crew was a little bummed out since there had been no mail delivered to the ship. The XO had decided that the crew could have liberty that night.

One way I would describe Djibouti is to imagine if the Earth had a rectum. That's Djibouti: It's underdeveloped, dirty, hot, and dusty, and in my opinion, it feels like a blemish on the face of the planet. Despite all this, I had a memorable experience there that evening.

The French maintain a strong military presence in Djibouti, which includes brigades from the French Foreign Legion, specifically the Demi-Brigade. That afternoon, two French sergent-chefs, non-commissioned officers equivalent to the U.S. rank of staff sergeant, came on board. I happened to be near the quarterdeck when they arrived, and out of curiosity, I asked the OOD about the purpose of their visit. He informed me that they were there to see if they could get a tour of the ship.

Since I had some time available, I decided to host our guests. I approached one of them, extended my hand for a handshake, and said, "I'm George Trowbridge, Chief Quartermaster. How can I assist you?"

The sergent-chef took my hand and, in English, introduced himself: "I am Lefebvre, and my friend is Sergent-chef Bonnet. We are from the Demi-Brigade here. Chief, is it possible to see your ship?"

I replied, "Yes, of course! Let me show you around." I then asked the OOD to issue visitor badges to them and started the tour, first taking them up to the bridge.

I spent over an hour showing my guests around the ship. I was impressed by their genuine interest and the insightful questions they asked. I concluded the tour by taking them to the Chiefs Mess, where we could cool off in the air conditioning and chat. Lefebvre's English was quite good, while his friend Bonnet's was not as strong, though he seemed to understand me very well.

Towards the end of their visit, Lefebvre invited us to join them for drinks at their club that evening. He said they could pick us up at 1830. His only request was that we wear our uniforms. Before they left, five of us accepted the invitation.

After dinner, Mike, Manny, Gene, Jamie, and I put on our dress khaki uniforms and garrison caps. We headed to the quarterdeck, where Lefebvre and another French soldier were waiting for us on the dock. Two military-style Land Rovers were parked there. We all left the ship, and within moments, we were in the two vehicles driving away from the docks toward the town of Djibouti.

It was a quick drive through town, then we passed near Djibouti Airport on our way to Camp Lemonnier, which housed the French Foreign Legion garrison. Soon, we parked near a building Lefebvre called the "Cantina." As we approached the entrance, Lefebvre told us that once inside, we all must meet and greet the club's mascot to gain entry to the bar.

Upon entering, we discovered a lobby area just inside, and off to one side, on a large cushion, lay a live, full-grown leopard. I immediately noticed that the leopard wore a collar with a light steel chain attached. Its chain was linked to the wall.

Lefebvre pointed toward the leopard and said, "His name is Grands Félins, or you would say, Big Cat. Go greet and pet him; it's okay."

Gene looked at me and said, "You're the junior chief; you go first."

I noticed a group of soldiers gathered near the lobby, watching intently. As I slowly walked toward the leopard, I heard a voice with a distinct Aussie accent say, "Go ahead, mate; he probably won't kill you."

Just as I got about 3 feet away, the leopard rose from its floor cushion and did a low stretch while licking its chops. I paused, bent down, and reached out to touch the top of the leopard's head. To my surprise, the big cat leaned its head against my hand, prompting me to start scratching, rubbing, and petting it. Suddenly, it began to behave more like a domestic cat and genuinely seemed to enjoy the attention.

After a moment, I stopped, stepped back, and said, "Gene, you're the senior man here; it's your turn."

Gene hesitated for a moment. I urged him, "Come on, don't be a pussy." Finally, he slowly approached the big cat, just like I had, and reached out to scratch its head. Afterward, Mike, Manny, and Jamie took turns petting and rubbing the big cat. With each interaction, the soldiers in the club cheered and yelled with excitement.

Greeting 'Big Cat' was an important tradition that newcomers had to follow to feel welcomed into the club. Before long, we found ourselves at the bar, enjoying bottles of Adelscott beer. This amber-colored French beer was both sweet and bitter, with a hint of whisky aroma.

It turned out to be a fun night. Around midnight, several of our new friends gave us a ride back to the ship. Gene had brought along some patches featuring our ship's logo and a ship plaque. In return, the legion soldiers presented us with several of their uniform tabs and unit patches. It was a great exchange.

The next morning, I found that mail from the U.S. had finally caught up with the ship. I received three letters from Jan and one from Angie, which caught my attention. I opened and read Jan's letters first. I set Angie's letter aside in my locker to read later. Since the ship was about to depart soon, I took the time to write a letter to Jan and delivered it to the ship's post office to make sure it was sent out before we got underway.

Later that morning, we departed from Djibouti. The pilot disembarked once the ship was positioned in the outbound channel and clear of the underwater reefs on the west side. We continued north to navigate past the Îles Moucha islands and reefs, then adjusted the ship's course to 078 degrees, beginning the first leg of our transit through the Gulf of Aden. Ultimately, we would pass through the Arabian Sea to the Gulf of Oman, then the Strait of Hormuz, and into the Persian Gulf.

It was late morning, the day after we left Djibouti, which was now approximately 400 nautical miles behind us. We were transiting through the Gulf of Aden, approximately 80 miles north of the Somali coast, and staying north of the Horn of Africa.

I was in the chartroom aft of the bridge, preparing the passage plan for transiting the Strait of Hormuz and entering the Persian Gulf. Suddenly, over the VHF-FM radiotelephone, a two-tone alarm signal sounded for about 30 seconds, followed by a voice stating, "Pan, Pan, Pan. I say again,

Pan, Pan, Pan. This is the Greek tank ship *Andora, Andora, Andora*. I spell Alfa, November, Delta, Oscar, Romeo, Alfa. Call Sign: Sierra, Victor, Victor Zero, Niner. I say again, Sierra, Victor, Victor Zero, Niner. My latitude is one-three, one-zero north, and my longitude is zero-five-zero, two-zero east; I require assistance. We are under imminent threat of being boarded by pirates."

The Greek merchant ship was transmitting an internationally recognized safety message. "Pan" is an "Urgency" safety message, indicating that the calling station has a very urgent message concerning the safety of a ship or the safety of a person. The law of the sea dictates that any captain or master of a vessel who hears a distress or urgency call must respond to such calls and provide assistance if able to do so, as long as it does not unduly endanger his own vessel.

The OOD called the captain to inform him of the merchant ship's Pan "urgency" radio call. I had already plotted the merchant vessel's stated latitude and longitude on the chart and determined their bearing and range. I estimated that the merchant ship was only about 22 nautical miles from us at the time of the radio call.

The captain arrived on the bridge, approached the VHF-FM radiotelephone, picked up the handset, and said, "Merchant vessel *Andora*, merchant vessel *Andora*. Call sign, Sierra, Victor, Victor Zero, Niner. This is U.S. Navy warship, USS *W.S. Sims*. Do you copy? Over." The captain paused and waited for a response. After about 30 seconds, he repeated the call.

After the second call, the merchant ship replied, "U.S. Navy warship, this is the master of the tank ship *Andora*. How copy over?"

The captain instructed the ship's master to switch to another channel, and communication was established on that frequency within moments. Meanwhile, we increased our speed to full ahead and established the course we estimated would take us to the Greek ship's position. We soon learned from the master of the merchant ship that two large boats had been following them for several days. The tanker's maximum speed was less than 14 knots, so they could not outrun the pirate boats, which were now closing in on his ship. To cover ourselves legally, the captain asked the master of the merchant ship, "Do you require our assistance and agree that we can render assistance?"

The ship's master replied, "Affirmative, I require assistance and will accept any assistance you may or can provide."

To proceed legally, we needed permission from the master of the merchant ship. We documented the radio call in the ship's log, and our radiotelephone was capable of recording radio calls. In CIC, they also made an audio recording of the call on tape. Legally, we were protected under international maritime law to proceed.

The master of the Greek tanker indicated that his ship was operating in ballast, meaning it was not carrying any bulk liquid cargo. He also informed us that his ship was headed for Gadani Beach, Pakistan. Gadani Beach is located on the Arabian Sea north of Karachi and is home to a large ship-breaking yard. Ships at the end of their useful service life are dismantled at ship-breaking yards like the one in Gadani Beach.

The tanker's master also clarified that because the ship was to be scrapped, there was a minimal crew on board, and they were not carrying any firearms. Therefore, they could not effectively resist if the pirates boarded his vessel.

In recent years, reports have emerged of Somali pirates boarding ships and taking them by force off the Horn of Africa. In some instances, the pirates executed the entire crew and disposed of their bodies at sea. The pirates would then sail the captured vessel to Gadani Beach, where they sold it for scrap, reaping substantial profits. Therefore, it is reasonable to assume that the pirates intended to seize the tanker for its value at Gadani Beach.

Our ship's crew had been trained in anti-piracy tactics, and we had conducted anti-piracy drills just days before during the "Suroit" exercises. Before deploying from Mayport, the ship was outfitted with M2 Browning .50 caliber heavy machine guns mounted on the 02-level deck on the port and starboard sides aft of the bridge. Additionally, one deck above the main deck on the 01 level and further aft, we were equipped with 20-millimeter (mm) Mark 16 cannons, mounted on both sides of the ship. The 20 mm cannons were belt-fed, fired a larger and more powerful round, and had an effective range of 2,000 yards (1 nautical mile) with a maximum range of 7,000 yards.

The order was given to man the .50 caliber machine guns and the 20 mm cannon stations. Each gun crew consists of a gunner, loader/spotter, and a sound-powered phone talker for communication with the bridge and CIC.

Within 30 minutes, we spotted *Andora*; it may have been one of the last surviving T2 tankers in the world. The T2 tanker was a class of oil tankers produced in large numbers in the U.S. during World War II. In the post-war years, many of these tankers were sold to shipping companies from foreign countries. The old T2s were likely capable of top speeds between 14 and 16 knots. No wonder the pirates in their smaller and faster boats could keep up.

As we closed in on *Andora*, we also spotted two smaller crafts nearby. One, a boat with a white hull, was about 200 yards directly astern of the ship, while the other, a blue-hulled boat, appeared to be trying to close in on the tanker at her starboard quarter. I don't believe anyone on the two pirate boats was aware of our presence as we continued to approach.

In just a few minutes, we had maneuvered the ship to a position off the port quarter of *Andora*. This location provided our gunners on the starboard side with a clear field of fire on both boats. The captain began to read the following statement prepared by CIC over the VHF-FM radiotelephone on channel 16:

> "Unidentified vessels on our starboard side, we are a U.S. Navy warship. You are violating Article 101 of the United Nations Convention on the Law of the Sea by attempting an act of piracy against a ship in international waters outside the jurisdiction of any state. You will immediately cease and desist your activities. You are ordered to turn your vessels away and leave the area. Failure to comply will be seen as piracy and aggression on the high seas and will result in the use of force against you."

The XO then repeated the same statement over the 1MC external and weather deck speakers. The pirates' reaction indicated they had heard and understood our message through the radiotelephone or the ship's 1MC. Many of them were in the open, waving what appeared to be AK-47 assault rifles and handguns, and some shouted something unintelligible. I moved to the starboard bridge wing with binoculars and began observing the pirates on both boats. I noticed that the wake patterns of both boats changed, indicating they were accelerating and trying to get closer to the tanker.

I turned to look for the captain, who had moved to stand beside me, and said, "Captain, they're picking up speed and closing in on the tanker." The captain did not respond verbally but nodded his head to indicate he had heard me.

Next, the captain turned, picking up the 1JV sound-powered phone handset to communicate with the deck gun stations. He said, "This is the captain, starboard gun stations, fire warning shots across the bows of both boats. Commence fire." Within moments, there were short bursts of fire from both the .50 caliber and 20 mm deck guns. Watching through binoculars, I could clearly see the geysers of water from each round's impact, just ahead of the boats. I noted that all of the pirates had taken cover and that I couldn't visually see any of them. The gunfire would continue for several more minutes.

While our guns were still firing, I moved to the 02-level aft of the bridge, where I positioned myself farther back from the starboard .50 caliber gun station. The .50 caliber gunner was firing short bursts, aiming just ahead of the white boat's bow. Suddenly, I heard a different sound from the .50 caliber gun. It seemed like the rate of fire between individual rounds within each burst had changed. At first, I thought it was just my imagination or that we might be taking fire from one or both pirate boats. At the same time, the gunner stopped firing the gun.

I overheard the gun station phone talker reporting to the bridge that there was a stoppage in the gun and that they had ceased firing. Where I stood seemed to be a safe distance from the gun. I watched as the gunner opened the gun's cover to access the ammunition belt, and then a loud "pop" was heard. The noise was a live round malfunctioning as the cover was opened, causing the cartridge case to rupture. The gunner looked at the station's loader and phone talker to ensure no one was hurt or injured. Then, he quickly used an extractor to remove the ruptured cartridge and threw it over the side. I heard the gunner say it was just a stoppage or misfire.

On hearing the popping sound, I suddenly felt a brief stinging pain on the right side of my face and ear. I reached up to check the area and concluded that nothing was wrong. I turned my attention back to the pirate boats. As I watched, I noticed a man on the white boat jumping up and waving a white rag or piece of clothing.

The captain must have seen it too because next I heard the phone talker say, "The captain has ordered cease fire." We slowed the ship's speed to maintain a position near the two boats, which both now appeared to be dead in the water. Throughout all this, the tanker had maintained its course and speed and was now several miles away.

As I made my way back to the bridge, I could see that pirates on both boats were waving white rags at us. I watched as the boats seemed to be slowly turning away. We waited, and after several minutes, it became clear that the pirates were giving up. The pirate boats appeared to be making way through the water as they headed southwest.

Once I was back at the starboard bridge wing, I overheard the captain say to the OOD, "Let's hold this position and drift for a while to make sure they really are leaving. Keep the deck gun stations manned, I'll be in CIC." Just like that, it was over.

I entered the bridge and Hampton, the QMOW, said to me, "Chief, what happened? You've got blood all over your cheek and ear." I reached up to touch my right cheek, face, and ear. When I pulled my hand away, there was blood all over my fingers.

"I don't know. I guess I'd better go see Doc." I turned and headed for the ladder to leave; I wanted off the bridge before anyone else noticed that I was bleeding.

I went below to sick bay to see if Doc Stein was in. Luckily, he was there. I pointed to the right side of my face, saying, "Doc, can I get you to check this out for me?"

Doc pulled up a stool and told me to sit down while asking what had happened. I described what I could recall while he cleaned up my face and ear. Then, he began a close examination.

After he finished checking, he said, "George, it looks like something small at high velocity punctured your right cheek, came out about a centimeter higher, and then went through the Helix part of your ear. It could have been a piece of shrapnel or a flying fragment off of something. It looks as if most of the bleeding has stopped on its own. Let's suture the openings shut; they'll be small and barely noticeable."

"You're the Doc; do what you think is best," I said. He laid out his suturing kit and supplies before going to work.

Doc looked at me and said, "You know, if what hit you had been about 2 or 3 centimeters closer to your nose, I could be fitting you for a body bag right now."

Doc sat at his desk, where my medical record was laid open, and began to write. I stood up and asked, "We all set?"

Doc responded, "Yes, we're good." I thanked him for his help and left. Next, I went to the Chiefs Mess to change my uniform shirt and clean up. I checked myself in the mirror and was pleased to see that the sutures were hardly noticeable.

Once in the Persian Gulf, our initial destination would be Sitrah Anchorage near Mina Salman on the island of Al Bahrayn, or as Westerners call it, Bahrain. Going to the anchorage would allow us to take on fuel, supplies, mail, and dispose of our garbage before we began our assignment in the Gulf.

The next day, I was getting some items from my locker when I spotted Angie's letter. I decided to open it. From reading what she wrote, things had changed, at least from her perspective. The idiom "Absence makes the heart grow fonder" echoed in my mind.

Angie wrote that she had evaluated our relationship while I had been away and that, upon my return to Mayport, she wanted us to be a real couple. She articulated her feelings, reasoning, and argument very well. She expressed how much she hoped I felt the same or was open to the idea. Don't get me wrong; I would have chosen Angie in a heartbeat if I weren't married. I folded her letter, placed it back in the envelope, and put it in my locker. Silently, I kept saying, "Shit, and shit again." Now I had a big problem.

On Friday, July 2, we transited the Strait of Hormuz and entered the Persian Gulf. In the days leading up to this, we noticed that the air temperatures increased daily, while the relative humidity remained low during the day but approached 100 percent at night. The horizon frequently appeared to have a brownish haze hovering just above it. Considering the weather and climate conditions, the XO decided that the crew should shift to their modified summer uniforms.

The captain made a radio call over a secure circuit to check in with USS *Coronado*, an Auxiliary Command Ship (AGF-11), docked in Bahrain. *Coronado* served as the Flag/Command ship for the Commander, U.S. Middle East Force. For operational purposes, the U.S. Middle East Force is referred to as "MIDEASTFOR."

Most top-side spaces, including the bridge, lack air conditioning. The summer air temperatures in the Gulf range from 97 degrees Fahrenheit over water to 115 degrees closer to land. The seawater temperatures generally range from 91 to 94 degrees Fahrenheit. Relative humidity is typically high at 95 percent or more. However, by combining these temperatures with the additional heat generated by the ship's boilers and the radiant heat from the ship's steel construction, the actual air temperatures on the ship's bridge alone can, at times, soar to 130 degrees or more.

The next day, we set the Sea and Anchor detail as we approached the Sitrah Lighted Bell buoy, the primary floating navigation aid marking the channel that leads to Sitrah Anchorage off Mina Salman. Within an hour, we had the ship safely anchored, and the anchor watch was set. We were here to receive several barges for refueling, taking on supplies, and possibly mail. The International Pollution Prevention laws prohibit ships from dumping garbage in any part of the Gulf's waters. We would offload all of the ship's garbage to the last barge arriving today.

From Sitrah Anchorage, we could often see the city of Manama on the island of Bahrain. Manama serves as a major trading and mercantile center. Most days, unless the dust haze was particularly thick, the skyline of tall buildings and hotels was clearly visible. On sunny but hazy days, the distant city reminded me of a magical island kingdom surrounded by desert.

Thus, we embarked on our three-month stay in the Persian Gulf during the year's hottest months. We would return to Sitrah Anchorage every eight to nine days to refuel and pick up supplies or mail. At some point, we might've been able to moor outboard of USS *Coronado* at Mina Salman for a day or two.

That night, we departed from Sitrah Anchorage and began our transit to our principal operation area (OPAREA) near the Strait of Hormuz. The OPAREA positions our ship between Iran and the countries of Oman, the United Arab Emirates (UAE), and Saudi Arabia. The run from Sitrah Anchorage to the OPAREA is 295 nautical miles, taking about 18 hours at 16 knots.

We were to patrol off the west coasts of Oman and the UAE. Generally, we should remain well offshore from Oman and the UAE, south of the Saleh Oil Field near the western end of the Strait of Hormuz.

Our position was meant to be tactical. It would allow us to monitor the Imperial Iranian Air Force traffic with our air search radar. Bandar Abbas and Chabahar fighter air bases are located along Iran's coast and form the northern part of the Strait of Hormuz. Before the fall of the Shah in 1979, the U.S. had sold Iran a number of F-14 Tomcat fighters and trained their pilots.

With the fall of the Shah during the revolution, the Imperial Iranian Navy was renamed the Islamic Republic of Iran Navy (IRIN). In the 1970s, the United States sold several aging destroyers to Iran: USS *Zellers* (DD 777), named *Babr*, and USS *Stormes* (DD 780), named *Palang*. Additionally, they have one former British destroyer named *Damavand*. However, the IRIN also had a diverse fleet of frigates, corvettes, patrol craft, missile boats, and minelayers. Bandar Abbas also serves as Iran's main naval base.

As the second year of the Iran-Iraq War unfolded, the Strait of Hormuz became a critical area of conflict. Both sides had threatened to target each other's energy exports, which are vital to global markets. Approximately one-fifth of the world's seaborne crude oil passes through this strait each day. The Iranian forces recognized that successfully closing the strait could significantly disrupt the global economy. If Iran chose to take hostile actions against shipping in the strait, whether through surface or air attacks, our ship would act as the first line of defense in countering these threats.

We arrived at the OPAREA around noon on Sunday, July 4. The area we were to patrol was marked on the navigation charts using the coordinates provided by MIDEASTFOR. Once the coordinates were plotted and connected, they formed a rectangular shape measuring 5.5 nautical miles wide and 10 nautical miles long. This rectangular area is generally oriented in a northeast-southwest direction. Thus, we had a new domain of 55 square miles of water in the eastern Persian Gulf.

We started our days of patrolling in our designated area. During our patrols, we generally maintained speeds of 3 to 4 knots, just fast enough to ensure steerageway. Our route followed a course of 030 degrees to reach the northern end, after which we turned around and headed back on a course of 210 degrees to the southern end. Each trip took about two hours, and then we repeated the process.

Poor visibility in the Persian Gulf can result from early morning fog, salt haze, or dust, with dust being the most prevalent. During the summer months, as rainfall decreases and temperatures rise, the ground dries out, leading to fine dust being lifted into the atmosphere. Dust storms and sandstorms can occur throughout the Gulf in every season, but they are most common in July.

It was our fourth day on patrol, and I was working in the chartroom while Franklin was on watch on the bridge. He popped in and said, "Chief, you've got to see this."

I followed him onto the starboard bridge wing, where he began pointing to the southwest. There, we saw what looked like a massive brown wall extending upward from the horizon and reaching high into the sky. I quickly realized a vast dust storm was coming off the desert. I rushed to one of the surface search radar repeaters on the bridge. After observing the display for several moments, I could make out the outline of the storm and saw that it was tracking in our direction.

We were about to experience the first of several dust-sandstorms that summer. On the approach of these storms, the OOD would alert the crew over the 1MC, allowing the crew time to close all doors, hatches, ventilation valves, fittings, and openings to prevent or minimize dust and sand from entering the ship's interior.

With everything shut and secured, it quickly became stifling on the bridge. The air temperature on the bridge during these storms often soared to over 120 degrees. On the bright side, the dust-sandstorms generally passed quickly. After a storm passed, the air is still hot stepping back outside, but it felt much better than the stuffy, overheated air that quickly built up on the bridge.

After several days, I noticed that the haze gray paint on the exterior bulkheads and decks had taken on a brown hue. After one of the storms, small drifts of sand would gather in some corners, resembling tiny snowdrifts.

A significant event occurred in my division during July. The pay grade E-6 selection list was released, and Mike Franklin was on it and would be advanced to QM1. On July 16, the command held a frocking ceremony for those advancing to the next higher pay grade.

I was happy for Franklin, and he was very deserving. I had been assigned to *W.S. Sims* to fill the QM1 (pay grade E-6) billet. However, viewed from a career perspective, we now had a QM1 and a QMC occupying the same billet. This situation was not necessarily beneficial for Franklin, as I was occupying the position he should hold. It also wasn't ideal for me as a QMC. I decided that right after the deployment, I would reach out to the QM Rating detailer about orders to a ship with an actual QMC billet.

Operating in the hot Persian Gulf required several lifestyle adjustments. The primary one was malaria control. Malaria is one of the deadliest diseases found in tropical and subtropical areas. We must take anti-malaria medication to prevent the disease caused by parasites. The crew had been taking malaria prophylaxis tablets weekly before the ship entered the Mediterranean Sea.

We need to take one tablet every Wednesday. For several days after each dose, many individuals experienced common side effects, including headaches, dizziness, nausea or vomiting, stomach pain, loss of appetite, weight loss, and feelings of nervousness or irritability. Personally, the main problems for me were the days of dizziness, nausea, and stomach pain, which were often accompanied by diarrhea, making it impossible to eat. Afterward, I had several better days, but soon Wednesday rolled around again. It was a vicious cycle.

Chilled water air conditioning systems cool the living and berthing areas. On many days and nights, the AC could not keep up. For sleeping, most of us placed towels over the mattress sheet and slept on the towels, which was much more effective for managing the dampness caused by constant sweating while trying to sleep.

The engineers secured the hot water system throughout the ship except for the galley. No one required a hot shower; the water temperature in the showers was tepid and adequate. The uniform standards were further relaxed for the crew. The only standing rule for those working outside on deck was that T-shirts were mandatory. One could get severely sunburned in less than 15 minutes.

On the bridge and other topside locations, watches and work were brutal. The sun constantly beat down, and air temperatures easily reached 120 degrees or more by noon. Any air that flowed through the bridge was hot and dry. At night, after dark, it could be even more uncomfortable. The air temperature would cool to maybe 100 degrees, but the relative humidity generally rose to 100 percent—the air condensed into water, saturating every surface, including human skin and clothing.

I put myself into the QMOW rotation to give the QMs more time between watches and additional time off the bridge. One evening, while talking with Mr. Marsk, who was the OOD, we were both drenched in sweat and feeling miserable. He surprised me when he asked, "Chief, do you ever feel like you're going to lose your mind up here on the bridge?"

I couldn't help but laugh and replied, "Sir, just the fact that we are here, doing what we're doing, already makes us certifiably crazy."

"Good, then it's not just me," he responded.

After another four days, we left our station and headed for Sitrah Anchorage again. It was time to refuel and maybe collect mail for the crew. While on the way, I wrote a letter to Jan. As I went through my locker, I noticed Angie's letter and decided to send her a letter too, hoping to end our relationship. I stared at the blank paper for several minutes, trying to figure out what to write.

What I wrote to her was short, direct, and to the point. In summary, I explained that we were just friends and that I didn't see us as anything more than that. I encouraged her to seek the kind of relationship she desired elsewhere. I concluded the letter by wishing her the best. After folding the letter, I placed it in an envelope for mailing. I believed what I had written would bring our situation to a close. With a sense of satisfaction, I dropped her letter, along with one to Jan, in the outgoing mail and then went to work.

The next day, we anchored the ship at Sitrah Anchorage. Before long, a tugboat towing a fuel barge came alongside. As is common throughout the Gulf, the daytime weather at the anchorage was mostly clear, although it was continually affected by a dust haze. The air temperature well exceeded 100 degrees, accompanied by an unrelenting hot and dry wind.

The afternoon at anchorage followed essentially the same routine as before. After the tug took the fuel barge away, another tug and barge arrived, delivering pallets of supplies and food stores. An "all hands" working party was formed, and everything was loaded on board within an hour. Finally, we off-loaded our stored garbage onto the barge, and our work was complete. The crew was happy because the supply barge brought the ship mail.

It is illegal to consume alcohol on commissioned U.S. Navy ships. The captain did the next best thing for the crew: The XO and supply officer arranged to bring about 20 cases of Schlitz, Pabst Blue Ribbon, and Budweiser beer, packed in large coolers, out on the last supply barge. Many crew members were surprised and happy when they heard the XO announce over the 1MC: "This is the XO; there is ice-cold beer available on the barge. There is a limit of two beers per crew member. For any interested crew members, come get your cold beer."

Not many crew members abstained. From the aft section of the 02-level, I observed as sailors queued up on the main deck to descend the ladder to the barge. Soon, about two-thirds of the crew filled the deck of the barge. I made my way down and boarded the barge; I, too, wanted my two beers. On a blazing hot afternoon in the Persian Gulf, it isn't easy to describe how refreshing that first big gulp of ice-cold beer felt. It was a wise decision by the captain, as it boosted morale.

In the late afternoon, just before sunset, we weighed anchor and got underway, leaving Sitrah Anchorage behind. After navigating through the outbound channel to the Sitrah Lighted Bell buoy, we secured from the Sea and Anchor detail and set our course eastward for the overnight transit back to the OPAREA near the Strait of Hormuz.

Our operations now appeared to consist solely of spending eight to ten days patrolling our assigned OPAREA and, as needed, leaving to transit to Sitrah Anchorage for fuel and supplies before returning.

The operation would have been utterly boring if it hadn't been for the ongoing personal battles each of us faced against the relentless heat. Most of us were somewhat acclimated to our environment. Chapped lips had healed, and what had once been sunburned arms, necks, faces, and legs had turned into dark-tanned skin.

At times, we experienced intermittent breaks when the Iranians chose to test our readiness. Occasionally, Iranian patrol boats would venture into the Strait of Hormuz and approach our position. We issued warnings to the Iranians over the radiotelephone, but they often ignored them. In response, the captain ordered the 5-inch/54 caliber gun mount to cycle and aim the gun barrel in their direction. This action consistently prompted them to change course and turn away.

On several occasions, watchstanders in CIC detected Iranian F-14 Tomcats flying inbound from Bandar Abbas. However, the F-14s would veer away at the last moment, not wanting to risk engaging with us and the possibility of being shot down.

On August 2, we received orders from COMIDEASTFOR to transit to Mina Salman, and moor outboard of USS *Coronado*. We would be in port at Mina Salman for three days.

The next morning, for the first time, we navigated the ship through the Sitrah Anchorage to the channel entrance of the Khawr al Qulayah basin and the channel to Mina Salman. USS *Coronado* was moored at the Deep-Water Jetty, a broad, 2,600-foot-long pier.

With the assistance of two Navy Landing Craft Mechanized (LCM) boats, the captain skillfully maneuvered the ship alongside *Coronado*. We secured from the Sea and Anchor detail and set the in-port watch for the first time since departing Djibouti nearly six weeks earlier.

The entire crew was happy about not being underway for three days, even though Bahrain offered limited activities. Well over 90 percent of Bahrain's population is Muslim, which means it's essentially dry of alcoholic beverages. This resulted in no bars, no nightlife, and no hell-raising. However, the opportunity to get off the ship seemed sufficient. The two main attractions are visiting the Administrative Support Unit (ASU) Bahrain and shopping at the souk in Manama.

It was a fairly quick walk from the end of the pier to ASU Bahrain. The crew cared about three things that ASU provided: a small Navy Exchange store, telephones, and a small club where they could enjoy a cold beer.

Outside the gate at ASU Bahrain, buses are available to take you to the central part of Manama. Attractions in Manama include the central market and the Gold Souk. It is helpful to check the daily gold prices while at ASU. If you plan to buy gold jewelry, you need to know the price for that day. The price per troy ounce varies depending on whether you want to buy 24, 22, 21, or 18-karat gold. You should also be aware of the current exchange rate between the Bahraini Dinar and the U.S. dollar. Lastly, remember that a troy ounce of gold is about 31.1 grams.

Buying gold jewelry here is quite different from buying it in the United States. The beauty or craftsmanship of the piece doesn't matter; it all depends on the purity of the gold it's made from and its weight. Once you express interest in a piece, the gold merchant will inform you of the gold's purity. Next, he will weigh it on a scale and provide you with the weight in grams or troy ounces. Finally, he will take a calculator, crunch some numbers for a few seconds, and then tell you what his price is.

Here's where being a good haggler really matters. First, you need to understand that the gold merchant's initial quoted price will be way too high. I'll use a great 22-karat gold woven chain necklace I bought for Jan as an example. After weighing the piece and doing the math, the merchant said the price was 900 U.S. dollars (USD). I countered with an offer of $50.

This is where the dance and theatrics began. The merchant reacted as if he was shocked and insulted by my offer, saying, "Mister, I cannot sell such a nice piece for so little! I have children, I have a home, I have bills. Please, please work with me. Can you pay $600?"

"Okay, how about $75?" I responded.

He repeated his polite rant, which concluded with a new price of $450. I countered with $100. This time, his rant was brief and ended with a price of $275. I offered $160.

The merchant looked at me for a second, then reached his hand over the counter to shake. "Okay, mister, just for you, I give you a special price, $175."

I took his hand, shook it, and said, "Deal."

That's how a deal at the Gold Souk works. If a customer doesn't attempt to negotiate or haggle to lower the price, the gold merchant will gladly take their money and consider them a fool. Just like with Jan's necklace, had I accepted the initial offered price, I would have overpaid by $725, which is quite close to its actual value in the United States.

The wiser crew members waited to shop in the souk before heading to the ASU club to enjoy a cold beer. The club wasn't much; it was simply a large room with a bar and plenty of tables and chairs. However, it offered cheap cold beer and excellent air conditioning. Stepping outside felt like walking from a big refrigerator into a blast furnace.

As mentioned, ASU has telephones that can be used to make overseas calls. However, calls were limited to 15 minutes, and the telephones were available only until 1800, when the building closed. On the second day at ASU, I tried calling Jan at 1630, which was 7:30 a.m. in Iowa. To my relief, Jan answered the phone. It was a good thing I called now; in another week, she and Mitch would be moving to Florida.

We received mail twice while in Bahrain. As always, I was happy to get mail from Jan. In the second delivery, there was a letter from Angie. I didn't want to read it, so I set her letter aside in my locker to defer the inevitable.

On Friday morning, August 6, the ship was again underway as we backed away from USS *Coronado*. Once the vessel was turned fair, we entered the channel through the Khawr al Qulayah basin. Soon, we passed through the Sitrah Anchorage area, outbound, returning to the OPAREA to resume our mission. It was back to the tedious yet somewhat relaxing routine we had grown accustomed to.

One professional goal I had been pursuing since the beginning of the deployment was to earn qualification as an Enlisted Surface Warfare Specialist (ESWS). The ESWS program was initiated Navy-wide in 1978 with a formal PQS qualification process. Sailors displaying the surface warfare insignia on their uniforms signified that they had demonstrated an advanced level of knowledge and skills in various areas of naval warfare.

The first week back on station was largely uneventful. That Sunday morning had pleasant weather. The day's heat had not yet settled in; the skies were clear, and the seas were calm. The ship was patrolling at a speed of 3 knots. Generally, on Sundays, we follow a "holiday routine."

Several crew members were already on the fantail at the stern, fishing by trolling with lures. The waters here are home to many fish species, including king mackerel, barracuda, grouper, cobia, and queenfish. Some good fish had already been caught.

I was on the bridge, standing watch as the junior officer of the deck and conning officer, working on ESWS qualifications. The captain came onto the bridge, looked around, and smiled at everyone. He approached me and the OOD, saying, "It's such a nice morning. I'll be back on the fantail. I plan to go fishing and relax this morning. If you need me, that's where I'll be."

About 45 minutes later, the bridge sound-powered phone talker suddenly made the report, "Man overboard, starboard side." The phone talker added, "The captain says Latham is over the side."

Immediately, the OOD ordered the sounding of the emergency signal on the ship's whistle. Next, the Boatswain's Mate of the Watch (BMOW) began announcing over the 1MC: "Man overboard, starboard side, Man overboard, starboard side, this is not a drill, this is not a drill. Man the rescue stations, muster the boat crew."

Since I had the conn, I gave the order to the helmsman, "Right full rudder." Next, I ordered the lee helmsman, "Engine ahead full." Being well-versed in man-overboard recovery methods, I began maneuvering to execute the Anderson turn. Within moments, the captain arrived on the bridge.

"Chief, do you have the conn?" he asked me.

"Yes, Captain, I do. Do you want the conn, sir?" I replied.

He looked at me and said, "No, keep the conn. Let's go pick this son of a bitch up."

I moved to the starboard bridge wing, taking a position so that I could monitor our heading on the gyrocompass. Once our heading reached 240 degrees from our original course, I commanded the helmsman, "Rudder amidships, steady as you go." I quickly determined the wind direction based on the smoke drifting from the smoke floats in the water. Fortunately, the smoke floats were close to Latham, marking his position. Next, I ordered the lee helmsman, "Engine ahead two-thirds," to begin slowing the ship's speed.

While maneuvering the ship, the captain told me and the OOD, "There I was, just hooked my first fish, and what do I see? Latham, floating by with one arm through a life ring buoy. The son of a bitch waved at me. Just like he was taught in boot camp, he had his boondockers tied around his neck."

"Anyone know what division Latham's in?" the captain asked everyone on the bridge.

The bridge phone talker answered, "Seaman Apprentice Latham is mess cooking."

"You mean Seaman Recruit Latham," the captain replied. Next, he addressed the BMOW, "Pass the word for MA1 Jensky to report to the bridge."

The boatswain's mate responded, "Aye, captain." Within seconds, he announced over the 1MC: "MA1 Jensky, lay to the bridge."

With some advice from the captain, I continued to slow the ship's engine and give rudder commands to the helmsman, maneuvering the ship so Latham was downwind from us. I was able to stop the ship and get it dead in the water, with Latham just forward of midships on the starboard side, about 30 feet away. Silently, I felt pleased with my ship maneuvering ability. Soon, Latham gave in and grabbed onto one of the life ring buoys with a lifeline thrown from the deck. I watched as the deck crew pulled him to the ship's side, and then a horse collar was lowered to him from the J-bar davit. Latham placed the horse collar over his head and then around his chest, and the crew hoisted him back on board. Within moments, the phone talker reported, "Deck reports Latham is safely back on board."

The captain turned to me and said, "Chief, two things. First, great ship handling job. It was like watching a pro. Second, get a watch relief. I want you to ensure that MA1 Jensky knows what he is doing. I want Latham on report right now. Get with Senior Chief Macrillo and have him convene a disciplinary review board (DRB), then take him to the XO so it's all legal. I'm holding captain's mast on that son of a bitch before lunch. Do you understand me?"

What else could be said? I answered, "Yes, Captain, I'll take care of it."

By then, MA1 Jensky had arrived on the bridge. I motioned for him to join me on the bridge wing. My first question for him was where Latham was at that moment. He replied that Latham was in sick bay with Doc Stein. I quickly outlined for Jensky what the captain had ordered. Then I instructed him to have one of the other MAAs always stay with Latham. Next, I instructed him to contact Senior Chief Holloway, the Chief Master-at-Arms, and relay the same information to him. Finally, I explained that the chiefs would convene DRB in the Chiefs Mess as soon as possible.

After one of our junior officers relieved me, I went below and found Jensky with Mick and Gene in the ship's office. I went over everything with Mick and Gene to ensure Jensky had informed them correctly. Gene said to me, "We'll be ready to hold DRB in about 10 minutes. Can you round up some of the other chiefs?"

"I'll take care of it," I told Gene.

The offense committed by Latham was a violation of Article 87 of the Uniform Code of Military Justice (UCMJ): "Jumping from a vessel into the water." Additionally, he was charged with a violation of Article 134 General Article, specifically: "All disorders and neglects to the prejudice of good order and discipline in the armed forces, all conduct of a nature to bring discredit upon the armed forces, and crimes and offenses not capital, of which persons subject to this chapter may be guilty."

As I entered the Chiefs Mess, I saw two other chiefs present. I asked if they could spare a few minutes for a DRB and explained the situation, assuring them it wouldn't take long. Within a few minutes, Gene, Mick, and MA1 Jensky arrived with Latham.

Gene chaired the DRB and read to Latham the charges of violations of the UCMJ against him. Then he asked Latham if he had anything to say. The kid stood there, still wearing his wet T-shirt and dungarees. I'll never forget the thick white cotton socks the kid wore, which slid down to where they were about halfway off.

Finally, Latham spoke, "Chiefs, I'm crazy; because I'm crazy, you need to let me get off the ship."

Gene asked Latham, "Is that all you have to say for yourself? Latham, do you understand how stupid and dangerous the stunt you pulled was? Do you know there's always the chance we would have never found you, and you would have died?" Latham just nodded and didn't speak.

Lastly, Gene said, "This is getting us nowhere. You're going straight to the XO; from there, you're going to captain's mast. Dismissed."

Gene told Jensky, "Get this man to the passageway outside the XO's stateroom; we'll be up in a few minutes with the paperwork."

The XO's inquiry was fast, and within minutes, we all gathered in the vestibule outside the captain's cabin. One of the ship's MAAs had set up the podium for the captain. I knocked on the captain's door, opened it, and said, "Captain, we're ready for you."

Captain's mast was brief. Captain Macdonald read the charges to Latham and then asked, "Latham, do you have anything to say for yourself?"

Latham reiterated the same statement he made at DRB and to the XO. "Captain, I'm crazy, and because I'm crazy, you need to let me get off your ship." Doc Stein stood off to one side of the vestibule.

The captain turned to him and inquired, "Chief Stein, I take it you evaluated Latham? In your opinion, is he crazy?"

"Captain, based on my interview, he is not crazy. He is distraught and probably under some level of self-induced stress, but mentally he's fit," Doc replied.

The captain returned to Latham. "Seaman Apprentice Latham, I find you guilty of violating Article 87 of the UCMJ: Jumping from a vessel into the water. I am reducing you to pay grade E-1, seaman recruit, and I fine you one-half month's pay for three months." The captain continued, "I also find you guilty of violating Article 134 of the UCMJ. Disorder and neglect to the prejudice of good order and discipline. I'm awarding you 45 days of extra duty."

The captain ordered, "MA1 Jensky take this man and get him out of my sight." With that, the captain turned, opened his cabin door, stepped inside, and closed the door. Captain's mast was over.

I'm sure everyone but Latham understood how much his intentional jump off the ship affected the captain. From the captain's perspective, one of his crew members, for whom he is responsible, could have easily lost his life. The Navy would have held the captain accountable if Latham had been lost at sea. That is the weight one must bear when commanding a Navy vessel.

Latham had been in the Navy Reserves, where he was required to participate in mandatory drills. Reservists must attend drills one weekend each month and report for two weeks of active duty for training each year. Latham refused to attend his drills the previous year and did not report for active duty. According to regulations, the penalty for reservists who fail to fulfill these obligations is two years of mandatory active duty. As a result, Latham ended up on board.

Latham had just reported on board the week before, while the ship was in Bahrain. Being an undesignated seaman apprentice, he was assigned to First Division, the deck force. Being new, the BM1 sent him to the mess decks for a 90-day tour of mess cooking.

Like many mess cooks, Latham was assigned to work in the scullery. As discussed earlier, working in the scullery is regarded as the worst mess cook assignment a sailor can receive. Enter Latham, a guy who didn't want to be here, much less be in the Navy. It is surmised that Latham had been told about Seaman Haney jumping overboard and how he got off the ship. On hearing about Haney, Latham was gullible enough to jump off the ship, believing he had found a way out.

After another five days of patrolling, we departed our OPAREA once more, heading for Sitrah Anchorage. That night, we received a message from COMIDEASTFOR with some news. We were scheduled for a four-day port visit in Karachi, Pakistan, during the second week of September. This still left us with more than three weeks before we would take a break from being in the Persian Gulf.

That night, I found time to write a letter to Jan for the outgoing mail the following day. At my locker, I took out Angie's latest letter, stared at the envelope for several seconds, and then opened it. I felt a twinge of anxiety as I read what she had written. She made it clear that she wasn't giving up on me. At least not yet. Her idea was that once I returned, we could discuss it. She would respect my decision if I still felt the same after a face-to-face conversation. She closed by saying that unless I had a change of heart, she didn't expect me to write her back. I folded her letter and placed it back in the envelope. Once again, silently, I was saying, "Shit, and shit again."

The weeks felt like they were dragging on. The heat and discomfort of the Persian Gulf in August were just as oppressive as they had been in July. The only real difference was that we had started to acclimate to the constant heat, humidity, and grime from the desert dust. Wearing sweat-soaked uniforms had become routine. The side effects from the weekly malaria tablets had lessened for many. Personally, my upset stomach and diarrhea now lasted only about a day instead of two or three. September couldn't come soon enough.

Finally, on Sunday, September 5, we left Sitrah Anchorage. This departure was different from the rest. We weren't headed for the OPAREA. Instead, we were going to the Strait of Hormuz, the Gulf of Oman, and then to Karachi, Pakistan. The transit to Karachi would take two days from Sitrah Anchorage.

Early in the morning on September 7, we began our approach to Karachi from the west, navigating offshore from the south coast of Pakistan. I had set the navigation detail. Much like the Persian Gulf, a continuous haze makes visual navigation difficult. I was fixing the ship's position by radar bearings and ranges to the coast. Finally, I recognized Cape Monze on radar, and soon we sighted Cape Monze lighthouse visually. Cape Monze is the western extremity of a sloping headland, which rises to a pointed summit.

We needed to time our arrival outside Karachi's harbor entrance to coincide with the tidal currents as they begin to flood towards land. This is due to heavy rollers and sea swells on the edge of the flats near the harbor entrance.

As we approached Manora Point, we spotted the light on the point at the harbor entrance. I advised the captain and OOD to set the Sea and Anchor detail for entering port. The captain used the VHF-FM radiotelephone to contact the Karachi pilot station. The pilot station responded immediately, saying they could see our ship visually and that the pilot boat was en route to us.

Soon, the pilot boat was alongside, and several minutes later, the pilot was on the bridge. There were lighted front and rear navigation leading marks indicating the center of the channel for entering the harbor. By the time the pilot arrived on the bridge, I had positioned the ship to enter directly into the channel. It was a short transit entering the harbor; within 20 minutes, we were docking at our assigned berth in Karachi's Lower Harbor.

About an hour after we docked, representatives from the U.S. Consulate came on board and met with the officers and chiefs in the wardroom. Their purpose was to welcome the ship to Karachi and provide a port briefing, informing us about the city, the sights, and the activities the crew could enjoy. They brought a variety of street maps and brochures for the crew.

The personnel from the consulate also warned that Karachi can be a violent and dangerous city. There are ethnic tensions, particularly between the Mohajir community (Muslim refugees who migrated from India) and other ethnic groups, including Sindhis, Pashtuns, and Punjabis. Political violence and clashes occur between rival political parties, especially involving the Mohajir community. Near the end of the briefing, it was recommended to the captain that crew liberty should expire well before midnight. The message was clear: In daylight, Karachi was safe; after sunset, Karachi was not safe.

It would be maximum liberty for the crew. Other than for the duty sections, there was to be no ship's work. The XO decided that liberty expired on board at 2200. To my surprise, I didn't hear of anyone unhappy about not having overnight liberty. This was the first real liberty port for the crew in a long time; I believe they were just happy to get away from the ship for a while.

Currency exchange vendors set up on the mess decks, enabling crew members to exchange their U.S. dollars for Pakistani Rupees at a fair rate. One benefit of our deployment thus far was that, aside from Bahrain, we hadn't had many chances to spend our money. I exchanged about $350 for roughly 5,740 Pakistani Rupees in preparation for going on liberty. Fortunately, the Pakistani Rupee is weak compared to the U.S. dollar, with $1 equivalent to about 16.5 Pakistani Rupees (PKR) at the time.

That afternoon, I tagged along with Mike Franklin and two of our junior QMs. The four of us found a taxi driver who agreed to the price we offered to take us to Saddar Town in Karachi. We were about to experience driving in Karachi. The taxi ride from the port to the town border was almost terrifying. Taxis are small, compact cars whose drivers know three speeds: Stop, fast, and faster. The first main road outside the port was Shahrah-e-Iran Road. We shared the road with buses, cars, other taxis, trucks, donkey-drawn carts, people-drawn carts, camel-drawn carts, and pedestrians. I caught a glimpse of a sign that read, "Two Swords Roundabout," and holy crap, we all found something to hold on to as our driver accelerated the taxi into the roundabout at full speed.

To distract myself from the worry that we might crash into something or someone, I focused on observing the buildings and walls along the road. The road was primarily lined with walls and propped against them were long rows of what appeared to be wooden bed frames, with webbing strung between the supports. I asked the driver if they were indeed beds. He gestured dismissively and, sounding disgusted, replied, "Slum people and beggars live here."

We were currently on Khayaban-e-Jobal Road. Our driver constantly swerved to avoid hitting other vehicles, carts, or pedestrians. I was struck by the contrast between the attractive buildings peeking over the walls, the street beggars, and the impoverished individuals living alongside the road. Another sign read, "Three Swords Roundabout." Once again, the driver accelerated, and we entered the large roundabout. I counted at least five near-misses before we exited onto the next road.

Soon, our driver pulled up and stopped his taxi along the street. He pointed down a side street and said, "Bohri Bazar is down that street."

I got out, feeling relieved to be alive, and paid the driver 35 PKR. For just a little over $2, the four of us enjoyed a 20-minute thrill ride that few carnival rides can match. I gazed around the streets of Karachi, unaware that I was about to encounter experiences unlike any I've had before.

CHAPTER 8

CROSSING THE LINE

Saddar Town is home to many of Karachi's oldest neighborhoods, filled with lively markets, century-old buildings, and narrow, crowded streets. We quickly found many things here that couldn't be found elsewhere. At Bohri Bazar, shops sell almost everything imaginable. You can find furniture, Persian rugs, wood artwork, brass art, and craft items of all kinds.

The people working in the shops were mostly Pakistani or Indian. I sensed that they were courteous, gentle, hardworking, and honest. Each shop owner or worker patiently displayed and explained their goods. The prices are a bit inflated but not outrageous, allowing some room to haggle. As is common everywhere here, haggling is expected.

We soon discovered that if one is a fan of nautical items, there is shop after shop selling salvaged ship equipment. The selection is endless: brass helm wheels, engine order telegraphs, portholes, and ship bells. No doubt, most of the items in these shops come from the ship-breaking scrap yard nearby Gadani Beach.

One street is lined with many shops selling handcrafted wooden figures, statues, and carvings. Most offer beautiful furniture with carved and brass-inlaid designs. At one shop in particular, we were amazed by the craftsmanship and beauty of the products made right in the alleyway behind the shop. The shop owner invited us outside to watch his craftsmen at work.

I call them craftsmen, but they were really a group of teenage boys and women. Some of the boys sat in the dirt with their projects on their laps, using small wood chisels and mallets to carve detailed designs into the wood. Others worked with tiny chisels and mallets, making small grooves to inlay brass strands as they went. It was fascinating to watch them work so quickly and skillfully.

There were several small fires with steel tripods. To create the brass strands for inlaying, brass washers were suspended on wires over the fires to soften them. When ready, one boy used pliers to remove each hot brass washer and moved it to a small anvil. He shaped each hot brass washer into a long, thin strand at the anvil using a small hammer.

Several women were busy preparing the basic ingredients for wood stains. They chewed betel nuts and other leaves, then spat the mixture into old coffee cans. Their smiles showed red-stained teeth and mouths, clearly indicating they were chewing betel nuts.

The production assembly line was impressive. When I returned to the shop, I found a beautiful matching coffee table, two end tables, and a small chest of drawers. I negotiated a great deal with the shop owner and bought them for 1,900 PKR, which was about $115. As a kind gesture, the shop owner also gave me a beautifully hand-carved camel for my son.

The shop owner insisted he would deliver my purchased items to the ship that evening. I usually wouldn't trust many people in different countries, but I had no hesitation with these folks here. The four of us browsed several more shops in various parts of Bohri Bazar until late afternoon. I thought it was best to take a taxi and return to the ship before dark.

Once back on the same street where the first taxi had dropped us off, I negotiated the fare with a taxi driver to take us to the ship. The four of us piled into the small cab, and the driver took off. His driving was much like that of the earlier taxi driver. We all found something to hold onto as the driver weaved in and out of traffic at the fastest speeds he could manage. When he stopped at the Lower Harbor near the ship, we were all happy to get out of the taxi.

After the short walk back to the ship, we went on board. The quarterdeck OOD told me that some items had been delivered for me and pointed to my packages sitting on the deck away from the quarterdeck area. I was pleased that the wood shop owner had kept his word. The shop owner had carefully wrapped each piece in heavy paper, secured it with twine, and wrote "Mr. George" on each package.

Fortunately, our division had a storeroom below decks where we stored excess navigation charts, publications, and other equipment that couldn't fit on the bridge or in the chartroom. I took my newly acquired items down to the storeroom and found space in the overhead above-the-top shelves to secure everything I purchased.

Over the next two days, Mike Franklin, Jamie, and I made several trips to Saddar Town, where we all bought various items. Along with the shops, there are other attractions around Bohri Bazar. In a small park, we came across a group of Indians with an elephant and several camels. They offered rides on both the elephant and the camels for a small fee. I chose to try the elephant since I had never ridden one before.

On the elephant's back, a large pad with a bench seat was secured using ropes that functioned like cinches, pulled tight under and around the elephant's girth. A makeshift ladder hung down from one side. Franklin climbed on board first, followed by me. The handler sat at the front section of the pad, resting his feet on the elephant's head. And off we went! It was a pretty cool 15-minute experience.

My last day in Karachi was a duty day, marking the end of my visit. While many people noted the city's lack of nightlife, its uniqueness somewhat made up for this. Although I wouldn't consider Karachi a must-visit destination for a return trip, my experiences there will definitely remain among the most memorable.

The next morning, we left Karachi's Lower Harbor, and within minutes, we passed the harbor's breakwater and entered the Arabian Sea, heading toward the Gulf of Oman. It was back to the Persian Gulf for us. How much longer, no one knew for sure. We knew the ship was scheduled to return to Mayport sometime in late November. The thing about deployments on surface combatant ships is that there are no guarantees about when you will go home. It's just part of Navy life; you accept it or hate it. Either way, your feelings about it don't matter anyway.

The visit to Karachi offered a brief break from the intense heat and dust of the Persian Gulf. The next day, we sailed through the Strait of Hormuz. We steered a northeasterly course at the end of the first leg into the strait near Didamar, where the island shimmered in the desert dust, reflecting rays of the morning sun. We then adjusted to a southwesterly course through the Strait of Hormuz and later turned westerly into the Gulf, passing among the islands southwest of Jazireh-ye Qeshm (Iran).

By midday, we reached our station in the OPAREA and started the routine patrol of our 55 square miles of Gulf waters, just like we had all summer. Being near mid-September doesn't change the weather here; it stays as hot and dusty as it was in July and August.

Our time in the Middle East had been challenging for the ship's engineering department. As a vessel with a steam propulsion system, our boilers must always remain lit and operational, even when we're in port. The enlisted engineering ratings, known as "snipes," have maintained a continuous watch in the hot boiler room and the main engine room called "Main Control." One savior for the snipes in main control is that the propulsion controls and auxiliary systems are operated or monitored from an air-conditioned booth. But all other work is carried out in the hot environment of the engineering spaces.

In engineering, snipes follow heat stress safety measures. There are parameters based on the Wet-Bulb Globe Temperature (WBGT) that specify the maximum duration individuals can be in hot environments, with durations varying depending on the work task.

Every hour, the QMOW calls 'main control' to request two temperature readings: the seawater injection temperature and WBGT, which are recorded in the ship's deck log. The WBGT is measured in the hottest areas of the boiler and engine rooms. It's not uncommon for the WBGT to reach 125 degrees Fahrenheit or higher.

Few people on the bridge felt much empathy for the snipes, as the air temperatures were usually equal to or even higher than those in the engineering spaces. One night, while I was standing watch on the bridge, Mick, the senior chief machinist mate, came up to discuss a matter with me and take a look around. He didn't stay long, and his parting comment was, "I'm going back to main control, where it's cooler."

After spending six days in the OPAREA, it was time to transit to Sitrah Anchorage to refuel and resupply. The next morning, after we anchored, the usual process of having fuel and supply barges come alongside began. Everyone was pleased that the supply barge also delivered mail from home. I was pleased to receive three letters from Jan, and I felt relieved that there was no mail from Angie.

From Jan's letters, I was relieved to learn that she was now in Florida. She and Mitch moved as planned in late August. She managed everything with the moving company, and our household items were in storage. To my surprise, my mother also drove to Florida with them. She settled into a furnished apartment in Atlantic Beach, which she said she liked and is close to Mitch's school. She also secured what she believed to be a good job with an architecture firm in Jacksonville Beach.

The apartment was just temporary housing until I returned home. Once home, we would look for more permanent accommodations. I was happy that my family was now safely in Florida. Most importantly, Jan had set up telephone service, so I now had our phone number. Hopefully, I would find a place to call home soon.

On that same day, we received news from MIDEASTFOR. On October 5, we would depart the Persian Gulf. However, we weren't heading home yet; our next stop was Mombasa, Kenya. Mombasa is located at the latitude coordinate of 4° 04.0' South, about 244 miles south of the equator. This means we would cross the equator from north to south on our way to Mombasa. For me, this journey meant I would finally shed my pollywog status and become a shellback. In the chartroom, I quickly calculated that we would "cross the line" on October 11, just one day before arriving in Mombasa.

For many sailors, becoming a shellback is a significant milestone. A sailor who has crossed the equator is initiated into the "Ancient Order of Shellbacks." After participating in the "Crossing the Line" ceremony and initiation, they have joined the ancient order. On Navy ships, news spreads fast. Excitement grew among the shellbacks in the crew at the thought of initiating their pollywogs.

Besides the news about crossing the equator, another boost for the crew's spirits was that there were only two more weeks until we left the Persian Gulf. That evening, we weighed anchor and departed from Sitrah

Anchorage heading for the OPAREA. Now, we knew when this part of the deployment would end and the next part would begin.

The next morning, we went back to the OPAREA and started our patrol. The week felt slow. When Franklin and I weren't on watch, we worked on the passage plan to Mombasa. Luckily, we had the charts and publications we needed. Overall, everyone's mood seemed light and cheerful.

I was growing more anxious for several reasons. Soon, it would have been nine months since I said goodbye to Jan and Mitch. By the time the ship returned to Mayport, over 10 months would have passed. I missed them deeply, and my feelings grew stronger as the deployment continued. I also had a strong gut feeling that Angie wasn't done with me yet, which worried me. One skill I've developed over the years is the ability to compartmentalize my emotions. It's an essential skill because it helps me function at the levels I need to maintain.

Several days later, we returned to Sitrah Anchorage for regular refueling and resupply operations. Once again, the ship received mail, and I was delighted to receive letters from Jan. Everything seemed to be going well for her and Mitch. She enjoys Florida, and Mitch does too. For me, November couldn't come soon enough.

That evening, we weighed anchor and returned to the OPAREA for our final patrol. The next day, upon arrival, we started the routine that had become all too familiar. No one seemed to mind, as the end was near. The heat and the constant dust blowing off the desert no longer bothered us. After four days of operations, we returned to Sitrah Anchorage one last time.

Today, we would top off the fuel to full capacity. From Sitrah, it's over 3,100 nautical miles to Mombasa, which meant eight days of steaming to arrive by October 12. After refueling, the supply barge came alongside for the final load. Later, I noticed that very little garbage was loaded onto the barge. Some mail was delivered, but I didn't receive any letters from home. By late afternoon, we were ready to go.

We weighed anchor for the last time at Sitrah. Instead of the OPAREA being the destination, we were heading for the Strait of Hormuz. The next morning, on October 5, after transiting the Strait of Hormuz and entering the Gulf of Oman, we bid farewell to the Persian Gulf. From the Gulf of Oman, our route would take us to the Arabian Sea and the Indian Ocean.

Everyone noticed some changes on the second day out in the Arabian Sea. October marks the transition between the summer and winter monsoon seasons, resulting in light and variable winds. During the day, air temperatures are around 85 degrees Fahrenheit, cooling to the high 70s at night. The sea water temperature is cooler, in the low 80s. This created a more comfortable environment for everyone on the bridge and those working on the deck.

As the crew prepared to cross the equator, they split into two groups: shellbacks and the pollywogs. The shellbacks were busy organizing the initiation ceremony for crossing the line, while the pollywogs worked on finding ways to disrupt the shellbacks' plans and activities. Each day, their efforts grew more coordinated. Since the captain was a shellback, very few resources were off-limits to their group.

Three days from Mombasa was Pollywog Day. It was a day for pollywogs to prank and outsmart shellbacks. Any shellback was fair game, from shaving cream pies in the face as they turn a corner in a passageway to splashing water on them when they pass through a door. No prank idea was off-limits as long as personal injury was avoided. The day could be seen as pollywog preemptive strikes against shellbacks before they took action.

That evening, all pollywogs received written subpoenas ordering them to appear "In the Highest Court of the Raging Main" on October 11, before "The Royal Court of Neptunus Rex."

Two days out from Mombasa, that afternoon, the "Pollywog Beauty" contest was held on the flight deck. The winner of the contest does not have to go through the entire initiation process but will sit in a place of honor with the Royal Court. The catch is that contestants must dress in drag and compete in a talent competition. Surprisingly, there were quite a few contestants.

The same evening, the Plan of the Day was handed out. Besides the detailed crossing plan, it also described the day's uniform for pollywogs. For chief petty officers, the uniform is, "A Skivvy shirt with 'PW' printed on the back, khaki trousers inside out and backward, no belt, Skivvy shorts worn over trousers, khaki hat cover (no frame), tennis shoes or old shoes."

One day out from Mombasa, the ship crossed the equator during predawn. The day of reckoning began at 0530, as all pollywogs were gathered up and herded by the shellbacks to the forecastle. From then on, all shellbacks were addressed as "Most honorable shellback." No pollywog was allowed to speak unless spoken to by a "trusty shellback."

Once we reached the forecastle, the shellbacks organized us into rows facing the bow. On command, we all dropped to our hands and knees. At 0600, Neptunus Rex announced over the 1MC that the cleansing of the filthy and slimy pollywogs was to begin. This process involved washing everyone with seawater from pressurized fire hoses. The cleansing lasted at least 20 minutes until the shellbacks were satisfied that everyone was clean, subdued, and compliant.

The next step was to get all of the pollywogs from the forecastle aft to the flight deck. Walking was not permitted. Movement was achieved by crawling on the non-skid decks or crab walking on hands and feet. Along the way, each of us was served our ceremonial breakfast, a dead fish, which we must carry clenched in our teeth. I chose crab walking and wore a pair of flip-flops on my hands as protection from the non-skid.

On the flight deck, the initiation began. First, you went through the enclosed canvas garbage chute filled with rotting garbage and who knows what else. Upon exiting the garbage chute, you had to be cleansed again with a fire hose. Then, onto the Royal Doctor, where you were examined to determine your ability to tell the truth in preparation for appearing before the Royal Court and Neptunus Rex. Of course, the visit to the Royal Doctor involved some doses of truth serum. Next you went to the Royal Baby, the fattest shellback with, I think, peanut butter and jelly smeared all over his bare belly. Before moving on, you had to kiss the Royal Baby's belly and then proceed to appear before the Royal Court and Neptunus Rex.

You could be taken to the stockade for a perceived infraction at any moment. While in the stockade, you might be pelted with eggs or half-rotten vegetables. Naturally, after some time in the stockade, you were then cleaned off with a fire hose and seen again by the Royal Doctor.

Finally, once the Royal Baby made a decision, you were ordered to appear before the Royal Court. The Royal Scribe read the list of offenses you were charged with and asks how you pled to each one: "Guilty or Not Guilty." Anyone foolish enough to plead "Not Guilty" might find themselves starting over at the garbage chute.

I pled guilty to each charge and repeated the same statement each time: "The truth serum I have consumed does not allow me to lie."

Finally, the judge said, "On behalf of Neptunus Rex and this Royal Court, we believe you understand the solemn mysteries of the deep, and from this day forward, you belong to the ancient order of shellbacks." It was over; I was finally a "trusty shellback."

Overall, the crossing-the-line initiation wasn't a big deal. It felt mild compared to my CPO initiation. It was a fun day for everyone involved. By noon, the ship was cleared of almost all of the lowly pollywogs.

The shellback initiation is entirely voluntary. I think we had two crew members who chose not to participate. It's not a big deal if someone decides to opt out. The only rule is that you cannot watch or take part in the celebration cookout.

I overheard some guys talking about their friend who had opted out. One sailor put it like this, "He's still my friend that won't change, but now I know he's a pussy, and he knows everyone knows he's a pussy." That's what friendship among sailors looks like.

After clearing the flight deck of debris from the initiation activities, the cooks started setting up the barbecue grills and tables. Soon, hamburgers, sausages, and hot dogs sizzled on the grill. The usual fare included baked beans, potato salad, and condiments. Like many others, I went below decks to shower and change, keeping only my flip-flops. I threw away everything else I wore that morning. Back on the flight deck, everyone seemed to be in good spirits, and why not? They were now shellbacks. We could all look forward to arriving in Mombasa tomorrow.

Kenya is situated on the east coast of Africa. Somalia borders it to the north, and Tanzania lies to the south. Mombasa, Kenya's main port, also serves as Uganda's primary sea outlet, as Uganda is landlocked.

The next morning, we began our approach to Mombasa. The city of Mombasa is actually an island of coral outcrops, measuring about 1.3 by 1.9 miles. The Mombasa pilot boat met us and came alongside about 2 miles from the entrance. We proceeded into the port once the pilot was on the bridge. From a navigational perspective, entering Mombasa is not complex, with few hazards to navigation. Once the ship is safely through the break in the offshore reef, it is just a short distance to the harbor on the Likoni River. Within about 30 minutes, the ship was moored at our assigned berth in Kilindini Harbor.

Kilindini Harbor is located very close to the old town area of the city. From our berth, we could see the Likoni Floating Bridge, a pedestrian bridge crossing the channel. The bridge links Mombasa Island to Likoni on the opposite side of the river. Mombasa connects to the mainland via the Makupa Causeway to the northwest, the Nyali Bridge to the east, and the Likoni Ferry to the south.

Shortly after docking, personnel from the U.S. Embassy boarded to give a port briefing to the officers and chiefs in the wardroom. The briefing covered many activities and sights to see in Mombasa. Mombasa offers nightlife, casinos, and shopping. Additionally, safaris are available at Tsavo East National Park, a short drive from the city. Another attraction is Nyali Beach, located just northeast of the city.

Mombasa's culture combines influences from Arab, Portuguese, British, and Swahili traditions. Part of the briefing included information about the Maasai: Guardians of the African Plains. Embassy representatives explained that it is common to see Maasai dressed in brightly colored shuka cloth or African blankets, often carrying a spear. They stressed that Maasai warriors still command attention with their presence.

The only downside of the embassy port briefing was the warning that certain parts of old town Mombasa are best avoided late at night. Street gangs are prevalent; they rob people of everything they have, even their clothing. The solution is simple: Don't walk through those areas, as cabs and taxis are cheap and convenient at all hours.

Later, currency exchange vendors boarded and set up on the mess decks. I exchanged $350 for 4,200 Kenyan shillings. For me, it would only be three days of liberty in Mombasa. Today's arrival date was October 12, and I had the duty. Being here with four duty sections for five days meant I would have duty again on the last day. Having the duty the first night in a new port wasn't all bad. The next day, you could get the scoop on the best places to go and the spots to avoid from those who went on liberty the night before.

I wasn't interested in going on a safari. I was more focused on shopping and relaxing at Mombasa's nightclubs. The next morning, Jamie, Manny, and I left the ship to go into town and do some shopping.

We spent most of the day wandering through the streets of Mombasa, browsing shops, stopping at a café for lunch, and making several stops for cold beers. That afternoon, I discovered a new favorite called Tusker Beer Lager. It's the best beer I've ever had, and that's saying a lot. When poured into a glass, the beer displayed a straw-yellow color, a brief foamy white head, and a distinctive malt and hoppy flavor.

Apparently, I had quickly developed an affinity for Tusker. That afternoon, we spent some time exploring more local shops. I found a set of items I had to buy: twelve Tusker glass lager mugs featuring the Tusker African elephant logo. The shop owner carefully wrapped and packed the mugs in a sturdy cardboard box. So, I carefully carried my box of glass mugs for the rest of the afternoon.

Later that afternoon, we brought our purchases onto the ship. While on board, I passed by the mess decks, where a vendor was taking orders for Tusker Beer Lager. The supply officer was nearby, so I approached him and asked about buying Tusker. He explained that the captain and XO quickly developed a liking for Tusker, and they thought it was only fair that if they were going to take some home, the crew should have the same opportunity. Why not? I went to the vendor's table, filled out the form, ordered five cases of Tusker, and paid for them.

After reviewing my available cash, I realized I might need to scale back some of my plans for Mombasa, since I only had about $250 left to spend. We left the ship and headed back to town, quickly finding a bar that matched our tastes. Once seated with an ice-cold Tusker, Jamie mentioned a casino on Nyali Beach he wanted to visit later. I agreed we should go, but I wanted a few more rounds and dinner first.

Later, we found a taxi and headed out of town, crossing the Nyali Bridge. Soon, we arrived and stopped at the Florida Casino. Inside the casino, I was struck by its beauty. Clearly, it's designed to attract wealthy Europeans vacationing there. Through the windows behind the bar, the beach and the Indian Ocean are visible. After a few more rounds of Tuskers, Jamie and Manny wanted to try their luck at the blackjack and roulette tables. I'm not much of a gambler, but I enjoy playing slot machines. I told them to go ahead, and I would be over by the slot machine area.

I went to the cashier window and paid 360 shillings ($30) for a small container of tokens. After scanning the various slots, I found one I liked, facing a window that looked out onto the moonlit beach. I had barely settled into my seat when a waitress approached to take my drink order. Of course, I ordered a Tusker.

I started playing the machine, inserting one token after another, but nothing happened—no winnings. I glanced at my container of tokens; there were about seven left. With a sigh of resignation, I put in one more token and pulled the lever. Expecting nothing, I realized I'd hit some winning combination, as about a dozen tokens dropped into the tray.

Scooping my winnings into my container, I inserted another token, pulled the lever, and nothing happened. I put in the next token and pulled the lever: another winning combination! This time, about two dozen tokens dropped into the tray. I kept playing. Every second or third pull of the lever seemed to result in a winning combination and a payout. Soon, my small container was full. I ordered another Tusker from the waitress and asked if I could get a larger container. She returned moments later with several containers.

I kept playing the machine, and the same pattern continued with a winning combination and payout every second or third pull of the lever. The waitress brought me more containers. After about another hour, six or seven containers, filled to the brim with tokens, were scattered around with several sitting on another chair I had pulled up beside me.

Around that time, a man in a tuxedo came over and introduced himself as the floor manager. Very politely, he said, "Sir, this machine is malfunctioning. I must ask you to move to another machine."

I looked at him and said, "But I'm winning, I shouldn't have to move."

"But I must insist. You may keep your winnings," he replied, smiling.

I noticed two large, serious-looking Black men standing about five feet behind the manager. These two guys decided for me, and I said, "Okay, no problem."

The manager turned to one of the large men, who handed him a small tray of poker chips. The manager then came back to me, offering the poker chips while saying, "Sir, thank you for your cooperation. Please accept these chips as a token of our appreciation; perhaps you would like to try your luck at one of the tables." I accepted the poker chips and decided it was time to cash in. I had no idea how much I had actually won.

Standing there, I told the manager I wanted to cash in. He directed the two big men to help me carry my containers to the cashier window. The clerk at the window started pouring my tokens into a machine, keeping a tally on a slip of paper. After counting all the tokens, I slid the tray of poker chips to him to cash in.

The clerk behind the window asked, "What notes would you like?" I wasn't sure what he meant. He saw I was confused and said, "Would you like to be paid with 100, 200, or 500 shilling notes?"

I understood and, almost jokingly, replied, "How about a mix of 100, 200, and 500 shilling notes?" He nodded in understanding and began counting stacks of shilling notes on the countertop.

When he finished counting, he said, "There you are, sir, 14,820 shillings." He then placed the shilling notes in an envelope and slid it across the counter. I was stunned; my mental math indicated that about $1,235 was in the envelope. I thanked him and walked away, folding the envelope and putting it in the front pocket of my jeans as I headed back to the bar.

Holy crap, in less than an hour and a half, while drinking about six Tuskers, I turned $30 into over $1,200. I guess there was no need to rein in my spending plans for Mombasa anymore. After all, I now had more money than I did when I arrived here.

Back at the bar, Jamie and Manny joined me later. Jamie was happy he'd won about $200 at the blackjack table. Manny, not doing so well, said he'd lost around $150 at the roulette table. I shared news about my winnings at the slot machine and what happened.

Jamie immediately said, "No way, you're full of bullshit."

I pulled the envelope out of my pocket, stuffed with shilling notes, and placed it on the bar while. "No bullshit."

"You're buying beers for the rest of the night," Manny said.

Mombasa is a maximum liberty port, meaning you don't need to be on board unless you have duty. After many more Tuskers, it was around 0400. Fortunately, the casino also has a hotel. We asked the bartender about the rooms. He nodded and stepped away from the bar. After several minutes, he returned with a room key for me and one for Jamie.

Looking at me, the bartender said, "The manager told me since you were a gentleman earlier, your room is comped (free)." He turned to Jamie and said, "Your room is a double; if you two don't mind sharing, it's a special rate for our American friends for 300 shillings ($25)."

After several rounds, we left the bar and went to our rooms. Mine was excellent, spacious, and decorated with luxurious touches. The bathroom was fully stocked with toiletries. I undressed and got into the king-sized bed, and within minutes, I was out like a light.

When I finally woke up, I checked my watch, and it was already past noon. I had slept deeply, better than I had in months. To my surprise, my hangover was minimal and manageable. In the bathroom, I found a robe and put it on. A card on the table provided instructions for calling room service for the free breakfast. I called room service and ordered breakfast with coffee and juice. Within five minutes, there was a knock on the door. I answered to find a waiter standing there with a tray. I motioned for him to come in, and he set the tray on a table. Then he opened the window blinds, revealing a glass door leading to an outside balcony.

"Sir, do you want breakfast on the balcony?" he asked.

"Yes," I replied.

He moved the tray to the balcony table and asked if I needed anything else. I shook my head no and handed him a 50-shilling note. What a life! The balcony overlooked Nyali Beach and the ocean. I sat for a long time, sipping coffee and orange juice while soaking in the stunning view. I felt happy and content; so far, Mombasa had been good to me.

Later, after showering and dressing, I went to Jamie and Manny's room and knocked on the door. There was no answer. Downstairs at the front desk, I checked out of my room. Then, I headed to the restaurant near the casino entrance and found them eating a late lunch. Manny had found out that the casino had a bar on the beachfront, which helped us decide how to spend the rest of the afternoon. We also agreed that after dinner, we would go back to the ship to change clothes. Jamie had heard about some nightclubs that sounded like fun.

That afternoon, we went to sit on the beach. We grabbed some beach chairs we found and settled in with a bucket of cold Tuskers from the bar. Spending a night off the ship felt great. None of us had been off the ship overnight during the entire deployment, which by now had been almost five months.

After sitting there for over an hour, I spotted something far down the beach. We watched for a while before realizing we were looking at people. As they approached, it became clear they were running in a single file along the shoreline. Soon, we could see the individuals clearly. They were very tall, slender Black men dressed in bright red cloth, all carrying what appeared to be spears. Jamie said first, "Maasai." We watched as they continued along the beach when suddenly the man in the lead turned, heading straight for us, and the rest followed, maintaining their single file.

As they grew closer, we could easily identify the red shuka cloths with black stripes, colorful beaded necklaces, and the fact that some carried not spears but iron rods. Their footwear appeared to be sandals made from recycled tires. We all felt a wave of apprehension as the Maasai approached.

All three of us stood as they came up to us. The lead man raised his hand in greeting. I counted 10 of them.

The leader said in very good English, "Hello, are you Americans?"

"Yes," I answered.

Next, he asked, "Do you have American cigarettes, Marlboro?"

"Yes," I responded.

Then he inquired, "May we each have one cigarette?"

I looked at Manny, who said, "Don't look at me, I smoke Kools."

I turned back to the Maasai. "We have some Marlboros and Kools."

"Okay, thank you," he said with a smile.

Manny and I passed out our cigarettes and lit them for each Maasai. They all seemed to enjoy themselves as they took long, deep draws on their cigarettes.

"Are you Maasai warriors?" I asked them.

While laughing, one of them answered, "Here we only entertain tourists; at home, we herd cattle." They were actually a friendly and engaging group, openly answering any questions we had for them.

After a bit, the leader said, "We must go, thank you, our American friends." He turned and started running back to the beach, and each Maasai fell into line and ran off. We watched as they faded into the distance far down the coast.

We headed to the casino restaurant and had a nice dinner as the sun set. Afterward, we caught a taxi to take us back to town and the ship. Once back on board, I noticed the currency exchange vendor on the mess decks. I wisely exchanged 10,800 of my shillings for $900. I stashed that money in an envelope and put it inside my locker.

I did something else I learned to do as a young sailor. I took my military ID card from my wallet and put it in my left front jean pocket. Then, I folded my remaining shillings and stored my money in my right front jean pocket. Finally, I placed my wallet in my locker for safekeeping. The idea was that if I got robbed, rolled, or got into some kind of trouble, my driver's license, credit cards, and other personal information would be safely stored on board.

After showering and changing into clean clothes, we left the ship again. Since it was now dark, we followed the advice of the Embassy staff and hailed a taxi. Once inside, Jamie told the driver to take us to the African Jungle Club. When we arrived at the club, a sign outside read, "The All-Night, 24-Hour African Jungle Club."

Once we entered, the place was huge. There were five different bars, five or more lounges, and a large oval-shaped dance floor. In the center of the dance floor was a big circular fountain with water spraying from the mouths of statues around its edge. A second-story balcony circled the dance floor. The music was loud; there had to be over 600 or 700 people here, and the dance floor was packed.

Luckily, we found an open table in one of the lounges, and a waitress quickly appeared to take our order. Naturally, we ordered a round of Tuskers. After a couple of rounds, Jamie decided we needed to do shots with Tuskers as chasers. From then on, every round included Tuskers and a shot of Jack Daniel's whiskey. The only interruptions to our drinking were the women who periodically came to our table asking us to dance. Who would turn down a dance with beautiful African ladies? Not us!

While on the dance floor, I noticed something I had missed earlier. Rigged on two of the second-floor balconies were large ropes with an eye splice at the end. People placed one foot in the rope's eye and pushed off, swinging across the dance floor above the dancers to the balcony on the opposite side, where more people waited to catch them at the end of the swing. I made a mental note to add that to my to-do list before the end of the night.

Time went on, with Tuskers and shots, dancing, followed by more Tuskers and shots. My self-assessment showed I wasn't drunk yet, but I had a nice buzz. I decided, before I got too intoxicated, to take a few turns swinging over the dance floor on one of the ropes. Why not? It looked like fun. I stood up from the table and told Jamie and Manny what I planned. They both shrugged; I think Manny said, "Go do your crazy shit."

I made my way through the crowd to one of the stairways that led up to a balcony. Once on the second floor, I found one of the swing rope locations and got in line, since there were four or five people ahead of me. After a few minutes, I believe it was a club employee who motioned me forward. He yelled over the noise, "Big white man wants to fly like Tarzan."

I stepped up onto a small platform at the balcony edge; he handed me the rope. I put one foot in the rope's eye, took a firm grip, and pushed off with my other foot. My swing took me right over the dancers, clearing the fountain statues, and then to the other side, where two guys grabbed the rope as I landed on the platform. It was a blast.

One of the guys asked, "You want to swing back?"

I nodded yes. I put my foot in the rope's eye, got a grip, and pushed off. Just as I left the balcony edge, I felt like I had vertigo or something, and I was passing out. I faintly heard screaming and then felt considerable pain in my right arm and chest. Within a moment, I felt wet. Then I came to my senses; I was lying in water, and I was in the fountain. I rolled over, found the edge of the fountain wall, and pulled myself to my feet.

Once I was standing there, several club employees rushed to the fountain to help me. One of them pointed behind me and yelled, "You broke my statue, you pay up, now."

I looked where he was pointing; sure enough, part of a statue was shattered on the floor. That's when things spiraled out of control. The yelling man slapped my face and then punched me in the chest. I looked at him as he went to throw another punch. I grabbed his forearm and, with my other hand, grabbed his belt, picked him up, and threw him into the fountain. Bad move.

Within seconds, club bouncers swarmed me; there were just too many. They dragged me off the dance floor toward the club entrance, where

Mombasa police were already waiting. I heard Jamie yelling from somewhere, insisting that we would pay and that there was no need for police. At one point, Jamie got close enough to me that I grabbed my cash and military ID from my pockets and handed them to him. Outside, near a police van, there were more police officers than I could count. Once they got me to the back of the van, they took turns hitting me with what I believe were hard rubber batons.

Once they were satisfied that I was cooperative or simply tired of hitting me, they loaded me into the back of the van. I heard Jamie yell, "Don't worry, man, we'll get you out."

Then the van started moving, and off we went through the streets of Mombasa. I hoped our destination was a police station, not some other place where they would just kill me.

After what felt like an eternity, the van finally stopped. The back doors opened, and I was dragged out and led into a building. Once inside, I felt relieved to see it was a police station. In an empty room, they took my shirt, belt, shoes, and socks. One officer searched my jean pockets and found only my handkerchief.

"Where's your money? Who are you?" he asked.

I replied, "I'm an American citizen and a member of the United States Navy. Our ship is docked at Kilindini Harbor. I want to call my ship and the American Embassy now."

It seemed my statements didn't sit well with him. He swung his baton, smacking me across the face. I was then led down a hallway, through a steel door, and into another corridor. We stopped outside what appeared to be a large steel cage with vertical bars. Inside the cage, it was dimly lit. One by one, black smiling faces appeared between the cage bars. The cage door opened, and I was pushed inside. With a loud bang, the cage door slammed shut. I looked around in the dim light and saw dozens of people standing or sitting in the shadows. My only thought was, *Holy shit*.

Off in one corner, there was some activity. It took me a moment to realize there was a gang rape in progress. I looked for an open spot along the walls. I spotted an opening along one wall and immediately took up a position on that wall, facing into the cage. Good thing is I'm big and can punch hard. For the next few hours, I repelled one advance after another, by beating the shit out of anyone that came near. Before long, it seemed everyone avoided getting close to me, which was my desired effect. I wondered why they didn't just come at me in groups instead of just two or three at a time.

After some time, daylight shone in a hallway window across from the cage. As it got brighter, I got a better look at some of my fellow prisoners and/or night attackers for the first time. I was the only white man in the place. At least I still had my jeans on; the rest were all butt naked. I looked down at my hands; every knuckle was covered in dried blood. There was more dried blood on my forearms, most of my chest, and torso. I assumed the blood was mine or possibly some of my attackers; it didn't matter.

I heard doors slamming down the hallway and yelling. I moved to the front of the cage near the door as I heard another door bang open. Coming down the hallway was Gene, followed by two guards. Gene might as well have been an angel dressed in white, shimmering in the daylight. He was wearing his summer dress white uniform, with ribbons and his command senior chief badge on his chest. When they reached the cage door, Gene turned to one of the guards and said in his best command voice, "Get my man out of there right now, you understand me?" The guard nodded, opened the cage door, and motioned for me to leave.

Out in the hallway, Gene examined me and asked, "Are you all right?"

"Yes, are we getting out of here?" I responded.

Gene nodded. "Well, you look like shit, but let's go."

He turned to the guard and inquired, "Where's the rest of his clothes?" The guard simply shrugged.

Gene demonstrated the power and camaraderie of chief petty officers. We looked out for each other. I had to leave the police station in just my jeans, without a shirt, and barefoot. Jamie and Manny were outside with a taxi waiting.

"We've got to find you a shirt and something for your feet; you can't go back to the ship looking like this," Gene said.

Luckily, the taxi driver knew where to go. He found us a shop where we bought a polo-style shirt and sandals. Jamie picked up a couple of towels and two large bottles of water.

Outside, he handed me the water and towels. "Use these to clean yourself up. Man, you've got blood all over you." I took the water and towels from Jamie, using my reflection in the taxi window as a mirror, and worked to wipe the dried blood off my face, hair, chest, arms, and hands. After cleaning up, I put on the shirt and sandals. Jamie handed me my military ID.

"Where's my money?" I asked him.

He looked at me. "What do you think we used to bail your ass out? And, your money didn't cover it all. It cost $500 and 10 cartons of Marlboros to get you out."

I could only reply, "Oh!" Then I said, "Well, it's a good thing those sons of bitches never found out my name. They only know that I'm a U.S. Navy sailor. You can bet your ass the Embassy or the Navy will never hear about the shit they did."

"The smartest move you made last night was when you handed your money and ID to me," Jamie said.

We all got back in the taxi, and within a few minutes, we pulled up near the ship. We returned on board and made our way down to the Chiefs Mess. I had cleaned up enough that my appearance didn't attract anyone's attention. I immediately went to the head and got in the shower. The hot water stung my face, scalp, and upper body. When I came out of the shower, I looked in one of the mirrors. I was surprised to see minimal bruising, but I had raised red welts, skin abrasions, and minor cuts all over my back, chest, and upper arms, courtesy of the Mombasa police and some of my fellow jail cage residents. Aside from a swollen cheek and minor cuts around my eyes, my face seemed okay.

I went to my locker, put on a clean khaki uniform, and returned to the mess. I checked the reefer for any leftover chow that the mess cooks might have saved. Jamie, Manny, Gene, and other chiefs sat around the table. After I sat down with some food I had found, Jamie asked, "Do you want to know how we knew where they took you last night?"

"Sure," I answered.

"Well, after watching the police whip your ass and throw you into the van, Manny and I got a cab and followed it. Once we made sure you were actually taken inside the police station, we came right back to the ship," Jamie started.

Gene took over next, "These two woke me up last night around 0230 and told me all about it. We sat here until morning, discussing the best plan of action. Just know that if we couldn't get you out of jail, our next move would have been to tell the XO. You're lucky we could pull it off and keep what happened in the mess."

Manny, the mess treasurer, piped in next, "George, including the cost of the cigarettes, you owe the mess $385. Let me know when you can pay."

I nodded, got up from the table, and went into the berthing area to my locker. There, I counted out $400 in cash from my stash. I returned to the mess, sat at the table, and slid the money across to Manny.

"That should cover it, right?" I said.

Manny smiled. "That'll do it."

I turned to Gene and said, "Thanks, I know you could've just gone straight to the XO, but you didn't. I won't forget."

Gene simply said, "The matter is closed." He continued, "I've always figured you for a tough son of a bitch, but now you've left no doubt about that."

Then Jamie said, "Hey, you probably don't know yet. When we leave here, we're headed for the Suez Canal and the Mediterranean."

That was good news and a sign that the last stages of the deployment had begun. I decided my visit to Mombasa was over. I would stay on board today, work on our passage plan to the Suez Canal, and get some rest.

Doc Stein entered and sat at the table next to me. He asked how I was feeling, and I told him I was okay. He said, "George, with all of the other people's blood you had on you, I want you to swing by sick bay today so I can do a blood draw and a blood culture. We'll do it again in two weeks to make sure you haven't picked up any bacteria or fungi from your exposure." I told him I would come by later.

Later, I went to the bridge and found the message from the Sixth Fleet. The message indicated that we would stop at Djibouti from Mombasa to refuel before continuing through the Red Sea to the Suez Canal. After the Suez Canal, the message also stated that our next port would be Palma De Mallorca, Spain. However, there was more information on the second page of the message. After Palma, we were scheduled to arrive in Mayport on November 16.

As usual, Franklin was already on top of things. He had QMSN Davidson busy making corrections to the essential charts and publications. From Mombasa to Djibouti, it's 1,632 nautical miles. From Djibouti to Port Said, Egypt, including the canal transit, it's another 1,374 nautical miles. I started working on the passage plan. After a while, Mike Franklin appeared on the bridge.

Franklin looked at me and chuckled, "Cut yourself shaving, chief?"

"Yeah, something like that," I replied.

He started organizing the navigation charts I needed to lay out the passage plan. Later, I decided to take a short break; I was tired. I went out to the bridge wing, facing the dock, and watched as crew members haggled with vendors on the pier.

Since arriving in Mombasa, vendors had set up on the pier selling wooden, hand-carved souvenirs. I checked their wares several times while coming and going from the ship, and what I saw was impressive. They offered carvings of nearly every wild African game animal imaginable. Many carvings also represent Swahili culture, featuring beautifully carved walking canes, ceremonial masks, spears, and other items. Crew members steadily bought items from them, noting that the selling prices decreased each day.

After lunch, I took a two-hour nap and then got up again. Before returning to the bridge, I stopped by sick bay for Doc to draw my blood. By late afternoon, I was satisfied with our passage plan. We wouldn't get underway until early afternoon on October 17, so there would be time in the morning to hold the navigation brief before we depart. I called Mr. Marsk in the wardroom and asked him to schedule the navigation brief with the XO. I was dead tired; it was time to get some solid sleep.

The following morning, I was in much better shape. I had slept for over 12 hours and now felt rested entirely. I looked at the watch bill in the Plan of the Day and saw that I had the afternoon quarterdeck OOD watch (1200-1600) and the mid-watch (0000-0400) that night. I planned to stand my watches and sleep as much as I could in between.

The next morning, October 17, I checked the Plan of the Day and noticed that the XO had scheduled the navigation brief for 0930 in the wardroom. Later that morning, after the navigation brief, I went to the dock to review the vendors' offerings.

Many of the vendors still had a large number of items. One in particular caught my eye. Spread out on a large canvas, he displayed an array of wood carvings of nearly every kind. Knowing the ship was departing soon, I sensed his urgency to sell.

I looked at him and asked, "How much to buy everything?" I noticed that my question surprised him.

He thought for a moment and said, "3,000 shillings."

"I'll pay you 1,800 shillings," I answered.

"2,000 shillings," he countered.

"2,000, huh? Okay, I'll buy your whole shop for 2,000 shillings," I replied.

He nodded and responded, "Yes, agreed, you buy everything." I shook my head, indicating yes. Since I hadn't exchanged more money for shillings, the vendor agreed to be paid in U.S. dollars.

I counted out $170 and paid him (2,040 shillings). He produced large burlap bags and carefully packed the wooden products into them. Once he finished, over a dozen large bags were stuffed full. As I picked up one of the bags, it felt heavy. Fortunately, there were some crew members on the dock. I asked them if they could help me move my bags on board. I told them that in exchange for their help, each of them could pick any two items. That seemed to motivate them, and within a few minutes, we had everything on board and down to our division's storeroom. I let each guy go through the bags and take whatever items they wanted. Everyone was happy with the deal. I closed the storeroom door and locked it. My purchases were securely stowed.

Getting underway today would officially mark the beginning of the long voyage home. Early that afternoon, we set sail from our berth in Kilindini Harbor. Once we were outbound on the Likoni River, we made our way a short distance through the offshore gap in the reef, where we disembarked the pilot. The passage from Mombasa to Djibouti would take five days.

As we secured from the Sea and Anchor detail, the XO approached me at the chart table and asked me to speak privately on the port bridge wing. I followed the XO out to the bridge wing. Once there, the XO looked around to make sure we were alone.

He said, "Chief, I heard a rumor that you had trouble in Mombasa. If you did, can you tell me about it? From the looks of your face, hands, and arms, something happened."

My deep-rooted survival instinct and cardinal rule to never fully trust an officer kicked in. I decided to meet bullshit with more bullshit.

"XO, I'm not sure what you heard? I had a minor accident in town, if that's what you're asking about," I replied.

He looked at me momentarily and asked, "What kind of minor accident?"

Here came my bullshit story. I started, "XO, I don't know how much time you spent in the old town of Mombasa, but in the shopping district, there are streets at different levels, with concrete stairs from one level to the next. I was going down one of those stairs with my arms full of packages. I must have tripped on something and gone headfirst down a flight of stairs to the street below. I got scraped up here and there and hit my head on something."

The XO looked me in the eye and said, "That's your story?"

I answered, "Yes, sir." He continued, "Well, chief, that's not the story I heard. But I'm glad you're okay." I walked away confident that the whole incident was now behind me.

Our passage plan took us northward offshore the coast of Kenya, staying well clear of the coast of Somalia until we approached the Guardafuy Channel. To save time, we would transit through the Guardafuy Channel off Cape Guardafuy and the Horn of Africa into the Gulf of Aden. These waters between Cape Guardafuy and two offshore islands called "The Brothers" and the third island of Abd al Kuri are known for being rife with Somali pirate activity. Still, as a naval warship, it was of no concern unless we encountered a merchant vessel being victimized.

My Enlisted Surface Warfare Specialist qualification board was held on October 20 while we were en route from Mombasa to Djibouti. I completed all the PQS requirements and sign-offs just before we left the Persian Gulf.

The qualification board involves nearly four hours of answering questions from the board members. The XO chaired the board alongside two surface warfare-qualified officers, our engineering and weapons department heads. Mick and Chief Fire Controlman Bob Aaron completed the board. The questions may vary from simple inquiries about equipment parameters to lengthy scenario-based questions. At the end of the board, the XO asked me to step out so the members could discuss their opinions and then cast their votes, either approving or disapproving of the qualification. I waited in the passageway outside the mess. After several minutes, Bob came out and signaled for me to return inside. The XO and the department heads stood just inside the mess.

The XO extended his hand to shake, saying, "Congratulations, chief. You are now our newest ESWS-qualified crew member. Great job."

The XO showed me my surface warfare pin and asked if he could pin it on me.

"Of course, XO," I responded with a nod.

That was it. From now on, the letters SW appeared next to my rate; it was now QMC (SW) to indicate surface warfare qualification.

On October 22, at 0630, we reached the pilot pick-up area north of Port de Djibouti. The Djibouti pilot boarded north of the port entrance, and we docked about 40 minutes later. Our stay was only about four hours, just enough to refuel. In my view, the place still looked like the same shithole it did in June. The only difference was that it seemed even more rotting food from the U.N. World Food Program was stockpiled on the dock.

That afternoon, we were back underway, clearing away from Djibouti and into the Golfe de Tadjoura. We would transit Bab al-Mandeb off the coast of Yemen that evening before midnight. The transit of Bab al-Mandeb was uneventful, and we continued northward to the Red Sea.

We needed to cover the 1,285 nautical miles to reach Port Taufiq, the southern entrance to the Suez Canal, by 1900 on the evening of October 25. We had to also inform the canal authorities of our intention to join the northbound convoy through the canal, which started at 0400 the following day. It felt like we were truly homeward bound simply because we were heading in the right direction.

The only thing we were lacking was recent mail from home. We didn't receive any mail in Mombasa or Djibouti. Our next opportunity to receive mail would be in Palma de Mallorca. Assuming everything goes as planned for the Suez Canal transit, we should reach Palma on the afternoon of October 30.

We transited through the Red Sea, utilizing the central passage. However, this time, we were traveling northbound. The weather was pleasant, and the skies were clear. The wind mainly came from the south and southeast, creating following seas that push us along.

On the afternoon of October 25, we passed the southern tip of the Sinai Peninsula on our starboard side and entered the waters of the Gulf of Suez. Once again, the shipping traffic here is heavy, with both southbound and northbound ships all around us.

By early evening, we approached the anchorage areas south of Port Taufiq. After contacting the Suez Canal authorities by radiotelephone, we were assigned an anchor position. Once anchored, we were instructed to wait for their arrival. I quickly set up an anchorage plan on the navigation chart.

Shortly after anchoring, the ship was surrounded by small boats, all claiming to be with the canal authorities and insisting that we must allow them to board. We learned in June that the people in these initial boats are just a ruse.

Later, some actual canal officials arrived to brief us on the transit through the canal and inspect our ship documentation. To ensure everything went smoothly, we presented each official with the standard fare of Marlboro cigarettes, Zippo lighters, the ship's coffee mugs, and baseball caps.

We remained anchored for the rest of the evening. Around 0230, the canal authorities contacted us via radiotelephone, instructing us to proceed to the canal pilot boarding area in the approach channel to Port

Taufiq. After weighing anchor and getting the ship underway, we navigated through the congested anchorage area to reach the pilot pick-up location.

The waterway surrounding the port was busy with pilot boats navigating the area and delivering canal pilots to their respective ships. We maneuvered into the channel, where several ships were already approaching. Soon, a pilot boat came alongside to deliver our pilots. One of the junior officers met them on deck and escorted them to the bridge.

The captain welcomed the pilots as they entered the bridge and offered them gratuities along with other small gifts. At 0330, our convoy of ships gathered, and we proceeded northward through Port Taufiq before entering the first section of the canal.

Unlike the southbound convoys, the northbound convoys travel the full length of the canal without stopping. We would slow down only long enough to disembark the pilots at the north exit in Port Said. We should arrive in Port Said and enter the Mediterranean Sea in the late afternoon or early evening. Then, we could bid farewell to the sand, dust, and heat of the Middle East.

That evening, we departed from Port Said, heading across the Mediterranean Sea to Palma de Mallorca. It would take us over four days to cover the 1,555 nautical miles to Palma. We were scheduled to stay there for five days, departing on Friday morning, November 5.

While en route to Palma, I visited Doc Stein in sick bay. He had some news: My blood culture showed no growth of bacteria or fungi. He seemed confident that I was in the clear.

The following afternoon, we arrived in the open bay of Bahia de Palma and began to approach Puerto de Palma, located at the head of the bay. The Palma pilot boat came alongside, and the pilot boarded. After navigating past the harbor breakwaters, we entered the inner harbor and approached our assigned berth at the Molls Commercial docks. Within 15 minutes, we were moored port side to the wharf.

It seemed impossible, but just under two and a half years ago, I boarded USS *Vreeland* here at the same dock for the first time. From this vantage point, Palma looked just as I remembered it. I made my way down to the mess. I was tired, but for some reason, being here in Palma made my mood uncharacteristically relaxed. Fresh coffee was brewing, so I poured myself a cup and took a seat at the table. Jamie, Manny, and Mike joined me at the table. Since we had all been to Palma before, our conversation centered on crafting our plans for what to do on liberty.

We sat there, just shooting the breeze for quite a while. There was a knock on the door, and then it opened. The postal clerk delivered a good-sized bag of mail. Jamie and Manny started sorting the envelopes and packages for everyone. Soon, five envelopes with letters from Jan were sitting on the table in front of me. Then Manny slid one more envelope my way. As I looked at the envelope to see who the letter was from, my relaxed mood vanished; it was from Angie.

I read Jan's letters first. I hadn't received mail from her since the last time we were at Sitrah Anchorage in the Persian Gulf. I was glad to learn that everything was going well for her and Mitch. To my surprise, she knew when we were scheduled to arrive in Mayport. Being an experienced Navy wife, she knew to contact the ship's ombudsman in Mayport to find out our schedule. She had arranged to take the day off from her job, and she and Mitch would be on the pier when we arrived.

After reading Jan's letters, I picked up Angie's envelope. I hesitated and then opened it. As I unfolded her letter, a photograph fell out. It was a picture of her wearing just a scant bikini. I had to admit, she was gorgeous. A cloud of doom was gathering over me as I read her letter.

To paraphrase what Angie wrote, she still hadn't given up on us. She said that once I was back, she needed me to tell her to her face that I didn't want her. The picture was included to help remind me of her. Then came the "Aw shit" line. She also knew the date the ship returned to Mayport and planned to be on the pier to meet me.

As I put her letter and picture back in the envelope, I noticed my hands were shaky. I took Jan's and Angie's letters to my locker and stored them away. I had a big problem and wasn't sure how or if I could solve it. Under these circumstances, there was no way Jan could ever know about Angie. Now, how could I ensure that happens?

My usual approach to solving problems that do not require an immediate solution is to set them aside for now. Experience has shown me that this tactic helps me maintain my sanity. My immediate plan? Figure out what I was going to do on liberty while in Palma.

I would have two duty days over the five days I was here, leaving three days free to go ashore on liberty. All first liberty nights in Palma started in the "Gut," with a visit to Texas Jacks. As I learned during my previous time in Palma, it also offered great Mexican food.

But not tonight. I had the duty. Luckily, I wasn't assigned to stand an OOD watch on the quarterdeck. I was exhausted from standing watch, working long hours, and the numerous navigation details to get the ship here. Tomorrow would be a better day for liberty anyway.

Primarily, married career sailors lead dual lives. Unless someone has experienced the life of a U.S. Navy sailor in sea-intensive roles, there is a general misunderstanding of our mindset and how we operate. When on sea duty, if we are fortunate, there are years when we have three or four months to spend with our families. We strive to be typical family men while at home. For the rest of each year, our lives are starkly different at sea or away from homeport. I mean, our lives now involve working endlessly every day.

For operational types like me, when the ship is underway, we are almost always under tremendous stress to perform every task flawlessly, usually while battling chronic fatigue. There are no excuses for failure, only reasons. Often, this is why, on our first night in a port, we prefer rest and sleep over drinking and hell-raising.

Conversely, our lifestyles and work styles make us unique individuals. One trait we share is that we can be relied on for opportunities that bring excitement, fun, or general mayhem, but as we mature, we learn to prioritize rest first.

It was Sunday, October 31, Halloween. Late that morning, I found pay phones on the dock that could make international calls. In Palma, we were 5 hours ahead of Eastern Standard Time in Florida. I wanted to catch Jan at home before she left for church. To my relief, she answered after several rings. After catching up on each other's latest news, the rest of the call was filled with both of us expressing our love for each other and our shared anxiety about finally reuniting.

Jamie, Mike, and I left the ship late that afternoon. In the port, we found a taxi to take us into town; our first stop was the Gut and Texas Jacks. The place was packed with sailors and tourists who had discovered it since my last visit. We grabbed a table from some tourists as they were standing up to leave. Eventually, a waitress made her way to our table. We each ordered two San Miguel beers, two shots of tequila, and a big platter of tacos. Out on the street, people were dressed in Halloween costumes to celebrate. With mutual cheers, we clinked our shot glasses and down the hatch! Let the night of partying in Palma's Gut commence.

One thing chief petty officers must exercise wherever on liberty is maintaining a certain level of discretion. For instance, when we walk into a bar where junior enlisted crew members are present, we never stay to drink or party with them. Instead, we should be friendly, perhaps buy them a round, finish our drinks, and then move on.

As we enjoyed our beer, tequila, and tacos, more and more sailors arrived at Texas Jacks. We decided it was time to move on. Eventually, we discovered spots free of sailors or tourists, filled only with local patrons. After visiting several more bars, we settled into one that suited us well. It helped that many patrons were friendly local women who appeared to be in their late twenties or early thirties. We communicated just fine with their limited English and our limited Spanish. It turned into a fun and relaxing night of drinking, dancing, and general revelry.

Around 0300, we found a taxi to take us back to the ship. Our night of fun in the Gut was complete. Once back on board, I made some fresh coffee and found some leftover chow to make a snack. I wanted to sober up a bit before hitting the rack. While sitting alone at the table, Jamie came out of berthing, poured himself a cup of coffee, and took a seat.

Throughout the deployment, Jamie and I became good friends. He had gone through a rough divorce the year before, which still bothered him. On several occasions, I served as his sounding board when he needed to vent his frustrations. When I had trouble in Mombasa, he had my back, showing that he was also a good shipmate. Jamie was very perceptive and intuitive. He surprised me when he said, "George, something is happening with you. Is there some trouble?" I looked at him momentarily, debating whether to tell him about my Angie situation. I decided to share what was on my mind.

I explained the whole Angie situation to him, including her plan to meet the ship in Mayport. Jamie sat silently, listening as I went over all the details and my concerns about Angie being on the pier to meet us, along with Jan and Mitch.

The thing about shipmates is that they share the same complex and sometimes harsh environments, where we remain strictly non-judgmental about how we conduct our personal lives. This is a significant part of the shipmate brotherhood.

Jamie sat quietly momentarily and asked, "What does Angie look like?"

I got up, went into the berthing area, and retrieved Angie's last letter from my locker. I quietly opened and closed the door to berthing and sat back down at the table. I pulled Angie's picture from the envelope and slid it across the table. He picked it up, gazed at it for several moments, then exhaled.

"Holy shit George, she's drop dead gorgeous," he said.

"Yeah, I know. She's also smart and fun to be with. And, now she represents a huge problem for me," I replied.

We both sat silently for a few minutes. Then Jamie leaned forward and said, "I have an idea. You want to hear it?"

"Sure," I responded. Jamie laid out his idea and plan for the day we arrived at Mayport. When he finished, he said, "It'll work, trust me."

I wasn't entirely sure, but I said nothing. After all, I had no plan, so I would have to hinge my hopes on Jamie successfully executing his and pulling off a miracle. After talking for a while longer, I took back Angie's picture and stuffed it into the envelope. I told Jamie goodnight and went into berthing, undressed, and lay down on my rack. Within moments, I was out.

When I finally woke up, it was late morning. I got up, showered, shaved, and put on a fresh uniform. When I went to the mess area, the mess cooks were preparing to serve lunch. I grabbed some coffee and settled into the lounge while waiting for mealtime. As I waited, I thought about Jamie's plan to help me once we got home. I don't doubt that Jamie would do as he proposed. I accepted that he could either succeed or it would backfire. I would have to rely on Jan's saying, "Everything happens for a reason," and see what happened.

By mid-afternoon, my hangover from the night before was nearly gone. Jamie wanted to go out, so Mike, Manny, and I left the ship with him around 1500. Somehow, Jamie knew where he wanted to go and directed the taxi driver to take us to another part of Palma that I wasn't familiar with. After we got out of the taxi, Jamie pointed to an outdoor bar across the street.

At the bar, we found a large table with an umbrella shading it. Once everyone was seated, Jamie made an announcement. He thought it would be fun to take turns ordering a round of our favorite mixed drinks.

He looked at me and said, "George, you start."

When the waiter arrived, I asked if they had Bacardi Rum, and he nodded, indicating yes. I ordered a round of Bacardi and Coke on ice. After our Bacardi and Cokes, Mike ordered gin and tonics. Then Manny ordered Jack Daniel's with ginger ale. Finally, Jamie ordered, of all things, margaritas.

The cool late-afternoon breeze, the shade, and the very comfortable chairs made me feel extremely relaxed. It didn't hurt that attractive women seemed to be walking up and down the streets everywhere I looked. After we finished our margaritas, Jamie said, "Let's go again."

I realized that what we were doing would lead to extreme drunkenness, but right now it didn't seem to matter. I ordered another round of Bacardi and Cokes. I'm not sure how long we sat there drinking, but it was dark when Jamie asked, "You guys ready to go?"

When I tried to stand up, I fell back into the chair. I was plastered. After another attempt, I finally made it to my feet. We started walking down the street. The only one who seemed to know where we were going was Jamie. If passing out while walking and still functioning at some level was possible, I managed to do so. Next, I realized we were indoors, all sitting around a table facing an empty stage with music playing. On the table in front of me was a bottle of San Miguel beer and a full shot glass of clear liquid. I looked around; Jamie seemed alert, but Mike and Manny look like they were in a stupor.

I knew my eyes were closed, but I could now hear different music. I struggled to open my eyes. It was dark inside except for the dimly lit stage. As the lighting came up, my attention turned to the stage. It took me a moment to comprehend what I was seeing. Yep, I could believe my eyes: a woman was having sex with a live donkey up on stage.

I glanced at Jamie, and he smiled as he watched. I leaned in and tapped the table to get his attention. When he finally looked my way, I said, "You are one sick son of a bitch!"

He smiled even wider and burst into laughter. I was too drunk to get up and leave, so I watched as men and women repeatedly took the stage to perform various sexual acts. As a sailor, I've seen a lot, but nothing like what I saw that night.

At some point, we left and headed back to the ship. I assume Jamie managed those who were not functioning at their best level. I recall returning on board, undressing in the berthing area, and struggling to get into my rack. I also remember getting up at least twice during the night to heave my guts out in the head—an effect of alcohol consumption, which has rarely caused me to do that.

The next day, I found some comfort in knowing that Mike, Manny, and Jamie were also suffering from terrible hangovers. I realized that my time in Palma was over. I needed to work on the passage planning to the Strait of Gibraltar, across the Atlantic Ocean, and back home. After lunch, I felt well enough to head to the bridge and start the passage planning work.

In the chartroom, I discovered that Franklin, as usual, hadn't been idle. All the charts for our passage were spread out on the chart table, with a note on top stating that they had been updated and corrected. I began working, albeit slowly, as my hangover still had a tight grip on me.

I had duty on the last day in Palma and finalized the passage plan in the morning. That afternoon, I conducted the navigation brief in the wardroom for our departure from Palma and our transit through the Strait of Gibraltar.

The next morning, Friday, November 5, at 0800, we maneuvered away from the dock at Molls Commercial. We navigated the ship through the inner harbor to the breakwaters and out into the waters of Bahia de Palma. Once the pilot disembarked, we set our initial course and increased the ship's speed to 16 knots.

It's 471 nautical miles from Palma to the Strait of Gibraltar. Around midday tomorrow, we would pass through the Strait of Gibraltar and enter the waters of the Atlantic Ocean. From the Strait of Gibraltar to Mayport, there are 3,740 nautical miles of open ocean.

The passage plan for the Atlantic crossing was a simple one, and I had used it before. At the western reaches of the Strait of Gibraltar, we set a southwesterly course that would take us to the latitude coordinate of 30° 23.0' North, which is also the latitude coordinate for Mayport. We would then turn to a course of 270 degrees (west) and sail parallel along that latitude toward Mayport.

Upon arriving in Mayport, the ship would have a 30-day standdown period. One half of the crew can take up to 14 days of leave and return, allowing the other half to take their leave period. I submitted my request and was approved for 14 days of leave starting on the day of our arrival.

The ocean crossing was uneventful, except for several days of heavy weather with high sea state conditions along the route. On November 16, at 1300, the ship approached the Florida coast. On radar, I identified the radar beacon on the St. Johns River (STJ) entrance buoy. I recommended a new course to the OOD to close in on the buoy. Shortly thereafter, we set the Sea and Anchor detail for entering port. In their dress blue uniforms, the crew assumed their stations and manned the rails. Once the ship passed buoy STJ, we steered onto the forward navigation range lights and marks for the channel through the 5 miles of breakwaters on both sides.

On entering the channel leading into the Mayport basin, we slowed in the basin approach channel to take on the docking pilot who boarded from one of the tugboats. The pier where we were to dock was lined with families and local media to greet our arrival. Within 20 minutes, the ship was alongside the pier, starboard side to, and all mooring lines were passed and secured.

I was on the starboard bridge wing, scanning the people lined up along the pier, trying to spot Jan and Mitch. My heart raced when I saw Angie holding up a homemade sign. My heart raced again when I realized she was only about 30 feet away from Jan.

Then Jamie appeared and stood beside me. He asked, "Is Angie on the pier?"

I looked at him and said, "If you look, you'll see the short blonde holding up the sign that says, 'Welcome Back, George.'"

Jamie peered over the side of the bridge wing. "Yep, I see her. Don't worry, man, I got this," he replied.

He turned and headed aft on the 02-level, disappearing down the ladder to the main deck. The captain had ordered the gangway to be put out and secured the ship's crew from their Sea and Anchor detail stations. USS *W.S. Sims* was home.

Staying on the bridge wing, I watched the gangway area on the pier. Within moments, I spotted Jamie heading down the gangway and onto the dock. He walked quickly, making a beeline straight for Angie. He stopped in front of her, said something, then reached for her sign, took it, and folded it up. Next, he put his arm around her shoulders, and they turned together, walking away from the crowd. I thought, *Only Jamie could pull something like this off*.

Now that the danger from Angie seemed to be over, I leaned over the bridge wing and started waving to get Jan's attention. She and Mitch saw me and waved back. I left the bridge and made my way down to the quarterdeck. At the quarterdeck, a line of crew members waited to go down the gangway and greet their friends or family on the pier. Soon, I made my way down the gangway and onto the dock. I spotted Jan and Mitch approaching me. Within moments, we were sharing a three-way hug. After breaking from our hug, I gave Jan a long hello kiss. Our 10-month separation was over.

As soon as we could, I brought Jan and Mitch on board, and we headed down to the Chiefs Mess. Upon entering the mess area, it was busy and filled with families. I left Jan and Mitch in the mess area, went into the berthing area, and grabbed my already packed bag, with my leave papers on top.

We were back at the quarterdeck within moments and left the ship together. I was surprised to see our car in the parking lot. She had contacted Mike's wife and retrieved our car from their house. I took the wheel to drive and said to Jan, "You'll have to give directions because I don't know where we live."

She laughed and said, "No problem."

On the way home, Jan had good news. When her boss learned that Jan hadn't seen me in 10 months, he insisted on giving her a week off with pay. Life seemed good. I had my family with me again, and it felt great. I didn't seem to have a care in the world right now.

CHAPTER 9

A CHANGE OF PACE

Jan directed me to Mariner Village Apartments, located about 2 miles south of the main naval station gate off Mayport Road. As soon as I could, I changed out of my dress blues. It felt great to be home finally. Next month, Mitch would turn 11. I hadn't been a big part of his life for a long time. We sat at the dining room table for a while, talking and catching up. Then, there was a knock at the front door. Mitch went to the door and answered it. Two boys were standing outside, wanting him to come out and play. Jan told Mitch he could go since she knew the boys and their mother.

As soon as Mitch left with the boys and we were alone, it was time for our real homecoming together. Now, I was finally home. Later that day, I gave Jan the gold bracelets and necklaces I had bought in Bahrain. I was thrilled to see how excited she was about the jewelry.

After several days at home, I went to the ship to collect the remaining purchases from Karachi and Mombasa. I pulled out the furniture and bags of wood carving items from the division's storeroom. Fortunately, some crew members were nearby and offered to help. The final task was to retrieve my five cases of Tusker Beer Lager.

The following week, I was still on leave. During the day, Jan was at work, and Mitch was in school. I decided to go to the ship to use the military telephone system to call the QM Rating detailer. Considering that I would now be in the Navy for a career spanning at least 20 years, I needed to explore assignment opportunities that are conducive to future advancement. I was less than one year into the five-year assignment on board USS *W.S. Sims*. Staying here for another four years would not position me competitively.

From the Chiefs Mess, I dialed the detailer's phone number. I was pleased when he answers instead of an operator. We discussed my assignment situation and the need for me to fill a QMC (pay grade E-7) billet. However, I expressed a preference for staying in Mayport. The detailer said he needed to put me on hold.

Once he returned to the line, he said, "I have good news. I have a QMC retiring from one of the newer guided missile frigates, USS *Estocin* (FFG 15), and she's out of Mayport." He continued, "This works out great because I need to fill that billet. It'll be a simple cross-deck transfer on March 1. Chief, will you accept these orders?"

"Yes, I will," I replied without hesitation.

He said, "Great, you can expect to receive your hard copy orders in less than a month." After ending the call, I was ecstatic and thrilled about the great news.

The Oliver Hazard Perry (FFG 7) class guided missile frigates, designated FFGs, were the newest ships in the Navy's fleet. USS *Estocin* had been commissioned into service less than two years earlier, making her a new and modern warship in my view. Fortunately, no relocation was required with these orders, so Jan should be okay with it.

Jamie walked in just as I was about to leave. He smiled and jokingly said, "I'm glad you're here. I want to talk to you."

"What's up?" I asked him.

He started, "Do you want to know how it went with Angie?"

I had been wondering, so I answered, "Sure. What did you say when you walked up to her the other day?"

"I told her that George's wife and son were here and that you are not going to ruin it for them. You're with me. My name is Jamie, so let's take a walk," Jamie responded.

I asked what she said. He answered that she said, "I never knew if George was married, but I don't want to cause him any problems."

"That was it?" I replied. He shook his head, indicating yes.

I thanked Jamie for bailing me out and told him not many people would do what he had done for me. Jamie wasn't finished.

"There's more to the story," he said.

I said, "Okay, what?"

Jamie began, "I thought, what the hell, so I asked her for a date."

"And?" I said.

He continued, "We went out last Friday night, and I've been seeing her every night since."

All I could say was, "Good for you, man. I hope it works out for both of you if that's what you want."

"Well, right now things are great," he replied. I reached over, slapped Jamie's knee, and told him I was going home. I was happy for both Jamie and Angie. I was also pleased that Angie was no longer my problem, thanks to Jamie.

The post-deployment standdown period concluded in mid-December. Due to the upcoming overhaul period, we would remain in port until January. For me, this was a much-appreciated break. I was home for Mitch's birthday and would be home for the Christmas and New Year holidays—rare occasions on sea duty.

Two things happened on the morning of December 22 that seem almost fortuitous. From the bridge, I watched USS *Estocin* pull into the basin and dock at berth B-2. Lines of people filled the pier, greeting her arrival after her first six-month deployment to the Mediterranean. I was impressed that she required no tug assistance to maneuver alongside the dock and moor.

Later that same morning, my orders to *Estocin* arrived. So far, I had kept my impending departure quiet and hadn't told anyone on the ship. I was still on the bridge when Gene called me and asked me to come to the ship's office. When I arrived at his office, Gene handed me my orders and asked, "Did you know these were coming?"

I replied, "Yes."

He looked at me for a moment before saying, "Well, the captain didn't and he's pissed. He wants to see you; he's on board and in his cabin."

First, I went to the Chiefs Mess, where I carefully read the orders. I was satisfied with everything and would transfer to USS *Estocin* on March 1, in just over two months. I placed the orders in my locker and sighed, thinking I might as well get the meeting with the captain over with. I liked Captain Macdonald; in my opinion, he was an excellent commanding officer.

I went to the captain's cabin. I paused, knocked on the door, opened it, and said, "Good morning, Captain. It's Chief Trowbridge."

Sitting at his desk, he gestured for me to come in and take a seat. While sitting by his desk, I noticed another copy of my orders on his desktop. He turned to me with a serious expression and asked, "Did you know about these orders? Is this what you want to do?"

"Yes, Captain, I knew. I spoke with the detailer last month, and he offered me these orders," I replied.

His response surprised me when he said, "Chief, I need you here; the ship needs you here. I can get these orders canceled if you agree."

I decided to be honest with him. I shared my thoughts about competing for future advancement and explained that remaining in a QM1 billet as a QMC wouldn't benefit my career. I also mentioned how much I enjoyed serving under his command, but it was strictly a career decision, not a sign of dissatisfaction. He nodded; as a career naval officer, I knew he would understand my position.

He responded, "Well, me, I mean we, will have to figure out how to get along without you. I want you to know, on so many nights at sea, I was able to sleep better knowing your vigilance was always at work in keeping my ship in safe waters." I replied, "Captain, Sir, that's the best compliment I've ever gotten, thank you."

We rose and shook hands. Outside his cabin door, I paused, thinking, *Well, that went a whole lot better than I thought it was going to.*

The ship was scheduled for a restricted availability overhaul in late January. Certain modifications to her weapons suite would require a partial weapons offload at the Naval Weapons Station in Charleston, SC. On Monday morning, January 10, we set off for the transit to Charleston. Early the next day, we began to approach the channel leading to Charleston Harbor. The Charleston/Cooper River pilot boarded the ship at the channel entrance, about 4 miles out. The transit through the harbor and up the Cooper River to the Naval Weapons Station dock took roughly an hour and a half.

The weapons offload was completed in one day. The next day, at 0630, we departed from the weapons station dock and navigated down the Cooper River to Charleston Harbor and out to sea, bound for Mayport. The next morning, we docked at a berth in the southern part of the Mayport basin, known as the Delta piers.

By the third week of February, I couldn't wait any longer. I wanted to see USS *Estocin*. I walked over to where she was docked and went on board. I asked at the quarterdeck to speak with their Chief Quartermaster.

"You want QMC Wilson," the OOD said.

The Petty Officer of the Watch called the Chiefs Mess, and after hanging up, he said the chief would be there in just a minute. After several minutes, a chief appeared on the quarterdeck. The OOD pointed toward where I was standing and said to him, "This chief asked to see you."

"What can I do for you?" the chief asked me.

I shook his hand and said, "I'm George Trowbridge, your relief."

He replied, "I'm Don Wilson. We've been wondering when you might show up." Don suggested we visit the bridge/pilothouse to show me around. As we made our way through a wide interior centerline passageway, I was struck by how clean and new everything looked.

Once on the bridge, called the pilothouse on FFGs, I was amazed by how different it was from any ship I had previously been on. Don began explaining the layout of the pilothouse and the various pieces of equipment. The key difference is that all ship control functions have been integrated into a ship control console (SCC), located in the center and forward area of the pilothouse. The SCC almost gives you the sensation of being in an airplane's cockpit rather than in a warship's pilothouse.

He explained the operation of the SCC, which is managed and monitored by an enlisted operator and the OOD. The SCC operator acts as the helmsman, lee helmsman, and operator of certain functions. From his position at the SCC, the OOD can monitor and control the ship's course and speed while overseeing the main and auxiliary propulsion units, weapon systems, and various alarm systems. Additionally, he has easy access to interior communication circuits, general announcing circuits, and radiotelephone communications.

Don continued by detailing that the division is part of the Ship Control (SC) department, which consists of three divisions: Ship Control, Communication, and Deck. The division officers include the Chief Quartermaster (SC-1 division), Chief Radioman (SC-2 division), and Master Chief Boatswain's Mate (SC-3 division). The only officer is the department head, a lieutenant.

These ships operate under the principle of minimum manning. Whenever possible, labor-saving devices and automated systems are used to replace manpower. For example, a traditional bridge watch team consists of two officers and 11 to 13 enlisted personnel. The FFG pilothouse watch team includes one or two officers and four to five enlisted personnel. The same approach has been applied to every department on the ship. FFGs are roughly the same size as Knox-class frigates; however, they operate with about one-third fewer crew members, both officers and enlisted personnel.

The SC-3 division officer had made one deviation from the FFG manning doctrine, which did not require non-rated or undesignated seaman from the deck force to stand underway watches. He believed his personnel needed to stand watches as SCC operators and lookouts in the pilothouse. His reasoning was sound. If any of his undesignated seaman wanted to strike for and pursue becoming a rated Boatswain's Mate, traditional watchstanding on a ship's bridge is essential knowledge and experience for the rating. He was looking out for the best interests of his people.

It was clear that FFGs signify a departure from the traditional Navy frigate: with a gas turbine-powered propulsion system, minimal crew requirements, a fully integrated combat system, two helicopter hangars, and auxiliary propulsion units.

Listening to Don, it was evident that he was very proud of his division. He had gone through pre-commissioning, the ship's commissioning, all the post-shipyard work and trials, and had recently completed their first deployment. He and Signalman 1st Class Bob Larson had taken a group of young men fresh out of "A" school and trained them to peak professional standards.

Don was retiring from the Navy after 22 years. His retirement ceremony would be one week after I reported on board. Don emphasized that he would dedicate as much time as possible to helping me get up to speed before his departure.

As we were about to leave, the captain climbed the ladder to the pilothouse. Don introduced me to Commander Richard Mackay, who had taken command of *Estocin* just several days earlier. He struck me as a soft-spoken, fair-minded, and highly skilled officer. My gut instinct told me we would get along very well. After chatting with the captain for a while, Don took me below to show me the Chiefs Mess.

Fifteen chief petty officers were assigned to the ship. The Chiefs Mess appeared vast compared to the one on board *W.S. Sims*. The entire mess was clean, modern, and well-furnished.

Don and I talked a bit longer before he walked me up to the quarterdeck. While in the Chiefs Mess, he gave me several ship information booklets to review. We said our goodbyes, and I walked down the gangway. As I walked away, I felt excited and enthusiastic about my new assignment. My decision to leave *W.S. Sims* behind seemed to have been a good one.

The following week, on Tuesday, March 1, I spent my morning checking out and leaving the ship. I drove around the basin, parked near where *Estocin* was docked, and went on board. I arrived on board early enough that by the end of the day, I had completed the check-in process and moved much of my gear on board. Don had already cleared his locker and bunk, so I could move into the mess.

True to his word, Don spent a considerable amount of time transitioning the division business to me and providing training on the pilothouse equipment and operations. On Tuesday afternoon, March 8, the crew assembled in dress uniforms on the flight deck, and the command held a suitable and dignified retirement ceremony for Don. All the chiefs and their wives gathered at the CPO Club for Don's retirement party that evening. The party also allowed me to get to know the other chiefs better and provided Jan the opportunity to meet their wives.

The captain, XO, and several chiefs emphasized one point: Top performers are prioritized by the Bureau of Naval Personnel to man the FFGs. Out of the junior enlisted personnel graduating from their respective "A" schools, only the top-tier graduates are assigned to FFGs. I was informed before finalizing orders that both enlisted and officer detailers must submit the candidates for performance standard screening before the orders are issued. The goal is to ensure these ships are manned by the best the Navy can provide.

As I had more opportunities to get to know my fellow chiefs and different crew members, one common thread I noticed among enlisted personnel, chiefs, and junior officers was a shared sense of pride in being part of the crew. Not one crew member gave me an impression of negativity or a poor attitude, which I had never experienced at my prior commands.

Another aspect I enjoyed about FFGs was that I was the division officer and reported directly to our department head. Every ship so far, I had always had a junior commissioned officer serving as the division officer. Though I got along well with nearly all of them, I saw them primarily as just being in my way.

I didn't have to wait long to get underway; we were scheduled for a two-week operation starting on March 17. For me, this was an exciting time. We were initially bound for a port visit in Key West, FL. My new navigation team performed flawlessly during the Sea and Anchor detail when departing Mayport. All of them had recently completed the Mediterranean deployment, and like all crews, they gained experience that put them at the top of their game. The distance from Mayport to Key West is just over 445 nautical miles, and we would dock in Key West the following afternoon.

I quickly grew to appreciate FFGs for several reasons. They have a propulsion system powered by two General Electric LM2500 gas turbines and two 350-horsepower Electric Drive Auxiliary Propulsion Units (APUs) that can extend from and retract back into the hull. Coupled with a single controllable reversible pitch (CRP) propeller, these ships are highly maneuverable.

The APUs can serve as bow thrusters for precise maneuvering at low speeds, such as during docking or departure. They can rotate independently from 0 to 360 degrees, and thrust can be applied either simultaneously or in sequence.

USS *Estocin* (FFG 15)

When used skillfully, the combination of the CRP propeller and the APUs reduces the need for tugboat assistance. These features make the FFGs much more efficient and effective for exact maneuvering than any ship I have previously been on.

With a five-blade CRP propeller, it offers quick acceleration and deceleration. Backing the ship does not require stopping the propeller shaft or changing its direction. The propeller shaft rotates at a constant speed; adjusting the blade pitch redirects the thrust, making it a more efficient propulsion system.

Key West Harbor is 151 miles southwest of Miami Harbor along the coastwise route. The harbor itself is located in front of the city of Key West, protected on the east by the island and on the other sides by reefs, sand flats, Wisteria Island, and Tank Island.

At the entrance to the approach channel to Key West are Sand Key Light, a skeleton tower, an abandoned white square pyramidal skeleton tower to the west, and a light structure marking Stock Island Channel to the east. Key West harbor can be accessed through breaks in the reef system, leading into the turning basin, which is large and deep enough for ships to maneuver to their assigned docks. The pilot boat came alongside, and the Key West pilot boarded just north of the "KW" buoy at the entrance to the Main Ship Channel.

When the ship was safely in the turning basin, I watched as the captain coached the conning officer on how to use the thrust generated by the APUs, in opposition to the thrust from the CRP propeller, and how to use the rudder to essentially steer the ship at an oblique angle to the dock—something a Knox-class frigate could never do. We docked at Pier D-2, in the northern part of the harbor northwest of Key West.

For many of us who had never been here, we were about to discover unique experiences not found anywhere else in a U.S. city. What we learned over the next several days while exploring the town was fascinating. It seemed to us that Key West's residents were a mix of biker gangs, old hippies, gay people, local natives, fishermen, bums, and some tourists. The old hippies and gay people were busy buying historic Florida-style houses, restoring them, and turning them into vacation homes. The bikers filled the bars when they weren't cruising up and down Duval Street. The local natives and some old hippies, now turned entrepreneurs, ran the tourist shops, diners, restaurants, and bars.

All that said, the place was excellent. The overall vibe was laid-back and relaxed, and no one seemed to be in a hurry. It felt more like being in a foreign port than a small city in the U.S. This time period of Key West was before tourism and cruise ships overwhelmed it, commercialized it, and destroyed its old Florida charm and uniqueness.

We got underway on Thursday afternoon, March 24, and backed the ship away from Pier D-2. Once the ship was turned properly into the outbound channel in the turning basin, we began our transit back to the Straits of Florida. We were now headed to Freeport, Bahamas. I was starting to think this trip felt more like one a cruise ship would make rather than a warship. It's only about 210 nautical miles north to Grand Bahama Island. To arrive by 0700 the following morning, our ship's speed was a leisurely 14 knots. We would spend the weekend in port at Freeport and then head north for a two-day training exercise in the Jacksonville Operating Area.

Early the following morning, we docked with our starboard side to the Main Wharf, Berth number 4, located just inside the harbor entrance on the east side of the port. Entering the harbor was a very easy Sea and Anchor detail. Once again, the crew had liberty here, and several good options were available. Near the port is a massive marketplace for local art, sculptures, artisan goods, souvenirs, and woven items. If you enjoy beaches, swimming, and snorkeling, Freeport is your destination.

On Monday morning, we left Freeport. Once we were well to the south, we shifted course to follow the Bahamas' Northwest Providence Channel toward the Straits of Florida, heading north to our operational area off Jacksonville and Mayport.

After several days of familiarization training on various ship systems, we arrived at Mayport on Thursday morning, March 31. The following day, we began nearly four weeks of intermediate maintenance availability and wouldn't get the ship back underway until April 25.

On the home front, Jan had been happy since last November. After returning from deployment, I had been home, except for a three-day trip to Charleston, the past two weeks, and a brief operation involving the aircraft carrier USS *Saratoga* (CV 60) and the submarine *Batfish* (SSN 681) during the last week of April. The date that had our attention was May 5, when we would set sail to undertake a two-month Special Operations (SPECOPS) in Central America.

Before leaving Mayport, the ship received a detachment of Cryptologic Technicians (CTs) and many cases containing their equipment. The detachment's job is to collect, analyze, and report on communication signals. Their equipment allowed them to gather and process airborne, shipborne, or land-based radar signals. They also had electronic intelligence receiving and direction-finding systems, digital recording devices, analysis terminals, and other computer gear. The detachment consisted of 12 enlisted CTs and one officer, a lieutenant junior grade. Crew members referred to the CT detachment as the "spooks."

The spook's equipment was stowed or set up in the helicopter hangars. A modular container was craned on board and rolled into the port helicopter hangar. The container was about the size of a standard 20-foot shipping container and secured with tie-down chains, then connected to the ship's electrical power. In addition, the container was connected to the ship's sound-powered phone circuit, giving the container internal communication capability with CIC and the pilothouse. This container system and its associated equipment package served as the spook's operations center.

On May 5, we departed from Mayport. The distance from Mayport to Limon Bay and the breakwater at Cristobal, the Atlantic entrance to the Panama Canal, is 1,498 nautical miles. Our planned transit speed was 16 knots. It would take four days to reach Limon Bay.

Once we cleared the St. Johns River breakwaters and were well off the coast, we set a course to proceed southward to the Straits of Florida. The next day, the ship progressed from the southern end of the Straits of Florida, then it steered a southeastern route along the northern coast of Cuba to the Windward Passage. We transited the Windward Passage between the eastern tip of Cuba and the western tip of Hispaniola. Then we came to a southwesterly course to proceed south between Jamaica and Haiti. Finally, the course was set to the breakwater at Cristobal and Limon Bay, where ships enter the Panama Canal waters.

We arrived at the Panama Canal Zone early on May 9. As our ship approached the Cristobal breakwater and entered Limon Bay, the Panama Canal pilot boarded from the pilot boat. Soon after, the pilot instructed the ship to begin maneuvering toward the first set of locks, the Gatun Locks. The Gatun Locks are truly impressive; the three successive lock chambers resemble a massive staircase. The lock area is mostly concrete, with buildings on either side. Beyond the grassy areas next to the lock, the tropical jungle of dark trees and dense foliage begins.

The last time I saw the Panama Canal was in 1973. That was when my ship, returning from our deployment to Vietnam, transited from the Pacific to the Atlantic Ocean. I've always believed the canal should be considered one of the man-made wonders of the world. Its length is about 44 nautical miles (roughly 50 statute miles) from the Atlantic coast to the Pacific coast. While crossing the Panama Canal, a ship is raised and lowered 85 feet. After passing through Gatun Lake and Gaillard Cut, the ship enters Pedro Miguel Locks and is lowered 31 feet. One mile downstream from Pedro Miguel Locks, the ship enters the Miraflores Locks where it is lowered approximately 54 feet to match the sea level of the Pacific Ocean.

As the ship moved along the lock wall of the Gatun Locks, small boats approached to deliver the canal line handlers. Then, wire ropes from small electronic locomotives called Mules were sent over to the ship. The Mules ran on steel rail tracks along the top of the lock walls and were positioned on both sides of the locks. After the Mules passed wire ropes to both sides of the ship, they were secured to the ship's deck bitts.

Once the wire ropes were secured, the Mules began to winch in, removing the slack from the wire ropes. The Mules were then used to tow the ship on the wire ropes beside the lock walls, and ultimately to maneuver the ship into each lock chamber while helping the pilot position it. This process was repeated at each lock chamber throughout the ship's canal journey.

When a ship leaves the Gatun Locks and enters Gatun Lake, it has been raised to the lake's level. Gatun Lake is a man-made lake covering about 164 square miles. The shipping channel through the lake is 15 nautical miles long. After leaving Gatun Lake, you reach the historic section of the canal, the Gaillard Cut, also known as the Culebra Cut, which extends about 8 miles through the Continental Divide of Panama, the highest point on the isthmus.

The second lock was reached after the ship passed through the Gaillard Cut. The first lock, Pedro Miguel, has one chamber and lowers the ship by 31 feet. From Pedro Miguel, the ship enters Lake Miraflores and travels 1 mile to the Miraflores Locks. The Miraflores Locks have two chambers, which lower the ship the remaining distance back to sea level.

As a military vessel, we left the last lock and traveled to the docks at Rodman Naval Station on the Pacific side of the Isthmus of Panama, across from Balboa. The canal transit took over eight hours, so the ship moored at the Rodman Naval Station docks around 1600 that afternoon.

The next morning, we received a briefing by personnel from USS *Blakely* (FF 1072), a Knox-class frigate. The subject of the briefing pertained to our assignment to surveil activities conducted by Nicaraguan Sandinista forces in the area of the Gulf of Fonseca and to provide assistance to CIA and/or U.S. military advisors supporting Contra forces operating in the areas around the Gulf.

At 1000, the ship departed from the Rodman dock. Once clear and in the outbound channel, we passed under the Pan-American Bridge (The Bridge of the Americas), heading toward the Gulf of Panama, then on to the Eastern Pacific Ocean. Nearly 860 nautical miles lay ahead from Rodman to our operating area near the Gulf of Fonseca. It would take just over two days to cover that distance at an average speed of 16 knots.

Navy ships must send a Movement Report (MOVREP) message before leaving a port or an operating area. The MOVREP message is formatted to report the ship's plan of intended motion. As we had found, everything about this operation was secret. Our MOVREP message reported our location at the dock at Rodman to a position about 1 nautical mile south of the Pan-American Bridge, which was designated "MOD OUT" in the message. This meant that the ship's movement ended there as far as the rest of the world was concerned.

The ship passed through the Gulf of Panama that afternoon and evening, entering the Eastern Pacific Ocean. By the next day, I was reminded how the waters in the Pacific Ocean were much different from those in the Atlantic. The ocean appeared smooth, with small waves and long ocean swells. It's common to see marine life such as whales, dolphins, sea turtles, and different species of sharks. The weather was great, with plenty of sunlight, azure blue skies, light winds, and calm seas.

During daylight hours, especially along the coast, the various volcanic mountains could be seen in the distance. The area along the Central American isthmus is sometimes referred to as the "Ring of Fire" due to the presence of 29 volcanoes from Guatemala to Panama.

The next two months could be described as an adventure because that's exactly what they would be for us. Our adventure involved monitoring activities around the Gulf of Fonseca, which was our main purpose for being there. However, other events revealed that an unknown entity was also watching us.

We arrived near the entrance to the Gulf of Fonseca on May 13. The frigate USS *Julius A. Furer* (FFG 6) was present. *Furer's* whaleboat approached, carrying its spook officer and members of its CIC team. The team from *Furer* conducted an extensive intelligence briefing with us in the wardroom.

The briefing included information on recently detected activities within the Gulf, including which CIA operatives, U.S. Special Forces, and Navy SEAL teams were active and how to communicate with them. Other topics addressed what the communist Sandinistas, now supported by Cuban forces, were believed to be doing on the Nicaraguan side of the Gulf. The discussion covered details about the Contra forces operating out of El Salvador and Honduras in areas around the Gulf's coastline and El Tigre Island (Tiger Island), located in the central northern waters of the Gulf.

It would be necessary to enter the northern area of the Gulf and loiter several miles south of Tiger Island under the cover of darkness every third or fourth night. The purpose was to rendezvous with boats from Special Boat Unit 20 (SBU 20), deployed here from the Naval Amphibious Base, Little Creek, VA. SBU 20's primary task was to support U.S. special warfare units operating in the area.

At this point in the briefing, they clarified that the rendezvous with SBU 20 boats was meant to provide fuel, ammunition, and repair parts. Additionally, as requested, we would supply rations and, when possible, offer the boat crews meals, showers, and other support.

This information now clarified why we took on certain unusual supplies before departing Mayport. We took on supplies of gasoline, crates of Mercury boat engine parts, Furuno radar and electronic equipment parts, Kevlar helmets, and body armor. Thousands of rounds of .50 caliber ammunition, 7.62 mm, and 5.56 mm cartridges were loaded. The load that made us curious was a crate of 81 mm mortar rounds and 40 x 46 mm grenades used in M79 grenade launchers.

Then came a warning regarding the rendezvous with the SBU 20 boats. On two occasions, *Furer* had thwarted local fishing boats attempting to approach the ship under the cover of darkness. The assumption is that they intended to surround the ship with fishing nets to trap it. *Furer's* crew had detected these attempts by the fishing boats using night vision devices and forward-looking infrared (FLIR).

One of the final topics discussed raised most everyone's eyebrows. Information was shared about events that happened over the past five days. On three separate occasions, near evening dusk, underwater lights were seen near their ship. The bridge and lookout watch teams all confirmed what they observed. On two occasions, the underwater anomaly lasted long enough for their sonar team to try tracking and listening through hydrophones, but they detected nothing.

The underwater light was described as a round or circular pattern, approximately 75 to 100 feet in diameter. The underwater object was far too large to be phosphorescent, as is sometimes observed in whale activity. On each occasion, the light was seen some distance from the open sea, moving swiftly and directly toward their ship. When the light came close, it moved directly beneath the ship and reappeared on the opposite side before disappearing. We now knew we also potentially had an unidentified submerged object (USO) to contend with.

They provided us with the exact latitude and longitude coordinates of their ship during each encounter. With the final details about the suspected presence of a USO or USOs in the area, the team from *Furer* concluded the briefing.

After the briefing, I went to the pilothouse to plot the coordinates of *Furer's* USO encounters on the navigation chart. QM2 Bob Faber was the QMOW. He observed as I plotted the positions on the chart.

"Chief, what are these positions for?" he then asked.

The look on his face was priceless when I told him about the reported USO encounters by USS *Furer*. I walked away, silently chuckling at his reaction to what I had told him.

Since leaving Mayport, I had been standing watch as the junior officer of the deck (JOOD) and conning officer, working toward my OOD "Underway" qualification. I discussed with the captain the possibility of having an enlisted OOD during my first underway period. To my surprise, he supported the idea; however, he required that I complete the same qualifications as any junior officer pursuing their Surface Warfare Officer (SWO) and OOD qualifications.

Besides standing JOOD watches in the pilothouse, I concentrated on training in CIC to familiarize myself with our electronic warfare and combat systems suite. I also made sure to spend time in the Central Control Station (CCS) to learn more about the gas turbine propulsion plant and its auxiliary systems. I was making good progress in getting the SWO qualifications signed off, leading to my OOD qualification.

We maneuvered the ship to a position about 2,000 yards south of the entrance to the Gulf. The spooks considered this distance optimum for conducting their surveillance activities. To avoid constant maneuvering, we set the engine program control to "stop," bringing the ship dead in the water. We drifted very little since the offshore currents were minimal. Our operation and the purpose for which we were here had begun.

During the day, in addition to the ships' surface radar, hand-held binoculars, the "Big Eyes" binoculars mounted on each bridge wing, and the human eyeball are used for visual surveillance.

At night, radar, binoculars, FLIR, and night vision devices are the primary surveillance tools. The FLIR camera and sensor module are mounted above the pilothouse, and the viewing monitor and camera controls are located inside the pilothouse. Large night observation (vision) devices (NODS) are mounted on each bridge wing, and night vision goggles are provided for the lookouts and Signalmen.

The first night at the station was free of any significant events. With the engine stopped, it was unusually quiet in the pilothouse. The only activity was when, about every 30 minutes, the QMOW worked to fix the ship's position using radar and visual compass bearings to objects onshore. I stood the evening watch (1600-2000). During the watch, we only got underway twice to reposition the ship. I was starting to think this operation could be as mind-numbing as patrolling in the Persian Gulf.

Earlier in the late afternoon, some crew members noticed large schools of mahi-mahi, or common dolphinfish, around the ship. It didn't take long for the deep-sea fishing rods to appear, and soon they landed one mahi-mahi after another. Several of our Filipino cooks heard about the fish being caught and came out on deck to fish. Mahi-mahi are relatively large fish, ranging from 3.5 to almost 5 feet long and weighing between 15 and 40 pounds. By dark, many fish had been landed. The cooks decided the entire crew would feast on grilled mahi-mahi for tomorrow's evening meal.

One person, Master Chief Boatswain's Mate Mac Blake, was not very happy about all the fish caught and cleaned on the flight deck. His deck crew had just recently resurfaced and top-coated the entire flight deck. As I heard it, he told the fishermen that he better not find even a speck of blood, fish scales, or any other mess on his deck, or he would have their asses in a sling. Unless they're stupid, no one takes what a master chief says lightly. Once it was dark, crew members requested permission from the OOD to turn on the lights, so they could see to clean the flight deck. They didn't want to face the wrath of the master chief not being happy with the deck's cleanliness.

As promised by the cooks, the following evening's meal featured grilled mahi-mahi. This firm white fish has a pleasant, mild flavor. The cooks served the fish with mango salsa, rice, and a tasty salad. I have to say, I'm now a new fan of eating mahi-mahi.

Another afternoon activity that many in the crew surprisingly enjoyed was the afternoon physical training (PT) sessions. The session involved about an hour of doing various calisthenics. Not everyone at PT was there voluntarily; several individuals exceeded the body fat standards and were required to attend by mandate from the XO. Whenever my watch rotation allowed, I made it a point to participate in the PT sessions. Exercise over time always makes me feel better, both physically and mentally.

That evening, we entered the Gulf to rendezvous with one of the SBU 20 boats. About 45 minutes after sunset, we slowly entered the Gulf of Fonseca, heading for the designated rendezvous point south of Tiger Island and east of Meanguera Island. I was on watch as the conning officer and arranged for QM2 Jake Sullivan, my most senior and experienced Quartermaster, to be in the pilothouse to ensure we kept the ship clear of shallow water. Meanguera Island is located near the middle of the Gulf, about 9 nautical miles north of the entrance. This island features irregular, cliff-lined shores and rises over 1,600 feet high at its central part. A tiny inlet lies close to the southeast extremity of the island, where we expected the SBU boat to emerge.

When the ship was 4,000 yards (2 nautical miles) from Meanguera Island, we secured the navigation lights and went dark. Using a flashing light with an infrared lens aimed at the island, the Signalmen began sending Morse code, Quebec November, and numeral 1: "You should come alongside my port side."

The deck crew rigged a pilot ladder over the port side at the midship station on the main deck. The deck work lights were illuminated but with blue filters installed to reduce their visibility. The Signalmen and lookouts visually scanned the waters around the ship using NODS and night vision goggles. The OOD routinely panned the FLIR camera back and forth to detect small craft or fishing vessel activity. The captain monitored all activities, rotating between the pilothouse and CIC.

Just as the forward lookout began reporting over the amplified sound-powered phone circuit that he had spotted a small boat off the port bow, the radiotelephone crackled to life: "November Mike Juliet Echo, this is Papa Bravo One Niner, over."

The OOD grabbed the radiotelephone handset and answered, "Papa Bravo One Niner, this is November Mike Juliet Echo, over."

"Roger, request permission to come alongside on your port side, we see your deck light, over," the reply came.

The OOD responded, "Roger, permission granted to come alongside; the pilot ladder is over at midships, and line handlers are standing by, over."

"Roger, making our approach on your port side, out," the reply came.

I had set the engine program control to "stop" about five minutes earlier, and now the ship was dead in the water. I had called CCS and asked them to bring another ship service diesel generator (SSDG) online to supply electrical power to the APUs. Once SSDG#2 was online, I ordered the helmsman to lower the APUs. We would hold our position here using the APUs rather than the main propulsion and rudder.

Within several minutes, the profile of a small boat appeared out of the darkness and maneuvered alongside. I watched lines being passed down, and the crew secured their boat. Then silence when the boat's coxswain shut down the engines. After about a minute, one after another, four men ascended the pilot ladder, coming on board. The blue deck lights were shut off, and now the ship was dark.

Promptly at 1945, Lt. j.g. Gary Munson appeared in the pilothouse to relieve me as the conning officer and take the watch. Before going below, I checked with QM2 Sullivan to ensure he was comfortable with our location and could fix our position accurately.

Moments later, I descended the two ladders into the bright lights illuminating the portside passageway below deck. I planned to spend time in CCS with the Engineering Officer of the Watch (EOOW) for training on an auxiliary engineering system. As I passed the mess decks, four guys dressed in jungle fatigues were seated at one of the tables, enjoying the meal the cooks had served. One looked familiar; even wearing camo face paint, it was no mistake. With his distinctive crooked nose, I knew it was QM2 Hamilton "Ham" Savinsky from USS *Vreeland*.

I walked over to the table and said, "Well, Ham, it's good to see you."

He looked startled, recognizing me. "George, I mean chief, this is crazy, what on earth are you doing here? The last I remember, you got out," he responded.

"It's a long story, eat your chow, we'll catch up with each other's stories," I replied.

I sat at the table closest to Ham, and we visited while he finished his meal. He introduced me to the guys with him, one of whom was his boat engineer. He said nothing, but I knew the other two were SEALs just from their mannerisms.

Ham had transferred to SBU 20 the year before. His unit's primary task here was to support special warfare units. This was his second 90-day operating cycle in the Gulf of Fonseca region. His unit was supporting SEAL Team Two out of Little Creek. His unit was made up of a small flotilla of six boats. Their boats primarily operated out of Puerto Amapala, located on the northwest side of Tiger Island. Typically, they patrolled the waters around Tiger Island, which belong to Honduras and Meanguera Island. Meanguera Island was of more interest since it is a possession of El Salvador.

His boat had come out to the ship primarily to obtain repair parts for one of the other boats in his unit. In talking with Ham, it was clear that he was proud to be a riverine warfare coxswain in charge of his boat and crew. After Ham finished eating, he insisted I look at his patrol boat. We went out on the main deck where his boat was tied up. He went down the pilot ladder first, and then I followed him.

Once on board, I was reminded that the federal government did not wholly fund the operation here. Ham's boat is an example of corporate, not government, backing. Ham explained that his boat was designated Patrol Boat 19 (PB 19). The boat was a commercial-built, 25-foot Boston Whaler, Frontier Series, with stern drives, painted drab olive green. The boat had been armored and equipped with one MK2 81 mm mortar with a piggyback M-2 Browning .50 caliber machine gun. Two M-60 light machine guns were mounted on deck tripods on both sides, plus his boat carried M79 grenade launchers and M-16 rifles.

The Frontier Series has a spacious pilothouse forward and a large aft deck. Ham explained that the twin inboard engines were the largest available, each providing 300 horsepower, totaling 600 horsepower for the boat. His navigation equipment mainly consisted of a Furuno radar and a magnetic steering compass. His radio setup included one I was familiar with: the AN/PRC-25 (Prick 25) transceiver, which operates on two VHF frequency bands. After exploring his boat, primarily using flashlights with red lenses, we climbed back up the pilot ladder to the ship's deck.

James, the Chief Storekeeper, was there with several boxes. Ham's crew member and the two SEALs stood by, ready to disembark. James secured the boxes in a small net tied on a tending line. While I said goodbye to Ham, the others boarded the boat, and James lowered the boxes down to them. Ham descended the ladder, and we pulled up the pilot ladder as soon as he was on board. The boat's engines roared to life within moments, and his crew member tossed off the mooring lines. I watched Ham's boat back away and slip into the darkness.

After Ham's boat departed, I went to CCS. I decided to limit my time there since it was getting late, and I needed to get up at 0315 the following morning for the 0400-0800 watch. As I walked into CCS, the EOOW monitored the raising and securing of the APUs from the console. Moments later, the pilothouse called to relay that power from SSDG#2 was no longer needed. I could feel the ship's motion as it was being maneuvered, and propulsion brought us up to speed. I knew we were headed out of the Gulf back to our near-shore station for the night.

The next day was uneventful as we drifted around at our station. That afternoon at 1545, I assumed the evening watch as JOOD/conning officer. The ship was lying with our heading generally east at about 100 degrees. About 45 minutes after sunset, the forward lookout reported to the pilothouse an area of illuminated water at about 080 degrees relative, just forward of the starboard beam. He believed the range was about 3,000 yards (1.5 nautical miles) and closing fast.

The OOD and I rushed to the starboard bridge wing and, with our binoculars, began searching the water's surface at the relative bearing reported by the lookout. After several moments, we spotted it. The surface of the water was undisturbed but illuminated. The OOD hurried to the 21MC and called sonar control in CIC.

"Sonar, do you have anything at 080 relative, at 2,000 yards and closing?" he asked.

After about 30 seconds, the response came over the 21MC from sonar control: "Negative."

Meanwhile, I called the captain on the Bogen telephone system. When the captain answered, I said, "This is Chief Trowbridge. Captain, we need you in the pilothouse."

Within moments, the captain stepped into the pilothouse. "What is it?" he asked me.

"Area of illuminated water closing fast," I said, pointing to starboard.

He swiftly moved to the starboard bridge wing. We could see it clearly at about 300 yards; it appeared to be a fully illuminated, sizable underwater object. It never slowed, but as it got closer to the ship, it became evident that its depth had increased, and it disappeared under the ship. We all moved to the opposite bridge wing in time to see the light reappear momentarily, and then whatever it was disappeared.

The captain told the OOD, "Call the IC (Interior Communications) shop and tell them I want two video cameras loaded with film in the pilothouse at all times." Next, he turned to me. "Chief, get the most accurate fix position you can, plus the water depth here, and the bottom composition."

"Yes, Captain," I answered.

QM3 Michael Willard was the QMOW. I instructed him to obtain a round of compass bearings for the onshore objects we had been using. I proceeded to the radar to measure the range to land features that provided a good radar return. Less than a minute later, with the compass bearings and radar ranges, I plotted a position on the navigation chart I knew was accurate. The fathometer and charted depth matched, indicating that the water depth here was 105 fathoms (630 feet). The chart showed that the bottom composition was sand and mud. On paper, I recorded the latitude and longitude coordinates for our position, the water depth, and bottom composition information for the captain.

The captain was still in the pilothouse. I walked over to him and gave him the information I had recorded.

"Chief, go ahead and make the log entry. Let's call it what it is: an unidentified submerged object," he told me.

Next, he turned to the OOD. "Get Chief Lambert up here. I want him to take written statements from everyone who saw anything." The captain left the pilothouse, saying, "I'll be in CIC," as he descended the ladder.

The OOD had the word passed over the 1MC for the Chief Master-at-Arms to report to the pilothouse. In several minutes, Joe Lambert came up the ladder and entered the pilothouse.

"Who needs me?" he asked.

The OOD was standing near me and motioned Joe over. The OOD described what had happened and how the captain wanted written statements from witnesses. Once the OOD finished, Joe exhaled.

"You got to be shitting me," he said. He recovered and said to the OOD, "I'll get right on it, sir."

Joe turned to leave. "George, I'll take your statement after you get off watch, okay?" he said to me. I nodded to him, indicating my agreement.

That was it; we were officially veterans of our first USO encounter. It struck me that what we had just experienced was similar to the USO encounter described by the team from USS *Furer*. Once these phenomena were reported, I assumed that the U.S. Navy would want to investigate further. None of us knew, but there would be more to come.

Later, after I was relieved from watch, I went to the Chiefs Mess. I had brought along notes I had made about the incident. Joe asked for my permission to tape-record the interview, which I granted. The concise interview allowed me to detail everything that happened with a fresh memory and my notes. Lastly, Joe asked me to provide the written statement as well. After about 20 minutes, I handed him my completed statement. In my mind, the whole thing was now history—nothing to dwell on.

The year before, the ship's store on board USS *W.S. Sims* had received some really great Fujica 35 mm cameras. Since they were reasonably priced, I bought one on a whim and resolved that in the future, I would do more sightseeing and picture-taking while on liberty in foreign ports and less drinking and hell-raising. I also resolved that night that my camera would be with me whenever I was in the pilothouse for the rest of this operation.

The next day essentially followed what had become the routine: drifting off the entrance to the Gulf and occasionally moving to give the spooks a better vantage point for their intelligence-gathering activities. The watch that morning had been uneventful. I worked on OOD watch qualifications for most of the day. Late that afternoon, I assumed the evening watch in the pilothouse. Promptly at 1945, Lt. j.g Munson arrived in the pilothouse to begin the watch relief turnover. The sun had set about 25 minutes prior, and it was now dusk. Mr. Munson relieved me of the watch just as

I was about to go below, when the forward lookout came over the amplified sound-powered phone circuit speaker with a report.

"In the pilothouse, this is the forward lookout. I need more eyes out here to tell me what I see."

I turned and went to the port bridge wing and looked up at the lookout stationed above the pilothouse. He was leaning over the railing, looking down at me while pointing aft.

He said, "Chief, what in the hell is that?" I walked further aft, and then I saw it too. About three-quarters of the upper main mast structure was emitting a bluish, almost violet color; then I heard hissing and buzzing noises. I had seen this phenomenon before; I knew it was St. Elmo's fire.

The weather was clear, which made me wonder. Typically, St. Elmo's fire primarily occurs during thunderstorms. The hissing and buzzing sounds are proportional to the strength of the electrical field. It is a weather phenomenon in which a corona discharge from a rod-like object, such as a mast, creates luminous plasma. It's like lightning but not quite.

"Chief, what on earth is that thing?" the lookout yelled.

I didn't realize it, but Mr. Munson stood behind me and echoed the lookout's question, "Yeah, Chief, what is that?"

"You're seeing something not many people get to see, St. Elmo's fire," I answered them both.

I noticed Jamey Holden, one of my Signalmen on the 02-level, slowly walking aft toward the mast structure. I yelled at him to stop and get back. I know that any object from which St. Elmo's fire emanates is in danger of being struck by lightning, since this type of discharge may be the initial phase of the leader stroke.

The buzzing sound ceased, and the bluish glow faded away after about 30 more seconds. St. Elmo's fire was done and gone. I'm disappointed there was no time for anyone to grab a camera and record the event.

I was still puzzled by the clear, nearly cloudless sky. I checked the radar to see if I could detect any rain squalls or weather patterns not visible in the darkness; the display was clear. To me, this appearance of St. Elmo's fire is somewhat of a mystery.

After the St. Elmo's fire experience, I went below to the Chiefs Mess. It was close to 2030, so I thought I would relax while watching recorded professional wrestling shows on TV before turning in. I had just sat down and began to relax when the Bogen phone rang. Mark Goddard answered the phone and listened for a moment.

"Yes, sir," he said and then hung up.

Mark turned to me. "Don't know what's up, but the OOD says the captain wants to see you in the pilothouse immediately," he said.

I left the mess and rushed to the pilothouse. I was momentarily blinded in the darkness as I reached the top of the ladder to the pilothouse.

I heard Mr. Munson say, "Chief, the captain is out on the 02-level aft of the pilothouse." I felt my way to the port bridge wing door, went out onto the bridge wing, and then headed aft along the superstructure. I looked up, and what I saw stopped me cold. White lights were arranged in a V-shape just above the highest antenna on the main mast. I continued aft to the open deck area on the 02-level. I found the captain in the dim light, looking up at the mast. When I got near him, he pointed up and said, "Chief, any idea what that is?"

"No, sir, it's not any weather or atmospheric phenomenon I've heard of. Sir, we need to get video and pictures," I answered.

"I've sent for Mr. Michel too," he replied.

A moment later, the officer in charge of the spook detachment, Mr. Michel, stood next to us. He had brought two of his CTs with him. They both held video cameras and immediately started recording. I counted seven lights in the V-shape; sometimes, I could make out a faint triangular shape.

"About how long has this been here?" I asked the captain.

"Probably about 10 minutes," he replied.

"Sir, I'll be right back," I said.

I turned, realizing I now had gained some night vision. I went as fast as I could to the pilothouse. Once there, I went into the chartroom to retrieve my camera and returned to the 02-level. I knew I had a fresh roll of 24 exposure film loaded.

I went aft, stopping where I thought I would have the best vantage point, adjusting the camera to optimize exposure in low-light conditions. I walked further aft, directly under the object above the mast, to a point where I could look forward and up. I took maybe six or more pictures. From this angle, I could make out the object's shape. It was a triangular-shaped craft, hovering about 30 to 40 feet above the main mast, but it made no noise; it was silent. The ship's beam (width) was 45 feet. I first walked to the lifelines on the port side and looked up. I estimated the outer reach of the craft's structure looked to extend 20 to 25 feet over the side of the main deck below. I went to the starboard side and estimated the structure extended about the same distance over the main deck. By my estimate, the craft spanned at least 95 to 100 feet from one vertex to the other corner.

Then the words came to mind: "Unidentified Flying Object." I was witnessing my very first up-close UFO. Holy shit. Questions came to mind,

Was what we took earlier to be St. Elmo's fire real? Or was what we saw something conjured up by this UFO?

I was taking what I believed to be the last exposures on my film. As I adjusted the lens, I watched the craft disappear from view. I lowered my camera while looking up. There was nothing there. The UFO had vanished faster than the blink of an eye. I returned to where the captain and Mr. Michel were still standing.

"Captain, Mr. Michel, can we agree that what we just witnessed was a UFO? Or should we call it something else?" I said.

The captain replied, "Let's call it an encounter with an unknown aerial object. Chief, will you call or get Chief Lambert and fill him in? I want interviews and statements taken."

On small surface combatant ships, any news takes about two minutes to travel throughout the boat. On my way to the mess to find Joe Lambert, crew members stopped me several times and asked, "Hey, chief, did you see the UFO?"

My answer each time was, "We don't know what we saw."

I've witnessed some odd things at sea, especially at night. I have seen orbs glowing in various colors dance across the sky. I have observed rows and other geometric-shaped lights floating slowly and quickly across the heavens, only to disappear as if someone flipped a switch. However, I had never experienced what I had just seen.

Once in the mess, I found Joe, Mark, and James in the lounge.

"What's up?" Mark asked.

"The captain wants to call something we saw an unknown aerial object." I turned to Joe and said, "The captain wants you to gather everyone, interview them, and take statements. So, you may have a long night ahead of you. When you're ready, why don't you start with me so I can fill you in?"

I spent the next 15 minutes telling Joe about the UFO experience. Mark and James listened to what I said during the interview. As Joe got up to leave, I told him I would write my statement and ensure he got it later. I also gave him a list of people he should interview and get statements from. After Joe left, Mark summed up our situation so far.

"So here we are in the middle of a covert operation to monitor and support a war that we're not in, where the saltwater fishing is great. Then we get harassed first by a USO, next some weird light is all over the mast, and now a goddam UFO. We should call this place the Twilight Zone."

I think Mark's summation said it best. I did add, "But let's look at the bright side, no one is shooting at us or trying to kill us. I agree that the fishing here is great, and I am hungry for more mahi-mahi. Plus, at least the USO and UFO haven't vaporized us with a death ray or something, so things are good." James looked at me momentarily, shook his head, and walked away.

The following morning, the captain held a closed meeting in the wardroom with the XO and department heads. I was aware of the probable topic of the meeting. The questions would likely be: Last night, should the captain have called the crew to their battle stations by setting General Quarters (GQ)? Should encounters with USOs or unknown aerial objects be handled as hostile and, therefore, a threat to the ship? We would soon get the captain's decision.

The word passed over the 1MC: "All chief petty officers not on watch, assemble in the Chiefs Mess at 1030."

Shortly before 1030, most of the chiefs were in the mess. A knock came at the door, and the captain and XO entered. The first table closest to the door was always reserved for the captain, the XO, or any department head whenever they visited the mess. Once they were seated, we had the mess cook serve them coffee before we dismissed him.

The captain told us that he had called Southern Command in Panama over secure voice radio early this morning to report the USO and UFO events. I noted he now used the term UFO, not unknown aerial object.

He paused before saying, "They left it to my discretion to handle these events. However, the point was made that, whatever I do, I must avoid at all costs giving the appearance that we are aggressive or about to take hostile measures."

The XO took over by saying, "Starting at noon today, we will shift from Watch Condition III to Watch Condition II, port and starboard watch sections. That way, if we need to, we'll already be in a fighting posture."

As a Quartermaster, I had observed how they bore the weight of being in command under different commanding officers. The captain had contacted Southern Command for guidance, and all they did was dump it right back in his lap, with conditions. I must say, though, this is normal. If nothing happens, well, all is good. If something does happen that endangers or damages the ship or crew, they could hold the captain responsible. The commanders would be free and clear since they left decisions to the captain's discretion. That's the military way.

Shortly after the captain and XO left, I heard the announcement over the 1MC that the ship was shifting to Watch Condition II at 1200. I went to the pilothouse to check the Watch, Quarter, and Station Bill for my division and spoke with SM1 Larson, who told me he would ensure the Quartermasters and Signalmen were set up for port and starboard (six hours on, six hours off) watchkeeping. I explained to him that the watch condition was only while we were at the station and that we would be relieved on May 25 by USS *Gallery* (FFG 26).

At this point, I should tell you about Seaman (SN) Jorge (hohr-heh) Dejesus. Jorge was born and raised in Puerto Rico. He was relatively tall, with red hair and a heavily freckled face. Jorge was an undesignated seaman assigned to the deck force, SC-3 division. He was 19 or 20 years old, had been in the Navy for less than one year, and was well-liked by everyone. Jorge was a hard worker and always tried his best. One trait that made him stand out was his way of talking. English was his second language, so often, especially if he was excited about something, he would slip into speaking without fully pronouncing or saying all the necessary words. If he couldn't fully describe something in English, Jorge made substitutions. He jokingly called it his Puerto Rican Spanglish.

Jorge was known for one of his unforgettable lookout reports to the pilothouse. The one that stood out went like this over the amplified sound-powered phone circuit: "In the pilothouse, this is Hohr-heh, the forward lookout. I see a ship at 070, at maybe 12,000 yards, 6 miles."

The OOD, smiling, reached for the phone handset to speak with Jorge. "Forward lookout, what kind of ship is it?"

"Sir, this is Hohr-heh, no tengo idea, I mean, I don't know, but it's a bihg ass shihp," Jorge replied.

Everyone in the pilothouse cracked up laughing at Jorge's unconventional report. After that, often different crew members would be overheard saying, "It's a big ass ship," or "It's a "BAS," the new acronym for Big Ass Ship.

Watch Condition II now shifted me to the hours of 1800-2400 and the morning watch 0600-1200. At 1745 that afternoon, I relieved Lt. j.g. Greg Hanlon as the JOOD and conning officer. So far, it had been a quiet day. Jorge was in my watch section and started the first hour of the watch as the SCC operator. The SCC operator, forward, and aft lookouts rotate stations every hour to maintain alertness.

The OOD was Lieutenant Donald Hannity. Lt. Hannity was my boss as the ship control department head. Shortly after taking over the watch, Lt. Hannity informed me that the captain wanted me in the conning officer rotation for docking, undocking, and underway replenishment. Then he told me I was the conning officer for the next docking in Rodman.

Lt. Hannity added that the captain had agreed that we could practice restricted ship handling maneuvering while at the station, as circumstances allowed.

Then he said, "We have some time right now. Are you ready?"

I replied, "Yes, sir."

We called CCS to notify them that we would be lowering and operating the APUs, so that they could ensure adequate electrical power on the system. For the next several hours, we practiced using the thrust generated by the APUs, in opposition to the thrust from the CRP propeller, and using the rudder to maneuver the ship at various lateral angles. We also did some runs of slowly thrusting on the propeller, against the thrust from the APUs, to walk the ship forward and aft. We wrapped it up around 2000, just as it got dark. I gained new respect for Lt. Hannity; not only was he a very proficient ship handler, but he was also an excellent coach.

Tonight was our fifth night on the station. The crew had taken to calling our area of operation Loco Station. It was dark, close to 2100, when the lookout, amplified sound-powered phone circuit came to life. The aft lookout reported an underwater light about a mile from the port side beam. He added that it was coming straight at us. As we ran to the port bridge wing, I overheard Jorge, now the forward lookout, on the speaker saying, "Big light in the water, on the port beam, gran luz en el agua."

I yelled at Willard, the QMOW, to grab my camera from the chartroom. Within moments, Willard was beside me, handing me the camera. The underwater light was about 300 to 400 yards away; I was surprised how well it showed up through the camera lens. I began snapping pictures as fast as I could take them, hoping I would catch something on film. Just like before, the area of illuminated water moved in and then went under the ship. We ran to the opposite bridge wing just in time to see the light reappear, then moments later, it was gone.

Lt. Hannity immediately picked up the Bogen phone to call the captain. I overheard him explain the USO sighting, mentioning that it happened so quickly that there was no time to contact him before it reached our position.

After he hung up with the captain, he said, "Chief, just make the log entries about the encounter. The captain doesn't see any point in doing interviews or taking statements."

"Yes, sir, I'll take care of it," I replied.

The following night, we had another rendezvous in the Gulf of Fonseca with boats from SBU 20. We secured the navigation lights and went dark as we entered the Gulf. I navigated the ship by radar to take us to a prearranged position east of Meanguera Island and south of Tiger Island. Lt. Hannity monitored the areas around the ship on FLIR, and the lookouts scanned the waters using night vision goggles.

Once the ship was at the rendezvous position, I ordered the engine program control to "stop." Soon, the ship was dead in the water. CCS brought another SSDG online to supply electrical power to the APUs. I ordered the helmsman to lower the APUs. Like the last time, we would hold our position here using the APUs. Now we waited.

After about 10 minutes, a voice came over the radiotelephone; it was one of SBU 20's patrol boats calling. Lt. Hannity answered the call.

The reply came, "Roger, request permission to come alongside your port side. We see your blue deck lights, over." Lt. Hannity responded, "Permission granted to come alongside; the pilot ladder is over at midships."

"Roger, two units approaching on your port side, out," the reply came.

Within five minutes, two boats were making up along the ship's side. From what I could see, these boats were Boston Whalers too, and they looked almost identical to Ham's PB 19. Our deck crew positioned the boats so that both crews could come on board using the single pilot ladder. I watched from the bridge wing as, one after another, the boat crews ascended the ladder, coming on board. The blue deck lights were shut off, and it was back to being a darkened ship.

James called the pilothouse to let us know his people would be staging supplies on the main deck for loading on the two patrol boats. The SBU crews stayed on board well over two hours. Later, I learned that the cooks served them meals, and several asked to take showers and if we could launder some uniforms. Later, when the boat crews were ready and back on board their boats, they prepared to depart. The deck crew lowered boxes and containers using nets and tending lines to the patrol boats. Boat engines roared to life, our deck crew tossed off the mooring lines, and I watched the boats back away, fading into the darkness.

I ordered the helmsman to de-energize and retract the APUs. Thrusting on the propeller with right full rudder, I twisted the ship around until our heading was fair, taking us south to the Gulf's entrance and back offshore. It was almost 2330, so my night's work was nearly over. Twenty minutes later, our watch reliefs took over, and I went below; another long day was complete.

Days six, seven, and eight at the station were reasonably uneventful. During the late afternoons, more crew members tried their hand at saltwater fishing off the flight deck. While on watch, Lt. Hannity continued coaching me further in ship handling tactics, permitting me to practice various maneuvers. I was pleased as my success rate and proficiency increased.

On the evening of day eight, we carried out another rendezvous with two more boats from SBU 20 in the northern area of the Gulf. Everything went smoothly. After the patrol boats departed, Chief Gunner's Mate John Jeggey visited the pilothouse. He told me they primarily supplied the patrol boats with ammunition, mortar rounds, and fuel. He assumed they may have been in or were going into some hot operations.

The following evening was our ninth night on station. Lt. Hannity was the OOD, and I was the JOOD/conning officer. QM3 Salsberg was the QMOW, Seaman Goddard was the SCC operator and helmsman, and Jorge and Seaman Banks were the lookouts. It had been quiet since we came on watch at 1745. At 2200, Salsberg began the hourly weather observation. He went out on the starboard bridge wing to go aft of the pilothouse to the weather instrument station mounted on the bulkhead. Moments later, I noticed Salsberg's silhouette in the door opening.

"Mister Hannity, chief, you need to come out here," he said.

As Lt. Hannity and I moved toward Salsberg, Jorge's voice came over the lookout's amplified sound-powered phone circuit: "In the pilothouse, this is Hohr-heh, there's a big ass thing floating over us," he said, his voice fading, "A bihg ass objeto, flotando encima el barco."

We looked up, and in the same position as the last time, we could see the triangular-shaped outline of something big directly above the top mast antenna, but this time, it showed only a single white light. Lt. Hannity's shoulder brushed mine as he quickly moved to the Bogen phone to call the captain. He came back out on the bridge wing, and moments later, the captain was beside him. Chief Operations Specialist Bobby Babcock, the CIC Watch Officer, came up to the pilothouse.

"What's going on?" he asked me.

I told him to go out and look up above the main mast, and he would see. He stepped out and stood by the captain on the bridge wing.

In moments, he returned. "I'll get some spooks up here with cameras," he said as he passed by me.

After a short pause, the captain turned to me. and said, "Chief, call CCS and tell them I want both gas turbines online immediately, and call us back when they're ready for 30 knots." I went to the 21MC and called CCS, relaying the captain's order. I could detect the EOOW's wonderment in his voice as he said, "Aye, aye."

It wasn't more than three minutes before the EOOW's voice came over the 21MC: "Pilothouse, this is CCS, gas turbines 1A and 1B are online and ready."

I answered back to CCS, repeating their report.

"Chief, take us to 30 knots, right standard rudder, let's see what happens," the captain said.

"Aye, sir," I answered.

Next, I turned and ordered, "Helmsman, set program control to 30 knots, right standard rudder."

Seaman Goddard repeated my order, "Aye, set program control to 30 knots, right standard rudder."

There isn't anything much more exhilarating than hearing the whine of two gas turbines as they come up to speed and feeling the kick of the ship as the five blades of the 16.5-foot diameter CRP propeller go to maximum ahead pitch and dig into the water, creating massive amounts of thrust.

The helmsman reported, "My rudder is at right standard, program control indicates 30 knots."

I answered, "Very well." I wanted to let him know I heard his report.

In less than two minutes, the ship was up to speed. The massive thrust generated by the propeller creates vibrations and resultant harmonics that rumble through the ship's steel hull and aluminum superstructure. I walked out to the starboard bridge wing and was hit by the relative wind our speed was creating. Looking aft, I could see the phosphorescence in the stern wake and rooster tail shooting 20 to 25 feet in the air. This is all part of what has quickly created my love affair with FFGs. I commenced a series of maneuvers by steering courses that created a zig-zag pattern. Then the captain entered the pilothouse.

"Reduce speed to 10 knots, call CCS, and tell them to resume single gas turbine operation. Take us back to our station," he told me.

"What happened?" I asked Lt. Hannity.

He replied, "Whatever it was just vanished. It's gone."

I asked him another question, "Do we need Chief Lambert to conduct witness interviews and take statements?" He shook his head. "No, I don't think so," he said. "Just make the appropriate log entries."

This was it—we had our second UFO encounter. The captain had decided to handle it less formally than he did the first time.

Nearing the end of our watch, we returned to our station just outside the Gulf entrance and resumed our regular patrol routine. At 2345, our watch reliefs arrived in the pilothouse, and we turned over the watch. The turnover took a few minutes longer than usual since there was more information to brief them about what happened during the watch. The following two days were routine, except on the second night, we carried out another rendezvous with SBU 20 patrol boats in the northern reaches of the Gulf of Fonseca.

Early the next morning, just after I took watch at 0545, USS *Gallery* (FFG 26) arrived on station. She was here to relieve us so we could go back to Rodman. Around 0630, the deck crew launched our motor whaleboat off its boat davits into the water. Soon, the officer in charge of the spook detachment, along with several CTs and some members of our CIC team, loaded into the boat. Within moments, our whaleboat was heading to *Gallery* to conduct the turnover briefing with them. I commented to Lt. Hannity that I would love to be there when the subject of our USO and UFO encounters came up.

He chuckled and said, "Yes, that could be interesting."

I was prepared to execute the passage plan to Rodman on our whaleboat's return from *Gallery*. Finally, around 0900, the whaleboat came back alongside. Everyone except the boat crew disembarked via the pilot ladder to the boat deck. The boat was secured to the davit falls, lifted out of the water, and ultimately secured in the davit cradle. The boat deck reported to the pilothouse that the boat was secured for sea.

The captain sat in his chair and said, "Chief, let's go to Rodman." "Yes, sir!" I responded.

I relayed to the conning officer to increase speed to 16 knots and steer course 160 degrees, starting our first leg of the transit to Rodman.

CHAPTER 10

NEXT UP

At times, the 12 days we had been at the Gulf of Fonseca seemed never-ending. By early morning on May 27, we were off Punta Mala, the western entrance to the Gulf of Panama. I was excited about the chance to conn the ship for today's docking in Rodman. By 1230, we were in the northern waters of the Gulf and approaching the entrance channel to Balboa and Rodman.

Lt. Hannity took over the navigation plot while we were in the entrance channel. As we approached the Pan-American Bridge, I assumed the conn. Soon, we passed under the bridge and entered the channel off Balboa, where I reduced the ship's speed to allow the pilot boat to come alongside. The pilot boarded as the APUs were lowered. When the pilot arrived in the pilothouse, the captain explained that he wanted him to advise only and allow me to conn the ship to the dock, and the pilot agreed.

When handling a ship in restricted maneuvering situations, such as docking, the conning officer must manage multiple actions. The primary task is controlling the ship's position relative to the dock using the thrust generated by the propeller and the force produced by the rudder. With FFGs, the APUs are in the mixed configuration and are now utilized as a type of bow thruster. Once close enough to the dock, the mooring lines are put over; the conning officer must now control the order in which lines are put over. Once the first mooring lines are made fast on the dock, handling the mooring lines on deck must be managed to assist in final maneuvering and positioning the ship alongside the pier.

We were assigned to a berth on the south side of Rodman Pier Number Two, where we would moor with our starboard side to the dock. In the channel well off the pier, I began to twist the ship around its pivot point to port by thrusting with the propeller, using the rudder and the APUs to complete the turn and align the bow with the pier face. Once aligned, I proceeded slowly and used the APUs to control the ship's heading in relation to the dock. I planned to approach the dock so that, when alongside our berth, the ship would be at an angle of about 30 degrees from the dock, bow in.

It couldn't have gone any better. Once the bow was close enough, I ordered the bow line (line 1) and the after-bow spring line (line 2) over to the dock. Once the dock line handlers secured line 2, I ordered our deck crew on the forecastle to take a strain and hold the line. I applied left rudder and slowly thrust ahead on the propeller, forcing the ship's stern to walk towards the pier. As we got close, I ordered the crew on the flight deck to put over the stern line (line 6) and the quarter spring lines (lines 4 and 5). The deck crews took the bow and stern lines to power on the capstans, pulling the ship into its final position alongside the dock.

With quiet pride, I acknowledged that I had done it—conning the ship alongside a dock for the first time.

Lt. Hannity approached me. "Chief, excellent job," he said.

I thanked him and reminded him of our practice; his patience deserved the credit. However, only the captain's opinion mattered. The captain had stayed near me throughout the entire docking process, never saying a word. Once all mooring lines were doubled up and secured, I ordered the APUs retracted and de-energized. I requested permission from the captain to order CCS to secure propulsion, which he granted. Only then did the captain call me out to the starboard bridge wing.

He turned toward me and said, "Chief, outstanding job. That was excellent." His words gave me a sense of relief and satisfaction.

"Do you have your SWO book handy?" he asked.

"Yes, sir, it's in the chartroom, let me fetch it," I said.

Moments later, I handed him my SWO book. He turned to the qualification section and signed off the docking evolution. He returned the book to me.

"I'll sign the next section when you successfully undock and get us underway," he said.

I thanked the captain as he walked away and went below. For me, so far, it had been a damn fine day. I hadn't noticed before, but near the head of the pier, two black vans were parked. As we secured from the Sea and Anchor detail, I counted eight men exiting the vehicles and walking down the dock toward the ship. With only mild interest, I wondered who they were, since two of them were dressed in dark suits—wrong attire for Panama's tropical climate.

The men in dark suits drew my attention just because of their clothing. Three of the men were carrying what looked like black suitcases. As soon as the gangway was out and secured, I watched as all eight came on board. I would quickly find out what these men were up to.

What had started as a good day quickly turned sour. I was hungry since I'd missed breakfast and lunch, so I went to the mess. Luckily, the mess cook had prepared a plate for me and had put it in the reefer. I grabbed a glass of milk from the dispenser and sat down at one of the tables to eat. In a few moments, the mess door opened, and a stranger in civilian clothes walked in.

He looked at me. "Do you know where Chief Trowbridge is?" he asked.

"Yes, I do," I answered. "Everyone, including the captain, knocks on the door before entering the Chiefs Mess. It's just a common courtesy. Have you ever heard of it?" What I said didn't faze the guy.

"I need to see Chief Trowbridge. Can you get him for me?" he said.

"Yes, I can. I'm Chief Trowbridge. What do you want?" I answered.

He responded, "I need you to go to the pilothouse right now. My partner is already there and waiting for us."

This guy quickly annoyed me; I looked at him briefly before saying, "Who are you and what do you want? By the way, you can see I'm eating right now, can't you?"

"Are you coming or not?" he replied.

I laughed and told him, "When I've finished eating, I'll come to the pilothouse. Can you spare five damn minutes?" Without saying a word, he turned and walked out the door. Around that time, Bobby walked in, the chief in charge of CIC. I asked him if he knew what was happening.

His answer surprised me: "These guys claim to be from the Office of Naval Intelligence, but I don't think so. I'm not sure who they are, but I'll bet there is no way that's who they are."

"Some of them are talking with the captain, XO, and all the department heads in the wardroom right now," he added. I told Bobby about the guy who had just been in the mess and what he wanted.

"See, ONI people would never act like that," he said.

I intended to finish eating leisurely and then go to the pilothouse. The Bogen phone began ringing; no one else was around, so I answered. It was SM1 Larson calling from the pilothouse. I could hear the urgency in his voice.

"Chief, there are two people up here, they won't identify themselves, and they're demanding to see all of the logbooks and navigation charts we used at the Gulf of Fonseca."

"I'll be right there," I told Larson. I hung up the phone and hurried to the pilothouse.

On stepping into the pilothouse, one of the guys was the jerk who had come to the mess earlier. The other was one of the suits.

"Gentlemen, what can we do for you?" I said.

The guy in the suit stepped toward me. "Chief, we need to see your navigation record books and logs, the deck logs, and all navigation charts used while at the Gulf of Fonseca."

"Well, there's a problem with me doing that," I answered.

"What's that?"

"Everything you just asked for contains information that is either classified or secret, and I have no idea who you people are," I said. "You guys ever heard of operational security, OPSEC? The XO or, at the very least, my department head needs to authorize me to release what you're requesting. Let me call my department head and see what he says."

I sensed that these two were accustomed to bullying others. I could also see that the jerk was getting irritated. I stepped to the Bogen phone and called Lt. Hannity's stateroom; there was no answer. Next, I called the wardroom, but no one answered. Lastly, I called the XO's stateroom, and there was no response. I hung up the phone.

"Until I can speak with someone in my chain of command, I won't release anything," I told him.

I turned to Larson. "Would you go see if you can find Mr. Hannity or the XO and tell them I need them in the pilothouse?"

Larson seemed relieved at having the chance to leave. "You got it, chief," he said.

Down the ladder to below decks he went. I stepped into the chartroom, grabbed two stools, carried them to the pilothouse, and set them down.

"Have a seat until Lieutenant Hannity or the XO shows," I said.

They both took a seat; I went out on the starboard bridge wing to avoid talking to either of them while we waited. Larson returned and came out on the bridge wing. He told me he had checked at the quarterdeck, and both Mr. Hannity and the XO were off the ship.

Finally, after about 15 more minutes, I spotted Lt. Hannity and the XO at the head of the pier, walking toward the ship. I asked Larson to go to the quarterdeck and meet Lt. Hannity, to tell him of what was happening, and that I needed him in the pilothouse. I noted that he went aft on the 02-level, using the vertical ladder to descend to the main deck instead of going through the pilothouse.

I watched as Lt. Hannity and the XO crossed the gangway. Within several minutes, Lt. Hannity stepped into the pilothouse, spotted me on the bridge wing, and came out. I noticed that as he walked by the two agents, he barely acknowledged their presence.

"Sir, can you tell me what's happening here and who these people are?" I asked.

He gave a dejected look. "Chief, we're not sure who they are, but the captain has spoken with Southern Command, and they told him to cooperate with them. These people claim to be ONI agents, but I think it's more likely they're from some other agency."

"So, I can surrender the logbooks, charts, and our records to them?" I replied.

He nodded. "Yes, Chief, you can."

"Okay, sir, we'll take care of it. Is this all about the USO, UFO events?" I answered. He nodded, indicating yes.

Lt. Hannity walked back through the pilothouse and disappeared down the ladder. I approached the two agents.

"Tell me again what you want, and I'll have my people get them for you," I said.

"So you'll cooperate now?" the jerk replied.

I nodded. "I just said so, didn't I?"

I had developed a strong dislike for this asshole. The guy in the suit stood up and handed me a list of what they wanted. I called down to the lounge for the ship control department berthing and found that my two senior

Quartermasters, Sullivan and Faber, were there. I told them to come up to the pilothouse.

When they arrived, I handed the list to Sullivan. "Give these guys everything on that list. I'll be in the Chiefs Mess. If they ask for anything not on that list, call me."

I turned to the two guys. "QM2 Sullivan and QM2 Faber will get what you want."

Then, I turned and went down the ladder. At the foot of the ladder, I noticed the door to CIC was partially open, and I could hear people talking. I continued below and then headed to the mess.

Some other chiefs, including Joe Lambert, were present when I entered the Chiefs Mess. I asked Joe if he knew anything more about what was happening. He told me he had been in the central office complex (CoC) when two agents came in, demanded reams of copy paper, and inspected the copy machine. Once the paper was given to them, they instructed everyone to leave.

"Before they let me go, they wanted all written statements and interview notes having to do with the USO and UFO sightings," Lambert said.

Bobby interjected, saying there were more agents in CIC reviewing all the logs and records, which led to him, along with everyone else, being kicked out of CIC. I informed them that two in the pilothouse wanted all the logbooks, documents, and navigation charts.

I decided to return to the pilothouse. Sullivan and Faber were still there, but the two agents had left. Faber was in the chart room. He had my camera and bag on the chart table.

"Chief, we told the one guy no, but he stripped the film out of your camera and took every roll out of your bag. I'm sorry, there was no time to call you," he said.

I told him not to worry about it and that it wasn't his fault. I thanked them for their help and told them to call it a day.

Later, I was sitting in the lounge in the Chiefs Mess. The Bogen phone rang, so I answered it. It was the XO. He asked me if Chiefs Babcock and Lambert were also in the mess. I told him they were.

"The agents want to see you, Chief Babcock, and Chief Lambert in CoC," he said.

I told him I would gather them and head to CoC. I rounded up Bobby and Joe, and the three of us went aft to the passageway leading to the CoC. As we approached the entrance, we were surprised to see Lt. Hannity, two other department heads, and four of our junior officers standing in line outside the door. I noted that everyone here, except for Joe, was a watchstander either in CIC or the pilothouse.

"Does anyone know what this is all about?" I asked.

Lt. Hannity responded, "I'm not certain, but I guess they're going to want us to sign some kind of nondisclosure statement."

We waited in line, and one after another, the officers were called in pairs of two. No one was in there for long, maybe two or three minutes, before exiting and silently walking away.

Finally, they called Bobby and me. Inside, the XO sat off to the side. The same guy in the suit from the pilothouse called me over to the desk where he sat. In a monotone voice, he delivered a practiced statement, stating that I shall never disclose, verbally or in written form, any information about the events I witnessed from May 14 through May 24. Additionally, in any form of communication, I would never reveal to anyone their presence on board or any interactions I had with them.

He slid a document to me and held out a pen. "Read paragraphs 2 and 3, then sign at the bottom of the document."

I glanced at the XO and made eye contact. He gestured, indicating I needed to sign. I read the two paragraphs, then signed my name at the bottom of the document.

"Thanks, Chief, you can go," the XO said.

I turned and left the CoC as they called the last one in, Joe. On my way back to the mess, I could only think, *This is all a cover-up*. Our government was trying to keep our encounters with USOs and UFOs, or whatever they were, quiet. The only rationale I can relate to is that our entire operation was covert; therefore, no matter what happened here, it never really happened.

The following morning, at officers' call, the XO handed each of us a document. His instruction was to read the document's content to our division personnel and remind them that our operation here is classified. As I started to depart, the XO pulled me aside to tell me that the smooth deck logs had been returned and to have someone pick them up later from his stateroom.

I had wondered about that. I know no one can legally confiscate a ship's smooth deck logs since they are part of the ship's official record and ultimately are sent for safekeeping to the National Archives in Washington, D.C.

During morning quarters with my division, I reviewed the document provided by the XO. Then I asked all of them if they understood. Each man indicated in the affirmative. My last comment was that what happened yesterday is behind us. I had asked Sullivan to go to the XO's stateroom and recover the deck logs. Later, while still in the pilothouse, Sullivan approached me holding a folder.

He opened the folder to show me the returned deck logs. "Someone was busy," he said.

I reviewed the logs and noticed that numerous entries had been redacted with a black marker. It was time to put everything behind us and enjoy what we could while in Rodman.

Panama City is just a short taxi ride away on the other side of the canal. I informed Lt. Hannity that I wanted to allow maximum liberty for my division, and he agreed. My immediate mission for today was to find somewhere to make a phone call home to Jan.

Rodman Naval Station has a small but friendly CPO Club, just a short walk up the hillside from the waterfront. Late that afternoon, a group of us walked to the club. I learned earlier that the club had phones capable of making international calls.

After several beers, I figured I'd better call Jan before it was too late. This was my first chance to call her since our departure from Mayport. After finishing my call with Jan, I decided it was time to do some serious drinking. Why not? We all need to let off some steam. We were on a naval base. And, it was only a short walk, drunk or not, back to the ship.

Mark, James, Bobby, and I visited downtown Panama City the following night. We discovered a club called "The Copacabana," designed to resemble the famous Copacabana in Rio de Janeiro. The place reminded me of the nightclubs often featured in old movies. The club was quite classy, with every waitress being drop-dead gorgeous and wearing outfits that left little to the imagination. Several bars were lined with more women than men. Along the bars, I couldn't spot a woman who wasn't stunningly beautiful. You could buy them drinks for about 10 times the price, and if you do, you could choose to have a date for the night.

Later, the floor show began with a celebration of the Brazilian Carnival. All the samba dancers were beautiful, scantily clad women in elaborate, colorful costumes. It was an excellent and entertaining show that surprisingly lasted several hours, showcasing different types of samba music and styles of samba dancing.

On Friday morning, June 3, we were tasked with loading supplies to take to the Gulf of Fonseca. James supervised the loading of supplies in the port and starboard helicopter hangars, while John Jeggey oversaw his Gunner's Mates stowing ammunition in the small arms magazines. During lunch in the mess, John mentioned that they had loaded some unmarked and sealed cases that the CT spooks had taken possession of and placed in their operations container. Several loaded items piqued our interest when James mentioned that two 14-foot, Zodiac-type inflatable boats in crates, with two outboard motors, were among the received supplies.

We would depart Rodman on Sunday morning to begin the transit back to the Gulf. Most chiefs, including me, would go to the CPO Club on Friday or Saturday night. Our time in Rodman, Panama City, and the Canal Zone had provided a welcomed break.

Early on Sunday morning, the ship set out from our berth. I filed our MOVREP message just before getting underway, reporting the "MOD OUT" position just south of the Pan-American Bridge. After the conning officer backed the ship into the canal channel, he turned the ship around to head down the outbound channel. Several minutes later, we passed under the Pan-American Bridge. According to our MOVREP message, we would soon officially disappear. We cleared the outbound channel 20 minutes later and entered the Gulf of Panama. On our arrival at the Gulf of Fonseca, we would relieve USS *Gallery* on the morning of June 7.

On Monday morning, during officers' call, the XO announced that at 0930, there would be a briefing in the wardroom for all principal pilothouse and CIC watchstanders. Just before 0930, everyone who was not on watch assembled in the wardroom. Lt. j.g. Michel, the officer in charge of the CT spook detachment, was present to conduct the meeting and the briefing. Once the captain arrived, he instructed Mr. Michel to open the meeting. We were about to learn that significant changes had occurred during our short absence from the Gulf of Fonseca.

Mr. Michel began by discussing numerous intelligence items they had gathered during our previous visit to the region. In the interim, Southern Command and the intelligence detachment aboard USS *Gallery* confirmed much of what they believed had been learned.

He emphasized that the operations between the Contras and Sandinistas had escalated into a hot war in some of the eastern areas of the Gulf. It was also thought that Cuban forces might be in the area. Our area of operation was now primarily in the Gulf, not offshore.

We learned that the Nicaraguan Navy had deployed one 60-ton patrol craft and two Israeli-built, 35-ton patrol boats into the eastern Gulf of Fonseca. SBU 20's patrol boats now had potential adversaries in the Gulf. They may need backup, and that would be us.

The Nicaraguan patrol boats operated from Puerto Corinto, approximately 40 miles southeast of the entrance to the Gulf of Fonseca. Their shallow-draft patrol boats travelled from Puerto Corinto to the Gulf, hugging Nicaragua's coast along detached shoals and reefs within the 20-meter (65.6 feet) depth contour, extending up to 4 miles offshore. Most of these waters were too perilous and shallow for our ships to enter. There was strong suspicion that Nicaragua was using the patrol boats to transport arms across the Gulf to leftist insurgents in El Salvador.

Additionally, Soviet merchant ships were reportedly entering Puerto Corinto, delivering military arms and equipment shipments. Nicaragua had positioned field artillery and tanks near the Honduran border, supplied by the Soviet Union.

In anticipation of President Reagan possibly calling for a blockade or quarantine of Soviet ships entering Puerto Corinto, two more FFGs would depart from Mayport and arrive at Rodman by the third week of June. Any quarantine or blockade would require two ships operating in the area instead of one. One ship would be assigned to the blockade/quarantine, while the other would manage the Gulf of Fonseca.

The briefing concluded with an edict, if you will, from Southern Command. No reports of USO or UFO activities or encounters would be accepted. Therefore, if anything similar to our previous encounters happened in that regard, it didn't happen.

I assume everyone else found the information provided and discussed in the briefing sobering. We might face the possibility of war, with logistic support hundreds of miles away. The nearest air support for us or any of our forces in the Gulf would need to come from Howard Air Force Base in the Panama Canal Zone. If things go south, we were essentially on our own.

Our ship was well-armed and fully equipped. We were confident that our well-trained crew could handle any situation. *Estocin* was equipped on deck with M-2 Browning .50 caliber heavy machine guns, M-60 light machine guns, and our Italian OTO Melara 76 mm gun to engage more comparable enemies. The 76 mm/62 caliber gun is a naval autocannon. It is remote-controlled and has a magazine capacity of 80 ready rounds.

We carry 36 Standard Missiles (SM-1) for anti-ship and anti-air operations, along with four Harpoon missiles. The SM-1 missile has an operational range of 40 to 92 nautical miles, while the RGM-84 Harpoon anti-ship cruise missiles have a range of 48.5 to 129 nautical miles. In addition, our ship featured a range of sensors and processing systems, including surface search, air search, and fire control radars, as well as outstanding sonar capabilities and electronic warfare systems.

Tuesday, June 7, at 0530, we arrived at the rendezvous position with USS *Gallery*, 6,000 yards (3 nautical miles) south of the entrance to the Gulf. Within 15 minutes, our motor whaleboat was launched into the water and departed for *Gallery*. Select members of our CIC team, several CT spooks, and Lt. j.g. Michel were on board.

The captain asked me to establish an operational area on the navigation chart inside the entrance to the Gulf. He wanted to keep the ship in relatively safe waters, with Punta de Amapala to our west and Punta Cosiguina to our southeast. He directed me to keep us south of Meanguera Island, avoiding getting closer than 2,000 yards from the island. This area would enable us to maintain a strong position to intercept and fully monitor any Nicaraguan patrol boats operating in the Gulf.

This patrol area also positions the ship to monitor marine traffic and activities near the entrance of the Estero Real River. The Estero Real River is a navigable river discharging into the southeast side of the Gulf, bordered by Honduras on its north bank and Nicaragua on its south bank.

After about 45 minutes, our whaleboat returned from USS *Gallery*. I watched as *Gallery* picked up speed and headed southeast, bound for Rodman. Our time here may be more interesting than our last visit, or it may not.

We maneuvered the ship to enter the Gulf waters and take station in our new patrol area. On the navigation charts, I had established a rectangular area, extending 12 nautical miles from east to west and 2.5 nautical miles from north to south. This area offered us excellent views of points that provided valuable assistance for both visual and radar navigation. Near the eastern end, and just south, lies Islas Farallones, a group of light-colored rocks located 6 miles west of Punta El Rosario. Punta El Rosario was significant to us as any vessel traffic to or from the Estero Real River must pass close by.

We noted that the presence of fishing vessels here was much denser. How many are fishing, and which ones were here to surveil us? We set up patrol legs at a speed of just 4 knots. This speed, steering east/west, would take approximately three hours each way, but it still provided the necessary maneuverability to avoid collisions with the fishing vessels. The fishing vessels were challenging since, being small and wooden, they give very poor return on radar and are difficult, if not impossible, to detect by radar alone. Detection of these vessels was primarily by visual means. For nighttime detection, we had to rely on FLIR, the NODS, and our lookouts with night vision goggles.

During lunch, Bobby sat at my table. I asked him if the subject of any USO or UFO activity had been broached during the briefing on board *Gallery* that morning.

"They either had no encounters, or if they did, they're not saying," Bobby answered.

Being here held an advantage for SBU 20's patrol boats and the SEAL teams. Now our ship would, in a sense, become their mothership from which to operate. The following day, instead of patrolling, we loitered near the eastern end of our area north of Punta El Rosario to support operations.

We rigged our boat boom early that afternoon to moor boats alongside the ship. The boat boom is an 18-foot-long spar secured to a gooseneck by a pin on the ship's side, positioned perpendicular to the hull. It hangs from a block and tackle secured to the superstructure. Strong lines suspended from the boom feature a metal thimble eye at their bitter end through which boats can pass and secure their bow lines. Several rope ladders hang from the boom, allowing boat crews to climb up, use the catwalk along the top, and come on board. With the boat boom extended, we could moor up to four patrol boats alongside at any given time.

Four SBU 20's patrol boats arrived at our position several hours later. The patrol boat crews secured their bow lines to our boat boom. I noted that Ham's patrol boat was not among them. I watched from the bridge wing as the boat crews and SEALs climbed up the rope ladders to the boom and came on board.

We soon learned the SEALs were on board to prepare for a mission, which involved unpacking, inflating the Zodiac boats, and setting up the outboard motors. The boats have four lifting points on their gunwales, so Master Chief Blake's deck crew fashioned bridles to lift them, get them over the side, and lower them to the water using a deck davit. On a long painter line, the two boats were towed along the ship to where the patrol boats were nested on the boom. Some patrol boat crew members tied the Zodiac boats to their patrol boats.

That afternoon, a briefing outlining the SEAL team's mission was held. That night, at midnight, the four patrol boats were tasked with taking a seven-man squad to an area north of the entrance to the Estero Real River. The patrol boats would transport the SEALs far enough to transfer them to the Zodiac boats, using these boats to reach their destination. The mission was to reconnoiter the coast and inland areas on the Nicaraguan side of the border with Honduras. An assessment was needed to determine the presence of artillery, tanks, and Sandinista or possibly Cuban forces. If there had been a troop buildup, it could mean an imminent attack on Honduras.

Our role would be to follow the patrol boats to an anchorage area in the eastern part of the Gulf, east of Punta El Rosario. This area is Chismuyo Bay, approximately 6.5 nautical miles long and 2.3 miles wide, with water depths sufficient for our 24.5-foot draft. Once the SEALs transfer to their Zodiac boats and were away, the patrol boats would wait. We were to position the ship at the southeastern end of the anchorage area. We aimed to cover from the Estero Real River north to the border between Honduras and Nicaragua. If necessary, and called for, we would provide gunfire support to the teams ashore with our 76 mm gun.

The captain said he wanted the navigation detail to be manned so that the ship could be piloted precisely in these waters. Once we arrived in the intended area, we were surrounded by shallow shoal water areas on three sides. We would go in a darkened ship posture, meaning no navigation or deck lights. The captain instructed me to develop a detailed navigation plan for the mission and to notify him once it was complete.

After the briefing, I spent some time working on the navigation plan for the upcoming mission. I called Bobby to the chart room, so he could review it from his CIC perspective. Once we were both satisfied with the plan, I called the captain to inform him that it was ready for his review.

The captain appeared at the chartroom door several minutes later, and we spent about 20 minutes reviewing and discussing the plan. Once he approved the plan, I notified Bobby of several minor changes and that the plan was a go.

That night at about 2330, I set the navigation detail. Several minutes later, the four patrol boats, fully loaded, backed away from the ship with the inflatable Zodiac boats in tow. Shortly, the sound of the patrol boat engines faded into the darkness. The deck crew reported to the pilothouse that the boat boom had been recovered alongside and secured for sea.

In the dark pilothouse, I heard the captain's voice ask, "Chief, are you ready?"

"Yes, sir, let's go," I answered.

I would pilot the ship to our waiting point using radar navigation techniques. We started from a point 3,000 yards (1.5 nautical miles) directly north of Punta El Rosario. I recommended to the conning officer that the helmsman steer a course of 116 degrees and maintain a speed of 8 knots. We needed enough speed through the water to offset an ebbing current flowing west-northwest toward the Gulf. Unless countered, the current would set the ship northwest and into shallow water. It would only take 27 minutes to reach the designated waiting position. I fixed the ship's position every two minutes by radar; we were making good our intended track.

It would be too dangerous and time-consuming to anchor; the plan called for lowering the APUs and using them to hold position. When we were 750 yards out, I requested engine program control to "stop." As we decelerated, the captain ordered the APUs to extend. I had set up radar range lines to Punta Condega to our northeast and Punta El Rosario to the west-northwest to maintain our position. As long as the radar ranges to these two points didn't change and the fathometer showed a consistent water depth of 22 feet beneath the keel, I knew we weren't drifting and were where we should be.

Radio silence must be maintained throughout the mission. It would only be broken when the patrol boats had extracted the SEALs and were at our position, or if the SEALs or patrol boats required our support. The waiting began in the dark pilothouse; everyone remained silent except to exchange necessary information. The plan included that once the patrol boats were outbound, they would hoist inflatable radar reflectors, allowing us to detect them on radar.

Our ship's radio call sign for this mission was "Mike Sierra One." Once the patrol boats arrived at our position, they would transmit our call sign over VHF radio to inform us that the mission was complete. Then, they would proceed to the prearranged rendezvous point, located northwest of Punta El Rosario. At that time, our ship would navigate out of the area.

Just before 0430, a voice came over the VHF radio: "Mike Sierra One." That was the signal we had been waiting for. The captain ordered the APUs to be retracted. I recommended the course and speed to the conning officer to take us out of the area and to the rendezvous point. Once the ship was back in deeper water, northwest of Punta El Rosario, I requested permission from the captain to secure the navigation detail, which he granted. All in the pilothouse could almost feel the release of stress levels.

Once at the rendezvous point, we brought the engine program control to "stop." The deck force deployed the boat boom on our starboard side, allowing the patrol boats to moor alongside and for the crews to come on board. Soon, the four patrol boats came alongside and moored to the boat boom. Two of the patrol boats had the Zodiac boats in tow.

In CIC, the SEAL team squad leader briefed the captain on the information they had gathered during the mission. Later, Bobby told me that the squad leader used the High-Frequency (HF) secure voice radio to call Southern Command to make his report. He added that they had learned there were, in fact, artillery and tanks present, but there was no evidence of any troop buildup in the area.

After breakfast, additional supplies were loaded onto the patrol boats. Shortly thereafter, the patrol boats, with the Zodiac boats in tow, backed away from the ship and headed north in the Gulf, presumably toward their base at Puerto Amapala on Tiger Island.

For us, it was back to our patrol area in the central Gulf, among the fishing vessels scattered everywhere. Now, since it was June, the daytime temperatures were higher than when we were here in May. Some crew members felt disappointed because the fishing here was poor compared to offshore. As ship's crews do, they quickly settled into the daily routine.

If any USOs were present, we assumed that the shallower waters in the Gulf would likely prevent any encounters. During several evening watches, the lookouts reported strange lights to our south offshore that seemed to move erratically. Three days passed before any SBU 20 patrol boats arrived for supplies and fuel on the evening of June 12.

On Monday, June 13, the XO came to the pilothouse and asked to speak with me in the chartroom. I followed him inside and watched him close the door.

He turned to me. "Chief, I need you to figure out the distance from here to the equator and then from where we would cross the equator back to Rodman." I told him I would have it for him in a few minutes.

"Fine, I'll be in my stateroom, just call me," he said.

As he turned to open the door, he paused. "Chief, you're a shellback, right?"

I replied, "Yes, sir, I am."

"Good, let's keep this between us for now." He opened the door and left.

I found a chart for the Eastern Pacific Ocean in the chart table. It didn't take long to compute that from the Gulf of Fonseca to the equator at the longitude coordinate of 84° West was 804 nautical miles, and from there to Rodman was 627 nautical miles, for a total of 1,431 nautical miles. At a speed of 16 knots, the trip would take 3 days and 18 hours.

I noted that we would be very close to the Galapagos Islands. I also calculated the distance to cross the equator at the longitude coordinate of 91° West, about 40 miles north of the islands. It only added a mere 110 nautical miles to the overall distance. My thought was that you never know; maybe if we could get permission to visit the equator, we could gain another day to explore the Galapagos Islands. I quickly checked the Sailing Directions publication and found anchorages deep enough to accommodate us at the islands of Santa Cruz and San Cristobal. I thought it might be worth mentioning this to the XO.

I called the XO and provided him with the distance he requested. Before hanging up, I shared the information about the Galapagos Islands, including the distance and time needed to visit. I could tell he was interested when he said, "Hmm, let me talk to the captain about that. Thanks, Chief."

Late the next afternoon, we saw two Nicaraguan Navy patrol boats enter the Gulf. They stayed close to shore off Punta Cosiguina on the east side of the entrance. They followed the shoreline northward, staying east of the rocks at Islas Farallones, then rounded Punta El Rosario. We assumed they were headed for the Estero Real River. We now had potential adversaries nearby.

The following week was relatively quiet. Several visits by SBU 20's patrol boats were about the extent of any activity. The days were spent patrolling east and west within our small area of the Gulf. Our presence may have precluded any forays by the Nicaraguan patrol boats because we had not seen or detected them since the day they arrived.

Since fishing was now a bust, the crew devised a new venue of recreation. On the flight deck, a volleyball net was set up. To prevent losing the volleyball over the side, someone had the idea to encase the ball in a mesh laundry bag, which was attached to a long section of braided shot line that was both strong and flexible. Now, every afternoon, after the PT session, the volleyball games continued until it was too dark to play.

Monday, June 20, the XO announced with a note in the Plan of the Day that when USS *Gallery* relieved us in two more days, we would head southward and cross the equator before returning to Rodman. I spoke with the XO later in the day and inquired about the possibility of visiting the Galapagos Islands. He replied that the captain felt he had already pushed enough to secure the extra time and fuel to cross the equator, let alone request more time and fuel to visit the islands.

I also learned from the XO that President Reagan had abandoned the idea of calling for a blockade or quarantine of Soviet ships entering Puerto Corinto. However, the two other FFGs that had been ordered to sail from Mayport were now docked at Rodman. With two more ships in the area, it gave us and USS *Gallery* the time and flexibility to visit the equator.

The crew quickly divided into the shellback and pollywog groups. The XO, Lieutenant Commander Len Gehrmann, demonstrated his creativity by planning various events and activities leading up to crossing-the-line. Naturally, his focus was on the pollywogs performing and earning their way to becoming shellbacks. He dubbed all pollywog events as "Estocin Style," followed by the specific title of the event.

USS *Gallery* had departed Rodman early to allow them to divert south first and cross the equator before heading north to the Gulf of Fonseca. This meant that when they relieved us, their entire crew would be shellbacks.

The morning of June 22, USS *Gallery* arrived at the offshore station. During the morning watch, the ship transited out of the Gulf and into offshore waters, 3.5 nautical miles south of the entrance.

A "Cheer Ship" was planned for *Gallery's* arrival. The pollywog uniform consisted of skivvy underwear, black socks and shoes, white hats or ball caps, and neckerchiefs or neck ties. Officers must also have their shoulder boards taped on their shoulders to indicate their rank.

As USS *Gallery* approached, our pollywogs lined up along the port side of the main deck and forward to the forecastle, running in place and chanting, "Boomshakalaka, shakalaka, boom shakalaka, and boom!"

Upon the command over the 1MC, "Attention to port," everyone faced USS *Gallery*, standing at attention.

The following command over the 1MC was: "Hand salute pollywog style."

All the pollywogs, in unison, did an about-face, dropped their skivvy underwear, and bent over in an en masse mooning. USS *Gallery* was close enough that the cheering and yelling from her crew on deck in reaction to the mooning could easily be heard.

After the pollywog mooning, while we brought the ship around to the course that would take us south to the equator, a turnover brief was held with USS *Gallery* over secure voice radio in CIC. At our speed of 16 knots, it would take a little over two days to reach the equator. These two days would be filled with events and activities organized by the XO and the other shellbacks. Having earned my status as a shellback just about eight months earlier while on USS *W.S. Sims* in the Indian Ocean, I was pleased that this time I was a participant in being an initiator, not the initiated.

That evening, the "Estocin Style–Beauty Contest" was held. The XO, decked out in his formal dinner dress uniform, complete with medals, was the emcee for the event. About 14 crew members chose to be contestants; the XO quickly dubbed the group the "Estocin Beauties."

I must admit that some contestants were incredibly creative with the costumes, fake hair, breasts, and makeup they had crafted. First, there was a dance competition held on the flight deck. A group line dance was followed by each contestant performing their solo dance to the music of their choice. A heavy, sizable rain squall forced the contests off the deck, and it was moved to the mess decks for the bathing suit contest. The overall winner of the competition earned a spot on the Royal Court of Neptunus Rex and was exempt from going through the complete crossing of the line initiation process.

Two more events took place en route to the equator: the "Estocin Style–Dog Contest and Chariot Race." The dog contest involved one pollywog dressed and outfitted to resemble a dog, while their handler was adorned in their dress white uniform. Each dog was expected to be on a leash, with the handler responsible for keeping their dog under control. The dog and handler were judged on the best tricks and stunts the dog could perform.

The chariot race was entertaining. I was surprised at how quickly the three teams built the wheeled chariots large enough to accommodate a driver, crafted from various parts and equipment. Four-man teams were harnessed to each chariot, providing the horsepower. Each race consisted of five laps around the flight deck. Both events were enjoyable for everyone involved, including the pollywogs and the shellback spectators.

The general workshop had provided each shellback with sections of old firefighting hose about three feet long, with handles made from duct tape. We all now had our shillelaghs, which we could use to bring the pollywogs to submission. For the crossing-the-line initiation, most shellbacks created costumes, wearing bandanas as headgear, sleeveless shirts, and jagged cut-off jeans or dungarees, along with flip-flops or tennis shoes. And of course, each would carry their shillelagh.

After 15 days in the Gulf of Fonseca, we had retained all the garbage on board. This meant we had plenty of delicacies to fill the garbage chute for the enjoyment of the pollywogs as they crawled through. The Chiefs Mess, having considerable experience with this, prepared adequate amounts of truth serum for all the pollywogs to enjoy.

The evening before, the XO included several notes in the Plan of the Day. Note 1: "The prescribed pollywog uniform of the day for crossing the line shall be white hats worn inside out (all rates and ranks), white T-shirts, and skivvy underwear. Footwear and knee protection are strongly recommended but not mandatory." Note 2: "All pollywogs will present themselves on the forecastle in the prescribed uniform of the day no later than 0530 for cleansing and breakfast."

On the early morning of June 24, the ship approached the equator. All pollywogs were gathered by the shellbacks and ordered to muster on the forecastle for the cleansing and humbling process to prepare them for their appearance before Neptunus Rex and his Royal Court. Once all the pollywogs were on the forecastle, the XO took an elevated position atop the guided missile launcher base. From there, he directed the shellbacks in organizing the pollywogs, who were now on their hands and knees for the early morning cleansing, with seawater sprayed from the firefighting hose nozzles. Any pollywog who resisted or protested was quickly subdued by groups of shellbacks wielding and slapping their shillelaghs.

Breakfast was served, consisting of large, pickled herrings. Each pollywog was encouraged to chew and eat their herring or at least carry it clenched in their teeth. Finally, once the XO was satisfied, the transfer of the pollywogs aft to the flight deck began. They were all required to crawl on their hands and knees. The shellbacks now had control, which was quite a feat since out of the crew, there were fewer than 30 shellbacks, leaving us outnumbered almost six to one.

Once on the flight deck, the initiation process began. Each pollywog's first trial was to crawl through a nearly 20-foot-long canvas chute filled with garbage. Joe Lambert, being our most portly of the shellbacks, was the Royal Baby. John Jeggey, as the most senior shellback, held the title of Neptunus Rex.

My role today was to serve as the Royal Doctor. I ensured that each pollywog was cleansed and made truthful before appearing before Neptunus Rex and his Royal Court for judgment. First, I sprayed them down with the fire hose, and then I administered doses of truth serum to each. Then, I asked each one, "Are you now ready to admit your guilt in purposely embracing the status as low-life pollywog scum?" If the answer was yes, I move them on to kiss the Royal Baby's belly. Those who answered 'no' had to start all over again at the garbage chute. Eventually, all answered yes, allowing them to kiss the Royal Baby's belly, then next appear before Neptunus Rex and his Royal Court and become a shellback.

I handed over my role as the Royal Doctor to another shellback and went to the pilothouse to relieve Jake Sullivan, the QMOW, so he could go through the initiation and become a shellback. We had pushed Lt. Hannity through the initiation early to enable him to relieve as OOD and conning officer. In addition to being the QMOW, I also assumed the lookout duties. For the remainder of the shellback initiation, we set the ship to automatic steering. The weather was clear, the seas were calm, automatic steering was set to a course of 034 degrees, and the ship's speed was 16 knots; we were bound for the Gulf of Panama. Soon, everyone in the crew would be able to claim the title of shellback.

The crossing-the-line initiation was over by 1100. Now, everyone in the crew was pitching in to clean up the flight deck. Next, everyone would go clean up and change. As soon as possible, the flight deck would become our steel beach. The cooks and crew would set up the barbecue grills, tables, and break out the food. Our cookout was a celebration for all who had crossed the line. The rest of the day follows a holiday routine for the crew, with no work except for standing watch. It had been a good day. One hundred percent of those who were our pollywogs were now shellbacks.

We arrived in Rodman early on June 26. We received news that our participation in the SPECOPS was now complete. We would stay here for three more days, and on June 30, we would make the northbound transit through the Panama Canal. However, we weren't returning to Mayport just yet.

During the late morning, several trucks and a crane drove down the pier to the ship. The CT spook detachment and all of their equipment were being offloaded. The CT's operations container was hauled from the port helicopter hangar and then craned onto a flatbed truck at the dock. All of their equipment was offloaded and loaded onto a large truck with an enclosed bed. Our understanding was that they will cross-deck over to another ship departing for the Gulf of Fonseca.

I was glad we were here today because June 26 is also Jan's and my twelfth wedding anniversary, and I would be able to call her to celebrate. Three out of the last four anniversaries were spent while we were apart. Maybe, in the future, I would be home for one of our wedding anniversaries.

That evening, along with some of the other chiefs, I went to the CPO Club to celebrate the end of our operation. Several people were ahead of me using the telephones, so while waiting, we had several rounds. Soon, one of the phones was open, so I made my call to Jan. I could tell she was pleased that I was able to call on our wedding anniversary. I also had news that we learned that day. We would arrive in Mayport on July 8 and would be in homeport for a while.

The following morning, at officers' call, the XO announced that we would be receiving a considerable amount of cargo items to be stowed in the helicopter hangers. With the CT spook detachment gone, now both helicopter hangars were empty. The hangers are good-sized as they are designed to house Sikorsky SH-60B Seahawk helicopters and all maintenance equipment. The hangers are over 80 feet deep to accommodate the Seahawk helicopter, which is about 65 feet long.

I already knew that after the canal transit, our next destination was Puerto Castilla, Honduras. Puerto Castilla is located on the north coast of Honduras, on the Caribbean Sea. It is the former site of one of the divisions of the United Fruit Company, which at one time operated all over Central America. During World War II, the U.S. Navy built a small base there to operate seaplanes from.

Later in the day, five enclosed bed trucks and a crane arrived at the pier. First, the crane delivered several pallet jacks and hand trucks to the flight deck. Master Chief Blake would supervise the loading, and our deck crew would assist the civilian workers in stowing the cargo items.

During the afternoon, I was in the chartroom working on the passage plan to transit the canal then to Puerto Castilla. QM2 Faber came into the chartroom and asked me if I knew why we were loading refrigerators and other appliances. I told him I didn't know. I walked to the starboard bridge wing to watch what was being taken off the trucks and craned onto the ship. Sure enough, many of the crates and boxes on pallets were brand-name appliances and other items.

At the evening meal, Master Chief Blake mentioned that the cargo loaded consists primarily of clothes washers and electric dryers, color televisions, water heaters, refrigerators and freezers, and gasoline-engine-powered electrical generators. He added that both hangars were filled to the point where we could barely close the hangar doors.

Early morning on June 30, as we set the Sea and Anchor detail, the Panama Canal pilot came on board. Once all mooring lines were free of the dock, we backed away from the pier into the canal channel, while twisting the ship to bring our heading fair with the northbound channel direction. About an hour later, we arrived at the first lock, Miraflores Lock. Then on to the Pedro Miguel Locks and the Gaillard Cut. While in Gatun Lake, we provide the pilot with a brief demonstration of the ship's impressive acceleration and stopping capabilities before continuing to Gatun Locks. After going through the Gatun Locks, we entered Limon Bay, where the Panama Canal pilot disembarked. It was around 1600 as we passed through the breakwaters at Cristobal and headed out into the Caribbean Sea.

The distance from the Panama Canal to Puerto Castilla is about 620 nautical miles and would take under two days at 16 knots. On the first 310 nautical miles of the transit, we steered courses east of north to avoid the numerous banks of reefs offshore from the eastern Nicaraguan coast. Once north of these dangerous waters, we could turn to a westward course, keeping the Quito Sueno Bank reef system to our south as we proceeded along the northern coast of Honduras to Puerto Castilla.

Puerto Castilla presented several navigational challenges for various reasons. First, the navigation charts issued were based on an outdated French survey from 1947. These charts depicted over-the-water areas, with depth soundings printed every few inches and wide white spaces in between. I questioned the accuracy and reliability of the charts. Secondly, the pilots were local fishermen who had only operated small fishing boats, yet Honduran regulations require the use of a pilot. Third, the wharf is not long enough to accommodate our ship, and the water depths are unknown.

I met with the captain and shared my concerns about the uncertain water depths. I suggested a contingency plan based on what mariners have done for centuries when entering unknown waters. I proposed that, if necessary, once we were about 2,000 yards north of Punta Caxinas, we should launch our motor whaleboat and keep it 100 to 150 yards ahead of the ship. The boat crew, equipped with a hand lead line, could take depth soundings ahead of the ship and report the findings over the radio. The captain agreed that this would be our contingency.

On the morning of July 2, we were steering the approach course to Puerto Castilla. I was using radar for navigation since Punta Caxinas and Cabo de Honduras were still not fully visible. Everyone in the pilothouse was keeping a close watch on the fathometer depths. As we neared Cabo de Honduras, a lighthouse was visible. This posed a problem because the lighthouse is there but not indicated on the chart. A tall water tank is to the east of the lighthouse, and it is shown on the chart. Since Cabo de Honduras is low, swampy, and wooded, it offers no other prominent landmarks. I was no longer sure that continuing inbound was a good idea.

I recommended to the captain that we slow to 5 knots to buy more time to figure this out without closing in on potentially dangerous waters too quickly. The captain nodded to the OOD, who instructed the conning officer to reduce our speed. I glanced at the fathometer reading, and we now had only 22 feet of water beneath the keel, which did not match the charted depths.

I turned to the captain. "The fathometer depth does not concur with the charted depth. Captain, I recommend we launch the whaleboat and use it to take soundings as we discussed."

The captain said to the OOD, "Slow to 3 knots, and order the deck crew to launch the whaleboat."

The deck and boat crews had been briefed on our contingency plan and were manned and ready to launch the whaleboat. Within minutes, the whaleboat was in the water and underway. I watched as the whaleboat passed by and moved to a position about 100 yards directly ahead of the bow. BM1 Bent tossed the hand lead line ahead of the boat; I waited until, over the radiotelephone, the depth on the lead line was reported to be 12 fathoms, 66 feet.

The captain turned to me. "Chief, does 3 knots work for you?"

"Yes, let's keep this speed," I responded.

Next, he turned to the OOD and said, "Keep us at 3 knots."

When the ship was about 500 yards northwest of Punta Caxinas, the whaleboat reported that a small boat was approaching them.

The radio crackled: "We think this guy may be the pilot."

We stopped the ship as the small boat drew nearer. Eventually, it came alongside the pilot ladder we rigged on the starboard side. Mr. Hanlon escorted a man to the pilothouse.

"Are you the pilot?" the captain asked the man.

The man responded, "Si, el capitan. Por favor, mi inglés es pobre."

I was thinking: *This sucks. The guy just told the captain, "Please, my English is poor."*

My solution was to call Jorge Dejesus. I suggest it to the OOD. The OOD called down to the deck crew to have him come to the pilothouse. When Jorge arrived the captain quickly explained to him that he needed him to serve as an interpreter for the pilot. From that moment on, all communication between the captain and the pilot went through Jorge.

The captain nodded at the OOD and conning officer and said, "Speed 3 knots." Then he said to the conning officer, "Have the helmsman steer in the whaleboat's wake."

Now back underway, the whaleboat stayed approximately 100 yards ahead of the ship and reported the hand lead line depth readings every two minutes. That's how we navigated the ship around Punta Caxinas and into the waters of Bahía de Trujillo. Soon, we spotted the wharf along the southern shore of Cabo de Honduras. As we approached the wharf, the captain ordered the ship to stop about 150 yards from it. Over the radio, the whaleboat was instructed to take depth soundings along the length and at either side of the wharf. It appeared we had between 40 and 45 feet of water depth, which was more than enough to accommodate our draft. As I suspected, the pilot had been useless. He mainly just stood around and watched, saying little.

Near the small wharf, various types of construction equipment were parked: bulldozers, road graders, front-end loaders, and cranes. I immediately recognized the equipment as belonging to the Navy Seabees because they were all painted the familiar drab olive green color. As we got closer, I could read the large letters and numerals stenciled on each piece of equipment: "NMCB-133." I knew these were Seabees from the Naval Mobile Construction Battalion–133, based in Gulfport, Mississippi.

It was clear that the wharf was under construction; the usable portion for docking was approximately 125 feet long, while the ship's total length is

445 feet. To efficiently unload our cargo from the flight deck, we needed to moor with as much of the flight deck adjacent to the wharf as possible.

The problem lies in how to moor the bow and stern of the ship. A solution emerged when a call came over the VHF radiotelephone with news that the Seabees had a plan. They suggested we send our bow line over, so they could secure it to a large tree, backing it up with a road grader. For our stern line, they proposed that we pass it ashore where it could be secured to two bulldozers. We could also put out two spring lines and breast lines to the wharf. The captain thought for a moment and then agreed to their mooring plan over the radio.

With slow and cautious maneuvering, we walked the ship to the wharf. Now, there were about a dozen Seabees present to handle our mooring lines ashore. The deck crews threw the heaving lines from both the bow and the stern. Once the Seabees had the heaving lines in hand, they used them to pull our heavier mooring lines to the shore. Once the mooring lines were secured, the deck crews, both on the bow and at the stern, cautiously took the lines to power on the capstans to remove any slack. Soon, we appeared to have the ship safely moored.

One officer, several chiefs, and other Seabees came on board once the gangway was out to the wharf from the flight deck. The whaleboat was moored outboard on the ship's starboard side; we would leave it in the water and use it again later today when we departed Puerto Castilla. Master Chief Blake and BM1 Bent met with the Seabees to review their plan for offloading the cargo we had brought from Rodman.

The Seabees positioned a crane with a long boom on the wharf. It was lunchtime, and they decided to offload after lunch because the trucks needed for transport had not yet arrived. Master Chief Blake invited the two Seabee chiefs to the mess for lunch.

During lunch, I was a bit surprised by how talkative the two Seabee chiefs were. I asked one of them, named Tommy, how they had transported all their heavy construction equipment from Gulfport to here. He explained that their equipment had been transported to Honduras aboard Amphibious Tank Landing Ships (LSTs). LSTs can essentially run their bow aground and, with their bow ramps, discharge wheeled vehicles directly onto a beach or shore. The chief told me their equipment had been offloaded from the LSTs on the Caribbean side at Punta Caxinas, west of Cabo de Honduras, because they considered it too risky to bring the LSTs into the waters of Bahia de Trujillo.

The other chief, named Hank, mentioned that they were essentially there to build the base up for the Honduran Navy and to establish a port facility with a functioning wharf and pier system. Someone asked Hank what he knew about the cargo we had brought. Hank explained some things as he understood them.

"What you guys have brought here are bargaining chips for the CIA," he said.

He continued by telling us that the word was that CIA operatives would visit villages and towns around Honduras. In many inland communities, people live in deplorable conditions, lacking access to electricity, sewer systems, refrigeration for perishable food, and safe drinking water sources.

He added that the CIA agents met with community leaders and convinced them that, in exchange for their young, military-age men, they would provide electrical power, food preservation systems, safe drinking water, and more. Many leaders accepted the deal. The young men were inducted into the Honduran military as Contra forces. They were primarily sent to the CIA base in the Caribbean's Swan Islands or Eglin Air Force Base in Florida for training.

"The CIA ran similar operations to build fighting and intelligence gathering forces from the Vietnamese people during the Vietnam War," Hank said.

Drawing from what I learned in the previous two months about the entire Contra–Sandinista war, everything Tommy and Hank discussed seemed logical. After lunch, when I went out on deck, I noticed seven or eight six-by-six (6×6) cargo trucks parked nearby.

While the cargo was being offloaded, I spent my time working on the navigation plan for departure. First, I needed to determine the actual position of the Cabo de Honduras lighthouse, which does exist but was not indicated on the chart. By using precise compass bearings and a stadimeter (handheld range measuring device) to measure the distance to the light, along with some assistance from radar, I accurately identified the location of the light structure and plotted it on the chart.

I spotted twin spires of a church in Trujillo, a town on the southeast shore of Bahia de Trujillo. Using the same technique, I identified the exact position of the church spires and plotted them on the chart. While scanning the shoreline with the Big Eye binoculars, I noticed what appeared to be two tall wooden or steel crosses on the hillside along the southwestern shore. The crosses were difficult to distinguish due to the wooded hills in the background. The front cross was shorter than the rear cross. From our position, the front cross appeared to be to the right of the rear cross. I realized I was observing a type of navigation range mark.

Boats and ships can use navigation range marks to stay in safe waters. When the marks appear aligned from the vessel's position, it indicates that the ship is in safe waters. The pilot this morning did not mention the marks. I silently swore under my breath, realizing the advantage we could have had today if I had known about them. I also identified the positions of the two crosses and plotted them on the chart.

While inbound, I plotted a series of estimated and dead-reckoned positions for the ship that correlated with the depth soundings and were supported by radar ranges to Punta Caxinas and compass bearings to the water tank. I reversed the track lines on the chart to facilitate navigation and piloting the ship outbound. I noted that the track line on the chart heading northeast from Punta Caxinas aligned almost perfectly with the hillside crosses. I was now confident that I had a solid plan with sufficient navigational aids to pilot the ship safely out of here this afternoon.

I called Bobby in CIC and asked him to come to the pilothouse to review the plan. After my briefing with Bobby, I shared the outbound track line information so that CIC could set up their navigation charts to reflect the same plan.

Later that afternoon, the cargo offload was complete. We set the Sea and Anchor detail for departure. I reviewed the navigation plan at the chart table with the captain, OOD, and conning officer. I pointed out that, in my opinion, using the whaleboat to take soundings wasn't necessary. Since we were moored port side to the wharf, I planned that once we were away from the wharf, we would turn the ship around so we could recover the whaleboat on our port side, where the boat davit is located. Once the whaleboat was recovered, we were clear to navigate out. The captain agreed with and approved my plan. All we were waiting for was the arrival of the Honduran pilot.

Nearly half an hour later, the pilot finally showed up. I noted the captain didn't bother to have Jorge act as an interpreter; the guy was useless anyway. We took in all mooring lines, using the APUs opposed to the rudder and propeller thrust, and walked the ship away from the wharf. When we were at a safe distance, the conning officer twisted the ship around for our first outbound leg. The deck and boat crews made quick work of recovering our whaleboat and securing it in the boat davit. We were ready to go.

Now that we had helpful aids to navigation for use, I was able to navigate the ship outbound accurately. We slowed off Punta Caxinas long enough to disembark the pilot to a waiting boat. I recommended the initial course to steer and the speed to begin our transit. Just north of Cabo de Honduras are three islands, Islas de la Bahia, or the Bay Islands. I planned to navigate through the deepwater passage between the middle island in the chain, Roatan Island, keeping Guanaja Island to our east.

We were not yet homeward bound. Our next destination was the Naval Weapons Station in Charleston, SC. From the Bay Islands, our passage plan took us north to the Yucatan Channel, then northeast to the Straits of Florida, and finally to the waters off the east coasts of Florida, Georgia, and South Carolina. The distance from Puerto Castilla to Charleston is over 1,250 nautical miles, and it would take us three and a half days at 16 knots.

The transit to Charleston was enjoyable. The weather was fantastic, and we were fortunate that, at this time of year, there were no tropical storms in the area to contend with. As we departed from the Straits of Florida, the seawater transformed into a deep indigo blue, characteristic of the Gulf Stream flowing northward along Florida's coast.

Early on the morning of July 6, we began our approach to the channel leading to Charleston Harbor. The pilot boarded the ship at the channel entrance, approximately 4 miles out. The transit through the harbor and up the Cooper River to the Naval Weapons Station dock took about two hours.

We were here to offload certain missiles and other weapons in preparation for the ship's upcoming restricted availability overhaul period in Mayport, set to begin on July 19. The offload would take more than a day and was expected to be completed by tomorrow afternoon.

The following afternoon, after the weapons were offloaded, we welcomed aboard some male relatives of crew members. This was the father-son guest cruise. Planning for this event began back in May when the ship was in Rodman. The guests could be fathers or sons of crew members. As soon as all the guests were on board, we set the Sea and Anchor detail for getting underway. The pilot boarded, and after his briefing, we took in our mooring lines and backed the ship into the Cooper River.

Now we were finally headed for Mayport and home. Two hours later, after disembarking the pilot, we were back at sea, heading south to the St. Johns River entrance. The weather, winds, and seas were cooperating, so the evening meal was a cookout on the flight deck for the crew and their guests. With only 170 nautical miles to Mayport, I adjusted our transit speed to ensure we arrived at the entrance to the St. Johns River by 0830 tomorrow.

The following morning, we docked at a berth in the Mayport basin at the Delta piers. Jan was waiting on the dock with Mitch. It was Friday, and I didn't have duty until Monday, which meant I had the weekend to spend at home with my family. The plan was to give the crew maximum time off for the next 10 days before the ship's overhaul work began.

The restricted overhaul period would last until early November. The Jacksonville Shipyard would conduct various repairs and updates to the ship's systems, which were expected to take about three months to complete. This offers something rare: close to a three-month break from going to sea.

For now, my adventures are on hold, at least until November. I planned to make the most of my time with family during that period. Reflecting on the 18 months since reenlisting and leaving my family on that cold January morning in Iowa, so much had occurred. In my mind, a career in the Navy is now solidified. I can't see myself doing anything else. However, it comes with a price: constant separations from my wife and son. Fortunately, I have Jan, who has always been fully supportive of me. Without her support and belief in me, I don't think what I'm doing would be possible.

Before Thanksgiving, we resumed underway operations for sea trials and combat systems testing, continuing until December 5, when the ship would return to Mayport. After a brief holiday break in December, we would depart from Mayport just two days after Christmas.

We were headed back to the Panama Canal, and we would celebrate New Year's Eve in Rodman, welcoming the New Year of 1984. From Rodman, we would transit back to the Gulf of Fonseca, beginning our second tour of conducting SPECOPS. We would find that the operational tempo and environment were now quite different. Our visit to Rodman would last only two days, during which we would replenish our fuel and supplies for the upcoming month. What transpires during the subsequent SPECOPS in the Eastern Pacific Ocean is another story for another time.

Without consciously realizing it, I have truly earned the fouled anchors I proudly wear. I have grown and accepted the responsibility of knowing that when situations become dicey, someone will say, "We need Chief Trowbridge," or "Go get the chief." I am now the chief. In every instance, I must bear the weight of leadership by carefully observing each situation, mentally orienting myself to fully understand it, making a decision, and then acting. That's what leaders do.

I now look forward to becoming eligible for advancement to senior chief petty officer (pay grade E-8). I firmly believe that *Estocin* will give me the experiences and qualifications I need to be highly competitive in the senior chief petty officer selection process. Until then, I will enjoy all the upcoming adventures that I believe *Estocin* has in store for me. In just two more years, the outcome will be that USS *Estocin* exceeds my expectations and more.

EPILOGUE

GETTING THERE FROM HERE

The eight years of my life experiences I've shared here have led to significant changes in my attitude, demeanor, and behavior. Maybe I'm a late bloomer, but it seems my adult formative years were between ages 23 and 31. I've heard it said that persevering through complex challenges builds a person's character. Granted, character is important, but learning from both failures and successes is equally valuable. However, we must apply the knowledge and wisdom gained from these lessons in the future, regardless of the circumstances.

As you now know, I have made mistakes and sometimes exercised poor judgment. However, throughout my journey, I learned about and came to believe in the concept of the "self-fulfilling prophecy." A self-fulfilling prophecy is a belief or expectation that affects a person's behavior, leading to the belief or expectation coming true. For example, if someone believes they can reach a goal and works hard for it, their effort and attitude can help make that goal a reality. On the other hand, if someone believes they will fail and doubts their abilities, that negative thinking can block their progress and lead to the failure they expect.

Over time, I came to believe in the existence of fate, or perhaps destiny is a more precise term. As fate or destiny would have it, I met Chief Warrant Officer Griffin during NAVET orientation in Orlando. Without his proactive actions, I would have accepted waiting three more years to qualify for advancement to chief petty officer after reenlisting. So, is my encounter with Mr. Griffin and the outcome resulting from his actions on my behalf a matter of fate or destiny? I tend to believe it was fate that brought me to the chief warrant officer, but I think it was my destiny to wear the fouled anchors of a chief petty officer.

After all, the life events I've shared here led me to follow my destiny. Was my destiny always crystal clear to me? Absolutely not. My time on board PTF 19 and the adventures gave me a period of rest and recovery after my first ship, USS *Rich*. Recruiting duty, good, bad, and as ugly as it was, provided me with the tools to succeed. On board USS *Vreeland*, I realized that I was quite skilled at using those tools. It wasn't until my time on USS *W.S. Sims* and USS *Estocin* that my destiny became clear. Before that, I was unsure about what to do, where to go, or what I would become.

Our subsequent SPECOPS at the Gulf of Fonseca concluded in March 1984. In the following six months, the ship's schedule remained busy with activities leading up to our next overseas deployment. This included five weeks at Guantanamo Bay, Cuba, for refresher training and readiness inspections, as well as two additional underway fleet exercises for readiness and training.

The rest of my time aboard USS *Estocin* was productive. I took on many additional collateral duties. During my free time, I studied and earned an associate degree. In August 1984, I reached one of my main goals: qualifying as an Officer of the Deck (Underway). The captain noted that, based on his observations, I was one of the few enlisted OODs on surface combatant ships in the Navy.

Serving as an officer of the deck underway is a major responsibility. The OOD is in charge of the ship and answers to the commanding officer for its safe and proper operation. This includes navigation, ship handling, communications, routine tests, and inspections. On most ships, the OOD is usually one of the department heads, typically a lieutenant.

During the summer, the ship welcomed a new Executive Officer, Commander Keith Broughton. A few days before we embarked on a three-week readiness exercise, the XO pulled me aside to inform me that the captain had met with the junior officers and department heads. The meeting's focus was on the role of commissioned officers in standing watches as Junior Officer of the Deck, CIC Watch Officer, and Engineering Officer of the Watch, all under the command of an Officer of the Deck, who, in this case, is a senior enlisted member still legally subordinate to commissioned officers. I asked the XO about the officers' consensus.

He replied, "Chief, I hope you'll be pleased to know that you are highly respected and have the confidence and trust of every officer. Not one of them has any problems being your JOOD, EOOW, or CIC Watch Officer. Several commented that they are excited to learn from you. I thought you would want to know."

I thanked the XO for sharing, knowing he didn't have to. I know that for many, on October 16—the day we left Mayport to start our six-month deployment to the Arabian Sea and Persian Gulf—there was a sense of relief aboard. We were free from inspection teams and unnecessary oversight by squadron and fleet commanders. We were free from endless fleet training and evaluator teams. Who would have thought sailors could be this happy to deploy?

For me, it was always a mix of emotions. I felt sad about leaving Jan and Mitch behind again. On the other hand, I love being at sea. I looked forward to the navigational challenges that deployments present for people in my profession. Most importantly, I would be standing watches in the OOD underway rotation.

Our deployment to the Arabian Sea and the Persian Gulf differed greatly from my experience on board USS *W.S. Sims* in 1982 in two main ways. Most of our time in the Persian Gulf occured during the winter months, which have more tolerable weather and air temperatures. Additionally, FFGs are equipped with larger, more efficient air conditioning systems. Even the pilothouse is air-conditioned. This time, it didn't feel like the Persian Gulf experience was a living hell on earth.

Mid-deployment, we even enjoyed a welcome break. While operating in the Arabian Sea, just four days before Christmas, we received orders to transit nearly 1,800 nautical miles to Thailand. We arrived on December 28 and anchored at Patong Bay. We spent seven memorable days in the small community of Patong Beach, welcoming the New Year of 1985.

After our time in Thailand, we returned to the Arabian Sea, where we operated with a carrier battle group for several weeks in the North Arabian Sea. We then resumed patrolling the Persian Gulf until March 2, when we began the long journey home.

USS *Estocin* returned to Mayport on April 6. During the later part of the deployment, I was aware that the senior chief and master chief petty officer selection boards were meeting in Washington, D.C. I felt competitive despite having limited seniority as a chief petty officer. I believe very few of my fellow Chief Quartermasters serve as division and navigation officers, are qualified underway OODs, and have as much qualification, experience, and sea duty as I do. Additionally, in my most recent performance evaluation, the captain noted that I was the top-performing chief petty officer in his command. It seemed like a winning formula, but you never know.

During the first week of the post-deployment leave and upkeep period, I received great news. I was the quarterdeck OOD during the morning watch. The "duty radioman" returned on board, completing the message run to the base communication station. He had a large manila envelope with him.

As he placed the envelope on the log desk, he said to me, "Chief, the E-8 and E-9 selection lists are in here. I'll be right back." With a grin, he added, "No one is supposed to see the list before the captain, now no peeking."

As soon as the radioman was out of sight, I checked the envelope, and it wasn't sealed. I couldn't resist. I pulled out the numerous message pages from the envelope. I quickly flipped through them until I reached the Quartermaster section. A big smile spread across my face as I read under the 'QMCS - Senior Chief Quartermaster' subheading, at position 26 out of 28 selectee names on the list, I found my Social Security number and "Trowbridge G." I quickly organized the pages and placed them back in the envelope. A few minutes later, the radioman returned and took the envelope.

As he picked it up and turned to leave, he said, "Now, senior chief, you didn't peek, did you?"

"Of course not," I replied, laughing.

Silently, I told myself, *You did it. All the work has paid off. See, self-fulfilling prophecy is valid.* Being the second-to-last selectee meant I was close to being the most junior Chief Quartermaster chosen for advancement to Senior Chief Quartermaster. The first person I wanted to tell was Jan, but that would have to wait until later today.

The following week, Captain Mackay held a pinning and frocking ceremony for me. Jan was there to pin on one new senior chief collar device, and Captain Mackay pinned on the other. I'm glad Jan could be part of the experience.

To distinguish a senior chief petty officer from a chief petty officer, a single silver star is placed at the top of the fouled anchor insignia and on the top of the cloth rate badge on the dress blue uniform. Now that I proudly wear the fouled anchors with the single silver star of a senior chief petty officer, my next goal is to earn the fouled anchors with two silver stars of a master chief petty officer. How will I achieve that? Just consider it a self-fulfilling prophecy.

GLOSSARY OF TERMS AND ACRONYMS

Auxiliary Propulsion Units (APUs) — Found on the FFG 7 class ships and consist of two 350 horsepower (260 kW) retractable electric azimuth thrusters for maneuvering and docking.

Boatswain Mate of the Watch (BMOW) — An enlisted assistant to the Officer of the Deck (OOD) during underway watches. The BMOW must ensure that all deck watch stations are manned with qualified personnel and all watchstanders in previous watch sections are relieved. The BMOW must verify that every person in the watch has been properly instructed and trained. A BMOW must be a qualified helmsman and supervise the helmsman if senior to the QMOW.

Bogen Telephone System — A computer-controlled voice system that serves as the ship's internal telephone system and replaces specific circuits traditionally associated with sound-powered telephones.

Central Control Station (CCS) — In all gas turbine-powered ships, the foundation of the CCS is the engineering control system. FFG 7 class ships use the engineering plant control system to both operate and monitor the gas turbine equipment.

Combat Information Center (CIC) — Most of the warfighting functions are handled from the ship's Combat Information Center (CIC). In peacetime steaming, CIC acts as the electronic "eyes and ears" of the ship, advising the bridge team on how to navigate and maneuver safely and serving as a backup to ensure everything is being done safely. In alert situations and combat, CIC takes the lead, with the bridge team maneuvering the ship, communicating to the crew, and ensuring all stations are manned and ready.

Conn or Conning Officer — An officer responsible for instructing the helmsman on the course to steer. While performing this duty, the officer is said to have the conn.

Department Head — As the representative of the commanding officer, the department head is responsible for and reports to the CO about all matters that affect his or her department. That includes administrative matters, the operational readiness of the department, and the general condition of equipment.

Division Officer — Division officers are responsible to and, in general, act as assistants to department heads.

Engine Order Telegraph (EOT) — On steam-propelled ships, two telegraph units and alarms must be installed, one on the bridge and one in the engine room. The order is given by moving the bridge unit's handle to the desired position on the dial face. This sends an electrical signal to the EOT placed in the engine room, whose pointer acquires a position according to the signal given from the bridge. An audible alarm sounds at both ends. Accordingly, the watch-keeping engineer acknowledges the order by moving the engine room EOT handle to the required position and takes the necessary action. This sends an electrical signal to the bridge EOT unit, causing its pointer to acquire the respective position.

Electronic Warfare (EW) — Examples of offensive Electronic Warfare include radio jamming (flooding a frequency with another transmission, for instance) or radar jamming (degrading radar signals through the introduction of deceptive decoys or "noise" that renders the device useless). Defense measures employ many of the same principles used in offensive electronic warfare.

Engineering Officer of the Watch (EOOW) — The EOOW is a direct report to the senior bridge/pilothouse watchstander, usually either the officer of the deck or the commanding officer. The EOOW is the officer or senior petty officer on watch in charge of the main propulsion plant and of the associated auxiliaries. An EOOW is primarily responsible for the safe and efficient performance of the engineering department watches related to the equipment in his or her charge.

Executive Officer (XO) — The executive officer (XO) is the aide or "executive" to the commanding officer. The XO is usually the next-ranking line officer aboard a ship. The XO is the direct representative of the commanding officer in maintaining the ship's overall efficiency. The XO's responsibilities include the command's assigned personnel. With the help of department heads, the XO arranges and coordinates all ship's work, drills, exercises, and policing and inspecting the ship.

FF — Navy ship class designation for Knox-class Fast Frigate.

FFG — Navy ship class designation for the Oliver Hazard Perry (FFG 7)-class Guided Missile Frigate.

Hawser — A strong, specialized wire rope or large circumference fiber line. Used primarily for towing and mooring. Hawsers are thicker and more durable than standard ropes or fiber lines.

Helmsman — The helmsman is a qualified steersman who steers courses prescribed by the conning officer.

Junior Officer of the Deck (JOOD) — The junior officer of the deck (JOOD) is the principal assistant to the OOD. Anyone making routine reports to the OOD normally makes them through the JOOD. The JOOD often has the Conn and serves as the Conning Officer during routine underway bridge watches.

Lee Helmsman — The lee helmsman who stands watch at the engine order telegraph (EOT) on the bridge rings up the conning officer's orders to the engine room, making sure all bells are correctly answered. On gas turbine-propelled FFGs, during special details assigned to assist the SCC operator by operating the engine program control and the APUs.

Lookout — The lookout watch man is assigned lookout stations and performs duties as prescribed in the ship's lookout instructions. Lookouts should be rotated at least hourly. They are under the direct supervision of the BMOW and OOD.

Main Control — The main engine room. On steam-propelled ships, the throttleman in Main Control operates the main engine throttles in response to orders received from the bridge on the EOT.

Main Deck, Decks, and Levels — The highest deck, extending from the ship's stem (very forward-most point of the vessel) to the stern, is called the "main deck." All decks below the main deck are numbered higher than "1" (2, 3, etc.). All levels above the main deck are preceded by a zero (01, 02, etc.).

Mooring Lines — Usually, a six-line mooring setup is sequentially numbered from forward to aft. Lines 1 and 6 (bow and stern lines) keep the ship alongside the dock. Forward lines 2 and 3 restrict forward and aft movement along the dock. After lines 4 and 5, these lines also restrict forward and aft movement along the dock.

Officer of the Deck (OOD) — The officer of the deck (OOD) is in charge of the ship and is responsible to the commanding officer (CO) for the safe and proper operation of the ship or station. That includes navigation, ship handling, communications, routine tests and inspections, reports, supervision of the watch, and carrying out the plan of the day (POD).

Program control — This mode of control takes a single ship's speed input via an integrated throttle and, using a computer processor, automatically schedules the gas turbine engine throttle position and propeller pitch to obtain the ordered speed.

Ship Control Console (SCC) — Located in the pilot house. In addition to the multiple systems that can be controlled at the SCC, the center section contains an integrated throttle that allows the bridge to control the speed of the ship. This is the most remote station where the ship's speed is controlled and usually is the station that has program engine control while underway.

Sound-Powered Telephone — Sound-powered phones operate using voice power and require no batteries or external electrical power source. Sound-powered telephone circuits are hardwired aboard ship to connect all primary and auxiliary spaces or operating stations.

Quartermaster of the Watch (QMOW) — The Quartermaster of the Watch (QMOW) is an enlisted assistant to the OOD while underway (and in-port on certain classes of ships). The QMOW assists the OOD in navigational matters and maintains the ship's deck log. Additional duties include reporting and recording weather changes and executing the required ship's navigational lighting changes. The QMOW, who must be a qualified helmsman, supervises the helmsman if senior to the BMOW.

1MC — This is the general announcing system, over which word can be passed to every space in the ship. The ship's alarm system is tied into it as well. Transmitters are located on the bridge, quarterdeck, and damage control central/central control station; additional transmitters may be located at other points on the ship.

21MC — Captain's command intercom. Differs from the 1MC system in that it provides two-way communications. Each unit has a number of selector switches. To talk to one or more stations, position the proper switches and operate the PRESS-TO-TALK switch.

ABOUT THE AUTHOR

George Trowbridge served over 20 years in the U.S. Navy and retired from active duty in 1992 as a Master Chief Petty Officer. His time on board his first ship, USS *Rich* (DD 820) had a lasting impact on him. The combat experiences he faced aboard that ship during combat operations off the coasts of North and South Vietnam in the final months of the war were significant events that shaped who he became. This motivated George to document the details of these important events in his first book, *Striking Eight Bells: A Vietnam Memoir*.

He served at sea on five different destroyers or frigates and on coastal-river fast patrol boats. George completed seven overseas deployments, beginning with Vietnam and ending with Desert Shield/Desert Storm. His shore tours included serving as a Navy recruiter in the Chicago metro area and later as a navigation instructor at the Navy's Officer Candidate School.

After retiring from the Navy, George spent several years sailing as a Merchant Marine Officer aboard various commercial merchant vessels. His experiences working on those vessels led him to become a training provider for the maritime industry. George has founded two maritime training schools and has managed two others in the Gulf of Mexico region.

George lives in Largo, Florida, and is now widowed. He lost his lifelong partner and beloved wife of 52 years, Janice, to cancer in July 2023. He is retired but still manages to stay active with hobbies, doing yardwork, and his longtime passion, writing.

www.ingramcontent.com/pod-product-compliance
Lightning Source LLC
Chambersburg PA
CBHW050253010526
44107CB00003B/311